library page • musical instrument repairman • mental hospital orderly • children's summer camp counselor • tester of sonubuoy underwater submarine detectors • Air Force cargo net weaver • university orchestra librarian • FM radio classical music programmer • injection-molded plastic stereo case maker • clothing salesman • babysitter • lawn maintenance worker • construction site accountant • restaurant dish washer • soap sample delivery boy • bookstore sales clerk • male feminist writer/lecturer and women's rights advocate • department store bicycle assembler • theater company general manager • technical theater laborer • editor, theater company newsletter • art, music, and theater critic • songwriter • playwright • music educator • private flute teacher • teen theater founder/director • writer/producer of musical comedies • college writing instructor • freelance magazine writer • picture framer • gallery manager • abstract artist association founder/coordinator • poet • elementary reading tutor • substitute teacher • Ogunquit Playhouse publicity director • actor • Edwin Booth Theatre general manager and publicist • solo and ensemble flute recitalist • theatrical set designer • traveling musical instrument demonstrator • civic band musician • abstractor of criminology research articles • founder/director of Artful Endeavors

Praise for
Happy Dawg Walks the Sad Man

"Ross Alan Bachelder has an in-depth understanding of the complex underbelly of the fine and performing arts—the issues, oddities, and machinations that color that world. With twenty essays describing real-life encounters, along with nine playful tiny novelettes, *Happy Dawg Walks the Sad Man* is sure to captivate you, educate you, touch your heart, and amuse you from beginning to end!"

—*Artist Anne Strout*
West Falmouth, Maine

"I first heard Ross Alan Bachelder perform at the Museum of Fine Arts in Boston while visiting the US, and then, in October 2011, when he played at the opening of my painting exhibition in Tauranga, New Zealand. He's a wonderful musician, an immensely talented writer, and a remarkably adventurous multimedia visual artist. *Happy Dawg Walks the Sad Man* is loaded with inspiring anecdotes, insightful observations, and the author's unique perspective on the ways of the world."

—*Artist Susan Harrison-Tustain*
Tauranga, New Zealand (www.susanart.com)

"Coquelicot, smaragdine, wedge: you'll find all sorts of new and delicious colors on the market, but they can't beat the many colorful tales, both real and imagined, in *Happy Dawg Walks the Sad Man*. Thanks to Ross's more than fifty years of immersion in the fine and performing arts as writer, musician, artist, and theater professional, he's become a wise and savvy observer of the human condition. *Happy Dawg* is crammed full of wry humor, tender moments, and powerful insights. Trust me: this is a 'gotta read!'"

—*Pianist and choral director Cheryl Stromski*
Greenland, New Hampshire

"To me, Ross Alan Bachelder qualifies as a true Renaissance man. While managing the Edwin Booth, my onetime play company in Dover, New Hampshire, he cheerfully accepted the role of Grandfather/Flute Player in *Death of a Salesman*, then wrote and performed the incidental music each night, live onstage, while dealing every day with the formidable nuts-and-bolts responsibilities that producing a successful play requires. He's also a man of rock-hard intellectual integrity—an inveterate seeker after beauty in all its ineffable, exhilarating mystery."

—Director, set designer, costumier, and visual artist
Edouard Langlois, Gresham, Oregon

"In the months before my dear friend and first cousin, Deborah Homer O'Leary, died, her friend Ross gave her permission to really step into being an artist and feel good about it. His support and encouragement changed her life; he made her think differently about herself. And she wasn't the only one; he's inspired many people over the years to overcome their fears and immerse themselves joyfully in the arts—and with the publication of *Happy Dawg Walks the Sad Man*, he's bound to inspire many, many more."

—Artist Elisabeth "Betsy" Rix
Woodside, California

Happy Dawg Walks the Sad Man

The Remarkably Varied Adventures of a Confirmed Arts Multiple

by Ross Alan Bachelder

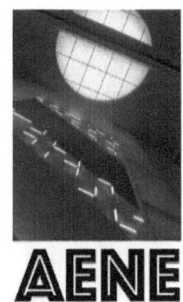

R. Buckminster Fuller © 2004 United States Postal Service. All Rights Reserved. Used with Permission.

Stamp image of R. Buckminster Fuller appears courtesy of the estate of R. Buckminster Fuller.

The Flute Guy © Susan Harrison-Tustain. Used by permission of Susan Harrison-Tustain (www.susanart.com).

Edouard Langlois © Michael Penney. Used by permission of Michael Penney (www.michaelpenneyphotography.com).

The caricature of the author that appears in the Afterword is used by permission of Tom Glover.

The portrait of the author appearing in the About the Author section and on the cover of the book © Michael Penney. Used by permission of Michael Penney (www.michaelpenneyphotography.com).

Happy Dawg Walks the Sad Man © 2016 by Ross Alan Bachelder. All rights reserved. No part of this book may be reproduced in any form or by any electronic or mechanical means including information storage and retrieval systems without permission in writing from the author, except by a reviewer, who may quote brief passages in a review. First edition.

Hardcover edition ISBN: 978-0-9969567-0-3
Paperback edition ISBN: 978-0-9969567-1-0
E-book edition ISBN: 978-0-9969567-2-7

Happy Dawg Walks the Sad Man is a publication of AENE (Artful Endeavors New England).

Edited by Nicole R. Klungle
Interior design by Nicole R. Klungle
Cover design by Damonza (Damonza.com)

Dedication

To Amy Bachelder Jeynes—a superb writer and editor, a deeply caring, remarkably insightful mother, and the finest daughter a father could ever hope to have.

Fig. 1. Portrait of the author drawn by his daughter, Amy, age six.

I Am an Artist

I am an artist:
I sing the jubilant colors,
Painting the emerald planet with passionate words,
Writing the elegant sound of incense in the sky,
And filling the languid silence
With laughing, undulating shapes.

I am a constant artist:
I roll my florid psyche in cool, botanical textures,
Gliding freely among slender, carbonate lines,
Sculpting the liquid contours of chords,
And whittling the delicate iambs
With sharp, glimmering, necessary knives.

I am a solitary artist:
I walk the luminous, moonlit fields,
Farming small, inanimate things,
Trolling the placid, perfumed waters,
And scouring the sweet green leaves of country lanes
To harvest the granite blue symmetry of clouds.

I am a talismanic artist:
I drape the heavens with fine, harmonious jewels,
Drawing pungent sap from the black recesses of sequestered
    souls,
Mining the stately architecture of indelible dreams,
And weaving the merry filigree of music
Into flavored, eloquent tapestries of decaying time.

I am an artist:
I dance the streets with calibrated eyes,
Turning slate into lapidary splendor,
Transforming barren soil into grass,
And alchemizing all that disappoints me
From common thing to transcendental star.

Ross Bachelder, 2010

Table of Contents

Preface
xviii

Acknowledgments
xxii

Chapter 1
Knowing Wendell Harwood
Lessons a Janitor Taught Me
1

Chapter 2
My Invincible van Gogh
Still with Me after All These Years
11

❦ Tiny Novelette 1 ❦
Kensington's Headache
23

Chapter 3
Out of a New England Storm
A Lady of the South Appears
25

Chapter 4
My Midwinter Romp in England & Scotland
34

Table of Contents

❦ Tiny Novelette 2 ❦
Tree Man and Balloon Boy Visit the Remarkables
79

Chapter 5
She Should Have Been a Buddha
The Story of a Friendship
81

Chapter 6
La Scala, Rock 'n' Roll, and the T
No Matter the Genre, It's All Music to Me
124

❦ Tiny Novelette 3 ❦
Harlequin, Columbine, and the Noblest of Callings
139

Chapter 7
My Improbable Journey to the Other Side of the World
And What Took Me There
141

Chapter 8
Franklin Case and the Loan
210

❦ Tiny Novelette 4 ❦
Gargoyle Goat and the Swamp Dwellers
223

Chapter 9
A Tale of Three Commissions
The Harbor-Scene Saw, Bernie and the King, and Shapes from Deep within Me
225

Chapter 10
Philadelphia Story
My Intoxicating Brush with Bucky
240

❀ Tiny Novelette 5 ❀
Weeping Wilma Saves the Lake
255

Chapter 11
The Precarious World of Arts Criticism
Dishing It Out and Taking It on the Chin
257

Chapter 12
The Art of the Assemblage
An Elegant Chaos, Joyfully Conceived
277

❀ Tiny Novelette 6 ❀
Barnaby Rupert's Obsession
303

Chapter 13
Theater in Small-Town New England
I've Done a Lot, and Loved Nearly All of It
305

Table of Contents

Chapter 14
The Friendly Toast
Second Home for the Nonconformist Diner
352

⚜ Tiny Novelette 7 ⚜
Penelope Brood's Dilemma
365

Chapter 15
The Story of Three Paintings
The Lobstermen's Lament, Rocky and Ellie May, and *Vito Ciccotelli*
367

Chapter 16
The Flute Guy and the Juggler
Saying No to the One and Yes to the Many
386

♣ Tiny Novelette 8 ♣
Little Miss One-Eye Finds a Lover
403

Chapter 17
The Instructor and the Mailman
My Precipitous Fall into Academia's Underbelly, and How David Stupple Helped Me Get Out
406

Chapter 18
Other People's Art
My Years as a Picture Framer
428

✺ Tiny Novelette 9 ✺
Reginald Ruffington's New Look
441

Chapter 19
Happy Dawg and the Sad Man
Art, Inhumanity, and the Quest for Happiness
445

Chapter 20
Our Incomparable Jennie
Fragments of a Life
453

Afterword
469

About the Author
473

List of Illustrations

Fig. 1. Portrait of the author drawn by his daughter, Amy, age six. viii
Fig. 2. Wendell Harwood at the piano, age eighteen, Ypsilanti High School, 1932. 5
Fig. 3. Wendell and Ross together, 1974. 8
Fig. 4. Wendell Harwood, pianist (and, from 1955 to 1969, head custodian in the EMU Department of Music). 9
Fig. 5. Left-hand drawing from the author's triptych *The Three Faces of Vincent*. 13
Fig. 6. Right-hand drawing from the author's triptych *The Three Faces of Vincent*. 15
Fig. 7. Middle drawing from the author's triptych *The Three Faces of Vincent*. 17
Fig. 8. Van Gogh and a Leaf, the author's portrait of Vincent. 19
Fig. 9. Kensington's Headache by Ross Bachelder. 22
Fig. 10. High Street, Somersworth, New Hampshire, at the height of the storm. 27
Fig. 11. The author in London, ready to tour the West End. 45
Fig. 12. Blind accordionist on Buchanan Street, Glasgow, Scotland. 58
Fig. 13. A magical moment at the Church of the Holy Rude, Stirling, Scotland. 72
Fig. 14. Tree Man and Balloon Boy Visit the Remarkables by Ross Bachelder. 78
Fig. 15. Deborah Homer O'Leary with Stuart Davis's *Hot Still-Scape for Six Colors—7th Avenue Style* at the Museum of Fine Arts, Boston. 87
Fig. 16. Deborah after our first trip to Boston's Museum of Fine Arts. 91
Fig. 17. Deborah outside A.J.'s Wood Grill Pizza, Kittery Foreside, Maine. 93
Fig. 18. Deborah, Ross, and Anne—the Three Artsketeers—at Silly's Restaurant, Portland, Maine. 95
Fig. 19. Ross trying to dance at the prom, Portsmouth, New Hampshire. 96
Fig. 20. Deborah—a gifted dancer—easily outshining Ross. 97
Fig. 21. Deborah and Ross at the Sanctuary Arts Fundraiser, Eliot, Maine, 2012. 102
Fig. 22. Deborah's Studio at Art on the Hill Studios, Kittery, well into the renovation. 104
Fig. 23. Deborah at the Greenland, New Hampshire, fundraiser, August, 2012. 107
Fig. 24. The ladder for Mobiles by O'Leary: Poetry in Motion, Directly to Your Door, September 2012. 116

Fig. 25. One of Deborah's mobiles on display at her home in Greenland, New Hampshire. 118
Fig. 26. Twilight Movement, dance-inspired sculpture by Deborah O'Leary. (Photo composition by the author.) 122
Fig. 27. Eric "The Showman" McIntyre at lunch in downtown Boston. 130
Fig. 28. McIntyre performing in the stifling heat of Government Center subway station, Boston. 132
Fig. 29. Harlequin, Columbine, and the Noblest of Callings by Ross Bachelder. 138
Fig. 30. My New Zealand travel shrine (gift of artist Anne Strout, West Falmouth, Maine). 146
Fig. 31. The Flute Guy by New Zealand artist Susan Harrison-Tustain. 160
Fig. 32. Gill Myers, who bought Susan Harrison-Tustain's portrait of the author, *The Flute Guy*. 161
Fig. 33. The author making music on Mount Maunganui, October, 2011. 163
Fig. 34. Cranky on his tractor, Tauranga, North Island, New Zealand. 169
Fig. 35. The airplane McDonald's in Taupo, South of Tauranga. 175
Fig. 36. Young couple punting on the Avon River in Christchurch. 177
Fig. 37. Damaged building buttressed after the Christchurch quake. 179
Fig. 38. Driving in Arthur's Pass, South Island—no simple journey. 182
Fig. 39. Sanctuary Bunkhouse at the top of Arthur's Pass. 186
Fig. 40. The author's accommodations at the Bunkhouse. 188
Fig. 41. Sanctuary Bunkhouse, the morning after the blizzard. 190
Fig. 42. The author outside the Bunkhouse, waiting for the kea. 192
Fig. 43. The author, happily windblown on the Doubtful Sound cruise. 195
Fig. 44. The TSS *Earnslaw*, Queenstown Harbor, South Island. 198
Fig. 45. Errol Bulling, the unofficial ambassador of Queenstown. 200
Fig. 46. Errol's juggling balls at the ready. 203
Fig. 47. The Flute Guy playing at Queenstown Harbor on his last day in New Zealand. 207
Fig. 48. Streetside diner Eifion W. Thomas, wishing the author well on the eve of his departure. 208
Fig. 49. Franklin Case at Haab's Restaurant, Ypsilanti, Michigan, on the day of our reunion (March 2013). 218
Fig. 50. Gargoyle Goat and the Swamp Dwellers by Ross Bachelder. 222
Fig. 51. Shapes from Deep within Me by Ross Bachelder. 238
Fig. 52. R. Buckminster Fuller U.S. postage stamp. 249
Fig. 53. "Once in love with Amy, always in love with Amy—that's me!" (Drawing by R. Buckminster Fuller for the author's daughter). 251
Fig. 54. Weeping Wilma Saves the Lake by Ross Bachelder. 254
Fig. 55. The Ghost of Emin Bey (assemblage, front and side view). 280
Fig. 56. The Ghost of Emin Bey (assemblage, interior view). 281
Fig. 57. Little Girl, Little Girl, What Does the Future Bring? (assemblage). 288
Fig. 58. Incantation (assemblage). 292
Fig. 59. Waste Not Thy Time on This Good Earth (assemblage). 299

List of Illustrations

Fig. 60. Barnaby Rupert's Obsession by Ross Bachelder. 302

Fig. 61. The author in one of his earliest onstage assignments, as a traveling minstrel in Moliére's *The Doctor in Spite of Himself* (Portsmouth, New Hampshire, 1977). 306

Fig. 62. Hackmatack Playhouse, still operating on the grounds of the Guptill Homestead in Berwick, Maine, after more than forty years. 309

Fig. 63. Miss Letitia Prism, Dr. Frederick Chasuble, and the Honorable Gwendolen Fairfax in Side Street Theater's production of Oscar Wilde's *The Importance of Being Earnest* (c. 1978). 314

Fig. 64. An award-winning portrait of actor, director, costumier, and set designer Edouard Langlois by portrait photographer Michael Penney. 321

Fig. 65. The author as Caiaphas in the Embassy Players' production of *A Remarkable Mary*, Portland, Maine. 331

Fig. 66. Skywave, created by restaurateur Mike Plumer for the Berwick Young People's Theater production of *The Shortwave Radio Connection*. 335

Fig. 67. Interior of the Friendly Toast, Portsmouth, New Hampshire (before the renovation). 354

Fig. 68. "Greetings from the Friendly Toast" (promotional postcard distributed gratis by the new owners after Melissa Jasper sold the Toast in 2013). 362

Fig. 69. The Unstoppable Thought by Ross Bachelder (illustration for "Penelope Brood's Dilemma"). 364

Fig. 70. The Lobstermen's Lament: A Way of Life under Siege by Ross Bachelder. 370

Fig. 71. Rocky and Ellie Mae by Ross Bachelder. 378

Fig. 72. Captain Vito Ciccotelli, U. S. Army, December 1945. 380

Fig. 73. Vito Ciccotelli (candid photo by the author). 381

Fig. 74. Vito Ciccotelli, Age Ninety-Four by Ross Bachelder. 384

Fig. 75. The author performing at Falmouth by the Sea Assisted Living, West Falmouth, Maine (photo by Anne Strout). 395

Fig. 76. Little Miss One-Eye Finds a Lover by Ross Bachelder. 402

Fig. 77. My friend Dr. David Stupple, Eastern Michigan University sociologist. 418

Fig. 78. The Stupples—David, June, Kyle, and Kelly—Ypsilanti, Michigan (1975). 421

Fig. 79. The frame shop and Franklin Gallery at Ben Franklin Crafts, featuring works by artist Judith Heller Cassell of Rochester, New Hampshire (October, 2011). 432

Fig. 80. Reginald Ruffington's New Look by Ross Bachelder. 440

Fig. 81. Happy Dawg Walks the Sad Man by Ross Bachelder. 447

Fig. 82. Our home on River Street in Berwick, 1978 to 1982. 458

Fig. 83. Jennie Gay in 1987, the year of her death. (Photo by Amy Bachelder Jeynes). 466

Fig. 84. Caricature of the author by artist Tom Glover. 469

Preface

Why, I've been asking myself, *in a world filled to overflowing with an astonishing, never-ending cornucopia of venerable tomes, new releases, and everything in between, would anyone want to read this book?*

Here, I hope, you'll find a few good reasons:

- If you've always yearned to be involved in the fine and performing arts, but don't know where to begin—and find yourself lying awake at night, uncertain of your abilities—then, regardless of your age, this book may be for you.

  It is *not* a how-to book. It *is*, however, the story of one man's joyful involvement in not one but many art forms, always in high-octane, revolving-door fashion. It's the story of a confirmed and committed *arts multiple*—a man incapable of specializing and thankful to be that way.

- If you've always specialized in one creative discipline—writer, artist, or musician—but wonder what it would be like to be deeply and simultaneously involved in all three endeavors, then this book may be for you.

- If, like me, you've been involved for years in several disciplines, but know from painful experience how hard it is to be taken seriously because of society's subtle and overt pressure to specialize, then this book may be for you too.

- And finally, if you value a serious discussion of arts-related issues, if you'd enjoy hearing about the many places that one arts multiple, living happily in New England, has traveled to, if you're fascinated with people of extraordinary character and accomplishment, who make a lasting difference in the lives of others—or if you simply enjoy a good story, well told—then this most certainly may be the book you've been looking for!

At this point, though, you may wonder why I came to write *Happy Dawg Walks the Sad Man* in the first place.

The answer is really quite simple: I've been passionately immersed in the fine and performing arts as both enthusiastic observer and inspired creator for more than fifty years now, and I decided it was time to share with others the magic of my many years of involvement. It's been a wonderful ride, and as I continue to pile on the years—I've now moved into the early portion of my seventh decade—I've no plans at all to get off the train.

Along the way, I've had a great many memorable experiences—some exhilarating, others less than rewarding, but all of them replete with either moments to be cherished or lessons to be learned.

Thanks to the arts, I've traveled to places I never thought I'd get to see, other than in the pages of travel books. I've developed friendships with people near and far, from every walk of life, who've made an enormous difference in the quality of my life and deserve to be remembered (you'll find some of them, richly honored, in the pages of this book). And I've enjoyed a wide array of multidisciplinary creative experiences as writer, artist, musician, theater professional, and fine and performing arts advocate.

I've spent time in England, Scotland, Canada, New Zealand, and dozens of cities and towns across New England and the Midwest, always in the service of the arts. I've founded and nurtured a wide array of creative enterprises, including a teen theater, an art association, and a fine and performing arts consulting service. I've taught either music or writing in several schools, performed frequently as a musician, created and exhibited dozens of artworks in several media, worked both on- and offstage as a theater professional in companies both small and large. I've written enough about the arts as an essayist, an arts reviewer, and a publicist to fill the pages of several books.

If you've done even one or two of these—or perhaps, like me, a sizable bunch of them—then you'll understand why, in spite of the bumps and bruises I've accumulated along the way, my "all arts, all of the time" lifestyle has been such a joy.

Happy Dawg Walks the Sad Man is a straightforward series of twenty informal essays, each a different encounter or series of encounters from my more than fifty years of passionate immersion in the fine and performing arts. And just for the fun of it, I've included nine short, short stories—light-hearted mini-adventures that I'm calling tiny novelettes—to give you a break from all that cogitating. They were written in response to nine eccentric drawings from a series I completed a few years ago while exploring the idea of spontaneous line work, or doodling.

The essays in this book—some alluding to events that occurred in the Midwest during the first thirty years of my life, others that occurred since 1974, when I moved with my wife and daughter to New England—are not arranged in any sort of chronological order. For that reason, there's really no compelling reason to read *Happy Dawg Walks the Sad Man* in order from cover to cover. After all, skipping around is one of the great and naughty pleasures of being a constant reader, with a mind entirely your own. So skip around and have fun doing it—and unless you tell your friends, they'll never know you did.

Altogether, the essays can be seen as both picaresque (because, for as long as I can remember, I've always leapt from one creative adventure to another and back again, whenever I felt like it), and Plimptonesque (because, like writer George Plimpton—who was famous for trying pretty much anything to get a good story—I've always been more than willing to try anything that might challenge me, intellectually and creatively, to grow).

I've included the novelettes—nine playfully eccentric fantasy pieces, set more often than not in actual but highly unlikely geographic locations—in my book because (1) it's important to me that my readers have a taste of the other, less conventional side of me, and (2) because I simply felt like it—writer's prerogative, I suppose. As I see it, the novelettes do a good job of revealing the peculiar, Jonathan Winters way in which I tend to view the world.

All art, all of the time: to the uninitiated, such a life can sound almost idyllic—a little too good to be true. But anyone who's been through it knows that a life in the arts is not all sunshine and roses; it would be foolish to suggest otherwise. Like humans everywhere, artists, writers, musicians, and theater people aren't perfect. Their egos are fragile, and in the heat of creative collaboration, they can be quick to ruffle one another's feathers. Anyone who's just beginning to get involved in the arts is likely to see that world as elitist, self-indulgent, and well-nigh unapproachable. Because of it, carving out a place for yourself in the arts can seem uncomfortably like a fraternity hazing.

And yet it doesn't have to be that way. In spite of what we read in books—and what we see in the vast majority of Hollywood films—the arts really *aren't* some lofty, exclusive club, accessible only to the affluent, highly credentialed graduates of prestigious universities. They belong to *all of us*, regardless of our backgrounds and social standing, and it is both our responsibility and our privilege to make them work for us—on *our* terms, not the terms of the self-professed cultural elite.

Preface

The arts have countless gifts to offer to anyone searching for a heightened sense of purpose, for insights into the workings of both ourselves and the larger world, or simply for a momentary but much-needed emotional lift. The more deeply we involve ourselves in creative endeavors of every kind, the greater is their power to inspire us, enrich us, and bring unmitigated joy into our daily existence.

It's important to remember, though, that in the arts, as well as in any other intellectual discipline, the goal should never be merely to fit in; it should be to find your voice—your own unique way of thinking and creating—and then to proudly speak your piece. Anyone who's full of energy and bursting with fresh ideas, valuable insights, and powerful convictions learns eventually that conformity is death to the arts.

As for me, I've long ago stopped worrying about where I fit in within that world. Just knowing that I've found my voice—no matter how inconsistent and unpredictable it might be on occasion—is good enough for me. I'm a proud, confirmed arts multiple—temperamentally incapable of specializing in any one creative endeavor, and infinitely happier now that I've stopped listening to the siren call of specialization and become my very own, multidisciplinary self.

If *Happy Dawg Walks the Sad Man* can manage, somehow, to persuade even a small handful of its readers—regardless of age, occupation, gender, spiritual beliefs, or political convictions—to stick their creative toes into the water, then wade in and immerse themselves more deeply in the fine and performing arts, then the writing of this book will have been more than worth the effort.

Acknowledgments

A book seldom comes to pass without the unqualified support of a small chorus of caring voices. I'm pleased to acknowledge the invaluable contributions of the following people, listed here in alphabetical order, who from the very beginning offered their constant encouragement as I conceived and then wrote this book.

Marilyn Bachelder of Berwick, Maine, a gifted musician, music educator, and woodworker—and my wife—who, after living with me all these years, must have wondered if I would ever find my focus as a creative. Like many others in my life, she finally realized that my alleged lack of creative focus is my focus—that I was never cut out to be a specialist, and have found immense pleasure and fulfillment as an arts multiple. Her support of my aspirations has been invaluable.

Stacey Camire of North Berwick, Maine, professional caricaturist, sign maker, and occupational therapist who loves to talk almost as much as she loves to draw, and is very good at both. Her constant encouragement and good cheer buoyed me on countless occasions as I wrote *Happy Dawg Walks the Sad Man*.

Karen Hayes of Portsmouth, New Hampshire, an artist and financial analyst who, from the very beginning of our friendship, sensed that I was born to do not one, but many things as a creative, and ought never to feel the need to apologize for my choice to avoid specialization at all costs.

Sharon Inman of Sherwood, Michigan, a high school classmate who has championed my creative work from the first moment we reconnected as classmates many years ago. For her remarkably steadfast support, I remain deeply thankful.

Amy B. Jeynes of Cincinnati, Ohio, a gifted writer and editor—and my daughter—whose guidance and encouragement were an enormous help to me in the early stages of my book. Because she also knows her way around a computer, she's come to my rescue innumerable times when software problems interfered with my work as a writer.

Anita Kimball of Tonopah, Arizona, a friend and fellow artist whose supreme optimism has never failed to shine a ray of brilliant sunlight onto my darker moments. The arts, together

Acknowledgments

with our pledge to be helpful and encouraging to everyone we encounter, have been the very foundation of our friendship.

Nicole Klungle of Saint Bernard, Ohio—the editor and designer of *Happy Dawg Walks the Sad Man*—who, while working with me on my book, showed me over and over again how knowledgeable, skilled, and attentive to detail she is as an editor. She plays her red pen like a Strad! I'm fortunate to have found her, and my book has benefitted enormously from her deep insight into both the book-writing process and the power of any kind of writing which, when cleansed of irrationalities, foolish digressions, and technical impediments, roars triumphantly to the finish line.

The late **Deborah Homer O'Leary** of Greenland, New Hampshire, a metal sculptor, jewelry designer, mobile maker, and onetime professional dancer, who, before her untimely death from cancer in September of 2012, earned a permanent place in my heart for the consummate beauty of her creative work, her extraordinary lack of pretentiousness, and her ability to maintain an almost Buddha-like serenity in an appallingly over-stimulated world.

Michael Penney of Durham, New Hampshire—an immensely talented photographer whose portrait of me can be found on the cover of this book. Michael is passionately immersed in everything photographic, and his finely crafted, deeply emotional works provide indisputable evidence of that passion.

Anne "Annie" Strout of West Falmouth, Maine, a nursing professional turned multimedia artist, who's absolutely fearless about trying new media and methods, and—when she's in her studio—more playful than a toddler in a sandbox. Being around someone as viscerally creative as Anne has been a constant inspiration for me whenever I find myself questioning my own abilities as a creative.

Lisa Bennett Toole of South Berwick, Maine, a certified Bowenwork practitioner, nutritionals consultant, artist, and equestrian who has always encouraged me in my creative work and applauded me for my moments of success. When I wondered, five years ago, whether a trip to New Zealand was possible or even advisable, she refused to accept any of my arguments against it. Her belief in me contributed importantly to my decision to stop my doubting and *go there*, no matter what.

Callum Toole (Lisa's son, also of South Berwick), an intellectually curious, remarkably compassionate young man who has always taken an interest in my work, and who has all of the mental and emotional tools he'll ever need to be a successful writer himself one day.

Happy Dawg Walks the Sad Man

Chapter 1

Knowing Wendell Harwood
Lessons a Janitor Taught Me

We can never really predict which of the thousands of people we cross paths with in our lives are destined to have the most significant influence on us—our values, our character, our future successes and failures. When in 1962 I first stepped onto a college campus as a freshman music student, I was certain the most influential of people would be my professors. After all, they had the power, and as sculptors of the mind they were destined to contribute mightily to the shape of my thinking, my ways of conducting myself in the world beyond the classroom, and my prospects as a young professional-in-the-making. But as a callow eighteen-year-old, bursting with optimism and eager to learn, I'd soon discover that knowledge and wisdom can be found not just in the classroom but in the most unlikely of places. And that, to my great surprise and everlasting gratitude, became the most important lesson of my college years.

Wendell Harwood—the name has a certain patrician, high-society panache, doesn't it?

And yet Wendell Harwood was a janitor by profession, toiling in the scuffed and battered halls of the music department at Eastern Michigan University in Ypsilanti, where I studied as an undergraduate student in the early 1960s.

Harwood first made himself known to me when, as an incoming freshman, I stepped for the very first time into the downstairs men's room of the Alexander Music Building and discovered him crouched in front of a stall, cleaning a toilet.

He was short and stout, probably in his late forties, with big, beefy hands and fingers like German sausages. His complexion was clammy and blue-veined; his hairline receded to the halfway point of his scalp. His blue-gray eyes had a distant, otherworldly look about them, as if he were anywhere but in the basement of an academic building, cleaning up other people's messes.

I would soon learn that Wendell didn't find it easy to look others—or perhaps even himself—straight in the eye.

"If you have to use the bathroom," he said, "I can come back another time!" He had a lilting tenor voice, but when he spoke, the words tumbled out willy-nilly, making it hard to understand him.

"Quite all right. I can wait!" I said, feeling very young and culturally distant from a man who in both appearance and circumstances was so dramatically different from the father I knew and the high school band director I expected to become.

He stood up and moved across the room, then began cleaning the sink opposite the stalls, humming quietly as he scrubbed. He was dressed from head to toe in threadbare, olive green work clothes. His shoes were deeply creased from untold years of down-on-his-knees labor as a janitor. The heels were dramatically worn down, causing him to walk with a waddle, like a wayward duck in a Disney cartoon.

When he'd finished his work, he gathered up his cleansers and rags, put them in a small, handled carrying case, and headed out the door. "All done!" he said. "Got to clean the practice rooms next. But I'll be back in the afternoon. I do the bathrooms twice a day, sometimes more. It never ends!"

Wendell the Invisible

I would see Wendell nearly every day in the music department that first year, mopping and waxing the floors, tending to the bathrooms, or polishing the practice room pianos. He never failed to say hello, then ask me how my classes were going. "Got to keep up with your studies," he'd say, "and put in your time in the practice room, too!"

The more I saw Wendell walking the halls of Alexander— we nearly always called it Alex for short—the more obvious it became that, when he wasn't being mercilessly stereotyped, he was being routinely and callously ignored. Except for the many times when someone needed his services, he was the Invisible Man of the music department. Students and faculty alike considered him certifiably quirky, perhaps even a little bereft of his marbles. He nearly always mumbled to himself while going about his labors, and much of what he said was slurred and nearly unintelligible.

One of the uglier and more persistent rumors was that he was known to sweep across campus each day at sunrise, check the bushes for piles of human waste, then shovel them into a bucket, bring them back to Alex and deposit them in the dumpster before reporting to work.

However ill-conceived were the various theories about Wendell, he was thought by and large to be little more than a kindhearted but hopelessly befuddled social outcast. The result was that people seldom if ever attempted to look beyond the mop and pail and ask themselves what else Wendell Harwood might actually have to offer other than his services as janitor.

As I worked my way through my undergraduate years, I came to see that the university community and its non-academic support staff actually inhabited two separate, patently unequal universes. Higher education has always been demonstrably hierarchical—an unabashed petri dish for the growth of social Darwinist ways of thinking. Social stratification, along with its unsavory consequences, was as rife and endemic at EMU as anywhere else in academia.

Anyone working from false assumptions—and far too many do, in every walk of life—would have been surprised to learn Wendell's real story. Not long after meeting him, I learned to my delight that he was a passionate lover of music, and that he had studied piano formally while a student at Ypsilanti's Roosevelt High School—a fact that more than likely explains why he sought janitorial work in the Department of Music at EMU rather than in some other department.

An enthusiastic tribute to Wendell, published in the 1931 Roosevelt High School yearbook, offers good, solid evidence of the extent to which Harwood's classmates admired and respected him for his musical accomplishments:

WENDELL HARWOOD

Paderewski—Wendell Harwood is to Roosevelt School as the immortal master. When this quiet, unassuming individual is seated at the keyboard, he assumes an entirely different personality. He becomes as one apart from him whom we have known. He calls from his instrument magnificent harmonies. He touches it softly, and it responds with minor strains of unspeakable sweetness. Our thoughts of Wendell as quiet and conservative vanish. While he plays, we discover that we do not know him at all.

Wendell has been the classical link in the class. He may be quiet and reserved, but he is always sure of a thing before he speaks. We all hope Wendell continues his study of the piano. It will make us proud to have known one who can assume the rank of a recognized artist.

Wendell was just seventeen when his father died unexpectedly in 1931, and according to the custom of the time, Wendell became the chief breadwinner of the family. The effects of the Great Depression were still being felt around the country, and Nellie, his mother, was both chronically ill and, for all practical purposes, unemployable. The circumstances he found himself in gave him no choice but to drop out of school, end his years of costly private piano lessons, and go to work. In 1955 he took a job as janitor at the Department of Music at Eastern Michigan University; he retired in 1969 after fourteen years of service.

More Than a Janitor

Harwood may have ended his formal study of the piano to make room for gainful employment, but he was clearly not a quitter. As I got to know him, I learned that for at least the past three decades he'd been leading a double life—working full-time and, with the support and encouragement of his mother, playing piano in his off-hours. From 1955 to 1969 he was both janitor and musician, and very good at both.

Entirely on his own, he'd developed a solid repertoire of classical and Romantic works for piano. Ludwig van Beethoven was his overwhelming favorite. "*Moonlight Sonata*—no better music on earth!" he'd say. Occasionally, when he saw me in a practice room, he'd take a break from his cleaning and play a few measures for me. In return, I'd play from one of the pieces I was working on as a flute player. We were making music across an enormous cultural divide, but in spite of our many obvious differences, we became friends.

One late-September evening in my freshman year, I shut myself into a practice room just off the balcony of Pease Auditorium to work on C. P. E. Bach's *Solfeggietto*—a piece I'd be required to play in front of a jury in less than a week. I'd just leapt headlong into an especially difficult passage when my concentration was broken by the elegant sounds of a piano coming from somewhere in the auditorium.

I put down my flute, opened the practice room door, and stepped out onto the balcony to see where the sound was coming from. The answer was just thirty feet below me, at the very center of the stage.

Fig. 2. Wendell Harwood at the piano, age eighteen, Roosevelt High School, 1932.

I sat down in front of the brass railing along the lip of the balcony and listened intently to the music. The scene below me was illuminated by a single, unshaded lightbulb dangling high above the Baldwin grand that had served so many visiting soloists with distinction for the better part of a century. A just-used mop and bucket lay in a puddle of water to the left of the piano, and hunched over the keyboard was a small man with muscular build and receding hair, bearing down with Glenn Gould intensity as he worked his way through the quiet middle movement of a Beethoven sonata. He was in ecstasy and lost to the world.

He was dressed as always in his workplace greens, but on this night, with hair all a-tangle and hands flying across the keyboard, he was an entirely different creature from the man on his hands and knees each morning in the music department bathroom, scrubbing away on the bowl of a toilet. Here at center stage of an empty auditorium, divorced for a moment from the tools of his trade, he was a latter-day Horowitz, playing to an audience of hundreds and wowing them with his pianistic gifts.

Arthritis—the result of years of exposure to bitterly cold water—had begun to gnarl and disfigure his hands, but his playing was still astonishingly fluid, with elegant phrasing, a soft but efficient touch, and remarkable control of his dynamics.

I waited until he neared the end of the movement, then worked my way down the staircase at stage right, strode down the center aisle, and stood at the base of the stage.

"Mind if I sit here and listen for a while?" I asked him. He finished the movement with a flourish, then turned toward the house and looked down at me. "No, not at all!" he said, displaying his characteristic warmth and aw-shucks diffidence. Tonight, though, it was seasoned with a tone of unmistakable pride.

As I settled into my chair, he rose from the bench, stood beside the piano, and bowed to an imaginary audience. It was a touch of humor seldom seen from him, tinged with regret at the thought of what might have been.

There for one moment, standing on that stage, he was a newborn butterfly, shedding his chrysalis and unfolding triumphantly to the welcome warmth of an imaginary sun. His working-class greens had become a tuxedo, and he'd become Wendell Harwood, concert pianist.

"How about an encore?" I asked, laughing.

"Encore? Well, sure!" he said, beaming.

He sat down again at the piano, flipped the tails of his imaginary tux, rubbed his hands together, then plunged into Beethoven's March from *The Ruins of Athens*, attacking the keyboard with all the energy and passion that had lain dormant within him over the years—years in which he'd uncomplainingly cleaned up after students too immersed in their adolescent dreams of greatness ever to imagine that the music department janitor, wed by circumstances to his mop and pail, might once have harbored dreams as ambitious as their own.

As he neared the end of the March, I thought of all of the men and women before him who'd reached for the stars but fell short of their destination, brought harshly back to earth by an unwelcome intrusion into what had been an inextinguishable dream.

A Piano for a Broom

He played the last thundering chord, and as the sound rose up into the hushed and hallowed atmosphere of the auditorium,

Wendell got up from the piano, grabbed the handle of his bucket, slung the mop over his shoulder, and waddled off the stage, smiling as he went.

For some reason he'd left his music on the piano rack, either because he'd forgotten it while lost in his musical reverie or because he'd planned to come back later in the evening for another performance. I decided to retrieve the music and return it to him in the morning, when we'd be sure to cross paths again at Alex. This time, though, he'd be both janitor and pianist, and I'd be both aspiring musician and kindred spirit.

As he disappeared through the wings off stage left, I hopped up onto the stage, plucked his music from the piano, then looked down at the keyboard. Smeared across the white keys from left to right was a trail of coagulating blood, drawn from the quicks of his jackhammer fingers as he'd pounded his way through the March. It was blood from a mighty battle, shed by a man who'd traded a piano for a broom, then learned somehow to live with the tragic diminution of his finest dream.

I went back upstairs to my practice room to continue rehearsing *Solfeggietto*, but I couldn't stop thinking of what I'd just seen and what it portended, not just for Wendell but for me.

By the time I'd worked through my undergraduate years as a music student and into a graduate teaching fellowship in the English department, the two of us had carved a curious, from-a-distance friendship out of the class-conscious polarity of the academic milieu. Every day, as he went about his rounds and I worked to perfect my musicianship and improve my skills as a writer, we were loyal chat-mates, sharing a beautiful but unspoken empathy with each other while talking about the simple things in life.

Without really knowing it, Wendell had become a teacher of sorts for me—an itinerant, mop-wielding professor of humble living. With his uncommon courage and ineffable grace, he'd taught me never to allow myself to be defined by the inevitable setbacks of living. At the same time, I learned to see in him qualities of dignity and nobility that some of the music department faculty, in spite of all their long-winded résumés, fancy suits, and elite credentials, couldn't rightly claim to have.

We Give and We Get, and Then

Wendell and I continued to share our day-to-day struggles whenever we happened to see each other in the course of our daily affairs in the music department. I'd tell him of my success-

Fig. 3. Wendell and Ross together, 1974.

es, and he'd tell me of his. Then, when a cousin of his suddenly died of a heart attack, Wendell learned he'd inherited a cool $150,000. For him, it was an unimaginable sum. Within a matter of days he'd ordered a Baldwin baby grand from a shop in nearby Ann Arbor. "I've always wanted a baby grand!" he said.

Then, in the summer of 1974, when he learned I was preparing to move to Maine in a few weeks with my wife and daughter—and that I had no piano of my own—he called me at my home and announced his intention to give me his old apartment-size upright as a going-away gift. "I'd hate to see you wasting away up there in Maine, unable to play!" he said.

I shook his hand and thanked him profusely, then arranged to have the upright moved into our apartment. It would eventually be strapped into a U-Haul for the trip to New England.

A week later, Wendell, who'd finally retired in 1969, came to Alexander Music Building and informed me that he had liver cancer and had been given only six months to live. Then he announced that he'd decided to will the baby grand to me. "I won't be playing it where I'm going," he said. "Might as well give it to someone who can make use of it!"

His days as a janitor were over, and he could now play his new piano whenever he wished, for as long as his health would allow.

I missed seeing him in the music department. We'd no longer be exchanging pleasantries and playing songs for each other, and Alex had lost one of its most loyal, self-effacing personalities.

Fig. 4. Wendell Harwood, pianist (and, from 1955 to 1969, head custodian in the EMU Department of Music).

"Good luck in Maine!" he said at the end of our last, awkward conversation together. "You'll hear from my lawyer about the piano. I'll take care of it right away!"

The months his doctor had promised him—precious time to play the piano without the interference of a day job—dwindled into weeks and then days. Just two months after he'd promised me the baby grand, I learned he'd passed away on September 5, 1974, at the age of sixty, less than two weeks after we arrived in Maine.

By then I'd moved the old upright into our apartment and settled into my very different life in New England. I waited patiently to hear from the lawyer about the contents of Wendell's will.

Finally, nearly six months later, a letter arrived. I tore it out of its envelope, read it eagerly from top to bottom, and discovered that nowhere in the will was there any evidence that he'd actually bequeathed the piano—or anything else—to me. He'd died before he could make it official.

"I'm sorry, Mr. Bachelder," said a note attached to the letter. Its writer would never know the not-at-all-acquisitive reasons for my sadness.

The heart mends, and in time my life began to pick up again where it had left off. I continued to play the small upright Wendell had given me, always mindful of the unique way in which it had come into my life. It was noticeably out of tune, and the felts on its hammers had become brittle and unresponsive, but it was okay with me. It might have been technically an upright, but it was a baby grand to me.

Many years later, when I played my piano late at night in my home in Maine, I imagined I could still hear snatches of Beethoven's March from *The Ruins of Athens* rumbling up from the soundboard and rattling the teacups on the shelf across the room. And had Wendell been there in the room with me, dressed in his tie and tux and spit-shined shoes, he'd have gone to the old upright, played the *Moonlight Sonata*, and made that instrument sing like it had never sung before—one more gift from an exceptionally giving man.

Chapter 2

My Invincible van Gogh
Still with Me after All These Years

In his tragically abbreviated life (1853–1890), artist Vincent van Gogh was much more than the gifted, astonishingly prolific painter he finally came to be in spite of his self-destructive behavior. He hungered unceasingly for approval of both himself and his art, and yet, more often than not, he was his own worst enemy. Long after his passing, he's become a case study in bipolar disorder—a man poetically enraptured and clinically depressed in equal proportion. He was as emotionally complex and paradoxical as they come—passionate but withdrawn, narcissistic but giving, fanatically driven but prone to ennui, intellectually brilliant but hopelessly obtuse.

He was also a deeply loving man, and yet he could be unspeakably small-minded and mean-spirited when, whether justly or unjustly, his fragile ego was under siege. Van Gogh was truly a survivor, and that quality in him, coupled with his incomparable vision as a painter, has made him the one person I've studied more thoroughly than any other person on the planet. I think he'd be astonished to learn just how profoundly he and his works have influenced countless artists and lovers of art, including me.

Vincent van Gogh has been an important part of my life ever since the early '60s, when, as a sophomore music student at Eastern Michigan University, I discovered and then eagerly devoured Irving Stone's histrionic page-turner of a novel, *Lust for Life*.

I'd recently declared a minor in English and American literature, and while Stone's over-the-top, quasi-scholarly opus would never have made the English department reading list—its wild popularity and pulp-fiction tenor had caused legions of indignant, stuffed-shirt academics to question its worth as reading material—it really revved up my literary engines.

I'd fallen into the rhythm of stopping off before my early morning classes to read over coffee and donuts at Roy's Squeeze

Inn, a charming little shoebox of a diner just across the street from the Department of Music. Luckily, the Squeeze Inn, with a stimulating mix of blue-collar workers, budget-conscious commuter students, and the occasional tenured professor in search of local color, made the perfect setting for a callow undergraduate eager to know more about not just van Gogh the painter, but van Gogh the man.

Many of the men who frequented the Squeeze Inn appeared to be truck drivers, carpenters, and mechanics. In their threadbare denims and matching shirts with company logos stitched to the pocket, they were dressed not to make an impression but to confront the demands of the workplace in practical, unpretentious ways. Perched next to them on the bright red swivel stools at the Squeeze Inn, the occasional visiting professor, tucked into his Harris tweeds, looked more like an eighteenth-century British dandy than a run-of-the-mill Midwestern academic.

As for me—at the time a wet-behind-the-ears nineteen-year-old with a stack of textbooks teetering next to my toast and eggs—I must have elicited many a chuckle from the more worldly-wise working stiffs around me. *Who does he think he is*, they must have wondered, *and what does he really know about life?*

Not much, I suppose. To them, I must have appeared to be all books and no experience. When not stuffed into a practice room, working on my skills as a flute player, I managed to find enough time to move from Stone's novel to whatever scholarly tomes I could find in the art history section of the university library. In them I finally discovered van Gogh's paintings and drawings—an astonishing cornucopia of works by a man possessed—an artist consumed by an almost fanatical need to get the things he saw down on paper or canvas before they had the audacity to get away from him.

Those books, copiously illustrated and rich with biographical data, really made their mark. For a short time, anyone who happened to be up early and on campus while I was an undergraduate would have seen an almost comically attired student strolling around at sunrise, trying hard to look like anything but a sophomore student of music. So completely immersed was I in Stone's colorful, near-tortured accounting of Vincent that I'd begun to weave into my persona the very characteristics most commonly associated with van Gogh: corncob pipe, bushy red beard, work boots, and a wide-brimmed straw hat that could easily have been snatched from van Gogh's head as he dozed in a field on the outskirts of Arles. It was my very own one-man play, performed each morning on the manicured lawns of a blue-collar campus.

Fig. 5. Left-hand drawing from the author's triptych *The Three Faces of Vincent*.

Anyone with an awareness of art history would have seen right away that I'd purloined my vision of van Gogh from both Stone's novel and the 1956 film *Lust for Life,* based on the novel and starring Kirk Douglas as van Gogh and Anthony Quinn as his truculent roommate, Paul Gauguin. And when I hopped up onto my stool each morning at the Squeeze Inn, I imagined that, at any moment, Vincent himself might come barreling through the door, drop his easel and canvases in the corner, and join me for breakfast. He'd have fit right in, and I'd have been revealed as an impostor.

Long after my years of university study, with a decade or two of real-life experience under my belt, I came to understand that the humble laborers I so often sat next to at the Squeeze Inn—men with steel-toed shoes, work-stained hands, and sun-parched complexions—were the kind of people van Gogh would have wanted most to paint, had he known them as I knew them.

It is common knowledge that van Gogh failed miserably at attempts to succeed in the more conventional occupations for which his parents and other family members thought he was best suited. He tried and failed at gallery sales, then took work as a book clerk, then attempted classroom teaching. And then he tried and then failed (perhaps most resoundingly) at the life of an evangelist. It ought not to be difficult for us to empathize. Many of us can look back with some discomfort, and perhaps even a little embarrassment, on a checkered employment history. It's the price we paid in our early years for attempting to please others while struggling to find out who we really wanted to be.

Few of us can claim to have been through as many trials and tribulations on our way to occupational fulfillment as Vincent van Gogh, and yet in his struggles to find himself, I began to see painful parallels with my own adolescent experience. If he and I had been contemporaries, we would likely have had much to say to each other about the need to free ourselves from the judgments of others and find our own, unique way in the world.

What was it about Vincent van Gogh, beyond the indisputable magnificence of his art, that has kept me and countless other van Gogh enthusiasts around the world devoted to him all these years?

Like them, I've bowed unapologetically before the altar of Vincent. I've stood in awe of his accomplishments—miracles on canvas that he managed to perform in spite of a steady drumbeat of setbacks and discouragements that would have caused the average artist to pour his paints down the nearest drain and turn his brushes into kindling.

I've drawn repeatedly from his drawings and paintings, trying in vain to unlock the mighty secrets of his one-of-a-kind line work, his passion-filled brushstrokes, and his dazzling color magic. Over more than fifty years, I've read all or parts of dozens of books about his life and his works. I've tracked down his

Fig. 6. Right-hand drawing from the author's triptych *The Three Faces of Vincent*.

paintings in galleries in New York City, Philadelphia, and Washington, DC, and from Boston to Indianapolis and back again. By the time you've finished this chapter, I may even have made it to the van Gogh Museum in Amsterdam to pay homage to the masterpieces so gloriously assembled there.

Clearly, I can't get enough of the man, but the question is why. The artistry of his work speaks for itself, so for my purposes I'll explore other explanations for my enduring passion for everything Vincent.

To begin with, I've always been in awe of the speed at which van Gogh painted in the last decade of his life—he didn't pursue speed for its own sake, and his was not merely a reckless speed; the speed at which he painted was a speed born of raw passion, combined with a level of mastery that few artists ever manage to achieve in their lifetime. One can almost see the sweat on Vincent's brow, hear the sound of the brush hitting the canvas, and inhale the pungent aroma of his oils simply by confronting one of his paintings head-on for the first time and drinking in its brilliance. Along with the speed and the mastery comes a certain come-what-may, go-for-broke fearlessness, and when van Gogh was in fiery combat with a canvas, he was as fearless as they come.

It's important to remember, though, that van Gogh didn't just pick up a brush one day and start turning out paintings like cars on an assembly line. He was remarkably well informed in the history of art, and to earn his stripes as a painter, he drew himself silly and worse in the early years, working at a furious pace, drawing and drawing and drawing again, until he saw irrefutable evidence of his growth as an artist on the sheet of paper in front of him. Vincent van Gogh was more an inspired workhorse than the idiot savant we've been led on occasion to believe he was.

I also admired Vincent for his growing indifference to socially acceptable behavior and material things. He grew up in a family in which respectability—wearing the right clothing, spending time with the right people, finding the right occupation—meant more than anything else. What meant the most to van Gogh were nearly always the things that meant the least to his parents, and those differences inevitably caused Vincent to seethe with anger and resentment. The more I learned about Vincent's troubled childhood—his chronic feeling that he was somehow unworthy of his parents' affection—the more similarities I saw in his upbringing and mine. Because of it, I found myself wishing I had had the courage to be as rebellious as he was when differences arose within the family.

Vincent van Gogh had a powerful work ethic, and to this day, when I think of drive and determination, I think of him. No matter what he tried to do or be in his early years, he gave it everything he had until he realized that it simply wasn't for him. When he finally got serious about painting, he became fully and passionately immersed in the one endeavor that meant more to him than anything else. Surrounded by the ignorance and disapproval of friends and family, he exuded intelligence at the easel and exhibited a level of courage and fortitude that few people—other than, perhaps, soldiers in battle—will ever experience. His accomplishments as a painter weren't some bizarre aberration; they were the result of careful observation, enormous labor, and a precocious insight into what makes a painting truly and lastingly succeed.

Fig. 7. Middle drawing from the author's triptych *The Three Faces of Vincent.*

Examples of van Gogh's extraordinary kindness and compassion are well documented in his letters to Theo, his sister Wil, and others. How many men do we know, for instance, who, like van Gogh, would take a prostitute off the streets, offer her a safe place to live and a chance to marry, and then, regardless of who the father might be, treat her children as his own?

How many men do we know who, while living in unimaginable squalor in the mining district of the Borinage, would take apart their beds, deliver them to a family whose children were cold and starving, then sleep on piles of straw?

And finally, how many men do we know who, while freezing at night in that same shack, would rescue spiders from their webs or leave saucers of precious milk for the mice who shared the appalling filth of their habitat with them? Vincent, who as a child living in Groot-Zundert had a passionate interest in animals and insects, did just that while living and working in the Borinage.

Fifty years later, while ministering to the lepers at his hospital in the village of Lambaréné in west central Africa, the famed philosopher, musician, medical missionary, and physician Albert Schweitzer would exhibit the very same reverence for life by insisting whenever possible that his fellow villagers step aside and allow vast columns of warrior ants—known to devour everything in their path, including humans—to march by without being stepped on.

Albert Schweitzer and Vincent van Gogh? At first glance they would seem like an unlikely match. Their lives were dramatically different, and yet it's obvious that in at least one important respect—their love and respect for animals—they were kindred spirits.

It could also be argued that they shared the same extraordinary level of intensity in their pursuit of an ideal. Both, in their own way, were willing to make great sacrifices in order to achieve their goals. Schweitzer, who became known around the world for his accomplishments as organist, scholar, and theologian, turned his back on prestige and public accolades and spent the better part of his later years caring for the less fortunate in Lambaréné. Van Gogh turned his back on conventional, socially acceptable occupations at every turn, and in spite of constant parental disapproval and the ridicule of nearly everyone around him for his odd appearance and eccentric behavior, he threw his heart and soul into his work as an artist.

One can only imagine what might have occurred if, through an accident of history, they'd met up with each other and discovered just how much, in spite of their many differences, they actually had in common. I can't help but think that Schweitzer would have found a way to help Vincent believe in himself when others, hard as they tried, failed to do so.

Because of his extraordinary perseverance, van Gogh was a powerful role model for me as I worked my way through my undergraduate years. Whenever my academic workload seemed insurmountable, I remembered Vincent's astonishing tenacity as a painter and worked doubly hard to succeed in both the classroom and the studio. And whenever I thought I might not be able to cope with the constant dissension within my family, I'd remember his courage while standing up against the harsh judgments and constant disapproval of his parents. Across what was obviously an enormous cultural and temporal abyss, he managed to help me believe in myself when others close to me seemed either unable or unwilling to do so.

A Postlude to Vincent

The popularly accepted theory that van Gogh shot himself with a pistol while painting in a wheat field on the outskirts of Auvers-sur-Oise was challenged by Steven Naifeh and Gregory White Smith in their biography *Van Gogh: The Life*. They contend that it was far more likely he was shot accidentally by one of two boys in possession of a stolen pistol and known to have repeatedly taunted Vincent because of his shabby appearance and peculiar ways. They go on to suggest that, out of compassion for the boys,

Fig. 8. *Van Gogh and a Leaf*, the author's portrait of Vincent.

van Gogh covered for them by saying on his deathbed that he'd shot himself intentionally. It would have been a way for him to end his life of suffering while simultaneously performing an act of mercy—a choice that would have been entirely compatible with the kind-hearted, compassionate man he was in real life.

A century after van Gogh's passing, he was remembered by 113-year-old Jeanne Calment—who as a 13-year-old was serving in her uncle's fabric shop when van Gogh came in to buy some canvas—as "dirty, badly dressed, and disagreeable," and "very ugly, ungracious, impolite, sick." She also recalled selling him colored pencils. Perhaps, had Calment encountered van Gogh at a better time in his life, seen van Gogh's paintings, and understood their brilliance, she would have died with a more favorable recollection of the man.

Sadly, he sold only one painting in his life: *La Vigne Rouge* (*The Red Vineyard at Arles*). That painting, rich in color and filled to overflowing with van Gogh's characteristic emotional intensity, is now in the permanent collection of the Pushkin Museum of Fine Arts in Moscow. Little could he have imagined that one day his works would come to be seen as world-class treasures, bought by private collectors and major museums for astronomical prices. In 1990, his *Portrait of Dr. Gachet*—the first of two versions—sold at auction in New York for a breathtaking $82.5 million. Allowing for inflation, that remains the highest price ever paid for a work of art at a public auction.

Vincent van Gogh paid a heavy price for his failure to understand the worst propensities of people, including himself, until late in his life. He was taunted by schoolchildren from an early age, misunderstood by his parents, rejected by women who couldn't accept his homely appearance and unsavory behavior, ridiculed for his refusal to conform to the dictates of conventional religion, and laughed at for painting to please not the academics but himself. The harder he tried to live from the heart, the more he was held in contempt for his refusal to conform. Tragically, in response to the intolerance all around him, he all too often acted in ways both inexplicable and inexcusable.

In the end, van Gogh was his own worst enemy. He lacked the critical self-assurance that would have allowed him to live his life the way he saw fit, regardless of what others might think of him. In Don McLean's magnificent musical paean to van Gogh, "Vincent (Starry Starry Night)," he spoke directly to Vincent, saying that the world was never meant for someone as beautiful as him. And yet, without the stunningly beautiful, emotionally powerful artworks Vincent left in his wake, the world as we know it, with all its ugliness and inhumanity, would be an infinitely less beautiful place to live in.

My Invincible van Gogh

Fig. 9. *Kensington's Headache* by Ross Bachelder.

❦ Tiny Novelette 1 ❦

Kensington's Headache

Being Tobias Kensington had never been easy. Born in the East London slums in the middle of the seventeenth century, he never knew who his father was or where his next meal was coming from. After the Great Fire of London in 1666, he was evacuated to the Moorfields area and forced to live with his mother in a cold and filthy tenement crawling with cockroaches, haunted by criminals, and lacking the most basic amenities.

Then, when he was a lad of only seventeen, the woman who brought him into the world was swept away by the bubonic plague, and he became an orphan. To make things worse, he suffered from inexpressibly violent headaches that left him horribly disfigured and caused nearly everyone to run with horror and revulsion when they saw him on the streets.

With no place to live and no one to be close to, he slept at night on park benches or in the rat-infested bowels of abandoned row houses. His was a wretched existence, and because of it he began to wonder if he would ever know a moment of happiness or feel the warm flesh of a beautiful woman against his own.

And then, one night, while dining on the contents of a half-eaten bowl of pottage from a back-alley trash can, he found a urine-soaked copy of the *Oxford Gazette*, and within it the remnants of a leaflet containing an announcement:

> This very evening, by order of the Queen, the underprivileged citizens of London's Moorfields district are hereby invited to a night of English country dancing at the Banqueting House, Whitehall. Regardless of the extent of your properties, your station in life, or your physical appearance, you shall be welcomed into the company of the Royals for this one and only time. Join us for a magical evening of reels, rounds, and longways, the warmest good cheer, and your choice of Ethiopian coffees, Central American chocolates, and the most delectable teas from Mainland China!

Elated at the prospect of even one brief moment of happiness, Kensington washed his clothing in the River Thames, combed the beetles from his hair, and headed to Whitehall. As he pounded the cobblestones from Cockspur to Charing Cross, throngs of hateful bystanders hurled stones and epithets at his aching head.

Finally, as he approached the grand facade of the castle, he saw a hundred guests dancing happily together by the light of tall, flickering candles.

"But who will ever wish to dance with the likes of me," he moaned to himself.

"I will!" whispered a woman with long golden hair and a gown of pure gossamer.

"But I am horribly disfigured by my headaches!" he said. "You'll run from me like all the others!"

"But I'm not *like* the others!" she replied. "Nor will I ever run from thee! The outward appearance of a man has nothing to do with his inner worth. You must trust me in this matter!"

Then, with his heart soaring to the heavens, he swept her up into his arms, and together they danced the night away. The very next morning, his headaches ceased to plague him, and his face was once again smooth as a new baby's bottom.

Chapter 3

Out of a New England Storm
A Lady of the South Appears

What would we do without surprises in our lives? It was Ralph Waldo Emerson who famously said, "A foolish consistency is the hobgoblin of little minds." I'm audacious enough to adapt his excessively quoted aphorism to my own selfish needs: predictability, I think, is the bane of a joyful existence. Serve me life in all its infinite variety—something delicious, never before on the menu. And that's just what Evangeline—a solitary figure from a faraway place, oblivious to the weather and oozing with charm—gave me on the night she came into my life. I may have embellished this story's cast of characters here and there, but everything else about this little melodrama actually happened.

As a child growing up in southern Michigan, I'd been taught from early on never to pick up hitchhikers. We had plenty of them where we lived, far out into the country and just off the edge of a busy highway leading from Jackson to Lansing.

The admonition was especially relevant for us as a family. We lived only a few miles from the notorious Michigan State Prison—a sprawling, heavily guarded penal institution made infamous after the release in 1962 of a shamefully hyperbolic B movie called *Jacktown*, directed by William Martin and starring the relatively unknown Richard Meade in addition to Patty McCormack of *Bad Seed* fame.

Every few months, as soon as news of yet another escapee had broken in the local media, we'd go into nuclear threat mode at our home. Why? Because the escapees had the unfortunate habit of walking past our home along U.S. 127 North while thumbing for a ride to anywhere but back to MSP. Add to that the fact that my mother was an Olympic-caliber alarmist, wired to fly off the handle at everything from the pop of a wad of bubble gum to the slam of a pantry door, and you have a volatile mix with a promise, however unlikely, of deep, deep trouble to come. We knew with rock-hard certainty that if a hatless man dressed in blue passed by our home in broad daylight, we'd not be going out to play for at least the next three days.

So well had I learned my lesson about hitchhikers that as a little boy I once refused to accept a ride from a neighbor who lived just down the road from us and had known us for years. And when as a teenage driver I came across a man whose car was stranded along a densely trafficked expressway, I ignored his desperate plea for a ride to the nearest filling station. As I pulled back onto the road, I could see him in my rearview mirror, shaking his fist and swearing like a drunken sailor. I felt like a heel.

So far, so good. By 1974 I'd moved to Berwick, Maine, with my wife and daughter, and even then I was still able to claim with unimpeachable authority that I'd never picked up a hitchhiker. It made me feel both proud and—in spite of what Jack Kerouac and his pals might have thought—socially responsible.

But then, one late December evening in the early '80s, my adherence to principle would be challenged yet again, along with my common sense.

My daughter Amy, then a junior high student, had gone out with me for dessert and conversation at Weeks Restaurant, a popular eating place on the edge of Somersworth, New Hampshire, just across the border from our home in Berwick. It was late January, and the threat of snow could be seen lurking in the slate-gray clouds gathered along the horizon.

We were acting on a longstanding tradition of going places together and engaging in one-on-one conversation—sometimes playful, sometimes serious—that I hoped would help nurture her growing intellect and strengthen the father-daughter bond we'd established long ago.

Our outings were always rewarding to me—the car was a four-wheel classroom where on equal terms we could explore any issue my daughter wished to explore, or just be joyfully, ridiculously silly. My recollection is that in those encounters I nearly always learned as much from her as she learned from me.

Shortly after we left the restaurant, laughing uproariously over some irreverent word game we'd just played for what seemed like the ten-thousandth time, we were engulfed in a blizzard so dense that we could barely see the cars ahead of us. The traffic was bumper to bumper in places, and High Street—the one and only path from downtown Somersworth to the bridge into Berwick—was blanketed with drifting, swirling snow.

As we worked our way down the hill and toward the state line, we could see a single rope of Christmas lights swaying violently in the wind above the bridge over the Salmon Falls River. On the bridge was a thick glaze of treacherous, utterly invisible black

Out of a New England Storm

Fig. 10. High Street, Somersworth, New Hampshire, at the height of the storm.

ice. We kept the wiper blades at full throttle while staring as best we could through the snowflakes trying their damnedest to cling to the windshield of our car.

At first the sidewalks appeared to be entirely deserted. Then a ghostly white apparition emerged from the heart of the blizzard, her pale arms flailing in the darkness. As we drew closer, we could see that she was wearing only a summery flower-print dress and a pair of tattered bedroom slippers.

"That's ridiculous," said my daughter. "There just can't be an old woman outside in this weather!"

"Can't be, but there is!" I said. "We'd better stop and at least offer to help her."

I eased the car out of the traffic, then pulled over to the curb and rolled down my window. A blast of snow swirled crazily onto the dashboard.

I shouted out the window, trying my best to cut through the roar of the wind. "Do you need help, ma'am? We've got to get you out of this storm!"

"Why, yes! That would be wonderful!"

I jumped out of the car, came around to the passenger side, flung open the door, and helped her climb into the back seat.

"Oh, thank you for stopping!" she said. "I haven't been able to find my house in this storm. Isn't it awful? Anyway, maybe you can help me get home!" I'd no doubt my daughter thought the two of us had lost our minds.

I turned down the heater fan, switched on the dome light, and looked at her with the help of the rearview mirror. In spite of the cold, and despite the fact that she'd never seen us before, she acted as if we'd known her for years and were picking her up for a trip to the beach. Entirely without prodding, she began to tell us about herself, releasing a puff of Southern charm into the stuffy, overheated confines of our car.

Her name, she said, was Evangeline Goody, and she was born and raised in Blue Mountain, Alabama. She appeared to be in her late seventies or early eighties, fragile as a wounded bird, with a generously freckled, strawberry complexion and delicate, praying-mantis hands. I realized that what I'd thought was a summer dress was in fact a faded lavender negligee trimmed with frayed, yellowing lace and decorated with tiny, pale pink rosettes. Resting on her breast was an antique broach with a red, Victorian-era rose in the center. Her hair was kept in place with a pair of matching Art Nouveau combs—the choice of well-dressed women nearly a century before.

"Where do you live?" I asked. "We'll take you there right away!"

"Oh, my house is up on the Hill, just beyond Pearl's Bakery," she said. Her voice, alternately soaring and plunging in pitch, was something between a Southern twang and a schoolgirl giggle. "We'll be there in a second or two!"

She must have been kidding. The hill she alluded to—actually named the Hill because of its position on a high ridge above and parallel to Main Street—was steep enough to be a driving challenge even on a normal day. In weather like this, it was pretty much impassable. I knew it was going to take a whole lot more than a few seconds to get us where we were going, but I wasn't about to let a raging blizzard get between me and a good deed. I drove across the bridge into Berwick, made a U-turn around the town hall, and headed back over the bridge into Somersworth.

Once we were back on High Street, I made a right turn onto Prospect and began the ascent. Just three houses up on the right-hand side, Evangeline waved her hand at a three-story home with a sagging wraparound porch and a red-brick side chimney. Above the front entrance was a porch light, barely visible in the falling snow.

"That's it!" She said. "That's where I live!"

We pulled into the driveway, helped Evangeline out of the car, and escorted her up a steep staircase to the landing. I rang the doorbell, and a diminutive, prune-faced woman wearing a corduroy bathrobe and with her hair in curlers peered out suspiciously from the foyer.

"We were heading back to Berwick when we found Evangeline down on High Street," I said. "This is my daughter, Amy. We thought because the weather is so bad right now, we should offer to bring your mother home."

"I don't understand," she said. "I ain't never seen this lady before! You've got the wrong address, mister."

"Oh, dear," said Evangeline. "It looked just like my house when we drove up to it!"

The head with the curlers on it glowered at the three of us, then the woman spun around, pulled her bathrobe tight around her, and slammed the door.

I figured it was an honest mistake. Who wouldn't have trouble recognizing her home at the height of a blizzard? We got Evangeline back down the stairs and into the car. To stop her shaking, we put a spare blanket around her shoulders. For a woman trapped in a tempest, ridiculously underdressed and temporarily homeless, she was remarkably calm and collected.

"What was the name of the street you said you live on?" I asked. We were yearning to find out where she lived, drop her off, and get home to our own warm beds.

"Oh, I'm so cold and confused right now, I can't for the life of me remember the name of the street!" she said. "Must be the next one over. If Hattie were here right now, she'd laugh at me. She always said I was scatterbrained."

"Who's Hattie?" I asked.

"My sister! She lives in Florida now. She's the youngest of the children, and the prettiest, too—though she could be difficult when she didn't get her own way. She's moved around so often, I can't always remember just where she lives at any one time! Anyway, I just know my house is right around the corner. Next street up!"

I was starting to worry, and not just about the weather. The snow was coming down furiously now, blown sideways by the force of the howling, gale-force wind. We drove back down Prospect, turned right on Market Street, then made another right turn onto Beacon.

When we'd made it nearly to the top of the hill, Evangeline waved again, this time more wildly. "That's the one!" she squealed. "It's got the big blue Christmas lights I brought up from Texas after my father died. I leave 'em up all year around. It's easier that way, don'tcha think?"

"Texas?" Amy whispered. "I thought she said she was from Arkansas—or was it Alabama?"

Once again we pulled into the driveway, tumbled out of the car, and climbed a set of stairs. This set was even longer and more slippery than the last one. The doorbell didn't work, so I pounded loudly on the door to make sure whoever was inside could hear me through the storm.

This time a twenty-something man answered the door. He was dressed in black from head to foot and had a bottle of Moxie in his tattooed right hand. He must have been at least six feet tall and was as skinny as a pencil. With Evangeline lurking shyly in the background, I took the initiative.

"Is this Evangeline Goody's home?" I asked, trying to sound fully in charge of a situation that was fast getting out of control. "We've just rescued her from the blizzard, and we figured you'd want to know she's safe and sound now!"

"Like, I dunno a lady named Evangeline Tweedy!" He scratched the back of his head, then took a swig of his Moxie and wiped his lips on his coat sleeve.

"Goody!" Amy said. "Evangeline Goody."

He belched into the swirling snow, then licked his lips and arched his brow—the one with the three tiny rings lined up like chicks in a hen house.

"Goody, Tweedy, Flabby—don't make much difference. And like I said, I don't got a clue about who this lady might be."

We were down the steps and into our car before Pencil Man had a chance to come to his senses and slam the door.

Later on, Amy asked me if I'd noticed his fingernails. "They were as long as Dracula's and painted black!" she said. "And he had a huge silver skull ring on one finger with a little glowing ruby in one eye and a snake coming out of the other!"

Welcome to Somersworth, I mused to myself.

Back in the car, Evangeline sat quietly now, with her hands clasped together on her lap and her chin lowered toward her chest. Her hair was still caked in places with patches of freshly formed ice.

"I don't know what happened!" she said. "I was so certain that was my home!" For the first time there was a touch of panic in her deep-South drawl. "And what have I done with my purse? My lipstick's gotten smeared. I need my pocket mirror!" She giggled, then leaned up toward the front seat. "A lady's not truly a lady," she said, "if she's not properly made up!"

"Tell you what," I said. "I'll bet the Somersworth police can help you find your home! Let's drive down there and talk with the dispatcher and see what they can do for you."

"Yes, let's do!" she said. "I've known Trudy—or is it Charlene?—for years. She always sends the police down right away when I lock the keys in my car." She went silent for a moment, then spoke quietly into the darkness. "I get confused sometimes—don't know what I've done with things, can't remember names—stuff like that."

Finding Evangeline's home had become a living nightmare, but we had no trouble finding the police station. It was on Main Street, just down the street from Somersworth House of Pizza, where it had always been.

For the third time, we piled out of our car and plunged headlong into what had begun to feel like the blizzard of the century. I ran up to the station entrance and pushed the after-hours buzzer, with Amy and Evangeline huddled behind me in the wind. The dispatcher quickly ushered us out of the storm and into the lobby. The words "Alicia: Dispatcher" were embroidered onto the lapel of her police jacket.

"What can I do for you?" she asked, ready after so many years of service to hear anything from a minor noise complaint to a major drug bust.

"Well, my daughter and I were on the way home to Berwick," I said, "and found this woman standing on High Street in the middle of the blizzard, with nothing on but slippers and a negligee! I thought we should ..."

"No need to go any further!" she said, smiling as she peered over my shoulder at the woman we'd begun to call Evie. "People drop off Scarlett pretty much every other week, no matter what the season. She's a wanderer, that girl. Ain't you, honey!"

"Scarlett?" I said.

"It's Evangeline!" said Amy. "Evangeline Goody!"

"Actually, we've been calling her Evie," I said, "and she seemed fine with that."

"Well," said Alicia, "it isn't Evangeline, and it isn't Goody. It's Scarlett—Scarlett Hamilton Biggs, to be precise. We know that because we checked the records a long time ago in order to know just who we were dealing with and where she came from. She was born in northeast Georgia, just outside Tallulah Falls. Lives now with her younger sister about a quarter of a mile from here, but slips out all the time without telling her about it, and starts in wandering again."

"I thought it was Alabama!" said Amy.

"Alabama, Arkadelphia, Davenport!" I said. "Doesn't make much difference at this point."

"Doesn't much matter where I came from," Scarlett laughed, "long as it's from the South! One thing I never forget is that I'm a Southern girl, born and bred!"

The dispatcher put one arm around Scarlett, gave her a motherly hug, and ushered her into the station's lobby. "We've got a cot and a patchwork quilt just for Scarlett," she said. "Makes her feel right at home. I'll give her sister a jingle, and she'll come over right away and pick her up."

Other than a handful of medical researchers and a growing army of geriatric caregivers across the nation, few people had heard of the word *Alzheimer's* when Scarlett began her wandering in and around Somersworth those many years ago. It was common then to assume that any oldster who habitually forgot who she was or where she lived was just a little screwy in the head—a harmless eccentric with stories to tell but no real ability to remember them.

In the late '70s, my own paternal grandmother, Marguerite "Margo" Hinckley, finally became one of that growing number of oddly behaving eccentrics—as odd in her own way as her brother, my great uncle Horace, who later in his life made a habit of eating his peas with a knife while dining in restaurants. We figured that, like Horace, Margo was just a tad goofy in her old age—until my father found her one morning in her apartment house, pouring soap flakes into a cereal bowl.

I paid one last visit to my grandmother before moving to Maine in 1974, and two weeks later she told friends she'd had a surprise visit from a nice young man with a bushy red beard and a sense of humor, but had no idea who he was. That man was me.

A year or so after we'd moved to Maine, Margo broke out of her Grass Lake, Michigan, Alzheimer's unit one morning and ran across an open field, peeling off her clothes as she went. Our beloved Grandma Hinckley—a rosy-cheeked Baptist who nearly always answered the door with a flowered apron around her waist and who kept a jar of sugar cookies on the mantle—had never had so much fun. By running buck-naked across that open field—a feisty young maiden on a springtime romp—she'd wiped away months of confusion and suffering and given herself what was likely the only moment of genuine liberation she'd ever experienced in her God-fearing, staid and proper existence.

I didn't know until many years later that Grandma's strange behaviors were the result of her having been systematically shorn of her precious memory. Nor was I experienced enough to understand what was actually happening when, in the midst of a powerful nor'easter, Evangeline Goody—AKA Miss Scarlett Biggs, the woman with the strawberry complexion and praying-mantis hands—came magically into our lives.

To understand fully the implications of what Margo and Evangeline had lost, I had to wait until many years later, when Margo's younger son, Lowell—my father—suffered the same fate as his mother and spent the last eleven years of his life in a nursing home. In his last few years there, he was increasingly unsure of who he was, where he came from, and the enormity of the gift he had given to his country—to all of us, really—while earning a Purple Heart in World War II.

There are days when, like any other mortal, I find myself praying in my own secular humanist way that in my old age I'll still be able to remember Scarlett Biggs, Alicia the dispatcher, and all the loyal friends and acquaintances who've given me so much pleasure over the years.

If, on the other hand, I should begin to lose the gift of memory and end up in a home, I'd want to be just like Grandma. I'd wait until the nurses weren't looking, then break free of my institutional chains and run buck-naked across my very own field of dreams. Like her, I'd want to move upward and into a more heavenly trajectory—into a world in which everyone would be as beautiful, warmhearted, and carefree as Evangeline Goody was that night while in the grip of a fierce nor'easter.

In our new and improved universe, I'd see Grandma Hinckley again and learn she'd stopped eating soap flakes and switched to Cheerios. As for Evangeline, whenever I saw her I'd have assurances that the sun would always be pounding joyfully down on her deep-South, strawberry complexion. And she would never again have to wonder either who she actually was or which house was truly her home.

Chapter 4

My Midwinter Romp in England & Scotland

Being a True and Faithful Account
of Ten Days of Joyous Perambulation
within and betwixt the Merry Municipalities
of London, Eastbourne, Brighton, & Loughborough

in England

& Glasgow, Stirling, and Aberdeen

in Scotland

during Which
I Met Many Wonderful People, Saw Many Exciting Plays,
Consumed Much Fine Cuisine, Visited Many Galleries,
Walked Many Miles, Saw Magnificent Architecture,
& Generally Flexed My Intellectual and Aesthetic Muscles
While Reflecting on My Great Good Fortune
For Possessing the Means, the Time,
the Health, & the Proper Disposition for

a Trip All Alone
of My Very Own Devising

Taken in Late February
& Early March of the Year 1997

Ross Bachelder

Verified and Authenticated by the Very Traveler Himself,
Living Now in the Old & Venerable Village of Berwick in Maine

Other than my countless journeys across the southern border of Canada while traveling between Maine and Michigan, my very first trip outside the continental United States was my solo trip to England and Scotland at the age of fifty-three. It was also a watershed moment for me, marking an end to my silly, self-administered ban on what until then I'd thought of as inexcusably frivolous, utterly unaffordable travel. I hope you'll join me now for a joyful recapitulation of that enthralling, life-changing odyssey.

I haven't always been so passionate about traveling. The idea that packing one's bags and heading off to some distant land was a wasteful, self-indulgent pastime had been deeply ingrained in me as a child.

My post-war, Detroit-area parents viewed travel as a luxury available only to the elite people of the world—people with money to burn. Their idea of an exotic destination was a lakeside cottage just ten miles from our home, where we spent just one hard-earned, contentious week. Money, they believed, was for practical things like lawnmowers and washing machines. To spend it on traveling was almost sinfully irresponsible.

I learned that lesson all too well. Long after leaving home and starting a family, I continued to avoid any but the least ambitious, most affordable travel adventures.

After my daughter grew up and married and moved to Cincinnati, I began to look more carefully around me and realized what I'd been missing after years of depriving myself of travel. While junior high school students across the country were flying casually to Paris for their end-of-the-year adventures, I was still acting like a clueless little gerbil, lost in a dense forest of plastic tubes, rushing off to nowhere in particular and back again.

England and Scotland Calling

By my early fifties, I decided I'd had enough of the cautious, sedentary lifestyle I was leading. It was time to answer the siren call of travel, and so, in the fall of 1996, bursting with enthusiasm and hungry for adventure, I scheduled a trip alone to England and Scotland.

The reasons for my choice of destination were both practical and emotional. To begin with, the two countries were relatively close by—a mere seven-hour flight over the Atlantic from my home in northern New England. Furthermore, if I were to fly in the off-season, a trip to England and Scotland would be eminently more affordable than travel to other, more distant lands. It was also important to me that England and Scotland were English-speaking countries. I didn't relish the thought of wrestling with a language barrier on this, my very first overseas adventure. I'd have enough to deal with just learning how to handle unfamiliar modes of travel and the British monetary system.

While saving money was of paramount importance, I wasn't about to travel to any old place just for the sake of traveling. I'd studied English and American literature in graduate school, so a journey to the British Isles seemed like a perfect fit for me. I'd be traveling to the very two countries where some of my most beloved literary figures—James Boswell, Samuel Johnson, the Lake Poets, and others from the length and breadth of the two countries, including, of course, Shakespeare—had actually lived and created long ago.

It also didn't hurt that at the time of my trip—February, 1997—I was deeply involved in professional theater as a pit orchestra musician, arts critic, and occasional actor. It made sense for me to combine my passion for live theater with my hunger for travel. I'd attend live performances from Eastbourne (south of London) to Glasgow, Stirling, and Aberdeen in Scotland, then come home to America and write about my experiences.

I'd never been on an airplane longer than two hours, so the six-and-a-half-hour flight from Boston's Logan Airport to London's Heathrow was a bit of a shock. Nevertheless, any discomfort I felt from being in the air so long was more than balanced by my elation at the prospect of arriving on the shores of a land with a culture I'd always yearned to experience firsthand.

I boarded my plane in Boston at 8:10 a.m., and by 6:30 p.m. British time we were preparing to land at London's famed Heathrow Airport—a huge, bustling enterprise that handles more international passengers than any other airport in the world.

Stormy Weather: London

As the plane began to make its descent, the weather began to deteriorate. Dramatic bolts of lightning slashed through the clouds around our plane, followed by deafening thunderclaps and a pounding rainstorm. We were being rocked by the most severe turbulence I'd ever encountered—a ride on the Tilt-A-Whirl, five miles up in the air.

"Things are a little rough out there tonight," said the soothing voice over the intercom, "so we're advising you to keep your seat belts on. We're in a holding pattern now because of the weather. Should be landing in about forty-five minutes."

It may as well have been an eternity. Round and round we flew in the dark, bouncing about in our seats like hot kernels in a popcorn popper.

As I watched the Wagnerian drama unfolding outside my window, the man next to me—a fashionably dressed fellow with bright red bow tie, professorial glasses, and receding hair—did his best to read the London *Times* between the inelegant lurches of our jetliner.

"Is this normal weather for landing at Heathrow?" I asked Mr. Bow Tie, trying to sound nonchalant as my eyes bugged out like those of Large Marge in *Pee-wee's Big Adventure*.

"Worst *I've* ever been in," he said without looking up from his newspaper, "and I've been in a whole lot of bad weather while flying."

"Think we're gonna make it down?" By now I was leaving claw marks on the armrests of my window seat.

"Hope so," he muttered. "I've got to meet with a client in an hour or two. Can't do that up here!"

Half an hour later, the plane was finally cleared for landing. As we banked left, aligned ourselves with the assigned runway, and dropped out of the clouds, we could see all of London spread out before us like some vast, Old-World territory—a multicolored terrestrial blanket dotted with twinkling, densely packed buildings and laced with streaks of slowly moving traffic.

Finally, we thumped and screeched our way onto the runway. We were safely on the ground, and we'd soon be able claim our luggage, call our loved ones, and go our separate ways into the exhilarating pomp and splendor of London.

Not surprisingly, it didn't happen quite the way I expected it to. Thanks to poor acoustics, oddly worded signage, and throngs of tourists too locked in to their own down-on-the-ground melodramas to be of assistance, I needed nearly two hours to navigate the intricacies of Heathrow.

I arrived at my luggage kiosk, and twenty minutes later my bulging suitcase came chugging toward me along the conveyor, tagged with an easy-to-detect green and yellow ribbon.

Unfortunately, I'd created a monster. Though it weighed at least as much as half a full-grown rhino, I managed somehow to yank it off the conveyor, drag it across the terminal sans wheels (my first big mistake as a traveler), then take the nearest escalator up to street level.

Seconds later I stepped out into an astonishingly diverse urban tapestry of people from around the world, wearing everything from trench coats and turbans to saris and tunics and swinging their briefcases in a frantic, oddly synchronized dash to points unknown. Though I was still fifteen miles west of Central London, the streets everywhere around me were clogged with London cabs, delivery vans, and double-decker buses tunneling willy-nilly through the vast canyons between skyscrapers.

I dove headlong into the swarms of pedestrians, and when a light ahead of me turned green, I stepped off the curb without thinking, and into an ear-splitting chorus of honking horns and obscene gestures. I scurried back onto the curb, half-expecting to see Mary Poppins float down with her umbrella, land beside me on the pavement, and escort me to safety. But mine was a very different reality: I was all alone in London now, and I'd need to learn right away how to fend for myself.

Once I'd gotten safely across the intersection, I sat down on a park bench, studied my London guide, then caught the Tube to Lexham Gardens, Kensington. I was only a few blocks from the Atlas Hotel now, but before settling down for the evening, I needed to get to a telephone and call my daughter in Cincinnati. We had a longstanding tradition of calling each other when we'd reached an exotic destination, and in my book, London more than fit the description.

I quickly found what I was looking for on Cromwell Road. It was one of those iconic but quickly disappearing London phone booths, the red-lacquered kind with partitioned glass panels on all four sides, a gently rounded top, and the distinctive crown logo repeated all around.

Inside, plastered on every available space, were colorful, flamboyantly designed cards advertising call-girl services. The cards featured voluptuous, steamy-hot women thrusting out their oversized breasts and flashing their come-hither smiles. Nearly all of them were overlaid with graffiti—crude, ad hoc sketches of private parts, underscored with words you're not supposed to utter in polite company, even in hardened, imperturbable London.

I called Amy and poured all of my most poignant first impressions into the phone—the terrifying descent into Heathrow, my first exhilarating encounter with throngs of homebound Londoners, my harrowing skirmish on foot against rush-hour traffic—then walked the six blocks to the Atlas Hotel. It would be the first of many B & Bs I would stay in while abroad.

As I approached the hotel, I saw a young man coming out from the lobby, cradling a huge vintage television, complete with rabbit ears and a rotor, in his arms. The power cord was trailing precariously behind him as he walked. I dropped my suitcase, rushed over, and opened the door for him; when he'd gotten a few feet down the street, he turned back just long enough to thank me for my assistance. "Cheerio!" he said over his shoulder, then stepped over to the curb and stuffed the television into the trunk of his car.

Where else but in London? I thought, then headed upstairs to my room.

Bobo's Bubbles

The next morning I struck out on my first walking adventure on European soil, still groggy from jet lag and carrying some items that needed laundering. Kensington Gardens was suburban in the big-city way, with an odd mixture of ivy-covered buildings, neatly manicured lawns, and stately shade trees lining nearly every street. Here and there one could still see signs of an earlier, more intimate neighborhood, with quaint mom-and-pop stores, ornamental gardens, and tile-roofed homes dotting the landscape. I figured it was only a matter of time before I'd come across a neighborhood laundry; it was that kind of place.

It didn't take long. Only a few blocks down from the Atlas, I found Bobo's Bubbles, a tiny, coin-operated laundry wedged between two nondescript office buildings. It was oozing with Old-World charm and telltale signs of urban decay. Music poured out onto the street from a portable radio on the floor just inside the entranceway. A homeless man was slumped against the building's facade, oblivious to the noise and dreaming his dreams of upward mobility and a nice, warm bed. Beside him was a beat-up grocery cart stuffed full of his earthly belongings and covered with plastic. Through the windows facing the street I could see a man with a plum-colored turban and a thick black beard moving his hips to the Stones' "Tumbling Dice" while sorting his clothes. I headed inside, stuffed my laundry into the nearest washer, fed my loose change into the coin slot, then disappeared into a book of short stories.

An hour later I was back out on the street with my laundry dried, folded, and slung over my shoulder. The homeless man had packed up and moved along for the day. Along the street where he'd been camping out was a colorful array of street vendors peddling jewelry, fresh fruit, and souvenirs to passersby. I bought a banana, walked my laundry back to the motel, and took a badly needed nap.

Later in the evening I ventured even farther out into the neighborhood. Several blocks away I found a restaurant featuring Indian cuisine and had a leisurely supper of chicken mughlai and whole wheat chapati. By the time I'd finished my meal and paid the cashier, it was dark outside.

As I exited the restaurant, nothing looked familiar. Should I turn left or right? I'd forgotten to make note of landmarks along the path to the hotel—a mistake almost as dumb as flying from America to Britain without wheels on my suitcase. The streets were deserted, and by now the stores everywhere had closed. With no one around to set me straight, I took a chance and walked several blocks to the left of the restaurant, but nothing—not one building, tree, or fire hydrant—rang a bell. There wasn't a phone booth in sight, and I'd yet to enter the cell phone era.

Me, lost in London! I wasn't about to worry, though. I shrugged my shoulders, turned around, and headed in the opposite direction. It was a beautiful, full-moon evening, with a warm summer breeze and fireflies winking high in the trees.

It was a fine time for walking, but I didn't see another soul for at least a dozen blocks. A night on a park bench wouldn't be the end of the world, but like the homeless man at Bobo's, I figured I'd be a lot happier in a bed.

I came to an intersection, looked left and right, and saw a stylishly dressed man with a full white beard and a cane, whistling as he walked toward me in the darkness. He looked to be in his late seventies.

"Lovely evening!" he said. "Out for a walk, are you?"

"Yes," I said, "but the truth is that I've wandered too far from my hotel—I'm not from around here—and I have no idea where I am."

"No need to go off your trolley!" he said. "Where are you staying?"

"The Atlas in Lexham Gardens."

"Smashing! I know right where it is. It'll be a doddle!"

Doddle? Whatever that was, I hoped it was a good thing to be.

He paused, then tossed me a look of genuine concern. "The Atlas? That's a good distance from here, mate. You must be truly zonked!"

Zonked? Another word I'd somehow failed to learn back in the States. But I needed directions, so I took the positive approach. "*Very* zonked!" I said. "And very lost! Any chance you could point me back to where I came from? I'd very much appreciate your ..."

"Quite!" he said. "And I'll do better than that. I'll walk you back! And no need to worry. I'll enjoy the trip."

We walked for twenty minutes or so, comparing notes about his life in London and mine in the States. When we reached the Atlas, I thanked Mr. Beard-and-Cane for his trouble and stepped into the lobby. Once inside, I watched him saunter down the street and into the night, whistling like Chaplin as he went.

South to Eastbourne

Before exploring London's West End, I needed to catch a late-night train seventy miles south to Brighton, then to the seaside resort city of Eastbourne. I'd arranged well ahead of time to see a Komedia-sponsored production of Michael Allen's *What's to Be Done with Algernon? (The Scandalous Life of Algernon Swinburne)* at Eastbourne Arts Centre. After the show, I'd be staying for two nights with Mickey and Barbara Wilson, the two people most deeply committed to and responsible for the artistic success of the Centre.

I'd arranged to meet Barbara near the train station lobby as close as possible to my scheduled 3:00 a.m. arrival. I was eager to meet her and eventually her husband, two rabid theatre enthusiasts who could be counted on to fill me in on the daily workings of their theater. It would be my first really meaningful interaction with citizens of any country other than my own.

Exhausted from three days of strenuous walking in London, I was happy to settle into my seat on the train to Eastbourne. I'd tramped dozens of blocks to the Blackfriar Pub on Queen Victoria Street; held on for dear life to a lamp post on a bridge over the Thames during a fierce, howling wind; watched the changing of the guard near Buckingham Palace; and stood mesmerized at the sights and sounds of teeming Trafalgar Square, where for nearly two centuries people both blue blood and blue collar had railed against injustices.

Tired or not, I was wild-eyed with anticipation as I stepped off the train in Eastbourne and headed to the lobby. To get there, I had to walk down a long, bleak, institutional corridor.

I was the sole passenger to get off the train and come into the station. Except for the rhythmic staccato of my feet against the floor, the place was silent as a tomb. As I walked along, trailing my suitcase behind me, I tried to imagine just what Barbara would look like and how she might behave on first meeting.

Finally, at the far end of the corridor, I saw a solitary figure emerge from the shadows—a woman with silvery hair, a pale blue jacket, and a warm smile, furiously waving what appeared to be either a beach blanket or a couch throw.

"Is that *you*, Ross?" she bellowed, her booming voice echoing down the corridor.

It was Barbara, the woman whose home I'd be staying in, and the object she'd been waving at me was an American flag.

"Yes, it's me!"

"Welcome to England!" she said. "And thank you for what your country did for us during the War!"

Her thank-you couldn't have been more perfectly timed. My father, Lowell Emerson Bachelder, had earned a Purple Heart after being wounded in action in Germany during World War II, then had returned to America along with thousands of other soldiers on the *Queen Elizabeth*. For this very British woman to remember after all those years just what America had done to help bring the war to an end, and then to acknowledge it to me in such a poignant way, added enormous significance to my trip to England. I went home with Barbara, met her husband, took a shower, and settled into the guest room for a badly needed sleep.

The next morning, I saw right away that Eastbourne was clearly not some backwater destination in an obscure, outlying district. A distinct aura of pedigree emanated from its sprawling parks, spectacular gardens, and ivy-covered stone walls. That it was so decidedly urban in spite of its quaint, rural flavor ought not to have surprised me. Founded around 1800 after the consolidation of four rural hamlets, Eastbourne now has a population of nearly a hundred thousand—the modern-day incarnation of an ancient community. It has an unimaginably rich cultural history. Roman ruins, including a Roman bath and the remnants of a paved road, are known to be buried beneath the town.

Charles Dickens performed at the Lamb Theatre in Eastbourne during the 1830s. Karl Marx and Friedrich Engels were frequent visitors, and Engels had his ashes scattered at his request at nearby Beachy Head—at 531 feet above sea level, the highest and most spectacular chalk sea cliff in Britain, notorious for having been the setting for so many dramatic suicides. Zoologist and agnostic Thomas Henry Huxley—the grandfather of Aldous Huxley, author of the acclaimed novel *Brave New World*—lived out his declining years in Eastbourne.

On the second night of my stay with the Wilsons, we piled into their car—a zippy, unpretentious vehicle of English manufacture—and drove into downtown Eastbourne to see Allen's play. On the way I learned that *What's to Be Done with Algernon?* is a semi-biographical play in three acts—each a monologue—based on the life of the eccentric Victorian poet Algernon Swinburne. The story of Swinburne's curious life is told by three people who knew him intimately: Benjamin Jowett, Master of Balliol College, Oxford; Mrs. Doris Addams, proprietor of Verbena Lodge (a brothel in St. John's Wood at which Swinburne was reputed to be a regular customer); and Theodore Watts-Dunton, the lawyer who lived with Swinburne for the last thirty years of the poet's life.

What helped make the Komedia production so captivating was that all three characters—Jowett, Adams, and Watts-Dunton—were performed by the very same actor, Jonathan Elsom.

In a pre-performance interview published in the *Eastbourne Herald*, Elsom talked candidly about the formidable challenges he would soon be facing onstage. "*What's to Be Done with Algernon?* is an enormous, terrifying, and exciting challenge for me," he said. "It's nerve-wracking to be in a one-man play, and this one tests my range as an actor, to say nothing of my memory!"

He need not have worried. Allen's play, originally intended to be a novel, turned out to be an enormous success. It was beautifully written and cleverly constructed—the perfect vehicle for one courageous actor to demonstrate the enormous depth and diversity of his onstage skills. The playwriting, costumes, set design, direction, and acting were altogether superb—evidence of a company working at an exceptionally unified, nearly seamless level of excellence not easily seen in small-town American playhouses.

After the performance I introduced myself to Elsom, traded notes with him about the world of small-venue theater and its unique demands, then helped him load the van for his next destination. I envied him for his carefree, swashbuckling life as an actor, and I couldn't help wonder if it might have been wiser for me to cancel the rest of my travel plans on the spot, then join him for his merry cross-country exploits, no questions asked.

Once back in Mickey and Barbara's home, we talked well into the early morning hours about their life in Eastbourne, my life in southern Maine, and the content and quality of theater wherever it was performed around the world. The next morning they drove me back to Brighton and left me off near the train station. "It's right up the hill!" they assured me. "It'll be an easy walk for you. You can leave your belongings in the Left Luggage facility at the top of the hill. Then you'll be free to spend the rest of the day exploring!"

I ought to have looked farther up that hill before sending them on their way. As they waved their goodbyes to me through the rear window, I realized that what they'd so blithely described as an easy walk was actually an appallingly steep incline, more than half the length of a football field. It might not have been so difficult had I not so foolishly invested in a suitcase without wheels before flying to England.

Off I went up the hill, straining like a packhorse and sweating profusely as I dragged the suitcase—a good fifty pounds or more of what seemed at the time to be an utterly useless array of items—up to the pinnacle. Then I hobbled over to the Left Luggage facility, thankful to have arrived standing up, and yanked on the door handle.

It didn't budge. "Must be stuck," I muttered to myself. I gave it another jerk or two, but nothing happened.

I lost my patience, and as I furiously rattled the door handle, an old woman with a gnarled cane, a kerchief tied under her chin, and a wart on her potato-like nose saw me trying and wobbled up behind me.

"Didn't see the *sign*, didja!" she cackled. "Left Luggage been closed for two weeks. Bomb scare!" She coughed loudly, then looked at me and shook her head. "England today ain't nothin' like it was when I was a young'un!"

I spent the next several hours shackled to my suitcase, trying to see the humor in what had become a pedestrian nightmare of embarrassing proportions. When my train finally arrived, I pushed the suitcase toward the valet, crawled into the first available seat on the train, and slept like a rock for the entire return trip to London.

Back to London: Life after Eastbourne

With my time in Brighton and Eastbourne behind me, it was time get back to London and see as many plays as possible before catching another train north to Scotland. I checked into the Atlas Hotel again, rested up for an hour or two, then took the Underground straight into London's fabled West End—home to nearly fifty theaters and, like Broadway in New York City, known around the world for the stellar quality of its productions.

I'd seen very little live, big-city theater before arriving in London. My passion for drama flowered only after moving to the East Coast in 1974 and discovering the vibrant theater scene in the cities and towns of northern New England.

My first taste of large-venue theater came in the mid-'70s in Boston, when I had the pleasure of seeing Katharine Hepburn (in *A Matter of Gravity* at the Shubert) and Hume Cronyn and Jessica Tandy (in *The Gin Game* at the Wilbur). Nothing, though— not even the best that Boston could throw at me—could have prepared me for the raw, heart-pounding excitement of standing for the first time in London's West End, gaping transfixed at the vast, multicolored forest of blazing marquees telegraphing

Fig. 11. The author in London, ready to tour the West End.

their competing messages of dramatic excellence against the jet-black, star-studded tapestry of late-night London.

I'd purposefully avoided buying West End tickets in advance. Call me wild and crazy, but I was determined to avoid the stultifying effects of excessive planning by doing no West End planning at all. I'd have to choose my shows on the spot, by the seat of my pants, and I couldn't have been happier at the prospect of not knowing which show I'd be seeing an hour after my arrival.

The Buddy Holly Story

My first choice—*The Buddy Holly Story* at the Strand Theatre, Aldwych, over *Miss Saigon* at the nearby Theatre Royal, Drury Lane—was made for reasons having little to do with the theater as an art form and a whole lot to do with its relevance to my life as an adolescent. I'd had a long-standing love affair with Holly, who came to prominence in America shortly after I entered my teen years.

My thrilling initiation into the world of rock—no more "(How Much Is) That Doggie in the Window?" and "Tennessee Waltz"!—came in the early '50s, through 45rpm records, including Presley's "Hound Dog" and its flip side, "Don't Be Cruel," followed by

Sanford Clark's obscure but hypnotic rockabilly hit, "The Fool." Before long, though, these seminal works were eclipsed, for me at least, by "Not Fade Away" and "Oh, Boy!"—early blockbuster hits for Buddy Holly and the Crickets.

Now, more than forty years after Holly, Ritchie Valens, and the Big Bopper were silenced forever in a plane crash near Clear Lake, Iowa, in 1959, the Buddy Holly influence is still fully integrated into my blood. He's had more to do with shaping my view of the world than any other composer I can think of, Beethoven and Stravinsky included. I wasn't about to miss a West End play about a musician who, in his painfully short career, influenced and inspired the Beatles, Elvis Costello, the Rolling Stones, Bob Dylan, Don McLean and a host of other legendary rockers and rockers-at-heart, including me.

While the glittering, pulsing marquee for *The Buddy Holly Story* was responsible for drawing me into the Strand in the first place, what was inside—an obscenely lavish set and over-the-top technical bravado—proved to be even more mind-numbingly extravagant. Once I'd absorbed the overwhelming grandeur of the visuals, I rolled like a kitten in catnip to the magical sounds of Holly's inspired melodies.

Both the music and the musicians were spectacular, but the story line was disappointingly flimsy. Because of it, I worried that my decision to choose *The Buddy Holly Story* as my first-ever West End production was foolhardy and misinformed. Furthermore, compared to the kind of intimate theatre I was accustomed to in northern New England, with its three-piece pit orchestras and tiny, church-basement-size audiences, Buddy Holly at the Strand seemed a little like trying to stuff all of Lower Manhattan into a shoebox, then crowing about the size and calling it art.

When the show was finally over, I burrowed through the densely packed lobby, walked to Victoria Station, then caught the Underground back to the Atlas, mouthing the lyrics from "Peggy Sue" and "Maybe Baby" along the way. I'd begun to feel conspicuously, self-consciously American, and wondered if the hundreds of Brits around me could tell I was a fish out of water, but I was deliriously happy to be there anyway.

Long after midnight and alone in my room, I poured myself a cup of Typhoo tea, munched on a Cadbury Wispa I'd picked up earlier at a nearby Tesco, then tucked myself into bed, dreaming that in just two miraculous, whirlwind days I'd conquered all of London and become the toast of the town. The next morning I woke to a cloud-free sky and the stirring prospect of seeing more—and then more again—of the gifts the West End had in store for me. I'd continue to prowl the streets of London, beholden to no one and praying that this wasn't all a dream that would soon fade away like Buddy Holly's hit and leave me a nonbeliever in a city of unbelievable riches.

I saw three more West End shows before leaving London, none quite as musically exhilarating as *The Buddy Holly Story*, but deeply rewarding in other, equally important ways. That they were so dramatically different in both style and substance was their greatest asset to me as a theater lover on tour. Seeing them one after the other, in three successive days, made for an invaluable educational field trip—a gloriously hurly-burly, real-life survey of the exceptional range and vitality of the London theater scene.

Jolson: The Musical

First on the list for my remaining two days in London was Essex and Bettinson's palpitating *Jolson: The Musical* at Victoria Palace Theatre, a spectacularly ornate, multi-tiered facility built in 1910 to replace a series of theaters built beginning in 1832 on the very same site. The current Victoria Palace has 1,550 seats, and in spite of various refurbishments and name changes, it has managed to preserve much of its original character. A gilded statue of prima ballerina Anna Pavlova, mounted proudly above the theater's facade, was taken down in 1939 before the London Blitz for safety reasons, then mysteriously disappeared. In 2006, an equally inspiring replica was installed in its place, bringing the Victoria Palace back to its original grandiosity.

As for the play, I remember being dazzled by the quality of Brian Conley's singing, the authoritative power and drive of the music, the undeniable splendor of the big-budget set, and the general excellence of the troupe's acting. I was not as impressed with the story as written for the stage. It seemed less a compelling tale of a legendary entertainment figure than a slick, aesthetically self-indulgent vehicle—a loosely tied together conveyance in which actors could parade across the stage, strut their considerable stuff, and pump up ticket sales to people on their maiden voyage to London and hungry for spectacle, with or without substance.

Jolson may have earned the Laurence Olivier Award for best new musical in 1996, but it left me less than overwhelmed. The monumental size of the hall—dozens of times bigger than what I'd been accustomed to in small-town northern New England—may have had something to do with my reaction to the experience. In a hall as big as the Victoria Palace, bringing audience and actors together on an emotional level—actually causing them to connect, deeply and lastingly—is always a daunting challenge. Only certain kinds of stage works, expertly conceived and brilliantly performed, have what it takes to make that connection.

The Lady in the Van: Maggie Smith at Queen's Theatre

The next night I made a precipitous leap from the in-your-face hype of *Jolson: The Musical* to Alan Bennett's quiet but amusing biographical play *The Lady in the Van*, starring none other than the celebrated British actress Maggie Smith (now Dame Maggie Smith).

As I gaped upward at the blazing marquees illuminating the West End, then walked along the sidewalk, elbowed by throngs of late-night tourists legging it to their chosen plays, it was the prospect of seeing Maggie—a supremely gifted actor's actor—live onstage that persuaded me to turn away once again from *Miss Saigon* and choose *The Lady* instead. What London first-timer in his right mind wouldn't jump at the chance to see a West End show starring a consummate professional—a woman who in several decades of acting on stage, in film, and on television has done Shakespeare with Sir Laurence Olivier and won an Academy Award for her performance in *The Prime of Miss Jean Brodie*?

I walked guiltily past *Miss Saigon*, looked back wistfully at what might have been, and in less than an hour found myself tucked into the second balcony of Queen's Theatre, another spectacular playhouse on Shaftesbury Avenue (next to the Gielgud) with a long, proud history as host to award-winning productions and world-class actors.

That night, with the more than capable assistance of playwright Alan Bennett, Dame Maggie would transform herself into the homeless, colorfully eccentric Miss Shepherd—a character based on a woman who in real life actually did spend fifteen years living in a van in Bennett's driveway.

I was so mesmerized by Dame Maggie's performance—*Pinch me!* I chanted to myself, *I'm really here!*—that I remember little about the story line. My only real excuse is that the play was less a fully realized story than a series of thespian vignettes, character-revealing exchanges between the early Bennett, the later Bennett, and the star of the show, Miss Shepherd. Described by one reviewer as "dotty and cantankerous," Shepherd lived a life some would think tragic, but others—sick to death of the rat race and the never-ending struggle to get ahead in the material world—might very well envy.

"The story," wrote Darren Dalglish in a 1999 review, "centres on [Shepherd and Bennett's] extraordinary relationship, which for Bennett was a source of intrigue, frustration, and compassion. Alan Bennett has skillfully used this strange event to create a play that reveals many insights into the mind of Bennett himself—his strained relationships with his mother, who was becoming senile, his insecurities, and his sexual identity."

Astonishingly, in the play's final scene, the broken-down van that Miss Shepherd had called home for so many years actually called *her* home. As I sat transfixed in my loge, the two of them—the woman and the van—glided with heavenly, high-tech grace up into the flies, making not a sound and reminding me that, with a strong enough vision, a sufficiently worthy script, and a fat enough pocketbook, nearly anything can be done in professional theater.

In a well-publicized review of the play, critic Paul Taylor related a conversation he overheard between two appreciative women outside the theater during the intermission. "She acts with every muscle," said the one to the other. "And this is so true," wrote Taylor. "[Smith's] performance is an object lesson in acting ... and like Alec Guinness [who was so brilliant in *The Lavender Hill Mob*, *The Horse's Mouth*, and a host of other performances on stage and in films], she totally submerges herself in the part. In *The Lady in the Van* she *is* Miss Shepherd."

Later in her career, long after I saw her in London, Dame Maggie enjoyed enormous public acclaim for her role as Professor Minerva McGonagall in the Harry Potter films, then appeared in the critically acclaimed drama *Downton Abbey* as Violet Crawley, the Dowager Countess of Grantham. Miss Shepherd, Professor McGonagall, Violet Crawley: there is something profoundly ennobling about seeing an actor onstage in her later years, playing roles entirely appropriate to her real-life age.

It's important to mention here that when I saw Dame Maggie perform at Queen's Theatre in 1997, she was only sixty-three—not nearly as old as Miss Shepherd, the character she played so masterfully on stage. "The costume and make-up department did a fantastic job on Miss Smith," wrote Dalglish, "making her almost unrecognisable, giving her a crumbed up dirty face, bulging eyes ... a black helmet, and a dirty brown overcoat." That she was able to pile on so many years in her characterization of Miss Shepherd was just another powerful testimony to her gifts as an actor of supreme skill and ingenuity.

Film and television, in collusion with the fashion, cosmetic, and pharmaceutical industries, worship youth while paying scant attention to either the reality or the beauty of aging. The result is that a very high proportion of Americans, young and old alike, equate *old* with *ugly* and will do anything they can to deny their own inevitable aging. More often than not, when they open their billfolds and buy into the fantasy of being forever young, they're only reinforcing the very stereotypes that will be used against them as they inevitably grow older. To chase the cult of youth into old age is tantamount to wishful thinking, and it leads to no good ends.

Shakuntala: A Sip of British Pub Theater

My final London theater experience before heading north to Loughborough and then Scotland was at the Gate Theatre on Pembridge Road, Notting Hill. I'd discovered it in my guide to London theater while preparing to bed down for my last night at the Atlas Hotel, my headquarters while in Kensington. I had no idea what might be showing or whether the theater would even be open on a Tuesday. In America, Tuesday is nearly always a dark day.

Happily, I learned the Gate was open for business. I took the Underground to Pembridge Road, walked a few blocks through a stream of pedestrians, and saw just what I was looking for straight ahead of me. I walked through the front door, past the customers lined up along the bar, and up the stairs to the second floor, where I was told the play would be staged.

It was even more intimate than I expected it to be—the polar opposite of the big halls I'd frequented only days before. And less than half the available seats were taken.

"What's playing this evening?" I asked the young man in charge of tickets. "*Shakuntala!*" he said, flashing a sincere, post-adolescent smile. "The show starts in twenty minutes."

Shakuntala? Strange title for a play, I thought. I had no idea what the word meant, but I figured I'd soon find out. I took a program, thanked the young man for his trouble, and settled into a chair near the back of the house, doubly excited for not having the faintest idea what I was about to see. To kill the time before curtain, I read through the early pages of my play program.

The Gate, the program told, opened in 1925 near Covent Garden, and until March 1941, when it was destroyed by bombing in the London Blitz, it had been host to such powerful stage luminaries as Robert Morley and Cyril Cusack. In 1979 the theater was reestablished, and since then it has continued to nourish and preserve its unique position in the broad and varied tapestry of English theater.

The play program was also replete with well-written notes about the origins and story line of *Shakuntala*. I learned that in Hinduism, Shakuntala is the wife of Dushyanta and the mother of Emperor Bharata. Her story is told in the Mahabharata and dramatized by Kalidasa in his play *Abhijnanasakuntala (The Sign of Shakuntala)*. The story, originating in the third century A.D. and deeply embedded in the sweeping cultural history of India, went something like this:

Following a passionate encounter with the mighty king Dushyanta, Shakuntala finds herself pregnant and rejected by the royal court. She gives birth in the forest to a son and assigns him the name Bharata. When the King tracks his former lover down and tries to take her back, she flatly refuses him. The plot takes turns both tragic and exhilarating from that point, and, as with all timeless stories, it has sent its lessons of romance and redemption into the hearts of countless readers for many centuries.

Absorbing the meaning of *Shakuntala* in the program notes was one thing; following the story line in live performance was quite another. Tired and distracted from a day of touring, I struggled to follow the action. It wasn't easy to connect the onstage dialogue with the characters listed in the program. I finally gave up, sat back, and enjoyed the spectacle. I remembered the magnificent costumes, the darkly lit, deeply evocative set, and the unquestionable skill of the actors. The performance was all the more poignant because of the close proximity of the players to the audience. That I had trouble making sense of the play really didn't dampen my spirits; I was having too much fun to allow that to happen.

Today, with a mere seventy-seat capacity, the Gate Theatre is the UK's only small-venue facility devoted to an entirely international repertoire. It continues to draw a wide variety of top-notch theater professionals into its ambitious productions. Jude Law, Rachel Weisz, and Sam Shepherd are among the respected, name-brand actors who've appeared there in recent years.

I left the Gate that night with a deep and abiding appreciation for the high level of artistry in London's pub theaters. I wanted to know more about both *Shakuntala* and the forces that have made live theater so generally superb in the United Kingdom, but my time in England was short, and Scotland's cultural riches awaited me. First, though, I'd make a brief but memorable stop in the central England town of Loughborough, home of Charnwood Community Theatre.

Loughborough: Industry and the Arts in Equal Measure

While Loughborough was just a little over a hundred miles from London, in character and appearance it may as well have been light years away. The city has fewer than sixty thousand residents, and while there is plenty of arts-related activity in Loughborough, its economy is heavily, proudly industrial.

The Great Central Railway—the UK's only double-track, main line heritage railway, harkening back to the days when steam locomotives were a critical component of the transportation industry—is in Loughborough. So are a host of other attractions, including John Taylor Bellfoundry, the world's largest bell foundry, which made the forty-seven bells for the city's Carillon war memorial in Queen's Park; Loughborough University, known far beyond the United Kingdom for its excellence as a teaching and research center, its strong links with business and industry, and its impressive achievements in sports; the Charnwood Museum and three other notable museums; and many well-preserved Art Deco and Victorian-era buildings.

Loughborough has no dedicated art gallery, but it is home to many impressive sculptures, including *The Sock* (also known as *Sock Man*), a bronze statue celebrating the town's longtime association with the hosiery industry. And until the Luddites destroyed John Heathcoat's lace-making machines in 1816, Loughborough was also renowned as a center for the manufacture of lace.

I stopped in the city of Loughborough expressly to visit Charnwood Community Theatre, an amateur drama group with a long, proud history and a reputation for no-questions-asked inclusion. CCT welcomes everybody into its productions, goes out of its way to try different things, and requires no auditions. It's the classic formula for community-based theater, essentially identical to what can be found in nearly every sizable town in northern New England. Charnwood, I was certain, would be a welcome contrast to the big-budget, heavily marketed West End theaters I'd experienced while in London.

Contrary to popular opinion, many amateur theater groups, when well-organized and populated with hard-working, idealistic actors, directors, and techies, can produce superbly performed plays. They're a critical part of the theater world and deserve the respect and admiration of anyone who knows that creative work need not originate in large population centers in order to be good. To think otherwise is to buy into the Darwinistic idea that good things happen only at the top of the aesthetic hierarchy in any creative discipline.

I hopped off the train shortly before 4:00 p.m. and found my way to the address for CCT listed in my guide to British theaters. It was a large, nondescript building that looked more like an office complex than a theatrical venue. After having had my socks knocked off by the splendor of so many West End play palaces, the venue was aesthetically disappointing. On reflection, I realized the emotions I was experiencing didn't sit well with me. *There you go,* I thought, *craving image over substance!*

I then remembered a fundamental truth about the theater world, articulated so eloquently by Peter Brook, the renowned British theater critic, in his book *The Open Door* (Pantheon Books, 1993). At the time, a South African director was exploring ways to bring live theater to Soweto Township, and when he lamented the near impossibility of establishing a theater in such an out-of-the-way place, Brook had this response: "I can take any empty space and call it a bare stage. A man walks across this empty space whilst someone else is watching him, and this is all I need for an act of theatre to be engaged." A rather stuffy pronouncement, but no less profound for that.

Having produced plays myself in more than one unorthodox venue—the basement of a Catholic church; a tiny rehearsal barn on the property of a rural barn theater; a ramshackle grange hall far out in the countryside, doubling as a social center and voting precinct—I fully understood Brook's assertion. The wisdom of his observation sent me back to a more reasonable assessment of the place I'd just stepped into.

How is it possible, I thought, *to judge the quality of a play company's work solely on the basis of its facility, without ever having seen the work itself?* I shelved my memory of Queen's Theatre, the Strand, and the Victoria Palace and strode confidently into the lobby of the complex, cleansed of my erroneous assumption and pumped for what I hoped would be an eye-popping amateur performance. With a name like Greasepaint Productions, I figured, how could they miss?

"Can I help you?" said a tall, stocky, good-natured fellow at the ticket window, dressed in faded jeans and sporting a warm green skull cap encircling a mop of wildly curly, copper-colored hair. (I never learned his name, but for our purposes, let's call him Nigel.)

"I'd like one ticket for tonight's performance," I said. "I've just come up from London—have been here from the US for the past week or so to write about live theater in the UK. I saw you listed in my guide, and would love to see one of your productions before moving on to Glasgow."

Once again, my habit of approaching the arts with devil-may-care spontaneity came back to haunt me. "Sorry," he said, "but we finished our most recent show on Saturday. Next show doesn't open until this coming Thursday."

It wasn't meant to be. I explained to Nigel that I had to be on the 11:00 p.m. train to Glasgow, so it wouldn't be possible for me to hang around in Loughborough until Thursday.

I was genuinely disappointed, but I wasn't about to go away empty-handed. "Sorry I won't be able to see your next show," I said, "but I've an idea. Any chance I could have a brief tour of your theater? Yours is the only amateur theater company on my itinerary, so at the very least I'd like to return to the States with some sense of how you operate—where you rehearse and perform as a company."

"Come with me!" he said over his shoulder, then strode down a long hallway off the lobby, his long legs moving him far ahead of me in a matter of seconds. By the time I caught up with him, he'd already entered a large auditorium—a gymnasium, really—with shiny parquet floor, cage lights high up on the ceiling, and tall windows all around. It was a beautiful facility, but obviously designed for sports, not live theater.

No stage, no curtain, no chairs: I had to remind myself of Mr. Brook's assertion that one needed only an empty space in order to produce a play.

"A very nice facility," I said, "but where do you actually perform?"

"Right here in the auditorium!" he said.

Then he shot ahead of me to the back of the auditorium, threw open a wide grey door, and spread his arms like the wings of a jumbo jet.

"Hussey Seating, North Berwick, Maine!" he bellowed. "Without them, we wouldn't really have a theater at all!"

Hussey, a series of rambling, unpretentious buildings on the outskirts of downtown North Berwick, less than ten miles from my home in Berwick proper, has been providing the seating for venues large and small—the winter Olympic games in Lake Placid, New York; the SkyDome (Rogers Centre) in Toronto; Comiskey Park in Chicago; the National Stadium in Riyadh, Saudi Arabia—since 1835.

I've kept my memory of Nigel's booming voice, authentic good humor, and playful demeanor with me for nearly two decades now. His off-the-cuff performance that afternoon, in the unadorned gymnasium of a municipal building in the city of Loughborough, was more than worth the price of a ticket. Live theater everywhere, whether scripted or spontaneous, ornate or spartan, has the power to bring us together and remind us of our common humanity. With Nigel's warmth and decency, he erased the vast distance between Loughborough and Berwick and made me feel entirely at home on British soil. That would be a hard act for anyone to follow.

It was now nearly 6:00 p.m. To while away the time, I toured the immediate area on foot, dragging my suitcase behind me and stopping to photograph whatever scenery and architecture caught my attention. When I'd had my fill of sightseeing, I found a small café, ordered a light supper, then read a chapter or two from my timeworn copy of Anderson's *Winesburg, Ohio*. It didn't matter that I'd read the book several times over the years; Wing Biddlebaum and the rest of Anderson's unforgettable menagerie of characters have always made splendid companions for me, wherever I might be traveling.

I stayed at my table until the café closed at 9:00 p.m., then made my way to the station. I'd not board the train to Glasgow for another two hours. By now the temperatures had fallen, and the stars were assembled against a still, ebony sky, twinkling their unspoken message to the few people still wending their way to their homes on the outskirts of Loughborough.

It was too dark to read now, so I walked a good half mile along streets dotted with what appeared to be abandoned factories and shuttered storefronts, barely discernible against the near-impenetrable darkness of approaching midnight.

Back at the station, rubbing my hands against the late February cold, I remembered the flute I'd brought with me to play, whenever possible, while in England. The station was empty of travelers (other than I) now and stood silently on the edge of an open field, waiting for someone or something to break through the darkness. I reached into my backpack for my flute case, assembled my flute, then blew several times into the mouthpiece to warm the sterling silver and make it playable.

I played parts of many songs that night—Gabriel Fauré's *Sicilienne* from *Pelléas et Mélisande*, Gordon Jacob's "The Spell" from *The Pied Piper*, and Paul Horn's *Shah Jahan*—but the melody that spoke most eloquently to me was Gluck's "Dance of the Blessed Spirits" from *Orpheus and Eurydice*. I'd been playing these pieces for many years in solo recitals and at special events, but here in central England, with the platform of a railway station in Loughborough as my stage, I sent melody after melody soaring up into the heavens, where they would leap from star to star, send their messages of aesthetic power and global unity, then drift back to Earth and warm the soil of a land far away from my home in northern New England.

When I'd finished the last, edifying note of "Blessed Spirits," I put my flute back in its case, stuffed it into my backpack, handed the conductor my ticket, and climbed onto the 11:00 p.m. train to Glasgow.

The Scotland Adventures

Now that I'd finished my exhilarating romp through live theater in and around London, it was time to try my luck in Scotland. I'd begin with Glasgow, the historic, culturally resplendent city that's lived far too long in the shadow of the more celebrated Edinburgh but is now happily in full Renaissance mode.

When I began planning my England/Scotland itinerary, nearly everyone—my friends, my co-workers, and complete strangers—seemed to be telling me with a straight face that the only Scottish town worth visiting was Edinburgh. "Stay away from Glasgow!" they chanted in near-unison, determined to take unsolicited charge of things and design my adventure to suit everyone but me. "There's nothing there worth seeing!"

They ought not to have wasted their collective breath. For me, a hidebound maverick without the slightest inclination to follow the herd in any matter, those were fighting words. If a splashy advertisement in the *New York Times* screeches that such and such a film is a must-see movie of incomparable excellence— the most enchanting film in decades!—then even the threat of incarceration wouldn't persuade me to go see it. The same goes for cities, anywhere on the globe.

I chose Glasgow instead of Edinburgh and have shed nary a tear of regret for my decision. Nothing worth seeing? Such an assertion is at best arrogant and uninformed.

The first artwork I saw after hopping off the train from London was a life-size bronze sculpture in the lobby of the Queen Street Railway Station, depicting a man and woman just reunited and locked in an exuberant embrace. A moment later I claimed my suitcases, then stepped out onto George Street, the main thoroughfare that would take me straight into the city center on foot.

My Midwinter Romp in England & Scotland

The weather was unseasonably warm for late February. The sky, a scintillating azure blue, was alive with rapidly moving clouds pushed rhythmically along by a vigorous early spring breeze. The leaves and flowers, just beginning to make themselves known to the city, added their irresistible perfumes to the faint smell of petrol coming from streams of downtown traffic.

The chaotic sound of shifting gears and shrieking tires dominated the area, but mixed into the typically urban racket were what sounded on first hearing like dozens of powerful radios, arranged in close proximity to each other, turned to full volume and simultaneously blasting their disparate musical styles into the atmosphere.

It didn't make sense until I got farther down the street and realized the sounds were coming not from radios but from an astonishingly large number of street musicians, all simultaneously plying their trade along George Street, indifferent to the competition wailing away at nearly every intersection. In one five-minute interlude I heard and then passed a trombone, a saxophone, a clarinet, a violin, a guitar, and finally an accordion—the one instrument that most captured my attention and dug deepest into the adventurous heart of me. Somehow, it was the perfect instrument—plaintive, romantic, and distinctly European in flavor—to welcome me into this, the city that no one had seemed to want me to visit.

I remember vividly that the accordionist—a diminutive, gnarl-handed old man with a black sailor cap, matching black jacket, and baggy pants frayed at the knees—was playing "Lara's Theme" from *Dr. Zhivago* as I approached him. A white cane with a red tip was propped up in the doorway behind him.

"How beautiful!" I said as he pumped the bellows on his accordion, weaving side-to-side while sending his musical love letter into the morning sunshine. When he'd finished the song, I stepped closer to him and put an appreciative dollar in his open accordion case. "Always a gorgeous melody," I said, "but even more beautiful on the accordion!"

"So you're a musician!" he beamed. "Then *you* play it!"

He slipped his beefy Popeye thumbs under the shoulder strap, then pulled the accordion deftly off his shoulders and handed it to me. I knew I wouldn't be able to play it with any proficiency, so rather than make a fool of myself, I thanked him politely, then handed it back to him.

He may have been blind, but he was obviously strong as an ox—a proud beneficiary of the principle that if one loses one

Fig. 12. Blind accordionist on Buchanan Street, Glasgow, Scotland.

sense, the other senses compensate. With the help of his engaging smile and one haunting, beautifully rendered melody, he'd managed to communicate passionately with a man he'd never met before and would never meet again—a man suddenly in love with Glasgow and hungry for anything the Glaswegians had to offer him.

The Tramway

Once I'd actually arrived in George Square, a sprawling center-city area designed in 1781 and named after King George III, I sat on a park bench and gawked at the imposing architecture, colorful springtime flowers, and towering statues of Robert Burns, Sir Walter Scott, and other luminaries of Scottish descent. By now I may have been filled to overflowing with memories of my time in London, but I was still more than ready to explore as much as I could in Scotland during my remaining seven days in the British Isles.

Before flying to England, I'd consciously avoided planning every last detail of my tour ahead of time. I made sure I'd allowed for pockets of time when I'd have no idea what I'd be doing next or where I would be staying. I figured that in Glasgow—a much smaller and more navigable city than London—I'd have no difficulty finding a place to stay. After all, I'd chosen to arrive in the British Isles in late winter, when travel would be considerably less expensive and not nearly as logistically challenging.

The British travel brochures assured me that because the tourist season was several weeks away—"Come to Scotland in the Off-Season and Have the City to Yourself!" they shouted—I'd have all the time I needed to see the sights, then take care of the more practical matters. I'd stop at several nearby bed and breakfast establishments, have a look inside, then choose the one that appealed most to me. Now that I was safely on British soil and fully in charge of my destiny, I was feeling powerful. With a little ingenuity, tempered by common sense, there was no problem I couldn't solve.

But as the Scots are fond of saying, my *bum* was *way oot the windae*. When good intentions are based on faulty presumptions, the results are bound to be disappointing. I trudged from B & B to B & B for a good two hours, with only my bulging suitcase as my companion, only to be told over and over again that there were no available rooms. "Busy week!" they'd say. "There's nothing available for you. Sorry, bub!"

Self-sufficiency was getting me nowhere, so I decided to seek help. But from whom? I was only fresh off the train—a certifiable greenhorn, loose on the streets of Glasgow—and knew absolutely no one in the city. Then it dawned on me to seek people of like mind and shared passions—theater people! I figured that, no matter where in the world we happen to live, if we're thespians, we're a family, and families take care of each other.

On a kiosk along the perimeter of George Square, I found an announcement for the current show at a theater called the Tramway. The name intrigued me. The announcement was multicolored and sophisticated in design, and the facility included an art gallery populated with what appeared to be high-energy modernist artworks by Scottish artists.

I got there as fast as my legs could take me, and right away, I knew it was my kind of theater. The Tramway—an abandoned tram depot and transportation museum—was severely scarred and discolored from years of exposure to the harsh Glasgow winters, then preserved as living testimony to the once-thriving industrial persona of the city. Inside I saw an entirely different universe—a cavernous, two-story facility lovingly transformed into a startlingly beautiful multimedia performance space featuring a mezzanine from which one could look down and see stunning, mural-size contemporary artworks.

I approached the ticket window and pleaded my case to a woman perched on a bright red stool and filing her nails. She had long, curly red hair, a Beatles-era mini skirt, and towering spike-heeled shoes. Her Scottish accent was captivatingly musical, and to my inexperienced ears nearly unintelligible. Nevertheless, it was beautiful, and so was she.

"You sound like an American!" she said.

"Yes, but right now I'm an *ugly* American! I've been looking for at least two hours for a place to stay, but no one has an available room. I'm here in Glasgow to write about the theater, and I thought someone at the Tramway might be willing to help me find a room—at least for tonight."

Ms. Spike Heels ushered me into a room buzzing with activity just off the lobby. People were hunched over computers and tethered to telephones, dutifully attending to the administrative chores so essential to live theater. For a marketing and publicity junkie like me, it was inspiring.

A woman at the nearest desk, with jet black hair, tattoos, and a nose ring, heard my story and looked up sympathetically from her computer.

"Can't find a room?" she said. "You're not the first! Don't know why, but accommodations are in woefully short supply here this weekend." She closed her computer, turned off the coffee maker, and reached for a telephone book. "I'll see what I can do for you," she said, smiling, "but at this point I'm afraid you ought not to be too optimistic!"

To make constructive use of my time, I had a good, thorough look at the artworks off the mezzanine, noting the marvelous way in which the architects had preserved the industrial integrity of the space when converting the once busy railway station into what appeared to be an immensely successful, multi-disciplinary arts center. The tracks from the railway were still embedded in the floor of the lobby, lending a powerful sense of both history and immediacy to the facility. Today, the Tramway is host to the work of artists, actors, filmmakers, and dancers from around the world, all of whom contribute mightily to the big-city vitality and cultural sophistication of Glasgow.

When I'd finished, I sat in the cabaret flanking the main performance area and leafed through a stack of travel brochures while sipping a Taylors of Harrogate tea. A half hour later, Ms. Nose Ring stepped up to my table and tapped me on the shoulder.

"Whew—I've found a room for you!" she said. "I swear it must be the only remaining room in all of Glasgow. Anyway, I've logged you in for the evening at McLays Guest House. It's on Renfrew Street—not far from here and convenient to several area attractions, including King's Theatre. It won't be the fanciest place in town, but it'll be clean and economical, and you'll have a safe place to bed down for the night!"

One should never accuse the Scots of being close-mouthed. Had I not slipped on my jacket and gathered up my brochures, I'd still be there in the lobby of the Tramway, listening to her warm-hearted, mile-a-minute chatter. But the afternoon was long, and I needed to secure my lodgings. I showered her with praise for her efforts, paid the waiter for my tea, and immediately caught a cab to McLays.

The Guest House

McLays Guest House turned out to be anything but a traditional B & B. It was cavernous. Its broad, multi-story exterior was made of pale beige stone, the main entrance was sandwiched between two imposing snow-white columns, and the entire edifice was topped off with a grey stone balustrade that added a touch of royal ostentation to the place. *I'll bet the inside is just as imposing!* I thought as I scrambled up the steps and stepped into the lobby.

Imposing? Hardly! The interior was austere and unpretentious, with threadbare carpeting and scuffed-up furniture straight out of the '50s. The plants in the lobby looked as if they hadn't had a sip of water in days.

None of this really bothered me. I've never felt a need to stay in luxurious accommodations while traveling. For me, frugality has always trumped pretension as a consideration—not just when traveling, but in all circumstances. Who did I need to impress while in Scotland? As long as McLays was as clean and economical as Ms. Nose Ring had promised it would be, I'd be a happy camper.

The man at the reception desk was tall and wiry, with a blue denim shirt and gray, closely cropped hair. He smiled broadly and handed me the key to my room. It looked as if it were more fit for a dungeon than a guesthouse. Somehow, the word *concierge* didn't fit the fellow I saw standing before me.

"Third door down in the basement hallway," he bellowed. "Number 14. An' I hafta say yer a damn lucky bloke. Usually we're silent as a tomb on a Wednesday, but for some reason we're stopped up this ev'nin' like a bad sewer! Turns out we had jis' this one li'l room still available. Lady from the Tramway called and begged me t' take you in."

He leaned over conspiratorially and planted his elbows on the counter. "Ain't none o' my business," he whispered, "but that woman sounded like one hot li'l chickie to me!" Then he tossed me a knowing wink, banged his fist on the desk, and unleashed a maniacal, ear-splitting guffaw.

I suppose I ought to have been at least a trifle flattered. He'd sized me up as just one of the boys—not a Glasgow fellow, but a fellow just the same. It helped me feel safe and secure in a strange but beautiful city, far from my home in Maine and badly in need of a rest.

"If you have inny questions," he said, "jis' ring me up from the phone in yer room. Worked the last time I checked 'er, innyway!" He handed me a copy of the *Daily Record* and a booklet of coupons from the local restaurants. "Plenty t' do round here!" he said. "Jus' down the hill from us is King's Theatre. It's a damn fancy place, with gold fixtures in the bathrooms and at least half a dozen balconies. I think they're doin' *Fiddler on the Roof* tonight. Should still be some o' the high-up seats available. Check 'er out, mate!"

I took the staircase to the basement, then made my way down a narrow hallway with exposed pipes and a slightly musty, off-putting aroma. The patchy, green-and-gray walls could have been replicated from the set of *One Flew over the Cuckoo's Nest*. I half expected to see Jack Nicholson come careening down the hallway with a network of shock treatment wires dangling crazily from his noggin, and with Nurse Ratched close on his heels.

Number 14 turned out to be long and narrow—a claustrophobic train tunnel of a room with an inordinately high ceiling and less than spartan appointments. The bed was more military than hospitable in appearance, the light fixtures were army barracks plain, and the bathroom was outfitted with a quirky sink-and-toilet combo that made me laugh out loud. I wondered if the walls might move slowly in on me during the night, squeeze me into a patty, then leave me out with the trash in the morning.

I called King's Theatre and reserved a ticket for the 8:00 p.m. performance of *Fiddler*, then lay down on a bed whose mattress looked for all the world like a sheet of plywood. I kicked off my shoes, doubled up the wafer-thin pillow beneath my head, and fell into a deep, therapeutic sleep. Visions of clog dancers, haggis[1] by the bucket, and multi-colored kilts ran past me like the trailer for a Scottish travelogue. When I woke an hour later, remarkably alert and refreshed, I realized I had less than an hour to dash down the street and make it to the performance. No time for haggis, thank God. As I approached the main entrance of King's Theatre, it loomed ahead of me like a Scottish castle plucked from some distant mountaintop and dropped inexplicably into the center of Glasgow. It was by any measure a monstrously large facility, with a forbiddingly dark, multi-story exterior made from slabs of red Dumfriesshire sandstone and influenced by the same High Baroque and Art Nouveau architectural styles that can be seen all around Glasgow.

King's Theatre opened on September 12, 1904. In 2009, more than a century after the theater was first erected, the city of Glasgow made a commitment to restore it to its former glory. The restoration came just in time for the commencement of the 2014 Commonwealth Games—an eleven-day, multi-sport extravaganza that drew thousands of sports-loving tourists into the town.

Today, King's Theatre seats an impressive 1,785 patrons on four levels: stalls, grand circle, upper circle, and gallery. One could puncture an eardrum sitting at the uppermost level, which is just where I landed, thanks to having gone out of my way to purchase one of the least expensive available tickets.

Had I made it to Glasgow many years earlier, I'd have been in very good company indeed. Over the years, many world-renowned actors and actresses have performed at King's, including stage luminaries like Sir Laurence Olivier, Sarah Bernhardt, Katharine Hepburn, and Tyrone Power. The Jackson 5 appeared at a Royal Variety Performance in the late 1970s. No stuffy, upper crust facility here; regardless of taste or social standing, there's something for everyone at King's Theatre— an egalitarian truth that Shakespeare and his fellow thespians would have vigorously applauded.

---

[1] Haggis: a popular Scottish delicacy consisting of a sheep's or calf's offal mixed with suet, oatmeal, and seasoning and boiled in a bag, traditionally one made from the animal's stomach.

As I settled into my chair, there was only one other patron at stage right—a friendly-looking woman with salt-and-pepper hair and a bright red jacket—sitting a few seats down from me. From where we were sitting, the people at floor level looked more like ants at a picnic than people at a performance.

We were ten minutes from curtain, so I took a moment to say hello.

"Do you come here regularly?" I asked.

"Nah, it's my very first time at King's." She smiled. "I'm a long way from home."

"Me too!" I said, lowering my voice. "I've come over from the States to see some live theater."

"Really!" she chirped. "I'm from the US too! Guess the Americans can't help coming here. Great town—And I'm a theater junkie, too!"

"Amen to that!" I said. "I'm having a fabulous time. Saw a half dozen plays in London just last week. So what part of the States are you from? I'm from Maine."

"You're kidding!" she responded. With just two minutes remaining until showtime, we were talking faster now. "I'm from Maine, too!"

By now, the coincidence had grown to monumental proportions. "What town, then?" I said.

"Oh, it's a town you've probably never heard of," she said. "North Berwick."

If I'd had a cup of tea in my hand, it would have been down on the floor of the balcony by now, shattered into a dozen pieces, every one of them as surprised as I was. As it was, I just threw my play program up into the air, then caught it on the way down.

"I'm right down the road from you, in Berwick!" I whispered as the house lights began to dim.

"Hussey Seating!" she squealed from behind her play program. "Just five doors down from my house!"

Such a small, small world! I marveled to myself as the overture began.

And what an overture it was! While performing as a pit orchestra musician in theaters from Portland, Maine, to Portsmouth, New Hampshire, I'd grown accustomed to working with only two or three other musicians for the run of a show. Since Glasgow was by my reckoning a very big city—nearly 600,000 at last count—I expected to be wowed by an orchestra of ten or twelve musicians. To my astonishment, I counted thirty-two players altogether at King's, including a cello, an English horn, and even a celeste (known by the purists as the celesta). It was a truly heavenly array of instruments, worthy of a professional orchestra. Under the direction of Graham Dickie, they were superbly unified as an ensemble.

Fiddler on the Roof, a traveling show produced by Pantheon (described with excessive modesty by its president, Jack Murdoch, as an amateur company), was jam-packed with energy and polished to perfection. With nearly eighty years' experience and well over two hundred productions under its belt—Pantheon staged its first production, *The Quaker Girl*, at Theatre Royal in Glasgow in 1927—one could easily see why *Fiddler* shone so brightly onstage at King's.

Rita Henderson, the artistic director and choreographer, obviously knew her stuff, and it showed in every nuanced moment of the production. The production I saw on that night more than lived up to Pantheon's lighthearted motto:

> Tis not in mortals to command success,
> but we'll do more: deserve it!

As the story roared along toward its heartrending conclusion, the entire population of the village of Anatevka, suffering under the relentless yoke of tsarist oppression against the Jews, was forced to pack up and leave its beloved city, then seek refuge in America and other more hospitable countries. It was a dark, soulful ending rare in musical theater, reminiscent of the closing moments of *West Side Story* and *Carousel*. And now, under far more desirable circumstances—a night on the town in the proud, culturally sophisticated city of Glasgow—I would soon be leaving, too.

The cast took its bows, and as the orchestra thundered to an end, I joined the audience in a well-deserved standing ovation. As I sat in the highest balcony of a storied playhouse, far away from my home in America, I looked back on my own several decades of work in the world of theater and felt a powerful kinship with everyone connected with the production, both onstage and off. For one magical moment I'd become one of them, bonded by the power and majesty of the performing arts.

A few seats to the left of me, Ms. Salt-and-Pepper turned briefly toward me, slipped back into her jacket, scooped up her shoulder bag, and disappeared into the darkening streets of Glasgow. I considered inviting her out for some after-the-show tea and conversation, but thought it best for her to be the author of her own Glasgow adventures, and I of mine. I knew it was possible we might cross paths again one day—we lived only a stone's throw from each other in the Berwicks—but if we did, it was more than likely we'd have no idea either whom we were looking at or where, if ever, we'd actually seen each other.

Outside the theater, the street lamps cast a warm, golden glow on the dozens of attendees who chattered amongst themselves as they scurried to their cars. It was time to leave the magic of live theater for their more prosaic existences in and beyond Glasgow. Humming "If I Were a Rich Man" to myself, I climbed the hill to McLays and found my way to my room.

How lucky I am! I thought to myself while dozing off. *I've got a nice warm bed in a quiet corner of Glasgow—all to myself—and not a care in the world for the next several days!* In a few short minutes I was sound asleep, dreaming of the many adventures awaiting me in the quaint, north-of-Glasgow towns of Stirling, Aberdeen, and Inverness.

But a peaceful sleep is not always an easy thing to achieve. Around 3:00 a.m., I was jarred out of my slumber by a violent knocking coming from somewhere in the hallway. *That can't possibly be for me!* I thought, still half asleep and hopelessly groggy. *Must be someone down the hall, ticked off about something.* I turned my face to the wall, pounded my pillow into shape, and tried my best to fall back asleep while the pipe suspended from the ceiling above me rattled and croaked in the darkness.

A few seconds later the knocking resumed, this time sounding more like the pounding of a jackhammer and accompanied by a foul string of epithets that would have made a Glasgow sailor blush.

"Myrtle!" the voice shouted. "You gitcherself out here *right now*, goddammit!"

My heart turned to granite as I bolted upright in my bed. The room was pitch dark and, to add to my misery, uncomfortably cold. My head was spinning, and in the confusion I couldn't tell the ceiling from the floor. I had no idea where the telephone was and wouldn't have known how to dial the service desk anyway.

With an abundance of adrenaline as fuel, I managed to crawl out of bed, crab my way over to the door, and reach for the security chain. Whether it was latched or not would spell the difference between my merciful escape and a violent, Jack-the-Ripper death at the hands of a madman.

"You fookin' beetch!" the voice roared. The bloke must have been in a drunken stupor. "I *know* yer in there! Now come out afore I come in an' *drag* ya out!"

With no hope of defending myself physically, I decided to ward off my attacker with a combination of Midwestern charm and the most generous dose of dripping sincerity I could muster.

"Sorry, sir," I purred, "but there's no Myrtle in here. You must have the wrong room!"

The only good news was my sudden recollection that the door to my room was three inches thick and made of iron—strong enough for a military prison. I knew now that the security chain was in place, and I figured the deadbolt was inviolable. I decided to wait him out.

"Send 'er out *now*, ya fookin' baw bag!" he railed. "I oughta come in there and tear yer pitiful goolies off, you worthless bag o' shite!" I had to give the man credit: he really knew his swear words, and he delivered them with an eloquence worthy of a grand opera.

Finally, my would-be assassin appeared to be running out of steam. His poundings grew less frequent, and his voice began to soften. "No Myrtle in here!" I whimpered. "Nope. You've surely got the wrong room, my friend!"

"Oh, *screw* it, then!" he bellowed. "I'll catch up with 'er in the *mornin'*, by God—I kin promise ya that!" Finally, I heard him begin to lumber down the hall, breathing like a prehistoric hunter-warrior, his knuckles dragging along the carpet behind him.

My strategy—the olive branch over the cudgel—had done the trick. Jack the Ripper was gone, and the room had grown blissfully quiet again—except for the furious beating of my heart. After a good twenty minutes of shaking from the bone-chilling cold and my residual terror, I managed somehow to fall back asleep.

The next morning I put on my street clothes, gathered up my belongings, locked the life-saving door behind me, and headed up to the service desk to return my key.

"Have a nice, long sleep?" asked the concierge, grinning mischievously as he tapped his nails on the service counter.

"Can't really say I did." I answered. "One of your guests—one of the more courteous ones, no doubt—pounded violently on my door around 3:00 a.m. He scared the crap out of me!"

"Really!" he said with an expression of manufactured astonishment. "I don't recall hearing any disturbances. None at all! Sure you wasn't dreaming?"

"Yes, I'm *sure*!" I snapped. At that moment I wanted badly to reach over the counter, grab the bastard by the throat, and demand a full refund, but I decided it was best to keep my cool.

"The guy insisted a woman named Myrtle was in the room with me, and he wouldn't take no for an answer. And he was swearing like a demented sailor!"

"Hmmm ..." said the clerk. "Maybe I was out on a trash run at the time—got only one fella on duty after midnight." Then he adopted a more conciliatory demeanor.

"Anyway, there just might be an explanation. I plum fergot t' tell the lady from the Tramway—*you* know, the hot li'l chickie!—that we'd booked the Irish national football team yesterday afternoon. They're in town for the Games. Took up every fookin' room in the place but the one we setcha up in!" Then he threw me another disingenuous wink and followed it with a sophomoric chuckle. "Let's face it, bub—whenever you mix up the Irish and the Scots and put 'em together in a pub, you can be sure there'll be a *whole* lot o' drinkin'!"

I tossed my room key over the counter, picked up my bags, and stormed out of the place as fast as my legs could move me. I loved Pantheon's production of *Fiddler on the Roof*, I was genuinely thankful to have found a bed to sleep in, and I was head-over-heels in love with the underdog city of Glasgow and its cultural riches. But I'd had it with McLays. It was time to head north and do up the rest of Scotland in something more akin to *style*. Off I went to the train station, hoping for better accommodations and dreaming of a good night's rest in the land of sheep and haggis.

Wallace Monument and Church of the Holy Rude

My first stay in central Scotland was in the breathtakingly picturesque town of Stirling—known as "the gateway to the Highlands"—seventy miles north of Glasgow. I'd arranged ahead of time to attend a performance of Harold Pinter's taut, emotionally harrowing drama *The Dumb Waiter* at Macrobert Arts Centre on the campus of the University of Stirling. First, though, I had two days to myself to explore the city and rejoice in its rich history and incomparable elegance.

By any measure—and perhaps especially from an American perspective—Stirling has an exceptionally long and illustrious history. Clustered around an imposing fortress and a medieval village, it has the look and feel of ancient Europe in every labyrinthine street and ivy-covered building.

I stayed at Argyll House on Causewayhead Road, in the shadow of the renowned Wallace Monument. Finished in 1869 and standing on the summit of Abbey Craig, the Wallace Monument was built to commemorate Scottish freedom fighter William

Wallace, who in 1297 defeated the British in the celebrated Battle of Stirling Bridge.

On the Saturday I climbed the monument, the weather, which had been warm and almost spring-like in the morning, abruptly turned violent. Shards of lightning filled the skies over Stirling, and as I climbed the long and winding staircase to the base of the monument, I was caught in a pounding wind- and hailstorm. I've always dearly loved weather extremes, so for me the storm was a gift from on high, lending its awe-inspiring power to the romance of the monument and all it stood for in the hearts of proud Scottish citizens everywhere.

Once inside the monument, I joined a dozen other tourists for a discussion of its history, then began a climb to the top—or almost to the top—of the tower. Two-thirds of the way up, we were told we could go no farther because of the exceptional force of the winds pummeling the monument at every point. "People have been sucked out of the turrets and down to their deaths from this very tower," said the guide. "As you can see, it's a long way down to the ground. And besides, we'd prefer to have you in town a while longer." I found little reason to disagree with his assessment.

The next day, relieved not to have been found lying at the base of Wallace Monument, crushed into bonemeal, I chose a more congenial activity—a regular Sunday service at the nine-hundred-year-old Church of the Holy Rude—a magnificent structure with a long, proud history—on St. John Street. Mary, Queen of Scots, worshipped there. The infant King James VI was crowned King of Scots there on July 24, 1567. On that same day, the Scottish reformer John Knox delivered the sermon. Historians have conjectured that a series of bullet marks, still visible on the church's tower, may date from the siege of Stirling Castle by Cromwell's troops in 1651.

While making my way to the service, I wondered what it would be like to sing with the congregation at a nine-hundred-year-old Scottish church, so I decided to find out. As is my custom when attending events of any kind, I arrived an hour early. A spectacularly beautiful graveyard lies along a ledge behind the church, overlooking the brooding, purple-tinged Grampian Mountain range—a part of the renowned Scottish Highlands. I've always been a fan of well-landscaped graveyards in beautiful settings, but this one far outdid any I'd ever seen for its melancholy aura and unspoiled beauty.

As I stepped behind the church and into the graveyard, a menacing bank of storm clouds fell into formation along the horizon. What had been a politely steady breeze quickly became a series of powerful gusts and then a gale-force wind. To avoid being swept violently to the ground, I wrapped my arms around the nearest grave marker, then held on tight, laughing fiendishly at the spectacle of my hair and jacket billowing out behind me.

I'm not usually superstitious. Nor do I have a history of belief in divine intervention. Still, while on this, my very first journey to the British Isles, I saw the first instance of what would turn out to be a mysterious, travel-related pattern: wherever I go across the planet, the fierce winds seem to follow.

The poet Christina Rossetti, a deeply religious woman, must have shared my deep appreciation for the wind when she penned these simple but eloquent words:

> Who has seen the wind?
> Neither you nor I:
> But when the trees bow down their heads
> The wind is passing by!

Whatever the reasons for the appearance of winds in my life, I never feel more alive and appreciative than when I'm at the mercy of a bracing, exhilarating wind. Add to it a warm spring rain, and I'm transported to heaven.

Inside the church, the wind was relegated to a whisper. A mood of quiet reverence, tempered by the reality of nine hundred years of Scottish history, permeated every corner of the sanctuary. The rows of glowing stained glass windows were breathtakingly beautiful. Here and there, the magnificent, carved wood architectural details added their splendor to the current Sunday services as they had to the community events that had been staged in the church over many centuries. The soaring stone arches along each side of the main worship area added dramatically to the grandeur of the place.

I chose a chair only a few rows from where the sermon would be delivered, determined to immerse myself as deeply as possible in the romance and immediacy of an event I knew with a certain sadness I'd never experience again. A smiling, rosy-cheeked woman next to me, probably in her sixties, thanked me for visiting and offered me a hymnal.

To begin the service, the pastor welcomed both the regulars and the guests to his church. "Are there any first-time visitors here today?" he asked. "Yes," I said proudly. "This is my first visit to Scotland. I've come over from America!" The parishioners turned toward me almost as a unit, first to satisfy their curiosity, then to register their approval at my presence.

I've never been one to wear my patriotic feelings on my sleeve, but here in Scotland, as I heard my voice echoing up into the highest reaches of the sanctuary, a powerful feeling of patriotism washed over me, enough to make me blush with pride. That I really am an American, with all of the rights, privileges, and responsibilities that come with the package, came home to me with remarkable force as I stood in the lofty, stained glass magnificence of the church.

When the sermon, delivered with restrained eloquence and a buoyantly irrepressible Scottish lilt, was over, I looked down at my program and realized it was time for the congregation to sing. I leafed nervously through the pages of my hymnal, found the assigned hymn, and cleared my throat while the organist played the introduction.

I sang with a curious combination of terror (that I'd make a fool of myself by failing to sing the correct notes) and elation (that I really was in Scotland, singing with the congregation in the very same church where Mary, Queen of Scots, had worshipped). That sense of triumph—the realization that I'd finally made it to England and Scotland—lifted my spirits, already higher than they'd been in years, to unimaginable heights. I wove my voice into the tapestry of voices around me, rode the sacred contours of the melody to its final, exultant chord, then got up once the service was over and mingled pleasurably with the congregants.

At precisely the moment I shook hands with the pastor and praised him for the wisdom of his sermon, the sun broke through the clouds and illuminated the stained glass windows along one side of the sanctuary, pouring their multicolored lights down the full length of the three pillars closest to me. I reached instantly for my camera, yanked it out of its case, and captured the image just before it dissolved with quiet elegance into the midmorning shadows. Afterward I returned my hymnal to the choir director, bid farewell to the congregants, and found my way back to my bed and breakfast, inspired and fulfilled beyond all expectation.

The next night I'd be at the Macrobert Arts Centre, watching a play performed by the Escape Artists, a small, emerging traveling company up from their headquarters in Cambridge, England, for a tour of Scotland. I didn't know which play I'd be seeing, but for me that was half the fun. Nor had I any idea why the troupe had chosen such a curious name for itself. Escape Artists? At the very least it was catchy and mellifluous, a stroke of marketing genius that suggested mystery and intrigue and was almost guaranteed to sell tickets to people from anywhere on the planet, including me.

Happy Dawg Walks the Sad Man

Fig. 13. A magical moment at the Church of the Holy Rude, Stirling, Scotland.

Pinter at the Macrobert Centre:
Doing *The Dumb Waiter* the Way It Ought to Be Done

Macrobert Arts Centre, a beautifully designed building on the campus of the University of Stirling (but no longer formally affiliated with it) is host year-round to a dazzling array of educational programs and cultural events, including film, dance, the visual arts, live theater, and multidisciplinary classes.

It is especially proud of its commitment to children's theater, boasting the largest child-oriented theater program of its kind in Scotland, serving every corner of the country. Since I'd written several plays for young people and run my own teen theater in Maine, I was certain a British children's theatre production would be of great interest to me. I learned instead that I was in for what was certain to be an adults-only experience: *The Dumb Waiter*, penned by the celebrated British playwright and political activist Harold Pinter. Needless to say, a Pinter play is in both style and substance anything but childlike.

Harold Pinter, who was born in 1930 and died in 2008, wrote twenty-nine stage plays and twenty-one screenplays over a long and illustrious career. He won a virtual cornucopia of prizes as a writer, including, in 2005, the Nobel Prize in Literature. He also wrote highly praised poetry and directed nearly thirty plays, including James Joyce's *Exiles* and David Mamet's *Oleanna*.

The Dumb Waiter, considered by many scholars and critics to be Pinter's masterpiece, is the story of two hit men, Ben and Gus, who are waiting in an austere and windowless basement room for their next assignment. As the plot unfolds, they make what appears on first hearing to be hopelessly inane, occasionally senseless small talk, which is interspersed with remarkably long patches of eerie silence that lend enormous tension and a feeling of claustrophobia to the story. Adding to the suspense of Pinter's play is the presence of a dumbwaiter—a small elevator used for moving food and tableware between the floors of a building—at the back of the room.

Food comes down periodically on the dumbwaiter, but neither Gus nor Ben seems to understand why it keeps arriving. Add to this emotionally charged drama a speaking tube that whistles and implied messages that never seem to reach their destination, and you have quintessential Pinter—questions without clear answers, human problems with no clean resolution. "There are no hard distinctions between what is real and what is unreal," Pinter once wrote, "nor between what is true and what is false. A thing is not necessarily either true or false; it can be both true and false."

I paid rapt attention to every vocal and visual nuance of the performance—the very definition of *taut* and *mesmerizing*—but this time around, I paid dearly for my swashbuckling, come-what-may approach to attending live theater. If I'd known which play I was about see instead of showing up blindly, I'd have been at least marginally equipped to understand what I was seeing.

After the performance, I hung around to congratulate Matthew Taylor, the director, and the two actors, Paul Malcolm (who played Ben) and Simon Hyde (who played Gus). To my great surprise, they'd set out a ring of chairs for us right after the performance, assuming all along that they'd be sitting down with me to discuss the performance.

I was more than a little intimidated by their readiness to engage me in conversation. I'd just been invited to trade ideas and insights with a group of seasoned pros—genuine theater aficionados who had every right to expect that I'd be thoroughly prepared for the encounter. Would they immediately see in my eyes that I hadn't sufficiently prepared for this meeting? The thought that I'd just been caught with my writerly pants down—another well-meaning American, in over his head and in danger of drowning—froze the blood in my veins.

"Thanks for attending our performance!" said the director. "It was really good of you to come all the way over here from America."

"You're ... uh ... very welcome!" I stammered. By now my once rosy cheeks had turned a chalky white, and my tongue was dryer than the floor of Death Valley.

"Any questions about the play?"

I wanted to come up with a question—*any* question—that would convince them I was up to the challenge of talking theater with them. I'd been thrown without warning into an ad hoc seminar populated with a group of stage-savvy Brits, born and bred in a country with a Shakespearean pedigree so intimidating that rank-and-file Americans have been playing cultural catch-up with them since at least the eighteenth century.

"Well, I do have one question I've been asking myself ever since the early moments of your performance." I cleared my throat and shifted nervously in my chair. "How on earth did the two of you manage to be so incredibly convincing in your roles as Ben and Gus? I've seen a whole lot of theater in America, but I don't think I've ever seen two actors disappear so thoroughly and convincingly into their characters!"

They looked briefly at each other, then at me, and then back again.

"I'm not sure what you mean," said Malcolm.

"Me either," said Hyde.

I'd been humiliated because of my lack of preparation for this meeting—knocked senseless in the first twenty seconds of round one, and clearly down for the count.

"Well, maybe I can help," said Taylor. "To begin with, I found over time that Paul and Simon are natural-born actors. It wasn't at all difficult to direct this play, because the two of them had a handle on their characters from very early in the game. They were very quick learners."

"But how?" I said. "They were so completely convincing that I pretty much forgot I was seeing two actors act. It was like being in the room with two genuine hit men while crouched in the corner and keeping my mouth shut for fear of detection. It was a masterful piece of acting! And both of you were so perfectly cast for physical type—wiry and muscular to a fault."

"And very good direction, too," said Malcolm. "Can't do it without that."

Both Hyde and Malcolm smiled broadly, and Taylor nodded his approval. "Well, hey," he said with a grin, "it helps that they've been around people a lot like Ben and Gus. Escape Artists uses reformed felons as both onstage and offstage talent—and sometimes the homeless and people with mental health issues, too—so I suppose we're bound to come across as convincing in a play like *The Dumb Waiter*."

Escape Artists ... Escape Artists ...

Escape Artists! What was it about me that allowed me to jump right over such a clever play of words while preparing for my trip? I'd loved the theater's name the moment I saw it in my fringe theater guide, and yet I'd somehow managed to fail to catch the meaning behind the words. In this particular case, I clearly didn't do my homework.

I wanted badly to pull a Kafka, turn myself into a vermin as monstrous as the one in *Metamorphosis*, and crawl ignominiously under the chairs and out the door of the Arts Centre. The underside of a rock was probably more than I deserved to call home. Miraculously, neither Taylor nor his two gifted actors—three consummate gentlemen, trapped in my moment of appalling ignorance—allowed me to see what must surely have been their astonishment.

Matthew Taylor, a Cambridge-based professional director, was brought to Wayland Prison in Norfolk in 1990 at the invitation of a group of prisoners who wanted to establish a drama group. Intrigued and inspired by the challenge of working in an unconventional setting, he established the Wayland Prison Drama Group and committed himself to helping the participants develop their acting skills. Next, he decided to found Escape Artists as an opportunity to help them avoid falling back into criminal activity. Within three years he began taking them on the road, and soon Escape Artists was on the path to becoming a fully professional theater company made up of released and rehabilitated felons working as actors, set and lighting designers, and administrators—everyone a typical theater requires in order to stage a production.

On the night I saw *The Dumb Waiter* at the Macrobert, Harold Pinter was listed on the programme (that's the way the Brits like to spell it) as an Escape Artists patron, along with actress Beryl Bainbridge, writer and broadcaster Sir Ludovic Kennedy, Stephen Tumin (the former chief inspector of prisons), and famed dramatist Timberlake Wertenbaker. Not bad for a company conceived in part by one-time prisoners, aided and encouraged by a passionately idealistic director, then staffed entirely by men who had either spent time in prison, struggled with mental health issues, or found themselves homeless.

After seeing his play performed by Escape Artists a few months earlier at Union Chapel in Islington, Pinter shared his opinion of the performance in the October 25, 1996 edition of the *Highbury & Islington Express*. "This [was] an excellent production," said Pinter, "highly intelligent, controlled, passionate. I enjoyed it very much." When a theater company can garner the praise of the very playwright whose work it has produced, it's nearly always certain the members have hit the bullseye as theater professionals.

Matthew Taylor, Paul Malcolm, Simon Hyde, and the other members of Escape Artists—with or without flashy credentials—were bringing something very different to the world of theater as we commonly experience it. They were hungry not for fame, but for what really matters in the arts: a kind of theater that's both aesthetically powerful and socially redeeming.

I doubt there could ever be a higher standard for live theater than the one Escape Artists set for themselves that night. Harold Pinter saw the beauty and nobility of their work, and the rest of us would be well advised to see what he saw, then pay homage to what he as playwright and social activist so fully understood: truly inspired, straight-from-the-heart theater has the power to make a difference in the lives of all of us, whatever our background and circumstances might be. Escape Artists had performed Pinter's *The Dumb Waiter* at a level of artistry that no other company—in any country, on any night—was likely to surpass.

In my two-week journey across England and Scotland, I managed to taste a little of nearly everything that modern British theater has to offer. Only a handful of people—especially among those with modest income and workplace inflexibility—ever get to embark on an adventure as thrilling and rewarding as the one I experienced. To have tasted the work of creative people in worlds far beyond my own was both a privilege and an opportunity.

What I saw in those two short weeks was far more than a mere sampling of live theater in the British Isles, in all its remarkable, richly textured variety. Those two weeks were also a chance to celebrate the ways in which, in spite of our cultural differences, we're all connected by an inborn human need to express our love of life through music, through dance, through art, through the written word, and through the glory and restorative power of live theater.

It doesn't matter, really, whether we're onstage or off, theater professionals or audience members. It's all theater, and we're all quite unavoidably the players. Since we're in it together, we ought to have as our goal a determination to wring every last bit of pleasure out of our wanderings, sharing our exploits with others through our creative work and learning about ourselves in the process.

There's really nothing quite like riding like a child on a carousel into a future of boundless opportunity and unbridled joy, fueled by a passion for the arts.

Fig. 14. *Tree Man and Balloon Boy Visit the Remarkables* by Ross Bachelder.

※ Tiny Novelette 2 ※

Tree Man and Balloon Boy Visit the Remarkables

One afternoon in the frigid month of February, Tree Man realized he was weary of standing sentinel in the vast pine forests of northern Maine, where he'd lived since he was naught but a seedling.

To compound the problem, there was very little nightlife near the Canadian border, so there was nothing for him to do but be a tree. And so, without a moment of undue deliberation, he decided to uproot himself, put New England behind him forever, and carve out a radically different life in New Zealand, home of the proud Maoris, the ever-elusive kiwi, the towering kauri tree, and scenery of breathtaking, heart-stopping beauty.

The thought of living alone in a new and unfamiliar land made him uncomfortable, so before departing to New Zealand, he headed southward from above the clouds—for unlike any other tree in the world, Tree Man could fly—to spend the evening with his friend Balloon Boy, hoping to persuade him to join him for a life of never-ending adventure in the Pacific Ring of Fire.

Balloon Boy, who had very few friends and who lived alone in a moss-encrusted cottage at the base of Shutdown Mountain in Lower Enchanted Township, was exceedingly thin-skinned and hypersensitive. Because of it, Tree Man always needed to avoid saying the wrong thing around him for fear he might be irreparably damaged by the slightest affront to his sensibilities. He must have said just the right thing, though, because late that night, while they whispered profundities and sipped herbal tea by a crackling fire, Balloon Boy accepted Tree Man's invitation. The next morning, as the loons glided over Enchanted Pond and a merry fangle of moose munched happily on a breakfast of lichens and bark, he tethered Ballon Boy to an interstice just beyond his chin whiskers, and together they drifted westward across the continental United States, over the wide Pacific, down the length of New Zealand, and into the happening South Island city of Queenstown, ringed by the sky-high Remarkables and replete with the most astonishing array of natural wonders.

"What a magnificent city!" shouted Tree Man over the mighty roar of the winds over Lake Wakatipu.

"Simply *marvelous*!" said Balloon Boy with a touch of Garbo in his voice. "But where can we possibly land? There are no open spaces, and I'm afraid we'll drown!"

Just then, Tree Man spotted the TSS *Earnslaw* chugging into Queenstown Harbor. "We'll land on the prow of the *Earnslaw*," said Tree Man. "They'll be happy to see us!" He eased up on the throttle, banked to the left, and began his descent, but just then a sudden gust of wind sent Balloon Boy careening into one of the *Earnslaw*'s red-hot, smoke-belching stacks, and before Tree Man could adjust his trajectory, Balloon Boy was burst into oblivion.

Tree Man decided right on the spot that he was even more thin-skinned than his hypersensitive friend. Then, without ever touching New Zealand soil, he finessed a smooth 180, headed straight back to the far north woods of Maine, reclaimed his spot of ground south of the Canadian border, and settled in for the night. Despite the loss of his dear friend Balloon Boy, he decided that living in the northernmost reaches of the Pine Tree State, with nowhere to go and nothing to do but be a tree, was really not such a bad way of life. And it was a whole lot safer, too.

Chapter 5
She Should Have Been a Buddha
The Story of a Friendship

When you've been fortunate enough to find a kindred spirit—a man or woman who shares your passion for things both achingly beautiful and essential for your happiness—then you'd be wise to grab onto that friend and never let go. When the connection is genuine, then nothing—not distance, not illness, and not death itself—will have the power to break the bond you've built together. Such is the power of a lasting friendship. Like the captivating smile on a Buddha's face, it's inextinguishable.

Deborah Homer O'Leary, who died on September 14, 2012, after a sixteen-month battle with breast cancer, was for me the absolute essence of the creative spirit, a woman who could not help but create, because creativity—our deep-seated, irrepressible drive to express ourselves, one way or another—was in her blood and soul and refused to be silenced.

Like nearly all truly creative people, she believed in peace and love, not violence and cruelty. Gentle, thoughtful, compassionate, funny, insightful—beautiful, inside and out—she was and will forever remain the antithesis of the mean-spirited people of the world. This is the Deborah Homer O'Leary I remember.

In the sixteen months I had the pleasure of her friendship, she quite effortlessly accomplished something that few people have ever done for me: she helped me grow as a person and feel better about the world. Few of us could ever ask for more than that from a friend. It's one person's unique ability to enrich another in lasting, transformative ways that distinguishes a true friend from a passing acquaintance.

The story of my friendship with Deborah cannot be separated from the story of her battle with cancer, which was a part of her life for nearly all of the less than two years we knew each other. For that reason, this will really be two stories in one: the story of the blossoming of a cherished, all-too-brief friendship and the tale of an artist struck down at age fifty-nine by a relentless, unforgiving disease that robbed her husband, Mike; her sons, Danny and Aiden; and innumerable friends and fellow artists—including me—of a creative gift that bettered all who were fortunate enough to have been touched by that gift.

Many of the interactions I shared with Deborah, especially during the last weeks of her life, are more than likely out of sequence in this narrative. Some may very well have happened on an entirely different day from the one I ascribed to them. It's understandable, though. I was experiencing our friendship not as a writer or reporter, but as a friend and fellow artist, shaken deeply by the revelation that a woman I'd only just met and begun to care for was suddenly facing a life-threatening illness.

Deborah—many called her Deb, but I loved the sound of the word *Deborah* and was never able to reduce her name to that more colloquial shorthand—was a one-time professional dancer, choreographer, and dance instructor turned visual artist. Her metal sculptures, jewelry, and mobiles were shot through with her innate gift and unbridled passion for the poetry of motion, qualities that define the very essence of dance as an art form. Tragically, her career as a dancer was cut short by a back injury, but that didn't stop her from becoming a popular and highly respected dance coach. And within the multidisciplinary world of the visual arts, through sculpture, jewelry, and especially mobiles, she found a way to sustain her love affair with movement.

In conversation, she never allowed people to allude to "the dance," which for her was the height of pretentiousness. Whenever someone dared to use the phrase, she didn't hesitate to deliver a swift and incisive rebuke. "La danse? Puh-*leeeze!*" she'd intone with one broad sweep of her graceful, dance-informed right arm, her eyes all a-squint and her nose pointed aristocratically toward the heavens.

I doubt that Deborah even thought of dance as an art form in the formal, academic sense of the term. For her, dancing was the body's joyful, inevitable response to the gift of life. She loved movement, and to her, the absence of movement was death. As she confronted the final days and hours of her existence—I had the privilege of her companionship several times in the last month of her life—I watched her eyes dancing artfully across an imaginary stage, even as the rest of her elegant body had finally lost its ability to move in anything like an artful way.

I first met Deborah O'Leary when she walked into the second monthly meeting of the KAA Seacoast Moderns, a group I founded late in 2010 under the umbrella of the Kittery Art Association. I conceived it as a place where lovers of abstract and experimental art could meet and interact with like-minded artists from the southern Maine / Seacoast New Hampshire region. Patterned after a similar group I'd coordinated at the Newburyport Art Association in Massachusetts in 2010, the Moderns were for me a concerted attempt to offer both an antidote to and a refuge from the suffocating dominance of traditional subject matter and approaches to art in this culturally conservative region.

She took a seat on the perimeter of the gathering that night, far enough away from me as moderator that I could neither read her expression nor quite make out what she was saying. She was wearing faded black jeans and a well-worn deerskin jacket. At her neck was an artfully understated pendant—a hammered metal, turquoise-colored bird with wings widely spread and poised to soar off into the sky, blessed with a gift for movement that humans yearn to emulate but will never really experience.

To begin the meeting, we went around the circle, asking the attendees to tell us their name, where they were from, and what they were doing as artists.

Artists from Portsmouth, Kittery, the Berwicks, the Portland region, and the North Shore of Massachusetts introduced themselves one by one, declaring their specialties and describing the extent of their experience as artists. Some expressed their pleasure at discovering a group of like-minded artists—a much-needed oasis for those inclined toward the unconventional and in need of reinforcement.

When we got to Deborah, she spoke with a quiet, uncertain voice. "Deb O'Leary," she said, shifting self-consciously in her chair. "I'm from Greenland, New Hampshire. I'm not really an artist. I do metal sculptures and mobiles, and some jewelry, too." She looked briefly at the artists sitting next to her, then finished her introduction. "I'm not sure I belong here. People keep telling me I'm a craftsman, but I like abstraction and want to spend time with others who like it, too."

I was charmed by her humility and touched by her quietude, but bothered by the intensity of her self-deprecation. Since I had the congregation's attention, I engaged in a little preaching.

"No matter what medium you work in," I said, "if you're actively creating, then in my book you're an artist! I don't believe in the arbitrary lines people have drawn between art and craft. It establishes a completely unnecessary hierarchy, then imposes it on creative people to make one camp feel less authentically artistic than another. In the worst sense of the term, its Darwinistic!"

"Well, maybe," she smiled, "but people keep calling me a craftsman. I've been typecast."

The people closest to her laughed knowingly at her remark. I continued the exchange, unable to help myself.

"Others can call us anything they wish, but only we can truly define ourselves, and that's a duty and a pleasure entirely our own."

I returned to my responsibilities as coordinator, worrying privately that to her, and indeed to everyone one else in the room, I must have sounded pompous and opinionated. I also couldn't help wondering if the people nearest the two of us could feel the creative energy radiating from that brief encounter.

The meeting droned on, and, like all first meetings of a newly formed group, our banter was polite but superficial. When it was time to adjourn, people cheerfully volunteered to put away the chairs, then began to file out of the room.

Once the crowd had thinned, I approached Deborah, suspending my duties as coordinator for the moment. "I'm really glad you came to the meeting!" I said.

"I'm glad, too!" she said. "Wish I could stay and talk, but I've got to get home now. My dog, Chance, needs to be fed and walked. See you next time!"

And with that she donned her jacket, picked up her tattered notebook, and slipped quietly out the door and into the night.

I saw Deborah at the next few meetings as the season began slowly to move from late-winter hibernation into emerging spring. Predictably, she sat on the margins of the group, talking softly on occasion to those to the left and right of her while I worked to keep the group's conversational train on track and on schedule.

It wasn't always an easy task. In moments of insecurity, I wondered how many in the group ever actually listened to my comments. And perhaps more than was necessary, I worried about Deborah. Was she glad she'd joined the group? If she wasn't, I'd have felt partially responsible. She was increasingly coming across to me as a serious, hard-working, idealistic artist—a woman of character and substance whose presence was clearly enriching the Moderns. I didn't want to be responsible for driving her away; we needed her in the group.

Then, while she lingered one night after a meeting—she was having a look at the current exhibit—I saw an opportunity to engage her.

"So! Do you get down to Boston regularly?"

"Once in a while," she replied, "but only if there's a good exhibit I want to see."

In the time I'd known her she didn't easily establish eye contact, so it was hard to tell if she was actually interested in talking. I decided to forge ahead anyway.

"Well, how about going down to the MFA with me sometime to see the Chihuly exhibit?" (If the answer was no, I figured the world would continue to go about its business, and we'd both be fine.)

"Sure!" she chimed, and for the first time since knowing her, I saw her eyes light up. "I've heard good things about Chihuly's work. I'd really enjoy seeing what he's able to do with glass. Like me, he's a sculptor, but just in a different medium."

We scheduled a trip to Boston for the following Thursday, and, as the week played out, I found myself hoping I'd finally found another person as driven to immerse herself in art as I am.

When the time for our adventure arrived, we met at a mall near Portsmouth, New Hampshire, left her car in the parking lot, and drove down together in mine, with me as the driver. Things were going smoothly until we approached the Newburyport exit. When she began to look annoyed, I realized she was wishing she were the one in the driver's seat.

"Why on earth are you driving so *slow*," she said. "At this rate, we won't reach Boston until the museum's closed!"

I was a bit miffed at her effrontery, so I gave her back a little of what she'd just dished out. "I'm just the cautious type," I said, "and especially when I have a passenger! Besides, I always try as much as possible to honor the speed limit." The last thing I wanted was to come across as a stuffy old man.

A short time later, we made it to Hilltop Steak House on Route 1 in Saugus—the one with the giant cactus and the grazing cows. It's no longer open for business, but it continues to be as deeply embedded in the Boston psyche as the Citgo sign and the Tobin Bridge.

"Look out!" she shouted.

"For what?" I shouted back.

"Whew!" she said. "I mean, did you even see that car coming?"

"Yes, and you don't need to worry! I really am on top of things when I'm driving."

She tossed me a half-skeptical, half-contemptuous glare—a sugar-coated arrow, straight toward the heart of me—then went on as if nothing had happened. Over the next several months I'd see that trademark, mixed-message smile many times. Rather than feeling threatened, I learned to love seeing it and hope for more. It spoke of intellectual honesty and strong convictions, and it kept me in check whenever I grew too sure of myself.

After a harrowing, duck-and-weave journey down Storrow Drive and through an urban labyrinth of streets, we arrived at the Boston Museum of Fine Arts, left my car in the parking garage, and entered the museum. We checked our coats and shoulder bags at the cloak room, then headed into the museum with cameras in tow. The facility had nearly doubled in size late in 2010, when the Art of the Americas wing was added to accommodate an ever-growing collection of world-class artworks. Because of it, we knew we were in for both a powerful aesthetic adventure and a real workout. The Americas wing was the fruit of both a formidably large endowment and the devotion of legions of Boston Brahmins—people with an unquenchable thirst for art and an appetite for the prestige it confirms on all who pursue it with cocktail in hand and wallet at the ready.

Our first stop in the museum was a visit to the Chihuly exhibit, tucked down under the Carl J. Shapiro Family Courtyard.

Born in Tacoma, Washington, in 1941, Dale Chihuly has become an internationally celebrated artist, a ceaseless promoter of himself and his material, glass. He perfectly matches the self-promotional persona of the modern-day, globe-hopping, entrepreneurial artist. And he's easily in the same league with shameless self-promoters like Salvador Dalí, famous for his melting watches, and the husband-and-wife team of Christo and Jeanne-Claude, the artists who in 2005 generated enormous controversy when they decorated twenty-three miles of Central Park pathways with 7,503 saffron-colored vinyl panels. (Why? Just because they could—and because they clearly had enough cash on hand to support their large-scale aesthetic dalliances.)

I was dazzled by Chihuly's exhibit—large, multi-colored glass sculptures of every imaginable size and configuration, all displayed in huge, rectilinear display cases. Altogether they came across as a deeply mysterious, crystalline magic forest, pulsing with tentacles and artfully illuminated to allow for maximum visual impact.

Deborah was not nearly as impressed. While I oohed and ahhed at every turn, snapping photographs and taking note of the powerful color combinations in Chihuly's glasswork, she padded furtively around the exhibit, giving it close inspection but saying not one word.

"So what do you think?" I inquired, eager for some confirmation, no matter how fragmentary, that she was glad she'd made the trek to Boston. "Pretty amazing, huh?"

She shot me the same highly skeptical, laser beam look she'd sent my way earlier in the day in response to my less-than-artful driving.

"I'm not all that impressed with these blockbuster exhibits," she said, underscoring her opinion with a dismissive swipe of her hand. "They strike me as entirely too self-indulgent."

I realized right then that Deborah O'Leary was never going to be an intellectual pushover. "Not the sort of mind somebody would be wise to mess with," I mumbled to myself, my ego a tiny bit bruised from the exchange.

We said goodbye to Chihuly, then headed upstairs, across the courtyard café, and over to the Art of the Americas wing.

The four floors of the wing, arranged from bottom floor to top—Colonial era to late twentieth century—are bulging with masterworks by John Singleton Copley, John Singer Sargent, Edward Hopper, Louise Nevelson, Lucian Freud, Jackson Pollock, and a host of other art history luminaries who've managed one way or another to rise like cream to the top of the aesthetic universe. They continue, however justly or unjustly, to set the standard for generations of artists following in their wake.

Once we'd made it to the fourth floor, with its impressive collection of landmark twentieth-century works, Deborah broke away from me and headed toward a wall with the paintings of Arthur Dove, Marsden Hartley, and Stuart Davis. She stepped up to a painting called *Hot Still-Scape for Six Colors*—one of Davis's most iconic jazz-influenced paintings—and instantly became one with its shape, its explosive palette, and its enormous creative energy.

Fig. 15. Deborah Homer O'Leary with Stuart Davis's *Hot Still-Scape for Six Colors—7th Avenue Style* at the Museum of Fine Arts, Boston.

A magnificent composition then came to life there in the museum, born of that always surprising, always delicious interplay between life and art. I yanked my camera out of its case, asked her not to move, then recorded the tableau. For one brief but exhilarating moment, O'Leary and Davis became *Deb and Stu*, on loan to the museum and in perfect harmony with both itself and the endlessly stimulating world of the visual arts. I considered myself more than merely lucky to be there.

When she'd exhausted her study of the Davis painting—a good ten minutes or more of heartfelt communion with one of her favorite artists—we walked through the other three floors of the Americas Wing, then headed downstairs for lunch at the Garden Cafeteria, just off the museum's courtyard. It's the inevitable choice of budget-conscious visitors, and happily free of the exorbitant prices and high-minded puffery of the museum's fancier restaurants.

The weather outside was beautiful, so we took our meals out into the courtyard and found an available table beneath a spectacular willow tree throwing its welcome shade down onto the lawn. A large, nonviolent army of pigeons and sparrows fell into formation around us, then joined us for lunch, fearless from years of begging, and waited eagerly for anything we might be willing to share with them.

After lunch we made one last stop at the Japanese Buddhist Temple Room up on the third floor. It had been one of my favorite places in the museum ever since I'd become a member more than twenty years before. I also knew that Deborah had wanted badly at one time to become a Buddhist monk, but was rejected for training because, according to the man who interviewed her at the time, women can't be monks. By now, knowing her as I did, I could easily imagine the indignation she'd suffered at the moment of rejection. "During the interview, he couldn't give me any convincing argument for excluding women!" she said. "I was just as smart as he was—probably smarter! I got up and walked out of the room without bothering to say goodbye."

We sat down together on the marble-topped ledge that runs along the wall to the left and right of the entrance to the temple. The room was enveloped in a warm amber light mixed with shadows cast onto the floor by the reverent gathering of Buddhist figures. In the fragile silence of the room, we imagined them talking quietly amongst themselves, indifferent to our presence, absorbed in divine contemplation.

Deborah sat nearly motionless, hands crossed on her lap. I could see a serene, benevolent smile building at the corners of her mouth. "It's very nice here," she whispered. "And I like the silence! Those Buddhists sure had the right idea: listening's more important than talking."

A rare, all-consuming tranquillity settled into my bones. For one precious interlude, I felt certain about the reasons I've been so passionately drawn to the fine and performing arts for so many years. For countless men and women, they're a guaranteed respite from the violence, disillusionment, and cruelty so rampant in our species—an antidote to hatred, a lamp of truth for anyone searching for a more meaningful way to cope with the sometimes daunting challenges of just being human.

The arts have an uncanny power to put the worst of human propensities in their place and turn us instead toward a more compassionate, more caring way to go about our lives. Beautiful things are peaceful things. When we surround ourselves with beauty, it becomes a shield against ugliness in all its manifestations.

As I sat next to Deborah in the supreme quietude of the Temple, I began to understand more fully the aura of serenity surrounding her, no matter where she was or what she was doing. And by so effortlessly and unselfconsciously embodying the Buddhist way, she was teaching me by example how to be more contemplative, more reverent, and—most remarkably—more at peace with myself. I was pleased that she was an artist, but I began to think she really should have been a Buddha, too.

Our mood was broken when three young women of Asian descent entered the room, talking happily amongst themselves in a language both liltingly musical and, to me, at least, incomprehensible. Their arrival was a signal for us to move along—to finish our tour of the museum, then slip out onto Huntington Avenue and into the Boston sunlight.

To catch our breath after nearly two hours of touring, we found a welcoming bench beneath a row of flowering dogwoods near the Northeastern University campus. Throngs of laughing students crowded the sidewalks during what appeared to be class change, and an unbroken stream of cars, trucks, and Boston cabs moved noisily down Huntington on their way to important, unspoken destinations.

Once again, the pigeons and sparrows assembled at our feet, calling plaintively for handouts. They'd have to do their begging elsewhere, because this time around, we weren't eating.

"They're having such fun, aren't they?" I said while shielding my eyes from the glare of sunlight. "Such a life of leisure—no wristwatch, no ornery boss, no unpaid bills, no urgent deadlines. They just hop from table to table, eat what they can scavenge, then fly up into the heavens without a care in the world."

"It's the good life, all right," she said. "And if they were artists, they'd have all the time they need to create. No pressure, no worry. Lucky little things!"

"When you think about it," I replied, "we're both pretty fortunate. I mean, you've got a wonderful little studio down in Kittery, we're both financially solvent, and you're lucky your husband doesn't resent the time you spend with your creative work."

"You're right!" she said. "I do have his support, and I do love my studio. But there's one little complication. I learned just last month that I have breast cancer."

It was like a rerun of *The Day the Earth Stood Still*. I could no longer hear or even see the traffic roaring past us, because at that moment there was no room in my head even to acknowledge its existence.

"There's a family history of it," she continued. "And now I've got to deal with the tests and the treatments and the time away from my studio. I'm not happy about it, but I'll fight it, and I'll get through it and get my health back again in a year or so."

She fed the birds the remainder of a cookie she had in her shoulder bag, then smiled at me. "They caught it early, so between the early detection and the treatments—all of which I've been told have a decent track record—the odds are still good."

I was too shocked to say anything other than what we've come to expect people to say in response to such unsettling news. "I'm so glad they caught it early!" I offered, trying my best to hide my obvious alarm. "And I'm sure the doctors will be right on top of this and will get you back into tip-top shape sooner than you think."

"Knock on wood!" she said, laughing. "Or better, on my studio door."

On the way home we talked about other things, beginning with art (Calder's soaring, monumental mobile, hanging in the fourth floor of the Americas Wing), then politics (the extreme right wing of the Republican party and what it has done to undermine this country's most cherished values), and, finally, the Seacoast Moderns (why she joined the group and the many pleasures it had given her).

Cancer was understandably off the list of items for discussion. Neither of us wanted to confront the reality of its arrival in her life—not then, on a beautiful spring day in northern New England, when the flowers were blooming and the world was full of possibilities. We retrieved my car from the parking garage, got back onto Route 1, then drove the hour or so along I-95 north and back to New Hampshire.

We reached the parking lot behind Art on the Hill Studios in Kittery around 4:30 p.m. Deborah had a tiny studio on the second floor, overlooking a towering, absurdly oversized chair enshrined inexplicably on the front lawn. On a different day I might have found it funny, but I'd learned only an hour ago about Deborah's cancer, and I was in no mood to be amused. With an unpleasant mixture of affection and foreboding, I decided I must have a photograph of her, not later but now—right there on the sidewalk.

Fig. 16. Deborah after our first trip to Boston's Museum of Fine Arts.

"You don't need to do that!" she grumbled.

"But *I do*!" I smiled. "I love having photos of my artist friends. And now I can add this one to the one I took of you at the museum."

I got my snapshot, and though she didn't think so, I was certain it was a beauty. Afterward, I thanked her for coming down to Boston with me, and we parted ways. Deborah went straight upstairs to her studio to work on a mobile, and I drove across the border to my home in Maine, wondering when I'd hear from her again and how I'd ever find a way to help her with what was obviously a difficult situation.

Though I wanted badly to know how she was doing, I didn't hear from her for nearly two weeks. Then, a day or two before the next scheduled meeting of the Moderns, she wrote and asked me to notify all of the members of her need to suspend her involvement in the group until further notice. In the letter she talked courageously about her hope for the future and her determination to beat the disease that no one wants to have.

> Hi, Ross,
>
> Thank you for your kindness—I really appreciate it. Yes, I am facing Western medicine square in the eye now and will have a double mastectomy pretty soon in Boston as I have a complicated case. After all of my attempts at homeopathic cures, I guess to save myself I have to say uncle and embrace Western medicine.

It's genetic—my sister has had six bouts with breast cancer, and my aunt died of it. I am just going to do what I have to do, and getting back to my work (which I have been unable to focus on at all lately) will save me. I'll be okay and love the thought that I'm part of the family of Seacoast Moderns. I will be a warrior—and in the meantime I'll try my damnedest to grow my art. Thanks so much.

My best,

Deb

Over the next few weeks, the gravity of Deborah's situation began to weigh more and more heavily on me. Still, I refused to believe for even one minute that she was in any real danger. To me, her illness was just a terribly inconvenient, entirely temporary circumstance. Since I'd never had to watch a close friend struggle with cancer, I was clearly in denial.

When Deborah stopped attending the meetings, the Moderns lost a significant portion of their excitement for me. It's remarkable that a woman as quiet and contemplative as Deborah was in those first few meetings had left such an indelible mark on our gatherings. It was also a reminder to all of us that silence can be more powerful than any amount of errant chatter in a crowded room.

During those first few monthly meetings, one other member of the Moderns appeared to come to care for Deborah as deeply as I did. Anne Strout, a jewelry maker, encaustic artist, and nurse from Falmouth, Maine, shared my respect and admiration for Deborah's most endearing qualities. The three of us became inseparable, and even after Deborah stopped attending the meetings, we continued to go places together, visiting galleries and sharing meals in Portland area restaurants that Anne knew well and had recommended to us. We'd discovered we had a great deal in common, including a fiery passion for the arts, a healthy dose of skepticism about the world around us, and a taste for hard-hitting, proudly irreverent humor.

The Great Lost Bear on Forest Avenue and Silly's Restaurant on Washington Avenue, near Munjoy Hill, became our favorites. There, between sips of tea and mouthfuls of pasta, we carried on, quite without inhibition, ranting about the state of the arts and poking the gas-filled balloons of pretentiousness at every opportunity. And when in Kittery Foreside, just down the road from Deborah's studio and across from Portsmouth Naval Shipyard, we'd spend time together at A.J.'s Wood Grill Pizza. She and Anne were crazy about the Greek salad, and I was hooked on their made-to-order pizza.

One of our favorite destinations while in Portland was always the Greenhut Galleries on Middle Street, just down from the Old Port area. We could count on Greenhut to feature the works of truly accomplished artists, generally free of the hyper-academic, pseudo-modernist clichés that tend to dominate the more heavily commercial galleries in any tourist-friendly city.

Among our favorites at Greenhut were Jon Imber, an astonishingly gifted semi-abstractionist who was stricken with ALS (amyotrophic lateral sclerosis) in 2012, then painted with his non-dominant hand until his death in 2014 at the age of sixty-three; Grant Drumheller, a highly imaginative portrait and still life painter who studied with Philip Guston and teaches art now at the University of New Hampshire in Durham; and Canadian-born artist Alison Goodwin, whose playful, richly colored works show the influence of Matisse, Klimt, and Giotto. All three artists managed to capture our collective fancy because of their spirited, nonconformist approach to painting.

One Saturday, after our usual visit to Greenhut, we decided to drive up Munjoy Hill and have lunch at Silly's Restaurant, the gay-friendly artists' oasis on Washington Avenue. The decor was perfectly suited to our off-the-wall, counterculture sensibilities, so we loved dining there.

Walking up the relatively steep grade of Munjoy Hill was no longer an option for Deborah. She'd begun to have persistent pain in her back and legs, so going by car was imperative. We left my Subaru in the parking garage and piled into Anne's car, a beat-up, emerald green 2000

Fig. 17. Deborah outside A.J.'s Wood Grill Pizza, Kittery Foreside, Maine.

Toyota Corolla belonging to her ninety-seven-year-old mother, Libby. Deborah settled into the passenger seat next to Anne while I stretched out behind them in the back seat.

"I call it the gramma car," laughed Anne as we pulled out into traffic. "That's because, like Libby, it's small and just keeps on running."

As we cruised up Congress Street, guffawing like three wild-eyed teenagers on the prowl, we were in friendship heaven.

"You know what?" I shouted from the back seat. "We're such a good fit, they should call us the Three Artsketeers!"

The name stuck and became the perfect *nom de plume* for our extraordinary camaraderie. It had become impossible for us to imagine that we might not always be a trio. We knew without ever needing to mention it that we'd grown to cherish our friendship, and nothing, we were certain, would ever interfere with it.

In spite of our penchant for nonstop humor, we did manage on occasion to have our serious moments. While bouncing up the hill toward Silly's, we got into a quasi-intellectual squabble about whether a craftsperson should also be considered an artist. It was a half-serious, half-comic recapitulation of that same self-deprecating question Deborah had posed at her first Moderns meeting. Anne and I were certain of our positions—the distinction between art and craft had no foundation in logic and was only good for making studio artists feel superior to ceramicists, jewelry makers, and others who work with their hands—but Deborah hung back, saying nothing. Her silence told me she was still having trouble believing that a mobile maker was as much an artist as anyone applying paint to a canvas.

"Of course a craftsperson is an artist!" I said. "Don't let anyone tell you otherwise. Calder was a mobile maker—the father of the genre, really—and his artistry is acknowledged around the world!" I sat up, moved close, and thrust my head between the two of them. "To argue that the two aren't one and the same is to make a false and utterly useless distinction. That's great news for the artist, horrible news for the craftsman!"

Deborah waited until we were done bickering, then turned around and smiled at me over her shoulder. "Well, maybe I *am* an artist, then!" She rolled down the passenger side window and shouted at the stream of pedestrians moving along the sidewalk. "Hey! You!" she squealed. "I'm an *artist*, damn it! I'm a fucking *artist*—and don't you forget it!"

It was a powerful moment. We laughed our way up the Hill and into Silly's, and as the waiter brought us our lunch, I couldn't help thinking that Deborah's raucous, curbside

Fig. 18. Deborah, Ross, and Anne—the Three Artsketeers—at Silly's Restaurant, Portland, Maine.

acknowledgment to the world—that she really was an artist, not merely a craftswoman aspiring to be an artist—was an important turning point in both her feelings about her creative work and her hope for survival.

After the Portland caper we returned to our respective lives for a while—Anne as a nurse about to retire to make more room for her art; Deborah as an artist and the mother of two college-age children, coping with an endless stream of doctor visits; and I as the manager of a frame shop and gallery in Rochester, New Hampshire.

Whether we were busy or not, the magnetic pull of our friendship persisted, and within a week or two I was on the phone to Deborah, proposing a short hop to the Friendly Toast in Portsmouth to share some much-needed art talk and see how she was doing.

I proposed a 10:00 a.m. get-together, and she showed up right on time. I could see her passing slowly by the windows along Congress Street as I closed up my computer and cleared the table for her arrival. For the very first time, she was using a cane, and that reality, combined with her gaunt features and the addition of a headscarf, brought tears to my eyes. They'd not be the last.

I watched her work her way slowly into the restaurant, past the booths full of chattering diners and the dozens of kitsch art pieces either decorating the walls or hanging from the ceiling. We loved the Friendly Toast as much as we loved Silly's, and right now, the Toast's playful, upbeat atmosphere meant even more to us than usual.

We were hungry but frugal, so we split an omelet—they're monstrously large and obscenely delicious at the Toast—and sipped from cups of No. 12 almond tea while laughing and trading stories about our creative work. "I'm working on another mobile," she said. "And I've got to make a bunch more jewelry for a show I've been juried into." She may have lost some of her mobility and much of her hair, but she'd not lost even one little snippet of either her indomitable spirit or her sense of future.

She'd also begun to talk openly about her cancer, and as difficult as it was to hear it, I was pleased that our friendship had evolved to the point where she could share her feelings without reserve.

Fig. 19. Ross trying to dance at the prom, Portsmouth, New Hampshire.

She took another bite of her omelet, then pointed downward with her fork. "None of these treatments—not the alternative treatments in Texas and not the more traditional treatments I've since taken here in the Seacoast—have really put a stop to the pain," she said. "It's harder for me to walk now, and I tire easily. My legs can't do what they were able to do just a few weeks ago." She polished off the last of her omelet, then wiped her mouth with a napkin. "I think I'm just gonna write 'em all off and take my chances."

I'd begun to be alarmed. I wasn't at all prepared to entertain the possibility that she wouldn't survive her battle, so hearing her talk so openly about giving up her treatments sounded ominously like capitulation to the enemy.

"Please don't turn your back on those treatments!" I blurted out. "I can't bear the thought of you suffering!" I felt a wash of shame for having revealed the depths of my worry to her. I'd always cried easily, but this was not a good time for tears. For Deborah's sake, I needed to learn to buck up, and fast.

Across the warmly lit confines of our booth—every table at the Toast featured its own nostalgic, endearingly peculiar lamp—Deborah saw my distress and tried to comfort me. "It'll be all right!" she said with a smile. "I've just got to eat the right foods and listen to the messages coming from my own body. A positive attitude can do wonders to combat disease. I'm not getting much of that from my doctors, so I'll have to do that for myself."

"That and humor." I said. "We can always find ways to laugh away the pain!"

"That shouldn't be hard," she laughed. "You and Annie and I—we're our very own SNL comedy trio!"

On the way home we stopped at FedEx/Kinkos to pick up some stationery supplies. On the sidewalk near the entrance were two mannikins, each adorned with a prom dress. One dress was canary yellow; the other was pale blue.

"What are you *doing*?" she said as I handed her my camera, dashed over to the mannikin with the yellow dress, positioned myself behind it, and struck a clumsy, ballerina-like pose. She got the joke, then joined in the fun.

She handed me the camera, then got behind the other mannikin and struck a pose that put mine to shame for its balletic grace and bell-ringing authenticity. She'd never be able to hide the fact that before her back injury she'd been a professional dancer and choreographer. Since then, her gift for movement

Fig. 20. Deborah—a gifted dancer—easily outshining Ross.

had found a home in the quiet elegance of her sculptures and mobiles.

Deborah felt little need to write as a condition of friendship. Nor was she a big talker. I've no doubt I exhausted her on more than one occasion with my loquaciousness. She was happiest being either alone with her art or across the table from a friend, communicating with her eyes, her naturally expressive hands, and her sparingly employed, film-noir voice.

I couldn't reasonably expect to get together very often with her. She was now on the medical treadmill, going with her husband several times a week for cancer treatments, all while doing her best to help her two sons prepare for college. Nevertheless, over the next two weeks I checked my e-mail several times a day, hoping against hope that I might find at least a brief note from her with assurances that she was okay.

After eight or ten days of silence, I finally heard from her by e-mail. This time we agreed to meet at Marshall's department store in Newington, New Hampshire, then go in her car to Me & Ollie's, a restaurant in downtown Portsmouth. In spite of the pain she was experiencing now simply from getting in and out of her car, she insisted on driving. In one respect, at least, I was glad: it was proof that she was stubbornly determined to get well again, and not about to relinquish control of her life voluntarily.

We ordered bagels with cream cheese, then grabbed a window seat along Pleasant Street and went on and on about the Seacoast Moderns and her latest projects. Even though she was no longer attending the meetings, she insisted on being kept in the loop. "You're still my family," she said, "and I don't want to lose touch with any of you."

She needn't have feared losing touch. Anne and I were now in it for the long haul, and Deborah might very well find herself getting more of us than she'd wished for.

We finished our bagels, then got refills on our tea. Deborah was in fine spirits, and I was glad, not only because I was eager for any sign that she was doing well, but because I wasn't at all ready to cut short our visit.

"I want to get going again on a sculpture I'm doing," she said. "It will have three dancers suspended inside a wire hoop, in an acrobatic pose. And I've got all sorts of other projects in mind!"

Her mood then abruptly took a downward turn. "I'm starting to worry about money, though," she sighed. "These treatments are expensive! And it won't be easy to find conventional employment. I've done hardly any conventional work. I've got to do something to raise some money, but I really don't know where to begin."

I sat back in my chair, absorbed what she'd just told me, then decided to take the plunge. "I could help you come up with the money," I said. "I've done tons of arts publicity over the years, and what it takes to do that could easily be applied to helping you raise money to help cover your medical costs."

"You don't have to do that!" she said with a touch of panic in her eyes. "We'll manage. Mike is working full-time. And besides, I *hate* publicity. And nobody knows who I am, anyway."

"Nobody knows?" I said, "Don't be silly! Of course people know who you are! You're known all over the Seacoast for your mobiles and your work as a dance teacher!"

I also knew she'd only recently won best of show in the sculpture division of the annual New Hampshire Craftsmen's Fair in Newbury, New Hampshire—an event known around the country for the quality of its juried, multimedia artworks.

I laughed, then dug in for the fight. Without really considering the ramifications, I was determined to put my publicity background to work for her. I was more than aware of her aversion to drawing attention to herself. She was clearly not a self-promoter, but I knew that some serious promotion was precisely what she needed. And because I'd come to value our friendship so much, I was more than prepared to do the dirty work for her.

Finally, after ten minutes of benevolent haranguing, she broke down and agreed to meet with me another time and consider my offer. The worst she could do, I figured, was to give me a flat-out no and be done with it. She'd yet to learn how really driven I can be when confronted with a worthwhile cause, but she'd soon find out.

We met a week later at Me & Ollie's, and after a grueling hour and more of *Don't you dare*s and *I won't have it*s, she capitulated. By mid-afternoon, Let's Help Deb!—what would become three separate fundraisers over a four-month period—was born.

The first fundraiser was scheduled for June 2 at Sanctuary Arts in Eliot, Maine, a onetime church transformed by sculptor Christopher Gowell into a thriving center for the visual arts. For several years, Deborah had been having her sculptures cast at Josh Dow and Lauren Holmgren's Green Foundry, located on the grounds of the Center. They and Christopher were more than happy to make room for Let's Help Deb! in their annual open house.

I engaged Way to The River—a band from Newburyport, Massachusetts, made up of musicians from many walks of life who play without charge for people in medical crisis—to perform live for the event. I then got in touch with a long list of Seacoast New Hampshire and southern Maine artists, all of whom agreed to donate artworks to the cause.

It was pouring rain on the day of the event, but the mood at Sanctuary Arts was festive and bursting with optimism. Several of Deborah's friends were there, putting the finishing touches on every phase of the day's scheduled activities. My job was to organize and label the dozens of donated artworks. As I ran back and forth between the main hall and my car with the items, soaked to the bones from the downpour, I saw Deborah pull up in her station wagon. As she rolled down the window and waved hello, I could see she was wearing a brand new hairpiece and a blouse in purple—her favorite color.

"So glad to see you here!" I said while opening the driver-side door for her. I knew it was getting more and more difficult for her to get in and out of her car.

"I'm glad, too!" she said. "But I've got bad news. I discovered another lump this morning while showering. They're popping up all over the place!" She turned off the ignition, grabbed her shoulder bag from the passenger seat, then stepped slowly out into the parking lot. "The cancer is spreading."

I wanted to stop right then, pull her out of the car and hug her to pieces, but it was raining hard, and both of us had responsibilities.

In spite of the rain, the turnout for both the open house and Let's Help Deb! was truly impressive. Dozens of Deborah's friends and fellow artists had come to support her, and her spirits were obviously buoyed by their presence. Way to the River played with great skill and gusto, fueled by both the enthusiasm of the crowd and the nobility of the band's purpose. That the drummer had only recently dealt with cancer himself only added to the poignancy of the day's events.

Tim Guldemond, a Newburyport dentist and the band's lead guitarist, took a moment to talk with the crowd of celebrants about the reasons they'd come to play. "So many of your friends have come here to support you!" he shouted to Deborah over the revelers. "You must be thrilled! Anything you'd like to say?"

As she sat quietly next to Betsy Rix, her first cousin and best friend who'd come from her home in San Francisco to spend time with her, the entire hall erupted in warm, sustained applause.

"I just want to thank everyone in this room for caring enough to come and help with the fundraiser," she said. "I love you all!"

She Should Have Been a Buddha

"And we should probably say thanks to Ross, who put this event together for you," said Tim. Polite clapping followed his acknowledgment.

"Yes, we should," she said. "He's been really helpful over the past few months. He's my best friend!" She paused for a moment, then looked at Betsy and a half dozen other women friends sitting next to her. "Well, my best *male* friend, anyway!" It was vintage Deborah, and it got a good laugh.

The band, known for always trying its best to honor requests, asked Deborah what song she'd like to hear. Play "Love Is All Around!" she shouted. "I've always been crazy about that song." They banged out the song, and several people in the crowd sang along with the chorus.

As the afternoon progressed, I watched Deborah from a distance, talking and laughing with her many friends and acquaintances as she moved about the hall. The music, the friendship, the laughter—all appeared to carry her round and round the room on a caring but fragile cloud of supreme optimism.

When I saw her standing alone for a moment, stranded in the midst of the crowd of well-wishers, I decided to chase her down and see how she was doing. She was leaning slightly on her cane, taking in the drama unfolding in every corner of the hall.

"I love this band!" she shouted over the noise. "I'm so glad they agreed to play for us. They're really good!" I nodded in agreement, then offered her one of the gingerbread cookies I'd collected on a napkin. We munched quietly together while watching the couples around us dance up a storm. I marveled at her ability in the face of a life-threatening illness to maintain her equilibrium. It was the Buddha in her, fast at work.

"I never get to dance," I said. "I'd ask you now, but you're such a good dancer, I'd make a fool of myself!"

I could tell from her expression that she really missed dancing of any kind. "I'd really like to dance," she said, "but right now the pain in my legs is pretty bad. We'll have to wait until I get better again. Maybe we can in a month or so."

She smiled at me, then held fast to her cane and began swaying rhythmically to the music. It was a short-lived, life-affirming gesture—almost like dancing—and then it was over. A moment later, two of her friends come along and ushered her off to the refreshment table. As I watched them reach for the chips and lemonade, I had a sinking feeling that the moment she'd swayed to the music was the closest we'd ever come to actually dancing together.

The fundraiser was a great success. We sold many of the donated artworks—jewelry, paintings, and a wide array of

Fig. 21. Deborah and Ross at the Sanctuary Arts Fundraiser, Eliot, Maine, 2012.

hand-crafted items. Across the lawn in the Green Foundry, Josh and Lauren sold dozens of personalized iron pull tiles to friends of both Deborah and Christopher, the woman who'd founded Sanctuary Arts and agreed to host Deborah's fundraiser.

A week later, Deborah sent me one of her rare e-mails, thanking me for my work on the fundraising and insisting—demanding, really—that I use her studio when she wasn't there. "I don't like the idea of my studio going to waste," she said. "Let's face it: I can't get there easily any more. I need to find a way to pay you back for the work you're doing, so the place is yours. You can go down there to paint and play music, write and relax any time. *Do it!*"

I couldn't bring myself to say no. Over the next several weeks I did just as she insisted, often two and three times a week. I rehearsed for various gigs as a musician; started and then finished my painting of a llama I'd seen and photographed in Ipswich, Massachusetts, three years before; gave flute lessons to my friend and fellow artist Anita Kimball; listened to classical music well into the evening hours; and generally used the studio as my very own, soul-mending sanctuary whenever I was in Kittery. It was a dream come true, and because it was a gift from a very special friend, it had infinitely more meaning for me than it would have had if I'd been merely a renter.

The first time I saw the studio, I fell in love with its quaint, turn-of-the-century schoolhouse architecture. There was one delightfully tall window at the far end opposite the door, and a funny little stained glass window high up in one corner, put there for no apparent reason other than to allow additional light to flow from one room to another.

Unfortunately, the army tank green walls caused what would otherwise have been a charming little artist's retreat to feel a little bit sinister and a whole lot claustrophobic.

I decided that a touch of honesty would be a timely thing. Over tea at the Toast one morning, I waited for just the right moment, then said, "You know, I really love your studio. It's a joy to be there. But it's kinda depressing, what with the morbid green walls and the lack of storage space." She frowned, then nodded her head in agreement. "I'd love to fix it up for you," I said. "With a little hard work and ingenuity, it would be an even better place for you to create in!"

To my delight, she didn't say no. I took that to be a yes, and over the next month or so, with help from both Deborah and my friend Anita, we rolled up our sleeves and got to work. In less than a week we'd finished painting, and the new color—a soothing, pale blue-gray called Spring Rain—made the room look and feel three times as big.

New shelving and a peg board for tools made the studio more organized and more efficient. Metal-working and jewelry-making equipment, long without a proper home, was finally secured to various work surfaces to make it more manageable. And the judicious placement of newly framed artworks—Deborah's beloved poster/portrait of dancer Nijinsky and a spectacular abstract by Kandinsky—helped transform her studio into an aesthetic tour de force. A colorful rug and some fresh flowers helped it feel more like a home, and with that last tender flourish, the studio had new life.

Deborah was ecstatic, and for the next several weeks she wanted more than ever to be there. "Health is everything," she said, "but being at work, making art in a beautiful space, is just as wonderful. I love my new studio!"

The next time I was in town, I dropped by the studio and saw the familiar white station wagon in the parking lot. She was there working, and I felt a rush of pleasure knowing she was still well enough to immerse herself in her art. Determined not to disturb her hard-won moment of serenity, I stood outside and looked upward toward the one big window in her studio, overlooking the giant chair and a freshly mowed lawn.

I could see her bent over the table just beneath the Nijinsky portrait, fully engaged in her work and lost to the more prosaic, worry-filled existence beyond her sanctuary. I left her alone, walked the short distance down the hill to Wallingford Square, and read from Robert Henri's *The Art Spirit* over lunch at A.J.'s Wood Grill Pizza. Henri's book—a heartwarming paean to the joys of creativity—made me feel connected to Deborah and gave me hope, however irrational, that she'd finally beat the cancer and return to the everyday rhythms of the life she'd been leading before her illness.

As the summer wore on, my energies were more and more devoted to raising funds for Deborah. My next break came when Marie Hussey, who lived near Deborah in Greenland, New Hampshire, saw the publicity for the Sanctuary Arts fundraiser and decided to get in touch with me by e-mail. "I know what Deborah and her family and friends are going through!" she wrote. "I lost my son Jason a few years ago from cancer. Not long afterward we founded the annual Summer Fun and Jason's Run to commemorate Jason's passing. It is time again for the event.

Fig. 22. Deborah's Studio at Art on the Hill Studios, Kittery, well into the renovation.

I'd like to invite you to set up a fundraiser for Deborah, here on the green."

How could I possibly say no to such an offer? I thanked her profusely, then scrambled to send the necessary publicity to the newspapers. Two weeks later, I gathered up all of the unsold items from the Sanctuary Arts fundraiser, added even more items to the list, then headed down to Greenland with my Subaru packed to the ceiling with artworks. In the trunk were two enormous bags of bagels donated by Panera Bread in Dover.

Deborah was much too sick to attend. By then she'd been reduced to hobbling with the aid of either her cane, her friends, or both. She could no longer drive, the nausea from chemotherapy was ever-present, and the pain from her cancer was intensifying.

As I pulled into the outskirts of Greenland, the weather was letter perfect—warm and sunny, with a gentle, early morning breeze. The birds were even more musical than usual as they chattered from tree to tree and waited for their share of the banquet being prepared by a small army of volunteers. I parked my car under a grove of trees and began to unload my cargo, but the warmth of the sun and the smiling, optimistic faces all around me couldn't erase the painful reality that Deborah wouldn't be there to witness the outpouring of love and concern for her.

I set up my Let's Help Deb! tent next to Lynn Marsh and Joanne O'Keefe, two longtime friends of Deborah who'd be selling an array of freshly harvested plants and flowers to raise money. By now the grounds were dense with visitors, and the air was replete with the joyful, carefree laughter of children.

Marie corralled my two bags of bagels and earmarked them for the more than one hundred runners who'd need to stock up on carbohydrates before the 5K race that would the proud centerpiece of the day. To the delight of the growing throng of celebrants, a live band, led by well-known Portsmouth attorney Lincoln Soldati and friends, began pumping out rock and pop oldies. Artist Mike Johnston of Durham set up his easel on the green and captured pen-and-ink vignettes of the activity unfolding all around him.

Right away, longtime friends of Deborah, along with complete strangers from all along the Seacoast and beyond, saw the Let's Help Deb! banner I'd hung between two trees and began stopping at the tent to express their concern for Deborah and to purchase jewelry, craft items, and paintings. Sales were brisk and continued throughout the day at the same heartwarming pace. I asked each visitor to sign a guestbook that would eventually be given to Deborah as a keepsake from the event.

By late afternoon it was time for the 5K race. I pulled together the unsold items in my tent and begin to load them into my car for the trip home. The crowd was thinning now, but small knots of friends lingered on the green, talking happily amongst themselves, working to reconcile their appreciation for the day's events with the nagging worry about Deborah.

As I loaded the last few artworks into my car, Lynn abruptly stopped what she was doing, nudged me, and pointed toward a beat-up white station wagon parked on the lawn just down from our display tents.

"Deborah!" she whispered. "She's here!"

I watched as Betsy helped her out of the car. She was only twenty feet away from my tent, but it took her more than a minute to get to a lawn chair with the help of Betsy, their mutual friend Bonnie, and her ever-present cane.

"I just had to make an appearance," she said. "I wouldn't have missed this for anything!" I didn't know whether to laugh or cry, so I did a little of both while hoping she couldn't see the tears welling up behind my glasses.

"Wait!" I shouted. "I need to have a picture of this!" She cheerfully cooperated, and I snapped a photo of her with the same astonishingly serene, all's-right-with-the-world smile I remembered seeing when we were together in the Buddhist temple at the MFA.

Smiling through the pain, she sat with her women friends for half an hour, laughing and talking while others packed up their belongings. I looked down and noted with amusement that the toes of all three women were decorated with garish, multi-colored nail polish. They were having too much fun to notice that I'd just captured a priceless thirty-toed portrait of Deborah and friends with my camera.

"I'm getting *way* too fat from all this summer eating!" said one of the women while munching on the contents of a bag of Fritos. Deborah glanced down at her gaunt figure and spindly legs, then cut loose with a deep, uninhibited belly laugh. "Now, being too fat is a luxury I'd *love* to have!" she said without a trace of resentment.

Bonnie interrupted the festivities to point out that Deborah really needed to go straight home and rest, but, ever the contrarian, Deborah would have none of it. She insisted on going out with all of us for a meal at Petey's Summertime Seafood restaurant in Rye, New Hampshire, one of her favorite restaurants. To get there we drove through several miles of emerald green fields lined with towering pines and shade trees, then found the restaurant, ordered fish and chips and a round of beers, and

Fig. 23. Deborah at the Greenland, New Hampshire, fundraiser, August, 2012.

spent the next hour sharing our observations about art and life and the little things that matter—anything but Deborah's deteriorating health.

Afterward we went our separate ways, and for the next few days I heard nothing from Deborah. Along with the silence came ever-increasing worry—a helpless feeling that even though we'd become very good friends, I could do nothing beyond the fundraising to help her. It didn't seem like nearly enough.

While visiting the Newmarket Creativity Center in New Hampshire one day in early August, I fell into a third opportunity to raise money for Deborah. Less than five minutes after I'd seen their exhibit space, I made a proposal for a 50/50 fundraiser to be staged there.

One half of the proceeds would help Deborah with her medical treatments; the other half would help the struggling Center cover operating expenses and stay open. The director happily agreed, and I immediately began planning and publicizing the event. Deborah had been a popular Zumba instructor at the Center, and everyone there knew and cared deeply for her. It seemed like a perfect collaboration.

We scheduled an opening for later that month, and on the morning of the event, I lugged dozens of artworks up a steep, formidably long set of stairs leading to the second floor. Then, with the help of several members of the Center, I hung the exhibit, including several of Deborah's spectacular mobiles, and arranged the details of the fundraiser.

Only a tiny handful of NCC members were in attendance, but the fundraiser went on as scheduled. As a musical tribute to Deborah, I performed "Sentimentale" from Claude Bolling's *Suite for Flute and Jazz Piano*, accompanied by longtime Seacoast area pianist Cheryl Lynne Stromski. Deborah wanted badly to attend, but the Center wasn't wheelchair accessible, and by now it would have been next to impossible for her to negotiate the twenty-one steps to the second floor entrance.

Later in the month I learned that the Center wasn't keeping its posted hours of operation, so I pulled the donated artworks from the Center and took them home, knowing that this would be my last attempt to stage a publicized Let's Help Deb! fundraiser. It was time for all of us to look for new and different ways to help Deborah conquer her illness and return to the active pursuit of her dreams as an artist.

Once the Newmarket fundraiser had run its course, I felt increasingly cut off from Deborah. She was in great pain now, heavily medicated and sleeping more and more in the middle of the day. Betsy, the friend and cousin from California who'd decided to stay in New Hampshire and help Deborah through her illness, informed me that her husband, Mike, understandably concerned about the effects of so many visitors on his wife's health, was determined to limit the flow of guests to their home in Greenland.

I wanted badly to pick up the phone and call her. I worried that she might think I'd stopped caring for her, but for a host of reasons I was reluctant to interfere. I decided to hang back, trusting that if it were meant to be, then one way or another I'd eventually hear from her.

She Should Have Been a Buddha

Each day, while at work at the frame shop and gallery in Rochester, I worried and worried. I'd become frustrated at the lack of communication and was at a loss to know just what I might do next to show my support for Deborah. Then, one morning, even more upset than usual, I confessed to the store's co-owner, Jean Ciccotelli, that while I wanted badly to talk with Deborah, I thought it inappropriate to call her.

"That's just plain silly," she said in her usual matter-of-fact way. "I mean, what harm can it do? I can tell you really care; you've been upset for weeks now. The only way you're going to be able to reach her and express your feelings for her is to call her. So get busy and call!"

I went immediately to the phone, and with my heart somewhere up in my throat, called Deborah. Betsy answered, and before I could fully explain to her why I'd called, she said, "Well, sure. Of course. Deborah would really like to talk to you. She wondered just the other day why she hadn't heard from you."

I'd finally broken through a wall of silence of my own making, and for me it was an important personal victory over self-doubt and insecurity. We talked for a good ten minutes, then arranged to meet at her studio the very next day to celebrate the improvements we'd made there. Anne, the third member of the Three Artsketeers, would come down from her home in Falmouth, Maine, to attend.

I had a key to the studio now, so when Anne arrived we went upstairs, set out the refreshments, and waited for Deborah and her friends to arrive.

When they pulled into the parking lot ten minutes later, Betsy was driving. Deborah was in the front passenger side, and Betsy's mother, Helen (well into her nineties), was alone in the back seat. We dashed down the stairs to greet them, and it was immediately obvious that Deborah was in great pain.

I reached into the open car window and hugged her, and it was also obvious that she'd lost considerable weight. Then Betsy came around to the other side, and slowly, with great care, helped her out of the car. Next came Helen, full of energy and warmth and clearly glad to be a part of things. The five of us stood together in the parking lot for a minute or two, then began to move toward the building's entrance.

We'd need at least a dozen steps to get to Deborah's studio on the second floor, so I asked her right away if she'd like some help getting upstairs.

"No way!" she said, clearly annoyed that I'd offered. "I'll get there myself, thank you!" She'd lost none of her feisty temperament, and it gave me hope that she was going to be tough enough to endure and then finally conquer her struggle with the cancer that had dominated the last year and a half of her life.

We fell into formation behind her and walked with her toward the entrance. Deborah, in the lead and fully in control, hobbled up the stairs as we silently watched her, listening to the clop-clop-clop of her cane and the shuffle of her sandals against the hardwood stairs. The possibility that this might very well be her last ascent into the studio became achingly real.

Once we were inside, the collective mood improved. We looked with pleasure at the new bookshelves and freshly painted walls, then savored the late-summer light pouring in through the one big window near the Nijinsky poster. Over the Danish Modern work table she'd bought the year before at a roadside sale was the Kandinsky abstract, bursting with energy and, along with Deborah's smile, lighting the room with captivating modernity. Each week for the past month or so I had put fresh flowers in a vase on the worktable, making sure their colors were in perfect harmony with Kandinsky's painting.

Chips were nibbled, stories were told, moments were remembered. We relished the presence of Deborah, back in the place she loved most with a handful of her most devoted friends and the beloved tools of her boundless creativity.

One by one, in our own careful way, we inquired into Deborah's condition. Her illness had advanced to the stage when it would have been foolhardy, in the face of her uncompromising honesty, for us to pretend that she was well on her way to recovery.

I fumbled for the most appropriate words and came up wanting. "Is the medicine working?" I asked. "Are you feeling better now than you were last week?"

"Not so bad right now, anyway," she answered. "The morphine is getting me through the worst of it. I have to tell you, though, there were moments at home when I was writhing around on the floor. The pain was the worst I've ever experienced!"

I'd never heard her speak so frankly about her suffering, and it was hard for me to hear. But like the Deborah I'd come to know, she immediately shrugged off the truth about her circumstances as if it were no more worrisome than a toe stub or a toothache.

In spite of her revelation, the conversation picked up right where it had left off. Helen, sitting quietly on a chair at the far end of the studio, told Deborah how important it was for her to have her rest. Betsy liked the studio, but wished it looked a little more like home. Anne admired the mobiles suspended from the ceiling and noticed the prevalence of Deborah's favorite color in more than one of them.

"Yup," Deborah laughed, "Color me purple!"

She then forced herself off her stool and asked for her cane. "I need to get along home now," she said. "And don't worry about me! Pain or not, the doctors are hopeful, and so am I. As soon as I'm over this pain, we'll have another party—a p-ART-y!"

We said our goodbyes and worked our way down to the parking lot. Betsy helped Deborah into her car, and Helen slipped into the back seat, carrying her ninety-seven years of joyful living with her.

I couldn't resist stealing another hug from Deborah. She hugged me back, then looked straight into my eyes with the puckish, trademark smile I'd come to love.

"By the way," she said, "*no more flowers*! They just die anyway." I absorbed the bluntness of her admonition, then stood wistfully next to Anne as we watched them drive away.

Over the next two weeks, I became more and more frustrated at the infrequency of my encounters with Deborah. She'd understandably stopped writing with any regularity. Our friendship had been interrupted by circumstances beyond our control, and however unfairly, I felt cheated of her company.

Is she thinking of me? I asked myself over and over again. *Did I make a fool of myself by exaggerating my importance to her?* I worried from dawn to dusk, hoping against hope for news of an improvement in her condition and yearning for even one small evidence of our continued connection as friends.

Then, one evening after I'd gotten home from work, I finally heard from her. I eagerly popped open the e-mail, hoping for a dose of badly needed sunlight.

August 4, 2012

Dear Ross,

Thanks for all you did. Now, I want you to take some of that money that's in the kitty and use it for the trip of your dreams. I got really bad news from the doctors yesterday. They give me less than a year to live. Kind of a shocker. Do you know of any really good shaman healers?

The gathering [the third fund-raiser in Newmarket] sounded so nice!

I also want you to have that studio and Annie any of my jewelry supplies, etc. Who knows what will happen, but once I get out of so much pain and can get to the studio to actually create a little more, I'll feel and probably be a whole lot better. The only thing that makes me want to give up is terrible bone pain. You very much inspire me and I really appreciate all of the love—if more people were like you the world would thrive.

Love,

Deb

PS: I'll call next week—so many tests and dr. appointments. Also, I hate to have you see me as I am now. xxxxxxxxx

I ought to have known that only Deborah's extraordinary honesty was capable of helping me to confront my denial and face reality.

Alone in my piano room I cried my heart out, then called Anne, the third Artsketeer, to tell her what I'd just learned. As a one-time nursing professional, she was more prepared than I was for the news, but no less shaken. Afterward, I wrote back to Deborah and assured her that she was beautiful inside and out, and that nothing—not even the ravages of cancer—could possibly change that. I then told her I wanted to see her again as soon as she was well enough to handle a visit.

She sent only two or three e-mails over the next two weeks, but I wasn't complaining. It meant everything to me to hear from her at all. In one of the letters, she wrote with disarming honesty about the progress of her cancer, which by now had spread to her legs, causing excruciating pain. "This stuff is voracious," she said. "I can't keep up with it!"

She was for all practical purposes trapped in her home now, unable to drive and increasingly dependent on family and nearby neighbors for routine help. And, thanks to the debilitating nature of her illness, she was being cruelly deprived of the pleasure of time in her studio—the one thing that would have given her the greatest satisfaction.

I wanted badly to see her again—to be a friend and companion at a time of her greatest need—but continued to feel I shouldn't interfere with her and her husband. It took her friend Betsy, now back temporarily in San Francisco, to nudge me into action.

"Just call Michael and tell him you'd like to speak to Deborah," she said. "When someone is as ill as she is, the family predictably circles the wagons in order to protect. As hard as it is for him, it is Mike's job to decide how much traffic his wife can handle, and who should be allowed to visit her." She paused, then added one more assurance. "Just call him and tell him frankly that you think it's important to come and support her. He'll listen!"

I called the next morning, and to my surprise Deborah answered the phone. I couldn't hide my elation at the sound of her voice. I then told her how much I'd missed seeing her and asked her if she'd like a visit. "That would be great!" she said. "Now I'll at least have something to look forward to!"

I drove straight to Greenland the next morning, full of an unsettling mixture of excitement and trepidation. It would be my very first visit to her home, and as I walked up the steps and rang the doorbell, I thought ruefully of the dramatic contrast between the home's tranquil exterior and the heart-wrenching drama unfolding inside.

Mike, who'd just been granted more time off from work to care for Deborah, greeted me with a warm smile and a welcoming handshake. It was evident from the look on his face that he was exhausted from constant worry and the demands of being available pretty much around the clock to care for his wife. "Deborah's in the living room," he said. "Go right on in; she'll be glad to see you."

I found her sitting quietly on the couch. Betsy was sitting next to her, administering a foot massage—a ritual that provided Deborah with at least temporary relief from the ever-present pain. Two longtime women friends were in the kitchen, preparing lunch for her: food carefully chosen to fight the nausea that resulted from her periodic doses of morphine. Music filled the living room, alleviating the inevitable sadness and foreboding that draped themselves like an invisible shroud over the home.

When the foot massage was done, Betsy headed out to the kitchen, and I took her place next to Deborah on the couch. Seconds later, Chance, the huge, black family dog who'd been sniffing at my pant leg to see if I was an acceptable guest, suddenly leapt up onto the couch, planted himself between the two of us, and licked me enthusiastically across every inch of my face.

It was a much-needed moment of levity, and thanks to Chance, the room filled with laughter. I hugged him while holding Deborah's hand, and when one of the women in the kitchen saw what was happening, she stepped into the living room and snapped a photo of the three of us just as Deborah put her head on my shoulder. It was a rare moment of intimacy in a room full of friends, and because of it I felt more connected to her than ever before. With any luck, I'd eventually have the photo as a remembrance.

As I continued to talk with her, I noticed a ring on her right hand, a simple wide brass band with a series of what appeared to be phoenixes engraved on it. I'd never seen it before, but thought it was just the kind of ring—unpretentious but beautiful—that Deborah would have been drawn to.

"What a gorgeous ring!" I said, holding her hand up in the air for a moment to have a better look.

"Take it, then!" she said, and slipped it gently off her finger.

"I assure you I didn't come down here to claim this ring!" I said, feeling silly and blushing deeply at the idea she might think I actually wanted her to give it to me. "I came to spend time with you!"

"No, I really want you to have it," she said, and handed the ring to me without a hint of regret. I slipped it onto my left hand, then thanked her profusely for her gift.

I then said my goodbyes to everyone, knowing that Deborah would soon need her all-important afternoon nap. Mike, badly in need of an hour or two of respite from his role as caregiver, headed down to the Coat of Arms, a pub across the street from Gilly's Diner in Portsmouth, to spend some well-deserved time with his friends. He knew Betsy and her other friends would take good care of Deborah in his absence. After he left, I slipped into the kitchen, called the restaurant, and instructed the bartender on duty to issue Mike a gift certificate for a round of drinks. I learned later that he happily shared it with his buddies.

Just before I left, I asked Deborah if she still wanted me to decorate the ladder we were going to put on top of the car as a part of the business we'd been planning together—Mobiles by O'Leary: Poetry in Motion, Directly to Your Door. She looked at me with feigned annoyance and said, "Yes, of course! But what I want to know is, when are you finally gonna get around to it?" We all chuckled at her irreverence, still there in abundance in spite of her obvious pain and our growing awareness that the time we were going to have with her was rapidly dwindling.

"Well, I can't do it today," I told her. "I'm a busy boy!" I walked over and ruffled her hair affectionately, then bent down and hugged her. "But I'll get right on it, finish it this weekend, then bring it down to you on Monday."

"S'bout time," she said, "but you'd better get busy. If you *don't*, I'm gonna need a *lot* longer ladder any day now!"

It wasn't until I was in my car and pulling out of the driveway that I fully appreciated the astonishing courage and inventiveness of her quip. On the way home, it gave me yet another reason to cry, but this time the tears were as much for the joy of knowing her as for the sadness of preparing to lose her.

I spent the better part of the weekend in her studio, working feverishly to finish the stepladder by Sunday evening. Knowing Deborah, I figured it had to be truly off-the-wall to impress her—goofy enough to speak eloquently to her offbeat, Monty Python sensibilities and give her a desperately needed lift the moment she saw it.

I made the uprights a bright canary yellow, then painted the steps fire engine red and added shiny, jet-black treads. Next came a series of shimmering purple streamers, blinking red lights, a tricycle horn, reflectors and trouble stripes, and finally two garlands of faux purple orchids. I prayed I'd managed to capture the playful aesthetic and sense of the absurd that helped seal our friendship nearly two years ago.

I showed up early Monday morning as promised, with the dramatically altered ladder hanging out the back of my Subaru. Mike helped me usher it into the living room, then took me aside and warned me that she was having a bad day and might not be able to visit. I handed Betsy a carton of popsicles—the only food that Deborah was able to keep down because of her recurring nausea—and she put them in the freezer.

While waiting for their decision I slipped into the living room and sat down quietly opposite sons Danny and Aidan, home from their respective colleges to be with their mother. Not long after my arrival, the silence was broken by a welcome burst of words from Deborah, who was now spending her days and nights in a beautifully appointed drawing room just off the entrance to their home, resting in a bed on loan from a local hospice.

"I've had enough of sleeping!" she said loudly. "I want to be in the living room." Mike disappeared into the drawing room, moved her gently from the bed and into a specially designed chair, then wheeled her out into the center of the living room where she could be with friends and family.

Once she'd settled into her chair, Mike and I brought the ladder in, parked it directly in front of her, and turned on the blinking lights. Mike reached over and gave the horn a good, robust honk.

"It's beautiful!" she said, and from the look on her face I knew I'd succeeded. Mobiles by O'Leary might never become a reality, but for that one precious moment, the idea of a traveling mobile business—entirely Deborah's—felt more real and more vitally important than reality itself.

The doorbell rang, and a small entourage of friends from Sanctuary Arts tumbled into the house. The mere sound of their exuberant chattering was beautiful music to Deborah, who had been their dear friend and collaborating artist for years and was thrilled to see them again.

As they entered the living room, Deborah's face lit up. Her eyes then widened with joy, and a smile, at once exhilarating and heart-breaking, spread like a Caribbean sunrise across her lips.

Christopher, the founder of Sanctuary Arts, and Lauren, who with her husband Josh runs the Green Foundry, came in and joined the growing crowd of well-wishers. They pulled up their chairs and formed a circle around Deborah, then told her, one by one, how much they loved her and appreciated her friendship over the years. Lauren took a moment to announce that the Foundry was busy right now, casting the sculpture she'd created only a few months ago for the annual New Hampshire Crafts Fair. "We'll be done with the casting in just a few days," she said proudly. "Then we'll make sure it's on permanent display in the sculpture garden!"

Deborah, who by now was constantly thirsty and craving moisture, asked someone to get her a popsicle. I jumped up and offered to get one for her, but Mike had already begun handing out drinks to the circle of friends. Deborah held him off with a polite wave of her hand. "The drinks can wait," she said. "First I want to have a popsicle with Ross."

Fig. 24. The ladder for Mobiles by O'Leary: Poetry in Motion, Directly to Your Door, September 2012.

Someone dashed out to the kitchen and grabbed the popsicles—"Get a purple one for Deborah!" I shouted after her. Then, while the others talked quietly amongst themselves, the two of us slowly and ceremoniously polished off our frozen banquets-on-a-stick, sitting in the center of the circle. I allowed myself to savor the ritual, knowing full well that it would be the last time I'd ever share a meal of any kind with her.

I came back again the next day without calling ahead. Mike had told me a week before to feel free to come by

She Should Have Been a Buddha

whenever I wanted to. This time, while I knew the home was exactly as I'd left it yesterday, it still seemed darker and less colorful than I'd remembered it.

I asked him if it was really a good time to be paying a visit, and he assured me it was. "She's made it clear to me that she really needs to talk with her friends," he said quietly. "I'll tell her you're here. I know she'll be glad to see you."

I waited in the foyer as he stepped up to her bed and asked her if she'd like to come out into the living room. She said no, and I could easily see why; she was too weak and too tired to make the move. From around the corner I watched him help her into a sitting position, and when he was done, he motioned for me to come ahead. "There!" he said as a look of the most remarkable kindness and understanding registered in his eyes. "Now the two of you can spend some time alone!" As he left the room, I knew I'd never really be able to thank him enough for his caring.

As we sat side by side in the late afternoon shadows, I told her how thankful I'd been to have her as a friend, and how much I appreciated the chance to be alone with her, even for a minute or two.

"We've had so many good times together!" I said, embarrassed at my obvious inability to hide my emotions. "I hope you know just how much I've grown to respect you and care for you!"

"I know!" she said quietly, staring straight ahead into the darkness. "I know ..." I worked to fight back my tears, but they just kept coming.

"I'll see you again tomorrow, then!" I said, trying for her sake to be more upbeat. She was silent, then with a voice both fragile and eerily distant, said, "Maybe ... and maybe not."

I realized then that she'd found a way to prepare me for the reality that she might not be here tomorrow—that it was time for her to let go.

Late on September 12 I called and learned that Deborah was indeed failing—that the end might be near. Nevertheless, Betsy and Mike assured me again that I was welcome to visit any time, so I promised to come back the next day.

I arrived early on the thirteenth, hoping to have one last visit with Deborah. Betsy, looking understandably tired and distraught, greeted me at the door, and as I stepped into the foyer, I could see Deborah beyond the door at the right, lying motionless in the half-light of the drawing room. Aidan, her oldest son, was sitting in the shadows just to the left of her.

I didn't want to intrude on their precious time together, so at Betsy's suggestion I stepped out onto the deck and watched

Fig. 25. One of Deborah's mobiles on display at her home in Greenland, New Hampshire.

the late-afternoon sunlight play on the lawn behind their home. Without really needing to try, I found myself reviewing the many adventures I'd had with Deborah and Anne over the past several months. The Three Artsketeers would soon become two, but I was still not at all ready to accept it as inevitable.

She Should Have Been a Buddha

Betsy then called me from the living room, where she'd been resting for a moment on the couch. Next to her was Chance, the family dog who'd suddenly jumped up onto that same couch only a few days ago and sat so proudly between Deborah and me.

"I think it's all right now for you to go in and have a moment with Deborah," she said, "but only a moment!"

I went in right away and found Aidan still sitting near her on the far side of the bed, holding her hand. I could hear her breathing slowly and steadily, but other than that she wasn't stirring. I stood uneasily just inside the door, moved by the sight of them but uncertain if I should stay. It was obviously their moment to be together, and it didn't feel right to for me to interfere.

Something had to give. Out of respect for the two of them, I left the room and headed reluctantly toward the front door. As I stepped out onto the front porch, Aidan called after me. "Ross! Don't leave!" he shouted. "Mom wants you here! She's listening, and I'm sure she needs to hear what you have to say."

I went quietly back to her bedside and took a chair on the opposite side of the bed, across from Aidan. I wondered if he realized he'd just given me a precious gift—a chance to have one last exchange with a friend and fellow artist who, with her quiet, Buddha-like demeanor, had come to have an enormous, lasting influence on me and countless other friends.

She lay motionless now, her eyes closed and her hands resting serenely on the blanket that cradled her gaunt but still elegant body. I reached down and took her right hand; Aidan still held her left hand firmly in his.

I wasted no time telling her how I felt, and once again, the tears began to flow. "I want you to remember what a wonderful friend and fellow artist you've been to me," I said, hopelessly caught up in the poignancy of the moment. "And I promise you Anne and I will take good care of Mike and the boys!"

I ran my free hand gently across her forehead, then stood up and said goodbye to her, taking care to thank Aidan for having the decency to call me back to her bedside. "We're still the Three Artsketeers!" I told her. "Nothing can ever change that!"

I then said a brief goodbye to Betsy and Mike, walked out into the driveway, and took a moment to collect myself before getting into my car. Less than a mile down the road, I pulled over and released a torrent of tears, knowing full well that I'd never see her again.

The next day, just after getting home from work, I found a message on my answering machine. It was Aidan, calling to inform me of his mother's death. Realizing how much I cared for her, he'd called me just fifteen minutes after her passing. Like father, like son; it was a gesture of maturity far beyond his years, and as with Mike, I wondered all over again how I could ever thank him enough for what he did.

When Mike had finally finished emptying Deborah's studio in Kittery, all of the metal-working and jewelry-making equipment she'd so lovingly set aside for Anne found new life in Anne's studio in Falmouth, Maine, an hour or so north of Portsmouth.

With the help of his brother, Mike staged a celebration in honor of Deborah at Sanctuary Arts, where she'd spent so many years at the Green Foundry and accumulated so many friends and admirers. Nearly two hundred people attended the event, featuring a slide show and home movies, including films of Mike and Deborah the day they married, of the two of them with Danny and Aidan as youngsters, and of Deborah performing at a dance recital. It was the first time I'd ever seen her dance professionally, and it helped me understand just how brilliantly she'd managed to invest her sculptures and mobiles with her own artistry as a dancer.

With Mike's blessing, I performed Claude Bolling's "Sentimentale"—the same piece I'd played for her at the August fundraiser in Newmarket—to pay homage to her and thank her for a precious two-year friendship. Since then it has become my unofficial anthem to Deborah and everything she stood for. Whenever I perform it in public, I dedicate it all over again to her memory.

Anne, who sat with me at the celebration, continued to find ways to express her love and appreciation for Deborah by staying in touch with Mike and his sons, bringing them a few of their favorite things on occasion, and planting flowers at their home in Deborah's memory. One of Deborah's most memorable mobiles, *Purple Ascendance*, hangs proudly in Anne's Falmouth studio, just down the hall from one of Deborah's favorite things—a single cowboy boot, artfully and whimsically decorated by Anne in honor of their friendship.

In my own studio in Berwick, I have a framed photo of Deborah—the one I took of her the day we were in Boston and I learned she had cancer—in a place of honor next to the mobile she'd given me in August. "Go and choose your favorite from the studio," she'd said. "I know you'll give it a good home." Nearby is the brass ring she gave me just two days before her death. Every few months, whatever the season, I make a pilgrimage to the sculpture garden in Newmarket to pay my respects to her and a sculpture of hers that's permanently on display there.

Postlude

Just what was it that brought Deborah, Anne, and me together, then in such a remarkably short period of time turned us forever into the Three Artsketeers?

There were many contributing factors—some circumstantial, others purely emotional. As luck would have it, we were all members of the Seacoast Moderns in Kittery, and it was our unexpected proximity that set the stage for a friendship that began quietly enough, then ignited into a spirit of easygoing camaraderie seldom achieved amongst groups of three.

That none of us were formally religious may also have contributed to our solidarity. We never really needed to worry about offending each other with an occasional outburst of irreverence. And because our view of the world was more pantheistic—more secular humanist than doctrinal—we were allowed moments of trenchancy that would have been well nigh inexcusable in more polite, God-fearing company. It was yet another manifestation of tolerance, a quality of paramount importance to the three of us. For creative people of every kind, it tends to come with the territory.

Most importantly, though, the three of us were equally immersed, day in and day out, in all things aesthetic. Anne is passionate about encaustics, fine art jewelry, African American music, and the blues; I'm obsessed with drawing, painting, found object assemblages, music, and writing; and Deborah was—and perhaps still is—deeply in love with movement of any kind, expressed with exquisite sensitivity through her magical, dance-influenced mobiles and sculptures.

Whatever our many enthusiasms, it was our passion for *making things*—our unremitting drive to produce one colorful, emotionally arresting artwork after the other—that brought us together and made our friendship indestructible.

And hand-in-hand with our shared passions was an unspoken commitment to peaceful coexistence. When we were busy creating beautiful things, we figured, we were far less likely to inflict pain and hurt on the people around us.

Since Deborah's passing, it hasn't been easy for either Anne or me to accept the diminution of the Artsketeers from three to two. We miss those action-packed outings, our moments of over-the-top irreverence, and our playful, six-legged quest for

Fig. 26. *Twilight Movement*, dance-inspired sculpture by Deborah O'Leary. (Photo composition by the author.)

the meaning of life, always with the arts as our search engine of choice.

Without ever needing to try, Deborah Homer O'Leary taught me many invaluable things. I learned from her the power of silence to speak eloquently about the things that really matter in life. I gained from her a greater appreciation for the absolutely essential part movement plays in sculpture, mobiles, and two-dimensional art forms. And I learned, merely by watching her in the last few weeks of her life, that it really is possible for us to accept our mortality with courage, dignity, and grace.

And finally, I learned from her what was surely the most important lesson of all: never to abandon a friend who's seriously ill and facing death. People with cancer and other life-threatening diseases may be severely compromised in physical ways, but in all of the other ways that count, they're fully alive and hungry for engagement. As the Three Artsketeers, we became inseparable, and from that first moment when we realized we'd become a trio, we knew that no illness, no matter how serious, would ever have had the power to come between us.

Just Another Little Death
(An Ode to Deborah's Studio)

Sure, it's tempting to think of it
As just another little death,
This ritual closing and emptying
Of the studio of an artist of the beautiful,
Gifted with an all-consuming sensitivity
To the things that really mattered in life,
Then cut short by some unforgivable medical savagery
In the very prime of her creative concupiscence,
Leaving behind a meager and yet elegant scattering
Of fragments of projects lovingly conceived
But cruelly deprived of their inalienable right to be finished
As they so richly deserved to be—
Left glowing but unfulfilled,
Scented with the cool blue intoxicating perfume
Of her invincible spirit.

Yes, the fragments—
Lying proudly on their cluttered, time-worn tables
In the still of a late summer night,
The windows open and inviting,
Taking in the sweet nighttime air and the rustling leaves
And the shimmering light of a vast white blanket of stars,
And wondering what happened to their maker—
Fragments yearning to be loved and made beautiful.

And with them the odd-shaped boxes and funny little bags,
And here and there small undisturbed asymmetrical piles
Of conceptual drawings and half-shaped coins of bronze,
Waiting patiently in the shadows
To be attached to their sterling silver chains,
Then pressed joyfully into service
Beneath the finely sculpted chins and swan-like necks
Of men and women from every walk of life
Who wanted nothing more than to have in their possession
One indestructible testimony to the soft-spoken power
Of an artist with a divine but unpretentious vision of existence,
And a supreme, unmatched ability
To breathe everlasting life into Ordinary Things,
Then send them out into the world
To warm the saddened hearts and feed the hungry souls
Of anyone ready enough and sensitive enough to receive them.

October 2, 2012
Dover, New Hampshire

Chapter 6

La Scala, Rock 'n' Roll, and the T

No Matter the Genre, It's All Music to Me

In a sane world—which is sometimes but not always an accurate description of America—no one can tell you who to vote for, what religion to espouse, or what a proper marriage looks like. So why should anyone be able to tell you which music is good or bad, serious or less than serious, enrapturing or stultifying? That power— the priceless ability to make your own aesthetic choices, then live by them without interference from the taste nazis of the world—is one of the greatest privileges of being a self-sufficient human in a true democracy.

The concert-going public has been conditioned for centuries to think of the world's most spectacular concert venues— Carnegie Hall, La Scala opera house, and the Vienna Konzerthaus among them—as the only places where truly knowledgeable music lovers and aspirants to musical knowledge can be certain they'll hear the most pleasurable music the human species is capable of producing, performed only by musicians at the top of their game.

Of course, there is some truth to these claims. There really is an elite, globe-hopping group of highly accomplished musicians, easy to replenish because of the overwhelming number of top-notch musicians waiting in the wings. And in spite of the often laughably pedantic, cutthroat dissections of their performances by the critics, they nearly always manage to deliver the goods. Their membership in that charmed circle of virtuosi pretty much guarantees they'll be booked into some of the most magnificent, acoustically superb concert halls on the planet.

The Very Important People within the classical music world— well-traveled soloists, conductors, orchestral musicians, and the unending entourage of marketers, publicists, and journalists they so depend on—can be seen as either intoxicatingly free to travel or hopelessly shackled to their look-at-me fame in an image-obsessed culture.

There's no question that the top performers have become the crème de la crème because they're astonishingly gifted, hard-working musicians. But riding the unforgiving hobbyhorse of absolute vocal and instrumental perfection must finally take its toll. In return for their privileged existence, they're often virtually incarcerated in their studios—forced by circumstances to gain and then maintain control of their required repertoire, and insulated from exposure to entirely different ways of thinking about musicality and excellence. World-renowned pianist Anton Rubinstein swore he never needed to practice, but few people in recorded history have ever been able to make such a claim. (On the other hand, Mr. Rubinstein may have had a genuine soul sister in one of my long-ago high school flute students, who—after I'd compassionately informed her that her musical skills had obviously taken a downhill turn—broke into sobs and wailed, "You told me I was good, so I stopped practicing!")

But contrary to centuries-old beliefs, especially those promulgated by class-conscious critics, smugly knowledgable historians, and hungry press agents, music does not have to be classical to be good—*really* good. Nor does it need to be performed by sought-after prodigies in world-class cities, in buildings designed by famous architects, to bring lasting pleasure to its listeners.

There really is another world out there that has not been informed by the tenets of the social Darwinist philosophy.

Social Darwinism is a nineteenth-century doctrine—thought by many to be an inexcusable misapplication of Darwinist evolutionary theory—in which the social order at any given time is thought to be a product of the natural selection of those persons best suited to the circumstances in which they find themselves. It often turns to the idea of biological destiny to justify the ascendance of some to the highest rungs of society, regardless of their actual ability, often at the expense of those who've been unfairly cast as inferior and therefore kept from moving up the ladder.

When I step back and take a long, hard look at the world of classical music—something I've been doing for many years in a less than scholarly way—I can't help but observe that many classical musicians, composers, and conductors continue to work from a presumption that any music outside the classical genre is somehow music of a lesser order, written and performed by people who for various reasons aren't equipped to handle more *serious* music. I've never worked from such presumptions.

While I'm without question a classically trained musician, and while I dearly love a great deal of the classical repertoire and perform a considerable chunk of it regularly, my tastes in music were actually formed in my earliest years—the 1950s—by constant exposure to entertainers like Johnny Mathis, Perry Como, Peggy Lee, and a host of other highly skilled but politely restrained softball pitchers of melody, played ad nauseam on the radio. For the most part, I loved and respected them, but without really understanding that they were actually singing songs marketed only to adult audiences and speaking directly to them. I didn't realize it at the time, but they were deficient in qualities that I, and countless others from that era, badly needed and secretly yearned for.

There was really nothing on the airways intentionally conceived for and then marketed to me—a young man with a healthy adolescent libido and a certain unexpressed animal rhythm deep within him, yearning to escape from the suffocating proprieties of the Eisenhower era. It wasn't until rock music finally exploded into prominence, with Bill Haley & His Comets, Elvis Presley, and Jerry Lee Lewis, that the raw, piss-and-vinegar part of me finally found a sympathetic ear in a handful of radio DJs—industry professionals who at least marginally understood average teenagers and began to talk directly to them through the 45rpm record.

I'd disappear into the solitude of my unfinished bedroom late at night, flop down on my bed, hold my portable radio tightly to my chest while staring up at the ceiling, and listen to American Top 40 until I couldn't stay awake any longer. One night, lost to the world and nibbling absentmindedly on the power cord of my Zenith, I got a shock so powerful that it left my teeth sore for weeks afterward. Somehow it was worth it, though, if only for the stolen pleasure of listening to music my parents didn't really understand and my father clearly detested. I never told them about the shock; it was my very own badge of honor, and I considered it none of their business.

The musical culture of the past several decades had gone into shock. Suddenly the Rolling Stones, Chuck Berry, Little Richard, Janice Joplin, and Bob Dylan were competing with Sinatra, Mathis, and Como for coveted airtime. Add to this my deep appreciation for jazz pianist Thelonious Monk, and the Hot Club of Belgium guitarist Django Reinhardt, and you can begin to understand just how many musical worlds I was inhabiting.

I was hooked on rock and listened to as much of it as I could, as often as possible. And yet, at the same time, I was studying the classical repertoire in private lessons and playing classical and popular music every day in high school—symphonic band arrangements of war horses like the *William Tell* overture, "Sleigh Ride," and "The Typewriter Song."

And then, when I entered college in 1962, certain I was destined to become a high school band director, rock 'n' roll music disappeared from my life.

Fresh from two weeks at Interlochen music camp as a scholarship winner, I'd been persuaded by mere proximity to esteemed conductors Harry Begian and William Revelli that I had a solid future as a classical musician. A deep, uncrossable canyon was suddenly formed between my rock 'n' roll universe and my life as a student of "serious" music.

Because I lived every day on that swaying bridge between two dramatically different musical epochs, I began to see myself privately as some sort of super-charged, duck-tailed "Rockin' Robin," dressed incongruously in white tie and tails—a man without a musical country to call my own. It took a few years of living in both worlds for me to understand that *all* of what I'd been exposed to—Como and Mathis, Reinhardt and Monk, Jerry Lee Lewis and Fats Domino, Stravinsky and Ives—was *my* music. To me, it was all exciting and beautiful, and no one could convince me otherwise.

I have a friend who's absolutely certain that two of my favorite musicians from those earlier times—Elvis Presley and Janis Joplin—were not really musicians at all. "Their voices were horrible!" he says. "Elvis just wailed like a stuck pig, and Joplin couldn't make a sound without the help of a bottle of Jim Beam and a pack of Marlboros. She ruined her voice—if she ever had one to begin with!" It should surprise no one that it is next to impossible for the two of us to have an informed, respectful conversation about music.

It's nearly always the non-musicians—people who've either never played an instrument or who lack the discipline to master the formidable pedagogical requirements of being a musician—who are the most unforgiving in their assessment of musical worth and technical ability.

To this day, there are still highly credentialed, technically proficient faculty members of major universities who continue to work from the erroneous assumption that the only serious music is classical music.

While studying music at Eastern Michigan University in the early '60s, I occasionally witnessed professors pounding on the practice room doors of any student who dared to play jazz, then ordering them to stop wasting their time with "inferior" music. It actually happened to me on more than one occasion. Since then, the Department of Music at EMU has come a long way toward recognizing the critical importance of jazz in any well-rounded music department curriculum. Eastern Michigan's Jazz Combo Program, coordinated by North Texas State University graduate Mark Pappas, is now an integral part of the Music Department's offerings.

Musicians who either can't find work in orchestras or don't aspire to an orchestral career may choose small ensemble work or strike out entirely on their own. One example is the refreshingly laid-back Kronos Quartet, whose repertoire is remarkably eclectic. Another is flutist Sir James Galway, who left the orchestral world after clashing philosophically with conductor Herbert von Karajan, then went on to become a world-renowned soloist.

One would be foolish to argue that university music departments—perhaps especially those of elite institutions blessed with a formidable endowment, top-notch faculty, and a steady flow of ambitious, goal-oriented students—aren't important incubators for what is new and exciting in any musical genre. But they're not the only place where good, fresh, exciting things can happen.

To find those places, one must be prepared to step out from under the academic bubble and into the real world—a world of infinite musical variety and untold riches. It takes a little digging, but you'll find them on the stages of bars and bistros in down-on-their luck cities like Detroit, Michigan (the fabled Bert's Marketplace on Russell Street), or Camden, New Jersey (Serengeti Jazz & Blues Café on Cooper Street); in public schools around the world, whose hard-working, deeply committed teacher/conductors are shamefully under-appreciated; in churches, in recording studios, and on cruise ships; and in isolated parts of the country where families are still playing remarkably sophisticated indigenous music in the privacy of their homes.

Enter the street musician.

Wherever I've traveled in large, tourist-friendly cities—with the exception of the more curmudgeonly municipalities who think of street musicians as loiterers and have enacted laws to ban them—I've inevitably come across an unorthodox sprinkling of musicians, some highly skilled, others technically shaky, adding their own unique beam of auditory sunlight to a cloudy day.

When I first stepped off the train in downtown Glasgow, Scotland, in 1997, I looked down Buchanan Street, the major pedestrian thoroughfare leading to the City Centre, and counted no fewer than twenty musicians—including a saxophonist, a clarinetist, a trombonist, a guitarist, and a dulcimer player—performing within a six-block area. You're also likely to find musicians tucked away in tunnels far below street level, fighting against the roar of the trains winding their way through the labyrinthine bowels of the city above them.

One of the most intrepid underground warriors in all of New England is entertainer Eric McIntyre. He's made his mark on the city of Boston in many ways over the decades, but in recent years he's been a frequent presence in the gritty, fume-choked entrails of the MBTA as a licensed, itinerant musician in what locals call the T.

Nearly every time I've come down to Boston, I've been able to count on seeing Eric performing for the hoards of tourists, commuters, and college students who pass through Government Center each day on their way to other destinations in and around the Boston/Cambridge corridor. He's been a Government Center fixture for well over a decade—as much a part of the MBTA network as any silver rail or push-pull train in the system.

Government Center was closed in March of 2014 for repairs and renovations and won't be open again until March of 2016, so I've no doubt Eric is busy now making music elsewhere in the MBTA. And when Government Center reopens, I expect to see him there again, plying his trade and pleasing the riders.

McIntyre is not just another musician, singing to the multitudes as they go about their affairs in what some like to call the hub of the universe. He's also Eric "The Showman" McIntyre—billed as an impersonator extraordinaire—and the spot-on reincarnation of another musician we've all known and loved for many years: Sammy Davis, Jr.

Every few days McIntyre can be heard singing some of Davis's most enduring tunes, including "The Candy Man," "That Old Black Magic," the lounge-lizard classic "Hey There," and "Mr. Bojangles," written by famed country singer Jerry Jeff Walker after an encounter with a street musician in a New Orleans jail.

McIntyre has no backup group. He has no guitar and no piano—only a harmonica, suspended on a holder near his mouth. His primary instrument is his voice, and he needs only a CD player, an amplifier, and a microphone to pour his heartfelt croonings out into the masses of MBTA travelers.

Like the dozens of other itinerant musicians who populate the T, McIntyre listens to the screeching of metal as the trains

Fig. 27. Eric "The Showman" McIntyre at lunch in downtown Boston.

arrive and depart, then arrive again on their relentless, clockwork meanderings. It's a combination avant-garde composer John Cage would have appreciated. McIntyre must also resign himself to the fact that in the minds of the majority of underground travelers, he's pretty much nonexistent.

But exist he does, and Eric "The Showman" made his mark on the city of Boston long before he ever imagined he'd be performing beneath the streets and sidewalks of the booming mini-metropolis he calls home.

McIntyre has performed at countless Boston area venues over the years, but one of his proudest moments was his appearance on the stage of Tremont Street's venerated Shubert Theatre, where since 1910 actors and entertainers like John Barrymore, Richard Burton, and Mary Martin have performed in tryout shows aimed at Manhattan's Great White Way.

McIntyre doesn't play the major concert halls these days. He's in his seventies now and must work around a foot ailment that limits his mobility. When he's not underground, it's likely you'll find him toiling at an agent-booked party or conference, or sharing his act with fellow residents at a nearby residential facility for seniors.

His dependence on recorded backup music—harshly distorted and nearly obliterated by the incessant screeching of trains—will never impress the critics, who are unlikely ever to pass through Government Center and listen to him, anyway.

Nor is The Showman ever likely to win a fashion award from the small army of twenty-something merchants above him, living like caged birds in the storefronts along trendy Newbury Street. To be sure, there are days when McIntyre, dressed in black and banging out "Mr. Bojangles" through the deafening roar of the trains, appears to have just stepped out of the television and into your home. But even the finest replication of Sammy's distinctive haute couture can't withstand the punishment of a day in Government Center, riding a cloud of air so moist and stagnant it sucks the starch out of even the finest shirt and turns the skin of even the most elegant Bostonian into fly paper.

No wonder, then, that few of them ever stop to drop a dollar—or even one thin dime—into the little box next to McIntyre's battle-weary amplifier. Most of them will never have to work to stay fresh as a flower while eking out a living in the sweltering heat of Boston's Underground.

The good news is that the deplorable conditions in which McIntyre and other itinerant musicians often have to work don't stop them from bringing genuine pleasure to the public with their music, however distantly removed from concert hall elegance and technical perfection they might be.

That distance between two radically different worlds—cultural, aesthetic, and pecuniary—can seem vast and unbridgeable. One learns from hard experience that in America, classical music does not come cheaply, while at the same time there is very little compensation for the music of itinerant musicians. In

Fig. 28. McIntyre performing in the stifling heat of Government Center subway station, Boston.

a Darwinist universe, what is often described as the best music in the world is inextricably woven into the fabric of the rich and powerful, with all of the illusions of superiority that membership in that fraternity implies.

To be fair, there really is a centuries-long tradition of excellence in the performance of classical music, regardless of either the affluence or the poverty of its practitioners. And the drive for excellence goes hand-in-hand with the noble intent and sublime emotions of the music itself.

What mesmerizes audiences the most at La Scala, the Konzerthaus, and other temples of musical perfection, with their plush red seats, stacked balconies, and High Rococo trimmings, is the sound of absolute mastery—of an almost inhuman command of what the average listener considers impossibly difficult music. Such music is often so overwhelmingly beautiful—so melodically exquisite and soaringly complex—that it appears to the layman to have been composed not by an earthly being but by some otherworldly God.

When gifted performers like Lang Lang, Yo-Yo Ma, and Ana Vidović are lost onstage in the exquisite nirvana of an especially powerful performance, one is tempted to wonder if the devil himself has had something to do with their musical gifts. One must never forget, though, that the work of highly skilled sound engineers—a luxury that the typical itinerant musician doesn't enjoy—also plays a part in that digitally recorded illusion of absolute musical perfection.

But let's come back down to earth again. What happens in the bowels of Government Center, or on the grimy, traffic-choked streets of Glasgow or Chicago, may appear to have nothing at all to do with what happens in the flamboyant world of touring virtuosi—a world born of conspicuous wealth, hierarchical privilege, and the succulent fruits of an educated life—but those two worlds are actually inextricably connected.

Why? Because music, regardless of its cultural origins, its musical genre, the man or woman who composed it, the trappings of the place in which it is being performed, or the level of proficiency of the performer, will always have the power to bring pleasure to those people who are disposed to find it pleasurable. All of the high-octane marketing and scholarly pedantry in the world cannot make people love a piece of music if their heart tells them it isn't lovable.

The third movement of Alexander Borodin's *String Quartet No. 2* is among the most sublime musical compositions I've ever had the pleasure of hearing. That Borodin was also a highly respected chemist is nearly incomprehensible. I've heard that quartet countless times, and yet I never really tire of listening to it. It feeds the soul of its listeners in a way that music by any other composer, in any genre, could never hope to do.

And yet the fact that it is a classical composition is not the reason it has such power to elicit profound emotions in its listeners. Classical or not, within the formidable demands and long-standing traditions of the genre in which it was written, it is the essence of musical perfection—the work of a great master of harmony, melody, and form.

Borodin is one of my great cultural heroes, but so are Janis Joplin, Elvis Presley, and Jerry Lee Lewis. Products of a very different time, bedeviled by social pressures unique to their era, they were nevertheless gifted in ways that Borodin could have never have imagined.

Joplin's soulful interpretation of George Gershwin's magnificent "Summertime" is the work of an emotional prodigy—a woman born to be musical, right down to the bone. She had a voice like hot, flowing lava and a heart as plaintively expressive as any celebrated diva pumping out an operatic aria for the fiftieth time on the stages of La Scala or the Konzerthaus.

For me and countless other armchair rockers, Presley's "Burning Love," Lewis's "Great Balls of Fire," and Joplin's "Summertime" continue to have the same magnetic allure as Borodin's legendary string quartets, but for entirely different reasons. These and similar gems of the emerging rock genre were full of pounding eroticism and intimations of a youth-driven rebellion against the heavily sublimated, painfully straightjacketed propriety of whatever music managed to get past the censors and onto radio stations in the '40s and '50s.

It's hard to comprehend how, within one brief but electrifying musical interlude, we as a culture went from Patti Page's insipid "(How Much Is) That Doggie in the Window" to Elvis Presley's hard-driving "Hound Dog" and its flip side, the irresistible rockabilly rhythms of "Don't Be Cruel." Together, they knocked the earth off its axis, provided a spectacular musical catharsis for millions of energy-deprived teenagers, and changed the world forever.

That Joplin, Presley, and Lewis and their contemporaries borrowed heavily from the great blues singers who preceded them didn't detract from the reality that they were themselves enormously gifted musicians. And just as importantly, they quite unintentionally became powerful missionaries for the spreading of the gospel of African American music into mainstream American culture—music that, in spite of its long, proud history, had been kept unfairly from the airwaves by the majority of white-dominated, ethnocentric radio stations.

While Joplin, Presley, and Lewis lacked the fancy credentials and privileged upbringings of Borodin and other venerated classical musicians, they had no shortage of the one quality that has allowed innumerable listeners to fall passionately in love with them as musicians: emotional authenticity. It's a quality marked by extraordinary intensity and a gut-wrenching sense of immediacy, and it doesn't come automatically with technical perfection. A great many highly skilled performers of the classical repertoire—people who dazzle us every day with astonishing facility at the piano and other instruments, including the voice—cannot claim to have within them what Joplin had.

Without that rare and highly prized gift of emotional authenticity, a quality that can be found, or found lacking, in any musical genre, musicians start to sound more like assembly line laborers while playing yet another masterwork from the essential repertoire for the fiftieth time. They become the pieceworkers of the concert hall circuit, and one has to wonder how much glamour there really is in that sort of calling.

The public's presumption of a dramatic disparity in form, content, and emotional intensity between the classical and rock genres is woven intimately into class differences and social stratification. Though a growing number of classically trained musicians have found ways to inject themselves into the rock and pop world, others, fearful of tarnishing their image within the performance community, have by and large chosen to keep a safe distance from the rockers. Exceptions to this unwritten rule can be found in orchestras around the country who, because of lackluster performance at the box office, have begun to bring pop musicians—and guest conductors (who in some cases aren't really conductors at all)—onstage to increase their revenue and pay their bills.

To find out why society continues so stubbornly to stratify the arts—to rank one discipline or genre, in the social Darwinist way, as either superior or inferior in relation to another—one must look beyond what the critics and historians are telling us with such maddening persistence each day. One must dig a little deeper.

Is it not telling, for instance, that one virtually never hears rock, folk, jazz, classical, or rap music played interchangeably on one radio show devoted to music? Keeping the various disciplines and genres separate makes it next to impossible for the champions of their various pet genres to engage with their listeners in a serious dialogue about the similarities between them.

Let's face it: the business of erecting false barriers between one art form or genre and another is great for business efficiency, aggressive marketing, and the bottom line, but damaging to the cause of a greater understanding of the nature of creativity itself. Mass production—and its inevitable consequence, specialization—have a great deal to do with the stratification of the arts.

In the '60s, James Galway was repeatedly hammered by stuffed-shirt critics for collaborating with British jazz singer Cleo Laine in the 1974 RCA album *A Beautiful Thing*. It brought his classical sensibilities into direct contact with the uninhibited rhythms and playful sensibilities of the pop world and elicited a remarkably poisonous outcry from the musical purists. Meanwhile, Galway was laughing all the way to the bank while marveling at the absurdity of the critics' myopic, self-aggrandizing ways.

The Beatles—as fearless as Galway when it came to thumbing their noses at the musical establishment—became cross-cultural pioneers within the rock world when they hired a small ensemble of classical musicians to add both a volcanic crescendo and a sustained piano chord to "A Day in the Life," the last track on the beloved *Sgt. Pepper's Lonely Hearts Club Band* album. Later, they did it again by weaving the aching, minor-key sonorities of a string quartet into the poignant tapestry of "Eleanor Rigby."

Classical performers like Dietrich Fischer-Dieskau and Elisabeth Schwarzkopf have most certainly earned their rightful place in the history of music. The best of the classical repertoire they bring to life so expertly is full to overflowing with beauty and humanity. But within the rock genre, singer/composers like Buddy Holly, Paul Simon, and Paul McCartney have also firmly established themselves as the masters of their craft, figures of great historical importance in the world of music. Excellence is excellence, regardless of where it comes from, where it appears on the world stage, and who's doing the performing.

But what of the legions of equally gifted musicians who have for various reasons—some legitimate and some of their own doing—failed to achieve rock-star notoriety? The hard-to-learn truth is that, in all things, there are degrees of excellence. Not everyone can have the same high level of proficiency in a given discipline; the cream always manages to rise to the top.

And so, let us pay homage to that vast infrastructure of musicians who, in spite of their relative obscurity and technical limitations, continue to make beautiful music. Beneath the multi-genre luminaries in the Darwinist pecking order are countless musicians who, while not as technically gifted as their more famous brethren, are no less essential to the promulgation of the arts as a humanizing, peace-loving component of any healthy society.

One way to express our appreciation for them is to go back for a moment to that nearly forgotten musical universe beneath the streets of Boston, where Eric "The Showman" and other less heralded musicians ply their trade with the same consistency and determination as more illustrious above-ground performers.

Regardless of how derivative his work as an impersonator may be, and regardless of the level of his technical proficiency,

Eric McIntyre is no less important to the world of music than composer and conductor José Serebrier, blues guitarist B.B. King, or anyone else in the music industry.

We hear story after story in the media about internationally famous musicians—Sting or Yo-Yo Ma, for example—who use their musical gifts to promote peace and wellbeing among the less fortunate. But it's critically important to remember that, contrary to popular opinion and the opinion of the vast, ratings-obsessed army of writers and reviewers, it isn't just the rich and famous among us who make the world a better place.

Eric McIntyre and countless other musicians who make a living in unconventional, unpretentious venues are altogether the essential infrastructure that unites musicians of every cultural stripe around the world. Without their work, and the work of legions of teachers of music in our public schools, music would cease to be the essential component of a peace-loving, aesthetically literate society.

The only lasting measure of a musician's worth to the world is whether he or she has brought pleasure to an audience, no matter how small or unsophisticated. Of all the places where music is certain to find an appreciative audience, nursing homes and assisted living facilities are the most fertile ground. It doesn't matter to the residents that they're ensconced in wheelchairs in the common room rather than in the topmost balcony of a plush-carpeted concert hall. And it doesn't matter that the performer they're listening to may not be the least bit famous.

To these people, *music* is the thing, not fame, not status within the social hierarchy, and not breathtaking technical brilliance. That makes them more powerful allies in the dissemination of worthwhile music than any season-ticket holder in an opera hall who doesn't know his Monteverdi from his Glass—who's more worried about the quality of his necktie and who designed it than he is about the emotional authenticity of the music he paid so dearly to hear.

If only one man or woman has had his or her spirits lifted by the moving lyricism of a simple song played by an average musician, then that one musician, at one moment in time, has succeeded no less triumphantly than the winner of yet another prestigious Tchaikovsky competition. And the all-important relationship between composer, performer, and audience will have been preserved.

Fig. 29. *Harlequin, Columbine, and the Noblest of Callings* by Ross Bachelder.

✣ Tiny Novelette 3 ✣

Harlequin, Columbine, and the Noblest of Callings

Barnabas Ridley loved to act. He'd played many prominent roles in amateur theater, but the role of Harlequin had always been his favorite.

When he was on stage dancing opposite the beautiful Columbine, he may as well have been in heaven, for he was doing what he loved most in the world to do. It never failed to amaze him that each night he was actually privileged to play suitor to a dancer of supreme gifts—a woman with the most fragile of limbs and an inborn perfume so delicate that it would often transport him into ecstasy.

So deeply immersed was he in the role of Harlequin, he'd invariably forget that in real life he was only Barnabas Ridley, master plumber, and that he repaired drainpipes and toilets for the greater portion of his living. He decided long ago that he'd never reveal the truth about his double life, not even to his closest friends.

If Barnabas Ridley had anything to do about it, Columbine would never know what Harlequin actually did to pay the bills, and his fellow plumbers would never know that, when he wasn't wielding a pipe wrench or unclogging a toilet, he was executing glissades and *grand jetés* on the stages of the most prominent dance halls in Europe.

To hide the telltale signs of his offstage existence, he always wore snow-white gloves and a mask that cleverly concealed his dense black beard and a grizzly network of scars from years of banging his forehead on the undersides of sinks. Nor did he ever allow the other dancers to see him in his plumber's uniform. It was his artful employment of subterfuge that kept his dual identity a secret.

But alas: things aren't always tea and crumpets for an actor! The man who played Clown each night always felt upstaged by Harlequin, who whether on stage or off seemed entirely too full of himself. To make matters worse, Clown had a secret crush on

Columbine, and was determined to win her heart by whatever means he could devise.

Then, one winter morning when a pipe in his apartment burst, he checked the listings for local plumbers and quite by accident chose the very firm where Ridley happened to be employed. Ridley, who had no idea where Clown lived, forgot to check the name of his caller, and when he drove to the address and stepped into Clown's apartment, covered with grease and lugging a toolbox, he discovered to his horror that he'd failed to remove all of his makeup from the previous night's performance.

His cover had been blown, and now the other dancers would soon know he made his real living not from dancing but from unclogging toilets and repairing pipes. All the other plumbers laughed and sneered when they learned Harlequin was a dancer, and he was ordered to turn in his uniform and surrender his license.

But even in the worst of circumstances, one must never give up hope! When Columbine learned that Harlequin made his living as a plumber, she found his profession not a matter of shame but the noblest of callings. After all, what sane person doesn't value a plumber?

The very next night they were back together on stage. Barnabas was granted a livable wage as a dancer, and in the spring, he and Columbine were married. And from that moment on, they knew they'd always be dancing together.

Chapter 7

My Improbable Journey to the Other Side of the World
And What Took Me There

In October of 2011 I traveled from my home in southern Maine to the North Island, Bay of Plenty town of Tauranga, New Zealand, to perform at the opening reception for an exhibit of artworks by internationally renowned New Zealand watercolorist Susan Harrison-Tustain. Altogether, I stayed nineteen days in the Land of the Kiwi, traveling 3,200 miles alone in a rented van, meeting many fascinating people, and taking hundreds of photographs along the way.

This is the story of that adventure and the events and circumstances that led to it. It is also the story of a man who, after two long-ago trips to England and Scotland, finally regrew his wings and embarked on a project that filled him with wonder and forever enriched his understanding of himself. New Zealand, like no other adventure, rekindled his passion for all things beautiful and mysterious, wherever they might be found.

In my mid-sixties, with two trips to England and Scotland under my belt and a long list of creative endeavors to relish, I still found myself yearning to travel to exotic destinations in distant lands.

The gulf between dream and reality would not be easy to overcome. I faced many heavy responsibilities as manager of a frame shop and gallery in Rochester, New Hampshire, and that reality, along with my freelance work as artist and musician and my late-in-life worry about money, kept me more or less grounded in northern New England. I was still able to take relatively ambitious day trips to explore art galleries and museums, paint outdoors, and perform as a musician, but my frequent small-scale adventures still weren't enough to satisfy the hungry traveler in me.

And then, in the spring of 2009, a door opened up unexpectedly on what would prove to be the opportunity of a lifetime.

It happened because of my work as a musician. I'd begun performing solo flute recitals on occasion in northern New England, determined to be more active and more ambitious as a performer. During my frequent trips to the Museum of Fine Arts in Boston—I'd been a member for nearly twenty years—I'd often hear the strains of a solo performer floating like a cloud of incense through the MFA's vast network of galleries. The presence of professional musicians, performing live at the museum every few weeks, added immeasurably to the experience of seeing so many spectacular artworks.

It was hard not to envy those musicians for their accomplishments. The difference between where I was accustomed to performing and where those musicians were plying their trade—amidst the architectural splendor of a world-class museum and surrounded by thousands of years of priceless masterworks—sent me into an emotional tailspin. I thought, *I'm not really ready to perform in a place like this! And they wouldn't want some nobody from Maine to come down here and play, anyway. They've got all the musicians they need, right here in Boston.*

I drove back to Maine that evening in an increasingly dark mood, plagued by lingering self-doubt. Once again, I wasn't achieving enough to allow me to feel good about myself. It had been this way with me, off and on, for many years. Without unequivocal evidence of achievement—of occupational growth and personal fulfillment—I knew I'd never be really happy in my professional work.

A few weeks later, during yet another trip to the MFA—this time in a noticeably better frame of mind—I heard a professorial-looking flute player performing with piano accompaniment in a corner off the downstairs lobby, just off the Huntington Avenue entrance. I paused, listened carefully for a while, then decided I was just as musically competent as he was.

Once again, I'd been inexcusably hard on myself—working from a posture of fear instead of a position of trust in my own well-demonstrated abilities. I was selling myself short for no good reason, and I had to do something about it. The very next day I called the administrators at the MFA and discovered how to qualify as a performer in the Afternoon Tea series. Within a few months, I learned that I'd been accepted without reservation into the series.

I signed on for seven consecutive monthly appearances, and just ten minutes into the first appearance, while I was playing from the balcony at the top of the grand staircase beneath the murals of John Singer Sargent, an incident occurred that would dramatically alter my vision of myself and lay the groundwork for another unforgettable travel adventure.

I'd just finished playing "Dance of the Blessed Spirits" from Christoph Willibald Gluck's opera *Orpheus and Eurydice*—an emotionally powerful piece, enriched and then carried along by the splendid acoustics of the hall—when a smiling, elegantly dressed couple applauded me from a distance. As I paused to sip a glass of water and rest my embouchure, they stepped up and praised both my playing and the incomparable beauty of my surroundings.

"What a beautiful piece!" the woman said. "And what a magnificent venue in which to make your music!"

Her companion nodded his agreement.

"I wish we'd remembered to bring our camera into the museum," she continued. "I'd love to have had a photo of this moment."

Lisa Toole, a friend who'd come down to Boston with me from South Berwick, Maine, to hear me perform, used her camera to take several photographs of me in performance, then promised to send them to the woman.

"Thanks so much!" she said, smiling, then introduced herself and her companion to us. "I'm Susan Harrison-Tustain, and this is my husband, Richard. I'm an artist, and we're here from our home in New Zealand, touring the United States and visiting various museums, including your Museum of Fine Arts."

She then gestured upward toward the vaulted ceiling. "It was such a treat to have come across your beautiful music as a part of our tour. And what a rewarding combination—these fabulous Sargent murals and the music of Gluck, one of my all-time favorite composers!"

The two of them lingered for a while to hear more of my performance, then slipped down the grand staircase and disappeared into the crowd of visitors in the ground floor lobby.

I finished my two hours of performing, packed up my things, and drove back to Maine, wondering how anything could ever top the excitement of that day's events. I'd finally proven to myself that I was up to Boston standards as a performer, and I'd impressed an out-of-town artist with my playing.

By the time I'd crossed the Maine border, dropped off my friend, and headed home, I'd begun actively wondering just what sort of artist Susan was. Modernist or a traditionalist? Armory Show or Colonial Britain? To find out, I went to the only source available to me at the time—the internet.

What I found was that Susan Harrison-Tustain is a proudly self-taught artist of the most extraordinary drive and accomplishment, with Romantic-era sensibilities, a palette reminiscent of the old masters, and an indisputable fountainhead of painterly expertise.

I then learned that, with the help of her husband Richard—a professional photographer, wine aficionado, and skilled event manager—she had put together an absolute juggernaut of a marketing plan for her career as an artist, including the publication of an impressive string of feature articles about her in *International Artist* magazine, workshops across Europe and in the United States, an ambitious online newsletter with an international reach, lucrative product endorsements, authorship of several best-selling self-help books for artists, and a growing number of eagerly sought-after instructional DVDs.

Harrison-Tustain was obviously a woman of taste and discernment, with demonstrated business acumen, an acute awareness of her growing status within the international arts community, and a deep, all-consuming pride in her hard-won success as an artist. *How fortunate*, I thought, *that I should have been performing in Boston when we crossed paths so unexpectedly.*

I thought about what she'd accomplished as an artist and what a fine life she'd created for herself in New Zealand, then went back to my own very different routine in Maine—my painting and drawing, my freelance gigs and solo recitals as a musician, and my work as manager of the frame shop and gallery in New Hampshire. In my quieter moments I continued to wonder what seed might have been planted as a result of our encounter in Boston, and what unimaginably beautiful flower might eventually push up through the soil and into the sunlight of my life.

Several months later, an e-mail arrived from Susan, dispatched from her home in the North Island town of Tauranga.

"As an artist, I do a lot of traveling for both business and pleasure," she wrote. "In my travels I always look for moments powerful enough to inspire and motivate me as a painter. Seeing you perform that beautiful composition beneath those Sargent murals, surrounded by such splendid architecture, has moved me to paint a portrait of you in performance. It should be done in six months, and then I'll be including it in an exhibit here in Tauranga in 2011."

A portrait of me? I marveled while sitting in front of my computer, scratching my head. *Why would anyone want to do that?* I began to wonder if I might simply have misread her letter, so I read it again. Sure enough, it was true: this woman I hardly knew, and whom I'd met only once quite by coincidence in Boston, really had decided to paint my portrait.

Not long afterward, I began to imagine what it would be like to actually go to New Zealand and see the exhibit she'd mentioned. As unlikely as it was, I began on a purely emotional level to find a way to get there. Late at night I'd preach to myself, trying without success to stop dreaming and fall asleep. *How badly do you want this?* I'd ask over and over again.

For the next several weeks I became a formidable two-headed hydra, deeply at war with myself, tossing and turning each night while dreaming terrifying dreams of cowardliness and failure. *Which head will be the victor?* I wondered. *The one that says, "No, it's not practical," or that other, more adventurous head—the one with a history of leaping over insurmountable barriers and choosing to believe in himself?*

More often than not, the less courageous head was winning. I was increasingly distraught at the very real likelihood that I'd once again choose the easy way out. Then, one afternoon while touring an exhibit at the Kittery Art Association in southern Maine, I confessed to poet Elizabeth Kirschner, a longtime KAA member, that I'd all but given up on my plans to go to New Zealand.

"I'll never be able to raise enough money for such an ambitious trip," I moaned to her. "It's just not practical."

Kirschner turned to me and raised her eyebrows.

"That's ridiculous!" she said. "Why would you choose to turn your back on such a fabulous adventure? If I wasn't about to go on a vacation myself, I'd stay right here in Kittery Point and not go anywhere until I'd convinced you that you *must* find a way to go to New Zealand!"

She was right, of course. Once again, I was running away from a very real, life-altering opportunity, allowing it to intimidate and then defeat me in a way that would be certain to cause me enormous regret and no small amount of personal shame.

I got up the next morning, went to my computer, and wrote to Susan, awash with determination and armed with a heaven-sent conviction that this time, the good head would vanquish the bad one and make real the travel adventure I'd been so fervently praying for.

I declared my intention not merely to come to New Zealand, but to perform at the opening reception of Susan's exhibit in Tauranga. Her answer was a resounding yes, and within days I'd opened a travel account at Kennebunk Savings in Berwick and scheduled an appointment with Horizon Travel of Dover, New Hampshire, to begin planning for the adventure. This was going to be an easy assignment for Nick, the youngest member of the team; he'd already been to nearly all of the places in New Zealand I was planning to see.

Fig. 30. My New Zealand travel shrine (gift of artist Anne Strout, West Falmouth, Maine).

It didn't take long for me to realize I'd need thousands of dollars to cover the cost of the trip. To raise the necessary cash, I ramped up my activity as a musician and submitted more artworks than usual to exhibit jurors, hoping to dramatically increase my freelance income. I began to get juried into various exhibits in galleries I'd assumed all along would never accept my works. And by bearing down harder than usual on the marketing of myself as the Flute Guy, I began to get more frequent paying gigs.

Most rewarding, though, was my decision to mount a solo exhibit of my multimedia work at my own gallery, just one month before my departure. I called it the New Zealand Sell-Off, and by pricing my pieces considerably lower than usual, I sold nearly two thousand dollars worth of artworks, many of them to a small circle of friends and fellow artists who knew how badly I wanted to go to New Zealand and had pledged to do what they could to get me there. I'd carry my deep appreciation for their support with me across the Pacific, then through all 3,200 miles of travel from Auckland to Queenstown.

Artist Anne Strout, a longtime friend from Falmouth, Maine, assembled a travel shrine for me, housed in a round tin container. In it was a delightful array of Lilliputian items commemorating my work as writer, artist, and musician. I vowed to mount it on the dashboard of my travel van, certain that its magical powers would protect me along every leg of my journey.

San Francisco: The Chinatown Layover

After nearly a year of planning and fundraising, the time to escape to New Zealand had arrived. Early in the morning of October 25, 2011, I took the C&J Trailways bus to Boston's Logan International Airport, then caught a six-hour flight to San Francisco. It would be the first leg of my trip to New Zealand and the first time I'd ever been west of St. Louis.

I spent most of the eight-hour layover touring portions of San Francisco with long-time Michigan friend Rob Imerson, who'd come down from his home in San Jose to show me the sights. We drove over the legendary Golden Gate bridge, wove our way through the roller coaster streets overlooking the Bay, watched a street artist ply his trade, and explored the colorful labyrinth of open-air markets in Chinatown. Strung high above the streets were long lines of freshly hung laundry, flapping like D-Day flags high above the sun-splashed neighborhoods.

When I came across a sidewalk bin full of sleek, multicolored fresh fish, I whipped out my camera and began photographing them. When the proprietor saw what I was up to, he raced out of the shop and ordered me to cut it out.

As delightful as my truncated romp through Chinatown was, I was eager to put San Francisco behind me and get to the airport, terrified that I might miss my flight to Auckland. Rob, who knew the city inside and out, understood my fear and leapt into action. After some truly artful driving through undulating hills and closely packed neighborhoods, he got me to the terminal with time to spare. Finally, the time had come to leave American soil and take the twelve-hour flight from San Francisco to Auckland.

We flew almost entirely at night. The flight was astonishingly smooth, thanks to the sheer size of the plane and the favorable weather. With the exception of the steady arrival of beautifully prepared food, and one disturbingly long episode of turbulence, the flight from San Francisco to Auckland was surprisingly uneventful.

Beautiful, Bustling Auckland

We landed on New Zealand soil under a blazing sun, but thanks to jet lag and the dramatic difference in time zones, I really had no idea what time it was. Nor did it really matter; I was too excited to care. Once out of the plane and into the terminal, I purchased a cell phone, had a quick snack at a tiny, stand-up McDonald's, then caught a shuttle to JUCY Rentals, a short distance from the airport. There I'd arranged in advance to pick up my rental van, complete with FM radio, CD player, and crude but functional sleeping quarters.

"Be JUCY, Live JUCY, Rent JUCY!" roared the company's blatantly youth-targeted slogan, which was displayed proudly on both sides of the yellow-trimmed, shamrock-green vehicle I'd rented for my odyssey. Right away, I loved its post-adolescent, "Look at me!" audacity, but in the heat of the moment, freshly arrived in what was for me a new and exotic land, I'd yet to consider what a sitting duck I was likely going to be. I'd be learning to drive on the left side of the road in an utterly unfamiliar country, behind the wheel of an absolute cartoon of a van that no policeman could possibly fail to see.

When the reality of what I was about to embark on finally hit me, I called up what little courage I could find and asked the JUCY representative for a test drive with coaching. He looked at me nonchalantly, with a touch of younger-generation derision at the corners of his easy smile, then shrugged his shoulders and said what teenagers around the world say with almost mechanical regularity: "No problem!"

He handed me the keys and slipped into the passenger seat to the left of me. "It'll be a snap!" he said. "Just remember to stay to the *left* everywhere you go." He then reviewed the contents of the dashboard, showed me where to sign the rental contract, and sat patiently with me as I made my first terrifying journey down a service road and back again, heaving and jerking like the madcap clown in a three-ring circus.

Auckland's JUCY Snooze:
Playground for the Unconventional Traveler

Not counting that blood-curdling test drive, my first really serious foray into left-side driving was into a dense tangle of big-city, rush-hour traffic in downtown Auckland. Even with the help of my first-ever GPS—and even though I was only an eighth of a mile away from my destination—I needed forty-five exasperating minutes to find the hard-to-spot entrance to the JUCY Snooze, the hotel I'd booked myself into for the first two nights. Once I'd managed to find the place, I parked my car triumphantly in the underground garage, pulled my suitcase from the storage compartment of the van, and noted with relief that there were still four fenders and two bumpers in plain sight, right where they ought to have been.

When I'd worked my way up to ground level and entered the hotel, I was instantly captivated with the playful, upbeat tone of the place. The lobby featured an image of a young and saucy, libido-tickling girl on the wall opposite the service desk. My assigned room was just as playfully conceived, and in bold letters on the wall over the bed were a few sage words:

> Sleep with your eyes closed,
> live with your eyes open!

"*My* kind of hotel!" I whooped. What that one heartwarming, life-affirming slogan was challenging me to do was precisely what I'd been trying to do for years. And now, here in New Zealand, I planned to do just that—and at breakneck speed—until that last bittersweet moment when I'd be forced to bid farewell to Kiwi soil and touch ground again in America.

Over the next two days I explored the city of Auckland on foot, relieved to have put off my baptism into expressway driving until the last possible moment. I made several excursions into the downtown area, gleefully absorbing the tone and texture of New Zealand's most populous city. Along every available walkway were rows of swaying palm trees; quaint, ivy-covered storefronts; and meticulously maintained beds of exotic flowers.

I also reserved the better part of a day for traveling to the outer extremities of the city. While Auckland has a fine transportation system, with sparkling clean, elegantly designed buses, I preferred to travel on foot. It would allow me to study the domestic architecture, admire the preened and pampered lawns, and take the pulse of the city by meeting and interacting with the locals.

I spent several hours exploring the Auckland War Memorial Museum—often alluded to simply as the Auckland Museum or AM—a beautifully designed facility with a rich offering of both native Maori and European-influenced art. The AM is considered one of Auckland's most iconic buildings, neoclassical in design and perched majestically on a grassed plinth (the remains of a dormant volcano) in the Auckland Domain, a sprawling public park close to Auckland's central business district. The interior of the museum is thoroughly modern and truly spectacular. The stunning, seven-story atrium, built of native kauri wood, dominates the courtyard and epitomizes the blazing ingenuity and cultural sophistication of modern New Zealand.

As a part of my visit to the museum, I attended one of the regularly scheduled Maori demonstrations, designed to give tourists unfamiliar with the Maori culture a glimpse into its proud, centuries-old cultural traditions. It featured poignant, first-person narratives and beautiful choral singing, culminating in a high-energy version of the Maoris' most celebrated dance, the world-famous haka. Afterward I toured the section of the AM devoted to Maori history and artifacts, and I marveled at their unmistakable artistry and ingenuity.

The Winter Gardens: Flowery Gem of the Auckland Domain

After the Maori demonstration, I walked through every last exhibit in the museum—at every turn brilliantly curated and elegantly displayed—then scrambled to find other things to explore while still on the outskirts of the city.

My first choice was the nearby Auckland Domain Wintergardens, built following World War I with funds generated from the Industrial, Agricultural and Mining Exhibition of 1913–1914, an event staged at the same site.

The Auckland Domain, established as a public park in 1844, had begun over time to be frequented by what many of the locals considered undesirables, so municipal leaders and Auckland residents decided together that something had to be done. The result was the Wintergardens, a magnificently landscaped, two-greenhouse complex whose elegant architecture is known to have been influenced by the aesthetics of the renowned Arts and Crafts movement that originated in England in the nineteenth century and spread rapidly to neighboring European countries.

The two greenhouses featured an amazingly fragrant potpourri of exotic ferns and flowers, so intoxicating that after more than an hour of taking in their perfumes and photographing them, I still found it difficult to leave the place.

While the Wintergardens feature an astonishing array of botanical wonders, not all of them can claim to be fragrant in the romantic sense of the word. In December of 2013, the Tropical House of the Wintergardens became the first place in New Zealand to have the giant *amorphophallus titanum* in full bloom. The plant can take ten years to mature, and the resulting flower is widely thought to smell of rotting flesh.

Auckland Zoological Gardens: Everywhere Stunning, Always Improving

The next day I turned my attention from flowers to animals, spending a rewarding afternoon at Auckland Zoological Gardens. It's only minutes from central Auckland, so I traveled there on foot rather than by bus in order to enjoy the beautiful architecture and landscaping along the way.

I've seen many zoos in my travels—Detroit, Cincinnati, and St. Louis to name just a few—and while the Auckland Zoo was noticeably smaller, it was no less well-designed, well-maintained, and animal friendly than the bigger facilities I've been to.

Auckland Zoo is home to the largest collection of native and exotic animals in all of New Zealand—875 creatures representing 138 species—including wallabies, kangaroos, emus, leopard tortoises, orangutans, ring-tailed lemurs, and, in the Australian aviary, rainbow lorikeets.

Like other zoos around the world, the Auckland Zoo has worked hard in recent years to improve its facilities and make them not only more humane for its animals but more appealing and informative for visitors. In September 2011, it completed the largest project in the zoo's history, Te Wao Nui. It covers more than one-fifth of the zoo's acreage and is dedicated to showing its visitors New Zealand's unique flora and fauna.

In April of 2014 it opened its newest exhibit, featuring four Tasmanian devils (three male and one female) who arrived from Healesville Sanctuary in Australia. The devils are there as part of an insurance population for the species and to raise awareness about the plight of this critically endangered marsupial.

In June of 2014, Dr. Jane Goodall, the world-renowned primatologist, conservationist, and UN Messenger of Peace, gave a public talk at the Aotea Centre's ASB Theatre, hosted by the Auckland Zoo. That event—a fundraiser to support Jane Goodall Institute projects—was sold out well in advance of Dr. Goodall's well-received appearance.

Central Auckland: North Island's Multicultural, Subtropical Oasis

Back in downtown Aukland, I kept close to my hotel in the evenings, sending e-mails to friends from the lobby, then prowling the neighborhood late at night, exulting in the subtropical climate with its profusion of tourists and locals; the area's wide array of restaurants, featuring cuisine from around the world; the musical trilling of birds of every imaginable kind and color; and, nearly everywhere I turned, gnarled, Hobbit-country trees and brightly colored, exquisitely perfumed flowers. To the eyes, ears, and nostrils of a New Englander, it all seemed the stuff more of impossible dreams than urban reality. Here in downtown Auckland, on only the first tentative leg of my nineteen-day tour, I was Alice with a beard and sandals, cut loose in Wonderland and pinching myself every three minutes to see if I really was alive and kicking.

The next morning I got up early, retrieved my van from the hotel garage, enlisted the help of a desk attendant to program my GPS, and then—with the sort of trepidation that comes with learning a new and formidably difficult skill—injected myself into the traffic-choked streets of downtown Auckland.

I ought to have known better than to take my very first spin on the expressway at the height of the morning rush hour. Everything seemed to be going well enough until I noticed driver after driver gesturing wildly out his window and over the top of his car. Had I a flat tire? Or perhaps a stuck turn signal? The gesturing went on for miles, accompanied by a cacophonous honking of horns and the violent pointing of that one human finger that has its very own traffic-related function wherever one happens to live on the planet.

I finally figured it out. In America, the fast lane is always on the left; in New Zealand, it is always on—you guessed it—the *right*. Once I got myself into the slow lane, where I belonged, I'd been baptized in the vehicular way, and driving in Auckland became noticeably more tranquil.

Six Nights in Tauranga: My Stay with Jennie and David

My next destination was the home of Jennie Reeve and David Karl in the city of Tauranga, a few miles across town from

Mills Reef Winery, where Susan's opening-night reception was to be staged with me as the cameo performer. My time with Jennie and David, a portion of whose home doubled as a bed and breakfast, would be my very first opportunity to talk at length with residents of New Zealand, and they proved to be superb hosts.

With them I experienced firsthand the warmth and conviviality that people rightfully associate with the New Zealand temperament. And when on my very first morning at their home they discovered I was laptop addicted—I'd boorishly immersed myself in my writing the moment I reported to the breakfast nook—I learned they were also remarkably patient and accommodating. David cooked a mean New Zealand breakfast for me, then gave me all the time I needed to pepper him with questions about life in New Zealand.

And then it was his turn. With refreshing candor and trenchant humor, David—a natural-born storyteller and stand-up comedian—cursed the Americans for exporting what he considered tasteless culture and offensive, market-driven mores onto Kiwi soil. He specifically alluded to the violent, misogynistic content often found in rap music and video games, promulgated by profit-crazed, ethically tone-deaf American businessmen.

I wanted badly to be a proud ambassador for the best things my country has to offer, but I had to concede that the worst of the lyrics in American pop music, not just in rap but in other genres as well, can make "My Country, 'Tis of Thee" a pretty hard sell when you're far away in another, more culturally homogeneous country. In spite of David's rather cynical take on some this country's music, he had many good things to say about America, and we realized we had a great many things in common, worthy of celebration.

Warming Up Is Essential: Two Gigs before Opening Night

While planning my trip to New Zealand, I'd intentionally scheduled two days off in Tauranga to prepare both musically and emotionally for my performance at Mills Reef Winery. More casual performances elsewhere in the city would be both an invaluable warm-up and a welcome diversion from the stress of worrying about how my performance at the Winery would go. I'd come nine thousand miles from my home in Maine to perform, and had just one terrifying chance to get the job done and done well. I'd intentionally put myself into a musical sudden death situation, and I felt certain I was up for the battle.

With the help of Susan's husband, Richard, I found two additional performance opportunities—one in a nursing home, the other in what we in America would call a high school but in New Zealand is called a college.

Melrose Lifestyle Care & Village: Rockin' with the Oldsters

I've played in many a nursing home or assisted living facility over the years as a part of my musical life, so the chance to perform at a home in New Zealand was really important to me. Performing in nursing homes can bring great personal and professional reward. Nursing homes are also an important reminder that, wherever we live, we all share a universal condition: our own inevitable, highly personal mortality. People don't stop needing cultural soul food just because they're older. Those of us still blessed with good health and a sound mind ought to do what we can to enrich the lives of those who are less fortunate than we are and closer to the end of their lives.

Richard and Susan had arranged a gig for me at Melrose Lifestyle Care & Village, a beautiful assisted living facility in Tauranga, not far from where the two of them live.

When I walked into the common area of Melrose to perform, I saw what had become an instantly familiar sight in my nursing home appearances: a large assemblage of people old and infirm, neatly arranged in rows and ready to be entertained. Some were alert and smiling; others were lost in some distant, melancholy reverie. Whatever their condition, all of them were eager for yet another splash of sunlight through the darkening window of their existence—an all-important break from the inevitable tedium of life in a nursing home.

After a warm and appreciative introduction, I flipped open my loose-leaf book of songs and chose Joachim Andersen's "Scherzino," a lightning-fast composition designed to enliven and captivate an audience. I banged it out with as much energy and enthusiasm as I could muster—I've always called pieces like this one "rip snorters"—then finished it with a necessary gasp and a theatrical flourish. Before anyone had a chance to applaud, one lone voice penetrated the room with a blunt, indignant entreaty: "Can't you play something we actually *know*?"

I smiled, then explained to the woman that I always mix genres of music in my performances. "You'll see," I said. "I'm sure I can come up with a song or two that you'll like!" Three pieces later, I played "America the Beautiful" and watched a large, appreciative smile spread like morning sunlight across her face as she clapped. I'd found the key to her happiness, and it was contagious. I plowed through another forty minutes of music—ragtime, jazz, Irish traditional, and a string of my most treasured, seldom heard etudes. When I'd finished my last piece—Charlie Chaplin's "Smile"—the room erupted in something akin to thundering applause. It may very well have been Charlie who did the trick, and thanks to him I went off to my next musical adventure feeling certain I'd brought a moment of pleasure to the residents of Melrose.

Soloing at Otumoetai College: "Growing [and Performing] the Otumoetai Way"

My next performance—the last before my scheduled appearance in Tauranga—was at Otumoetai College, a colorful, attractively designed facility not unlike the best we see in America. Richard came with me for the performance, and with characteristic warmth and understated humor, introduced me to a roomful of polite, attentive, and disarmingly silent teenagers.

I thanked the students for coming, put my songbook on the stand, and dove headlong into my performance, hoping to send a spark of wonder into the hearts of at least a handful of the kids in the audience. After a half dozen pieces, I realized it wasn't going to be an easy sell. I decided to try another, very different approach.

"Now I'd like to involve one of *you* in the performance," I said. "Music can be both a solitary pursuit and a rewarding social experience. Musicians should play with other musicians as often as possible. So is there anyone out there who plays flute and would like to come up and perform a duet with me?"

The answer came in the form of a pervasive, stone-cold silence. A shudder of adolescent unease rippled through the group as they glanced nervously at each other, perhaps fearing I'd call on one of them and put him or her on the spot.

Still no response. As I scanned the glazed-over eyes of the gathering, I realized it was time to throw in the towel and move on to another strategy.

Just then, a young girl of Asian descent—I'll call her Adrienne—raised her hand. "I'll do it," she said with a mere wisp of a voice. A dozen students turned toward her and watched her closely as she brought her flute to the front of the room.

After she'd had a moment to look over the work I'd put on the stand—a fast-paced, rhythmically challenging movement from a Telemann sonata, transcribed for two flutes—we plunged into the piece, leaping from passage to passage, determined for our own very personal reasons to come across with a credible performance.

As we polished off the last high-flying notes of the movement, her classmates clapped long and hard—not for me but for Adrienne, who'd shown them by example what courage and belief in one's abilities can do. Under emotionally challenging circumstances, she'd played flawlessly, with impeccable timing and a full, rich tone. She had that all-important killer instinct—an inborn desire to confront adversity and slay the musical dragon. It's the kind of fearlessness that both athletes and musicians must have in abundance if they hope to succeed.

I praised her for her accomplishment, thanked everyone in attendance, grabbed my flute and music, and headed back to David and Jennie's place to prepare for what would be the most important part of my New Zealand adventure—my cameo performance at Susan's opening reception.

I knew that, like Adrienne, I'd need that killer instinct to get through the reception. And here in New Zealand, far away from my home in Maine, I'd just been reminded of a paradoxical truth about the nature of the teacher-student relationship: the young sometimes have the power to teach their own teachers a thing or two about what works and doesn't work in the course of living.

The Mills Reef Performance

Finally, the day of my Mills Reef performance had arrived. I woke early, had a breakfast of scrambled eggs, multi-grain toast, and New Zealand–style bacon, then took a walk in the neighborhood surrounding Jennie and David's home to work off the tension that's an inevitable part of preparing to perform.

Back at home, I arranged the clothing I'd be wearing for the performance. Out of respect for Susan and Richard, I figured I'd better go all out, with dress pants, a tie—a rare choice for a man who once wrote an essay called "Necktyrrany"—and a Scottish tweed sport jacket I'd bought just for the occasion at my local

Goodwill Industries outlet for an astonishing fifteen dollars. Whenever I could, I needed to save my hard-earned money for travel expenses.

After I'd had a quick nap, we piled into David's car and headed to Mills Reef Winery to settle in and prepare for our part in the reception. David would be the resident problem-solver for the day's event; I'd be the featured entertainment.

Finally, the years of not believing completely in myself were about to step aside and make way for a happier moment. I really was on New Zealand soil, and I had less than an hour to prepare for the performance. To relax, I put aside my worries and tended to the more perfunctory chores that come with being a performer. I hung my sport coat on the back of my chair, put Gluck's "Dance of the Blessed Spirits" on the music stand, assembled my flute, and tested the hall's acoustics with passages from Mozart's Concerto no. 2 in D Major—passages I'd used for many years as a pre-performance warmup.

David, who'd helped performers for other special events on many occasions, fetched me a glass of ice water and put it on a stool next to the music stand. Hydration is the essential medicine for dry mouth syndrome—an affliction that's crippled the embouchure of many a wind instrument player in the midst of performance. Another entirely unwelcome mid-performance occurrence—wobbly knee syndrome—is its dreaded companion, and I prayed that neither of them would strike me this evening. *No time for manufactured crises!* I thought. It was time to shake off my insecurities and get down to business.

As the time for my appearance grew closer, the function room began to fill up with visitors. Soon there was standing room only, with more than three hundred people jammed into the elegantly appointed hall, eager to see the results of Susan's four long years of painting.

I wriggled through sharp elbows and stifling heat to the very back of the hall, where I'd been told to wait until I was introduced. It was difficult to see the front-of-the-hall proceedings, but I could hear Susan introducing her longtime friend Sir Ray Avery to the chattering assemblage of guests. Avery, a world-renowned scientist, philanthropist, engineer, inventor, and artist, had become a beloved cultural icon in New Zealand, and Susan was both proud and pleased to have him as an honored guest at her reception.

Then it was time for me to perform. As I worked my way through the dense forest of arms and legs, I heard Susan speaking with the aid of a handheld microphone: "... and we're honored to have Ross Bachelder here tonight—the Flute Guy—who's come all the way from Boston to perform for us!" Of course, I really wasn't from Boston, but under the circumstances, it was all right with me. I'd only enough room in my head to repeat an urgent, morale-boosting mantra: *It's do or die*, I chanted to myself. *Time to put that killer instinct to work!*

I broke through the front ranks of the assemblage, took my place in front of a lectern doubling as my music stand, thanked Susan and Richard for making my appearance possible, then dove headlong into my performance.

The human mind is the most astonishingly complex and versatile machine—at its best a nearly infallible computer, capable of performing the most demanding tasks while thinking of things entirely unrelated to them. I heard myself play the first mood-setting note of the Gluck, then began to careen with roller-coaster abandon through the exhilarating ascending passages of the song.

And yet, in mid-performance, I began simultaneously to revisit utterly unrelated events in my life—the day in 1968 when my daughter came into the world while the Beatles' "Hey Jude" was playing on a nearby jukebox; walking across a flower-strewn meadow beneath a spectacular canopy of stars on my first night in Scotland; reviewing lost dreams and personal triumphs over what seemed like countless decades; and whistling to myself while peeling potatoes in a diner to earn money for college.

And then, while roaring along the precarious hills and valleys of Gluck's masterpiece, I became intensely aware of my own skeleton. I imagined I could see with perfect clarity the brilliantly orchestrated interplay of bone and sinew, heart and lungs—all of which, in harmony with my killer instinct, had kept me standing erect and made possible this and all of my other myriad performances over the years. I'd become a living, breathing anatomical drawing by da Vinci, and I found myself reveling in my connection to all who'd passed before me and would take my place on the human stage in the future.

As I saw my skeleton standing there, tall and proud, exultantly in motion, I felt both breathtaking awe and deep appreciation for the gift of good health that had allowed me to perform successfully for so many years. For one exhilarating, evanescent moment, alone in performance and dependent on no one but myself, I felt as if nothing, not even death itself, could take from me what I'd accomplished on this day.

I finished the last poignant notes of the piece, took my self-conscious bows to sustained applause, then worked my way back through the crowd, emerging with enormous gratitude and a mile-wide smile on my Flute Guy face.

How I managed to hold myself together both musically and emotionally while completing an intensely emotional, do-or-die performance in the faraway land of New Zealand continues to be a great and unfathomable mystery to me. I'd promised myself I would pour every ounce of energy, emotion, and love into that performance, and as I look back on that day, I feel certain I accomplished my mission. It was time now for another glass of water and a moment of private, unapologetic self-congratulation. I smiled broadly at no one in particular, then reached for the glass and took a long, rejuvenating drink. Then a handful of guests, including Susan and Richard, came up to me and offered their congratulations.

The Gill Myers Story: Iron Maiden with a Heart of Gold

In attendance that night was a woman who came up to me with Susan shortly after the performance. Friend of the artist? Fellow musician? I wondered why such a classy, elegantly dressed woman would have anything but a passing interest in me. A moment later, I had the answer.

"How nice of you to come by and say hello!" I said as we shook hands. She had a sparkling smile, a willowy figure, and a firm, authoritative handshake. Right away, I could see that she was in exceptionally good physical condition.

"My pleasure!" she responded.

"I thought you'd like to meet Gill Myers," said Susan, with a smile even more lively than usual. "She just purchased my portrait of you!"

That portrait—the one she'd painted after seeing me perform at the Museum of Fine Arts in Boston several years ago—was just ten by twelve inches, and yet it had managed to capture both the drama of that moment and the highly individual details of my face and hands with masterful skill and sensitivity.

Many artist's renderings of musicians in performance capture them in awkward, less-than-flattering moments, with head unnaturally twisted, mouth distorted, or hands positioned incorrectly in relation to their instrument. Such was not the case with Susan's portrait of me. It was right on the mark in every respect—a genuine triumph within the always difficult genre of portraiture.

Why, I asked myself, *would anyone—especially someone from thousands of miles away, with whom I have nothing in common and*

Happy Dawg Walks the Sad Man

Fig. 31. *The Flute Guy* by New Zealand artist Susan Harrison-Tustain.

who I will probably never see again—choose to buy that painting? I thought it best not to ask, so I simply thanked her for her interest in my portrait.

Once Susan had completed her mission, she left the two of us alone and disappeared jubilantly into the crowd of well-wishers.

We hit it off right away. I learned that Gill, a warm, effervescent onetime nurse, had (like many other Brits) emigrated to New Zealand a few years ago. Having traveled to England twice myself, I immediately recognized the British inflections in her voice. Things had begun to calm down, so I decided to go ahead and ask her why she'd chosen to buy my portrait.

"Because it was so beautifully painted," she said. "And because I loved the story behind the artwork: American musician meets New Zealand artist in Boston; artist goes back to her home country and paints musician's portrait; and then that same musician comes all the way to New Zealand and performs at the opening reception of an exhibit that includes that very same painting. It's that story, along with the quality of Susan's painting, that motivated me to invest in your portrait."

"You certainly made Susan happy this afternoon!" I said. "And you've made me happy, too! I can't really find the words to say how much I—"

"By the way," she interjected, "in half an hour I'm going with a friend to a recital across town—a really good string quartet. You can join us if you'd like."

She needn't have bothered to ask. I'd have happily agreed to go coatless to the steppes of Russia with a woman who only a few moments ago had cheerfully purchased a portrait of me for an astonishing six thousand dollars.

Why me? I marveled. Why me? Then I gathered up my belongings and headed out the door with Gill Myers, proud owner of an unlikely portrait painted by a consummate artist who just happened to be in Boston five years ago on the day I played the music of Gluck at an afternoon tea.

Fig. 32. Gill Myers, who bought Susan Harrison-Tustain's portrait of the author, *The Flute Guy*.

We attended the recital, and it was a technically flawless, emotionally powerful performance—a fitting end to what was certain to become a more than merely memorable day of music.

Afterward, Gill asked me what I intended to do for the next day or two while in Tauranga. "I'm hoping to climb Mt. Maunganui," I said. "I've heard the view from there is spectacular!"

"Whoever told you that is right," she said. "My friends and I climb it nearly every week. If you like, I'll climb it with you tomorrow!"

The next morning I woke to a blazing subtropical sun and masses of cotton candy clouds draped everywhere around the horizon. We'd agreed to meet at a small café just off the base of Mt. Maunganui—actually a long-extinct volcano—which rises majestically above the tourist-friendly municipality of Mt.

Maunganui in the North Island's Bay of Plenty region. The mountain, known officially by its Maori name, Mauao, is known by the locals as the Mount.

We enjoyed a breakfast laced with lighthearted conversation about Gill's life in New Zealand, then walked a few hundred yards to the base of the mountain and began our ascent. Gill had sunglasses and binoculars; I had my camera on one shoulder and my flute on the other. For the last several years I'd been committed to leaving my musical thumbprint on every memorable landscape I'd encountered in my travels. I'd done it alone by moonlight beside the tracks of a remote train station in central England; from a fire tower atop Mt. Magalloway in Pittsburg, New Hampshire, just south of the Canadian border; and, while on a *plein air* painting excursion, from a flower-blanketed meadow in the verdant, deer-plentiful hills of southern Vermont.

Ahead of us I could see the Mt. Maunganui trails, beautifully manicured and maintained, making their serpentine way up and around the mountain. Here and there were flocks of sheep, happily munching the grass on plots leased to farmers as a way to feed their animals and keep the Mount well-trimmed and attractive for the never-ending influx of tourists. "This will be a great adventure!" I said.

"We'll be at the top in no time!" said Gill.

"In no time" is by any measure a subjective thing. In a matter of minutes, I needed to stop and catch my breath; not so with Gill. She charged ahead another fifty feet, not realizing until she glanced over her shoulder that I wouldn't be conquering the Mount as easily as she'd hoped. She waited politely until I caught up with her, then smiled compassionately as I leaned against the nearest tree and panted like a hound dog in a heat wave.

"Oh, dear!" she chuckled, a look of genuine pity in her wide-awake, ready-to-rumble eyes. "Many of the people around here walk the full height of the Mount several times a week! We New Zealanders are always outdoors, walking or playing sports."

I stood up, wiped the sweat from my brow, and prepared to continue our ascent. Was this how Gill Myers of Tauranga, the purchaser of my portrait, was actually going to remember me? The mere thought was too painful to contemplate.

We resumed our climb, and half a dozen stops later we arrived at the summit. Gill glided with maddening ease around the perimeter of the mountain while I collapsed onto the ground and lay gasping for what seemed like an eternity. I stared up at the laughing, sneering clouds and wondered what I'd done with my long-forgotten Planet Fitness membership card.

Eventually I got back on my feet and began to explore the top of the mountain. The view from the pinnacle was nothing short of spectacular, with throngs of tourists far below us, either walking the pristine beaches or dining leisurely along the glittering necklace of restaurants bordering the town.

Across from us, on a plateau-like clearing, was a handsome, fashionably dressed athlete doing a lightning-fast series of push-ups. He was trim, tanned, and sculpted as beautifully as a Greek statue. I watched him pumping away with unimaginable speed and an almost balletic precision, and lamented that I'd become one of the great and growing multitude of out-of-shape Americans, exercising little, eating unwisely, and gaining yet another belt size with each accumulating year.

"Oh, he's just training," Gill smiled, without the slightest hint of exhaustion. "He's one of the All Blacks. They never lose a moment to stay in shape by exercising." *And neither does Gill*, I thought ruefully.

After gathering what was left of my composure, I remembered with pleasure that I'd slung my flute over my shoulder and brought it with me up the mountain. It was time to honor my commitment to myself and make some music in yet another exotic location.

Fig. 33. The author making music on Mount Maunganui, October, 2011.

I took the flute out of its case, walked to the rim of a cliff overlooking the beach, and tested my ability to produce a tone against a bracing mountaintop wind. (The aperture of the mouthpiece of a flute can't handle more than the one precisely aimed column of breath—the column that makes it possible to produce a tone on the flute.) Once I'd found the right position, I took a good, deep breath and delivered Gluck's "Dance of the Blessed Spirits"—the song I'd played first at the MFA in Boston, then at Susan's opening in Tauranga—into the shimmering blue sky.

I had no idea who, other than Gill and a handful of climbers on their way to the mountaintop, might have heard me play that song. Nor did it really matter. In a world scarred by violence and diminished by a steady onslaught of ugly, soul-shattering noises, a musician can do worse than making his own intensely personal contribution to serenity.

The next morning, Gill took me to an exhibit at Tauranga Art Gallery, a beautiful facility in the western Bay of Plenty, specializing in exhibits of European-influenced and indigenous Maori art. The art on exhibit was beautiful, but I was restless, knowing today was likely to be the very last time I'd ever see Gill Myers, the woman who just two days ago had purchased my portrait and given me such a well-timed emotional lift.

We said our goodbyes, and the moment of our parting became the dress rehearsal for what was certain to be an even more dramatic play within a play—my actual departure from New Zealand soil in just twelve days, never to return.

The Coromandel and the Cop: A Snail's Pace in the Rain

On the night before the last of my six days with Jennie and David, I asked them to recommend one last day trip before my departure to the South Island. Right away, they suggested a tour of the Coromandel Peninsula, and the very next morning, long before sunrise, I was off and running to points north within the North Island.

My JUCY van—a garishly painted, stripped-down affair—was what spoiled American drivers, accustomed to luxury and a high-quality ride, would derisively call a crate. Residents of Detroit would call it basic transportation.

I should have known what an easy target my van would prove to be for New Zealanders, who've always been known to harbor a certain ill-concealed contempt for tourists—especially the ones who've never driven on the left side of the road before arriving in New Zealand, and have no choice but to use the country's convoluted, mountaintop roads for driving practice. The van was also a powerful cop magnet—a four-wheel scarlet letter for the police, whose job it is to assimilate inexperienced foreigners into the local driving culture.

For an American driving in the wilds of New Zealand, on the western tip of the Ring of Fire, it would be full-scale war—survival of the fittest—and here I was, alone in a ridiculous green and yellow van with a come-hither babe on its flanks, up against a vast army of seasoned natives with a tourist-negative chip on their shoulder, in cheerful collusion with New Zealand's finest and ready for battle.

It didn't take long for the enemy to find me. I'd had a fine time touring the Coromandel, but while driving back to David and Jennie's place late that night, I was suddenly enveloped in a pounding rainstorm so powerful that I could barely see the edge of the road, let alone the road signs and lane markings.

In spite of the tempest, I drove ecstatically on, propelled by a touch of Steve McQueen swagger and feeling just short of invincible. Not bad, I thought, for a neophyte driver in a strange land, driving in less than ideal conditions.

Then an ominous, pulsing red light appeared in my rear view mirror, distorted by the rain but unmistakable in origin. The police! I'd done something wrong, but I hadn't the faintest idea what it might be.

Somehow, in the raging, film noir darkness of the storm, I found my way to the edge of the road, turned on my trouble lights, and waited as the officer got out of his squad car and walked toward me, drenched with rain and holding a flashlight.

I could hear the rain pounding down on his cap as he stood at the driver's side window, then leaned downward, the better to see my quivering countenance in the shadows of the car's interior.

"Good evening, sir!" he said. "Do you know why I've pulled you over this evening?"

"Not really!" I said, employing my patented Midwestern, aw-shucks sincerity while fishing my driver's license from the glove compartment. "Is there something wrong with my van?"

"Not that," said the officer, who was young, Jimmy Stewart handsome, and astonishingly polite as he reviewed my license and passport.

"Actually," he purred, "I couldn't help notice how slowly you've been driving for the past few miles. In fact, I've gotten several calls from drivers who were concerned about your slow driving. They think it's dangerous. I need to warn you that we have legal minimums for road travel in our country. I'm afraid you're going to have to drive faster. Drivers in New Zealand can be ticketed for driving too slowly."

"*Driving too slowly?*" I said. "I've only just arrived in your country. I'm still getting acquainted with your roads, and in a blinding rainstorm at that! Under the circumstances, I thought driving cautiously would be the most responsible approach to getting from one place to another—especially until I'm more accustomed to your rules."

He smiled uncomfortably, then leaned even closer toward me through the window. "And by the way, is there any chance you've been drinking? Our drink-driving laws are very strict here!"

Drink driving? What a funny way to say that! I thought to myself, hoping he couldn't see the look of incredulity on my face.

"No, sir!" I said. "I think I average one beer every two years. And I can assure you that even if I were a drinker, I'd never drink drive!" It sounded ridiculous, saying it that way, but I figured that if New Zealanders say, "drink driving," then under the circumstances I'd be wise to say it that way myself.

I reminded the officer that for an American tourist on his very first trip to New Zealand, driving on what I considered to be the wrong side of the road, I was doing pretty damn well.

"Well, okay, Mr. Bachelder," he said. "I do understand!" He smiled again, and I took it to mean I wasn't about to get slapped with a whopper of a ticket. *They probably call it a "move violation" in New Zealand,* I thought to myself, chuckling.

"I can see you were trying to do the right thing!" he continued. "Unfortunately, I'm obligated to respond to any driver complaints I get while on duty." He put his ticket pad back in the pocket of his rain slick, then tipped his water-soaked hat.

"Tell you what," he said, "I've decided to let you go on your way without a citation for just this once, but in future" (it was endearingly British of him to drop the word *the*, I thought) "do try to observe the kilometers-per-hour minimum while you're driving here in New Zealand. Drive safely, now. And I sincerely hope you're enjoying your visit."

I think I heard him say, "Cheers!" as he walked back to his squad car and drove off into the darkness. And though he was the nicest policeman I could ever have hoped to encounter—I would have been proud to call him my grandson—I was exceedingly happy to see him go.

Cranky and the Van: Roadside Savior to the Rescue

The next morning I loaded up my van, said my heartfelt goodbyes to Jennie and David, then headed out onto the main road leading south from Tauranga and toward the vast, otherworldly expanse of the South Island, certain that unimaginable adventures were waiting for me. Though I was obviously alone in my van, I behaved like a toddler in a toy store, yelping and yippee-ing my way into the left-side traffic of Tauranga with pounding heart and—per executive order of the good folks back at the JUCY Snooze in Auckland—*eyes wide open*.

Unfortunately, moments of ecstasy have a habit of caving in to the vicissitudes. Just two hundred or so yards down the road, I heard the violent honking of a horn, then looked into my rearview mirror and saw a truck bearing down on me, its driver waving frantically for me to pull off onto the side of the road.

"A policeman in a pickup?" I groaned. "I thought I'd seen the last of the cops up in the Coromandel!"

The driver, a husky, middle-aged bear of a man dressed in gray shorts and a navy blue jacket, came dashing up to me with a look of raw fury on his face, all the while pointing at the right front tire of my van.

"Have you seen these tyres?" he bellowed, his face redder than a bullfighter's cape and getting redder. (*Tyres*—that's how the British spell it, and I was in a very British country.)

I stuck my head out the window and peered down at the side of the road. "Why—have I got a flat tire?"

"No, you haven't got a flat. But I'm surprised you haven't got *four* of 'em. Your tyres have hardly any tread *left* on 'em! It's a goddam *disgrace*, the condition o' them tyres!"

I sat there in my van, and though I didn't really think I'd done anything wrong, I felt my face turn crimson with shame. I've never been a car person, so I didn't really think the tires were all that bad. In my world, a tire that goes consistently round and round without exploding is pretty much all right with me.

"So who rented this fuckin' van to you, bud?" He was scratching his head now, clearly dumbfounded that I'd made it as far as I had.

"The JUCY company up in Auckland," I said, looking only half as sheepish as I was feeling at the moment. "They were nice to me. I thought it was a really good deal."

"You got their *number?*" he roared. "I'll be callin' them assholes and tellin' 'em just what I think of 'em for rentin' this death trap to an innocent American! Gimme' that fuckin' card!"

I decided to call him Cranky—the perfect name for a man filled to overflowing with righteous indignation. And yet I could tell, somehow, that beneath the rough, John Wayne exterior, he was gentle as a lamb.

I handed Cranky the JUCY card I'd left on the dashboard, and he immediately dialed up the outlet where I'd picked up the van just six days ago. Then I got out and stood next to him on the side of the road as he raged into the phone. "I'm standin' in the middle o' the road here in sunny Tauranga, with a four-wheel piece o' shit you got the nerve to call a van!" he said. "Only a fuckin' *moron* would rent this vehicle out. The tyres [there's that British spelling again] on this crate are balder than a baboon's ass!"

He stopped to catch his breath, then went right back at it.

"One more mile in the mountains with these tyres, and our American friend woulda gone straight off the edge of a fuckin' *cliff*! Now gimme your *boss's* number. I'm gonna call him when I get home and give him a piece o' my mind, too." He shut off his phone and strode back to his pickup, then ordered me to get into my van and follow him. He'd become a lumbering, fulminating grizzly.

I didn't know why, but I completely and unconditionally trusted the man. Because of that, I did exactly as he ordered, and together we drove half a mile down the road to what turned out to be a garage and repair shop just off the edge of the highway. Apparently it was his very own business, and that gave me hope that Cranky really knew what he was doing.

"You go ahead and pull that piece o' crap into the garage," he said, "and I'll get it up on the lift and make sure everything's all right!"

While Cranky inspected the undercarriage and thumped all four tires of my van, I looked around the garage. It was a classic of the genre. The cement floor was blotched and spattered with oil stains. The windows were so caked with the dust of decades of servicing vehicles that the sunlight had to fight to gain admittance. The walls were covered with fan belts, radiators, fuel pumps, and head gaskets—nearly anything that's ever been put under the hood of a truck to make it run.

"I'll have this sorry excuse for an automobile ready for ya in two shakes of a lamb's tail!" he said, laughing. (Not a surprising turn of phrase, since New Zealand is virtually carpeted with sheep, and lamb is by far its most popular dish.)

Two of the four tires failed to pass muster, so he replaced them with a pair of suitable spares from the tire rack at the back of the shop. Once they were on, he finished his inspection, tightened the clamps on the tailpipe with a mechanical flourish, and with one push of the hydraulic release button brought my JUCY rental back down to earth. He then wiped the grease off his paws and stood back to admire his handiwork. A thoroughly contented, job-well-done smile spread across his face.

I thanked him once again for his work on the van, then pointed toward an enormous, brick-red tractor parked along one wall inside the garage—just one of many tractors parked on the property. "One question before I push off," I said. "Why do you have so many tractors?"

Cranky's face lit up like the fourth of July. I'd inadvertently found the one thing, other than rescuing travelers in distress, that meant most to him in the world. "Tractors!" he shouted. "You'll find American-made tractors all over New Zealand, tucked away in garages just like this one. I'm crazy 'bout tractors! Got a half-dozen of 'em and counting. But *this* baby—he slapped the fender so hard it rang like the call bell in a boxing ring—is a McCormick Farmall Diesel, the 270 MD. It's my pride and joy!"

Fig. 34. Cranky on his tractor, Tauranga, North Island, New Zealand.

I'd no reason to doubt either his credentials or his sincerity. An emblem painted proudly on the side of his tractor near the engine housing read "Member: Central Southland Vintage Machinery Club." I asked him if he'd be willing to hop up onto the tractor and pose for a snapshot, and he scrambled up with all the energy and enthusiasm of a kid on a jungle gym.

Once I got my photograph, he climbed down from the tractor and presented me with a brief, ad hoc treatise on the history of the Farmall brand and its importance to the world of agriculture. I could tell that if I'd given Cranky the stage, he'd have been happy to catalogue the entire history of farming, from prehistoric times to mechanization. But it was time for me to get back on the road and head south, and he had more important fish than me to fry.

Cranky had become my roadside savior—a fascinating character in an equally fascinating land. Together we'd managed unexpectedly to forge a cross-cultural, transoceanic bond. We became two proud ambassadors of our respective countries—one a diminutive American on an outsize musical mission, the other a towering Kiwi who knew his engines inside and out and could swear like a pirate when his gifts as a troubleshooter were needed.

Cranky the mechanic is proud of his country, proud of his craft, and eager to help strangers in distress. He's the quintessential New Zealander—outgoing, unpretentious, helpful, and kind. I'd see many more people like Cranky in my joyful perambulations over the next few days, but none would be more appreciated and more permanently etched into my memory than Cranky. In a remarkably resourceful land, men and women like Cranky are the most precious resource of all.

Working My Way to Christchurch: Railways, Glowworms, and a Flying McDonald's

Once I'd finished my work as musician, squeaked past the police, and—thanks to Cranky—gotten my van on the road again, it was time to say goodbye to the Bay of Plenty region. I needed next to work my way down the remainder of the North Island to Cook Strait and then Christchurch, the city struck by a devastating earthquake in February of 2011. While I'd scheduled myself ahead of time into some of the Top 10 Holiday Parks in the South Island, I decided to choose the rest of them by the seat of my pants to preserve my coveted spontaneity as a traveler.

Driving Creek Railway and Potteries: A Train Ride in the Clouds

High on my list of North Island, must-see attractions was Driving Creek Railway and Potteries, a most unusual enterprise tucked into the hills of the quiet fishing town of Coromandel (called Coromandel Town by the locals to distinguish it from its namesake, the Coromandel Peninsula).

Famed New Zealand author, potter, and kiln-maker Barry Brickell built the country's only narrow-gauge mountain railway from scratch, beginning in 1975, to carry clay and wood to his mountainside kiln. Since the railway's completion in 1990, it and the adjoining pottery-making facilities have become a major destination for tourists, scholars, and pottery enthusiasts from around the world. The kilns on Brickell's property were designed and built by Brickell himself, using bricks made on-site from clay taken from the very same property. (Why a man with the name of Brickell should become a master brick-maker is one of those inscrutable mysteries that will likely never be solved.)

Interestingly, Brickell's railway has become more than merely a workhorse for the transporting of construction materials. It has also allowed him and his successors to maintain an ambitious, long-term project to replenish the country's forests, once teeming with coniferous *Agathis australis*—commonly known as the kauri tree. Beginning around 1840, these towering, majestic trees, sometimes matching and even exceeding the sequoia in height and circumference and known to have antecedents tens of thousands of years old, were either accidentally or intentionally burned, destroying nearly half of the existing kauri trees in New Zealand.

More than half of the remainder were then exported to Australia, Britain, and other countries, and the balance was used locally to build houses and ships. Much of the timber was sold for a return sufficient only to cover wages and expenses. By 1900, less than 10 percent of the original kauri survived. It is estimated that today, only 4 percent of the uncut forest can be found in small pockets scattered about the northernmost regions of the North Island.

A significant portion of the proceeds from both the train ride and the sale of items at Driving Creek Railway and Potteries is diverted into an ambitious, long-range plan to preserve the spectacular native forest cover and put an end to soil erosion for all time—a noble cause combined with a thoroughly entertaining, family adventure.

After exploring the area at Driving Creek where Brickell's pottery is made and sold to visitors, I took the one-hour trip by narrow-gauge rail, along with dozens of other tourists of all ages from around the world.

The tour was both highly informative and, in a back-to-childhood way, innocent fun. For one heart-warming New Zealand hour, we were the little engine that could—a real-life train set grown large, weaving its way through the lush, subtropical forestland purely for pleasure. We chugged musically along through narrow tunnels and over cleverly constructed bridges, laughing and comparing travel notes until we arrived at the top of the ridge, climbed up onto a sprawling observation deck called the Eyefull Tower, and reveled in a 360-degree view of the island-studded Hauraki Gulf and surrounding forestlands. Once back on the ground, we disembarked, said our goodbyes, and went our separate ways—a wildly heterogeneous swarm of travel-happy ants, cut loose from Driving Creek to continue our explorations in Kiwi country.

Glowworms Abundant, Down in a Cave

It is fair to say I've had a few loves in my seven decades of living—infatuations both small and large—but high on the list has to be my brief but passionate love affair with *Arachnocampa luminosa*.

I met her—well, actually, tens of thousands of her—in November of 2011 in the Waitomo Glowworm Caves, located in the Waitomo area of New Zealand's North Island. Waitomo is a twenty-eight-mile network of limestone caves and grottoes linked to the Waitomo River.

Arachnocampa luminosa, a genus of five fungus gnat species, have a luminescent larval stage that's akin to the larval stage of glowworm beetles. The species are endemic to New Zealand and Australia, dwelling in either caves and grottos or sheltered places in forests. They're not completely alone down there, though. They're destined to live their brief lives—amiably, I trust—with eerily silent armies of albino cave ants, giant crickets, and a host of microscopic creatures we've neither the time nor the space to talk about here.

That I first laid eyes on the glowworms while they were hanging from the walls and ceilings of caves only added to their glamour and exoticism. And since I am an inveterate lover of both the nighttime and the rain, it helped that the environment in those cool, cathedral-like caves—first explored in 1887 by local Maori chief Tane Tinorau, accompanied by English surveyor Fred Mace—was wet as a sponge bath and darker than a mole hole.

Dark, yes—but punctuated by tens of thousands of tiny, pulsing, suspended glowworm larvae, assembled on the stage of a vast, underground theater and entertaining their human visitors by simply hanging down, lighting the path of our boat ride, and being incomparably beautiful creatures.

We began our tour on foot, starting at the top level of the cave and the Catacombs, then taking shorter and shorter steps as we descended deeper and deeper into the cave. There are three levels altogether, linked by a deep limestone shaft called the tomo. Every inch of the way, I gawked and gasped as if I'd just witnessed the very first flight of the Wright brothers.

At the second level, called the Banquet Chamber, we learned that the traces of smoke above us offered unassailable evidence that early visitors would habitually stop to eat there while exploring the caves. Hearing that, I felt a profound connection to all of the New Zealanders—and especially to the Maori people, its earliest settlers—who had preceded me into the caves over the centuries.

We'd all hoped to pay a visit to the largest formation in the network of caves—called the Pipe Organ—but on the night I took the tour, tourists were barred from the area because of the very real possibility that hazardous levels of carbon monoxide might accumulate in the chamber. That we didn't make it to the Pipe Organ really did nothing to dampen my spirits, though. I was in such a state of euphoria while in the caves—a feeling I'd experienced in equal measure when first touching down on New Zealand soil only a week before—that only the collapse of the entire network of caves could have deprived me of my pleasure.

We reached the third and final level, including the Cathedral, the demonstration platform, and the jetty, a short while later. The Cathedral is an enclosed area nearly eighteen meters (sixty feet) high, with rough, paved surfaces that, in combination with the high, vaulted ceilings, give it extraordinarily good acoustics. A number of famous singers, including the renowned diva Dame Kiri Te Kanawa, have performed here since the caves were first opened to the public in 1889.

We concluded our tour with a magical boat ride through the Glowworm Grotto. For me, the name alone engendered enormous excitement. The system devised by the original designers of the caves as tourist attraction—a train of diminutive boats, moving slowly and methodically along a narrow, meandering canal with the help of heavy ropes and raw muscle—was both enormously inventive and oddly low-tech. That getting around the caves was almost entirely dependent on the strength and concentration of part-time employees was both touching and disconcerting. I ought not to have been concerned for my safety, though. I learned later that many of the people responsible for our safe passage through the caves were descendants of Chief Tane Tinorau, connected spiritually and genealogically to the founder of the Glowworm Caves. They were obviously proud of their association with the enterprise, and expert at what they do.

Once out of the Glowworm Grotto and back on land, we boarded our excursion boat and chugged our way back across placid, moonlit waters to the mainland. I left the caves with a heightened appreciation for the beauty and complexity of our natural surroundings and our sacred, inviolable connection to all of the living things of the earth.

It was time now to drive south toward Wellington, exploring what I could in the North Island along the way. I drove south of Waitomo, traveled through the outskirts of Rotorua, then wound my way through Tokoroa, Orakei Korako, Waimangu, and Waiotapu—towns with wonderfully exotic Maori names and powerful allure, especially when you're from staid, bread-and-butter New England. By early afternoon I'd been on the road for several hours and was both fatigued from driving and ravenously hungry.

Dining in Taupo: Not Your Usual McDonald's

To the southwest of Rotorua, and just east of Lake Taupo—the largest lake in New Zealand—was the tourist-friendly town of Taupo, known around the world for fascinating thermal attractions and a wide array of opportunities for outdoor adventure. I headed straight to Taupo, eager to take a break from my driving and find a good, hot meal.

While driving south from Waiotapu, I saw a McDonald's restaurant sign on the outskirts of Taupo. I knew before ever landing on New Zealand soil that I'd need to be frugal about meals—I'd spent several thousand dollars already to make my trip a reality—so McDonald's restaurants, with their modest prices, unhurried wayside inn metabolism, and ubiquitous

Fig. 35. The airplane McDonald's in Taupo, South of Tauranga.

Wi-Fi access, would more often than not be my eatery of choice while in the country.

I worked my way into the city with stomach rumbling and nerves frayed from the surprising density of traffic all around me, then saw the Golden Arches looming ahead of me like an upside-down W. Bingo. Like Sid Caesar, Ethel Merman, and their friends, I'd finally tracked down those elusive palm trees and found just what I'd been looking for—a place, however humble, where I could relax awhile and feed my face. Perhaps it wasn't such a mad, mad, mad, mad world after all.

While pulling into the driveway of the restaurant, I saw the propeller and part of the left wing of a vintage aircraft protruding from around the corner and to the left of the building. *Probably a war memorial of some kind*, I figured. *How nice!*

I bought my lunch and cut through the children's play area, and just ahead of me was the most extraordinary McDonald's seating area I'd ever seen. The additional seating for diners was the airplane itself—a beautifully preserved, decommissioned DC-3, painted red and white to match the color scheme of the restaurant. It was an American, fixed-wing, propeller-driven airliner, the speed and range of which revolutionized air transport in the 1930s and 1940s.

I headed up the ramp like a schoolboy on recess, settled into a window seat, and set my lunch down on a table similar to the desks in a one-room school. At the far end of the plane's single aisle was the perfectly preserved cockpit, enclosed from floor to ceiling in plexiglass to allow visitors to see what the pilots saw every day while flying.

The plane, designed and built in 1943 by the Douglas Aircraft Company, was one of three used by South Pacific Airlines of New Zealand from 1961 to 1966. Taupo mayor Rick Cooper had come across the plane in 1985 during a stopover in New Plymouth, and bought it on the spot for twenty thousand dollars. He'd planned to refurbish it and use it as his office, but when a representative from the McDonald's Corporation saw the plane, he fell in love with it and made an offer. The result was the airplane McDonald's, seen each year by tens of thousands of tourists and chosen by voters in a competition as the number one most unique McDonald's among more than thirty-five thousand units around the world.

New Zealand is still a young and adventurous country, filled with swashbuckling visionaries who are more than ready to take risks and experiment with fresh approaches to marketing. It may help explain why the McDonald's restaurants in that country often appear to be more innovative in both architecture and decor than those in the States. Examples of unbridled imagination and entrepreneurial daring abound in Kiwi country, in restaurants, office buildings, airports, and other venues too numerous to mention here. Such a free-wheeling approach to commerce and culture makes for a vibrant, exhilarating lifestyle and draws people from all over the world—including me—to experience first-hand New Zealand's youthful exuberance and aesthetic swagger.

I finished my meal at McDonald's, headed south to Wanganui, stayed overnight in a nearby Top 10 Holiday Park, then drove the next morning through Otaki, Waikanae, and Paraparamauru. My stay in the North Island would soon be over.

To get to the South Island, I would need to take the Interislander Ferry across Cook Strait. It proved to be a three-hour, pitch-black excursion from Wellington in the North Island to the South Island town of Picton. Because I'd unwittingly scheduled the trip as an overnight adventure, I failed to see anything but darkness during what was described in the Interislander brochure as "one of the most beautiful ferry rides in the world." As pleasurable as the nighttime excursion was, I couldn't help wondering if being charged the full amount for a trip across the Strait—minus the scenery—might have been a bit unfair. The concept of truth in advertising ought to have been applicable to the Interislander, too.

The City of Christchurch: Thoroughly British, Incomparably Beautiful, Still in Recovery

After crossing Cook Strait and landing in Picton, I wanted very much to explore Blenheim, Kaikoura, Hanmer Springs, and other towns south of Wellington, but my time in New Zealand was growing short. Furthermore, I'd already committed myself to a tour of Christchurch—that preened and pampered bastion of all things British—before heading south to Queenstown.

I knew ahead of time that any pleasure I'd find on arriving in Christchurch was sure to be tempered by sadness. In February 2011, just a few months before my scheduled trip to New Zealand, the city was hit by an enormously destructive earthquake followed by dozens of equally devastating aftershocks. A hun-

Fig. 36. Young couple punting on the Avon River in Christchurch.

dred and eighty-five people were killed in the quake, and hundreds of buildings were either damaged or destroyed.

I'd studied the history of Christchurch while preparing for my New Zealand adventure, so I knew that high on my list of must-see attractions would be the 130-year-old ChristChurch Cathedral, thought by architectural historians to be a masterpiece. Before the quake it had loomed majestically over Cathedral Square, employing its Victorian charms to lure tens of thousands of visitors into the heart of the city. Tragically, it was severely damaged in the quake, along with many other historic buildings. It was as if someone had torn the Christchurch pages from my guide, and then, for no good reason, crumpled them up and thrown them away. The quake was an offense to all who had worked so hard to make Christchurch a culturally sophisticated, aesthetically pleasing destination.

I arrived on the outskirts of the city in mid-afternoon, determined to explore what I could in the downtown area, then walk through as much of the renowned Hagley Park as my time and feet would allow. The clear blue skies, moderate sunlight, and a gentle breeze were ideal weather for the trek. I found one lone parking place along Harper Avenue, grabbed my flute and camera, and headed straight into the center of the city, studying the British-influenced architecture, manicured lawns, and myriad species of flowers as I went.

School must have gotten out just as I reached downtown, because the sidewalks everywhere were teeming with laughing, rosy-cheeked adolescents with textbooks under their arms, all wearing black skirts or trousers, bright red ties, and crisp white shirts or blouses. It was tempting to believe I'd landed in the tree-lined quadrangle of an elite London prep school, and I half expected to see Trafalgar Square and the changing of the guard around the next corner.

The Avon River, with meticulously groomed banks and overhanging willows, was at every turn breathtakingly elegant. A small armada of ducks floated serenely in formation beneath a storybook bridge worthy of Wordsworth and the Lake Poets. The ducks were followed by a young, fresh-faced couple, obviously in love and punting their way to an afternoon of pleasures that only a city as spectacular as Christchurch could hope to provide.

Farther down the river, the mood wasn't so romantic. A crew of laborers, wearing rubberized bib overalls, construction hats, and bright yellow vests, were up to their waists in water, dredging the river bottom for debris left over from the recent earthquake. They were just one small contingent among dozens of quake recovery workers positioned strategically across the city

Fig. 37. Damaged building buttressed after the Christchurch quake.

of Christchurch, hired for the express purpose of making the decimated downtown area once again safe, hygienic, and fully habitable.

I walked around the perimeter of downtown Christchurch, searching for evidence, however small, of the quake's fury. It didn't take long for me to find what I was looking for. Here and there I began to see multistory buildings with caved in rooftops and boarded-up windows. Some of the most historic edifices—most notably ChristChurch Cathedral—had been shored up by massive, buttress-like structures meant both to preserve what was left of the building and to protect passersby from falling debris.

The closer I looked, the more structural damage I saw in buildings that at first glance appeared to have been entirely untouched by the quake and its aftershocks. Some had hairline cracks here and there in their facades; others had sizable bites taken out of their corners, as if some fierce, granite-munching gargoyle had stopped in uninvited for supper and snatched whatever it wished from the table, entirely at random. On really close inspection, still more buildings proved to be slightly askew from ground level to apex, leaning oddly in ways that were at first unsettling and then, finally, just plain frightening.

I began to feel a little like an ambulance chaser, seeking that most reprehensible of thrills: evidence of other people's suffering. The words *There but for the grace of God go I* came to mind as I moved with quiet reverence from one painful example of destruction to another.

From the moment the first terrifying tremor struck central Christchurch and wreaked havoc on ChristChurch Cathedral—the pride and joy of New Zealanders everywhere for as long as anyone could remember—the city itself was transformed into a haunting reminder of the power of senseless destruction to demoralize a people and rob them of their greatest, most enduring triumphs. Some analysts have speculated that downtown Christchurch won't be fully habitable until more than a decade has passed.

Nevertheless, the very human drive to repair and rebuild after a disaster was evident to anyone who looked closely at the destruction in Christchurch. While exploring the city, I came across what a handful of locals identified to me as the future site of what would come to be known as the Transitional Cathedral or Cardboard Cathedral—an elegant, architecturally distinctive replacement for the stricken ChristChurch Cathedral. Designed by Japanese architect Shigeru Ban and begun on July 2012, the Transitional Cathedral opened to the public in August 2013 and quickly became both a beacon of hope and a source of immense pride for the citizens of Christchurch and all of New Zealand.

Hagley Park: Horticultural Tour de Force in a Proud, Intrepid City

Once I'd had enough of tracking down evidence of the quake's destructive power, I shifted my emotional gears and headed out on foot to Hagley Park. I'd allowed enough time for three more hours of sightseeing in Christchurch—affectionately called Garden City by the locals—and I was about to learn that I'd need every one of those hours even to scratch the surface of the park's 165 hectares (407 acres).

Hagley is really much, much more than a park. In addition to showcasing an astonishing array of trees from around the world—some of the oldest, tallest trees anywhere in New Zealand—the park has several specialty gardens designed to commemorate important historical events. Beautifully designed foot bridges and walking tracks crisscross the length and breadth of the park, allowing visitors to navigate the twists and turns of the Avon River. Nestled into one serene expanse of the park is the small but elegant Bandsmen's Memorial Rotunda, standing proudly in the center of a blazing springtime ocean of yellow daffodils—the happy result of the planting, in 1933, of more than sixteen thousand bulbs in the area surrounding the rotunda.

By 3:00 p.m. I'd walked several miles altogether in the park and taken dozens of photographs of its magnificent flowers and trees. Still—though I'd already played indoors at Mills Reef Winery in Tauranga, then outdoors at the top of Mt. Maunganui—I'd yet to pay homage to the wonders of Christchurch by playing at least a song or two at Hagley Park.

I found a quiet spot beneath a grove of trees, and as I began playing—this time, not familiar songs but improvised melodies—two colorfully dressed old women, probably in their late eighties, stopped and listened while chatting amiably together. Once I'd finished my songs, I exchanged pleasantries with them, asked them to take a picture of me for the record, wished them well in their travels, and went on my way.

My next adventure would be far away from the splendor and sadness of Christchurch, along a winding path toward the West Coast of the South Island. In a few hours I'd be driving to the top of Arthur's Pass—the only way, other than by air, that one could ever hope to reach the Kumara Junction Highway, the township of Hokitika, and the rest of the incomparable natural wonders along the zigzag path to Queenstown.

Arthur's Pass

A trip across Arthur's Pass—the highest and most spectacular pass across the Southern Alps—had been at the top of my New Zealand itinerary from the very beginning. While studying my maps in the months leading to my departure, I came back repeatedly to the little red dot along Route 73, imagining what it might be like to cut through the sky-high mountains paralleling the West Coast. The images of the Pass in my *Eyewitness Travel Guide* whipped me into an armchair frenzy of anticipation. Could this region really be as Shangri-La spectacular as the travel journals made it out to be? I'd soon find out.

Just the two-hour drive to the base of the pass was reason enough for me to fall head over heels in love with every inch of the region. It was late October when I began my approach—early spring in New Zealand—and everywhere around me, flowers were just beginning to bloom in the sweeping, aromatic expanse of meadowland. Though the place was bursting with springtime energy, I could see the snow-capped mountains far up ahead of me, breaking through the clouds and reaching exultantly toward the heavens.

When I finally got to the starting point of the ascent, I saw a sign as big as the side of a small building, positioned strategically on the lawn near the entry point of the Pass. In blazingly electrified words, it fairly shouted its ominous message to the tourists:

WARNING
If you don't have chains on your tyres, you're on your own!

Now, isn't that special! I thought. *A ridiculously out-of-season message, and a waste of electricity, too.* Clearly, as in every place where humans are in charge, the out-of-touch bureaucracy was alive and well in New Zealand. Even in the land of the Kiwi, change must be glacially slow to happen. I photographed the flowers, popped a CD into my player, and headed up the Pass.

The first thing I noticed was the complete absence of anything close to a straight line anywhere on the ascent. "Mount Medusa" might have been a more appropriate name for the Pass.

Fig. 38. Driving in Arthur's Pass, South Island—no simple journey.

Arthur's Pass is a marvel of engineering savvy and constructional derring-do, comparable in its scope to the design and construction of the Panama Canal, the Hoover Dam, or the Brooklyn Bridge. It's beautifully designed and meticulously maintained—a proud monument to the astonishing expertise and back-breaking labor of both its makers and its preservers. All along the roadway are bright yellow poles, positioned to keep drivers in line and safely distant from the dramatic cliffs that plunge everywhere from the edges of the roadways. While working my way cautiously up the Pass, I could hear the musical rush-and-gurgle of water streaming down the mountainsides from high above the road.

Trying to drive responsibly while gawking at the stunning vistas all around me proved to be among the greatest challenges of my trip through the Pass. For the entire ascent, I gripped the steering wheel of my van with white-knuckle determination, intensely aware of the possibility that I might lose my focus and plunge hundreds of feet down into a spectacular, man-eating gorge. Fortunately, the designers of the Pass included a great many pull-off areas for people who simply had to stop and stare at the breathtaking, awe-inspiring scenery.

The most harrowing challenge of the climb had to be the presence of a relentless parade of deafeningly loud, monstrously large logging trucks, hidden from view around nearly every hairpin curve. They weren't just vehicles for the conveyance of logs destined for fuel and construction; they were huge, hungry lions, waiting ominously to pounce on and then swallow up any lesser vehicles whose drivers lacked either the muscle or the means to protect themselves.

At first I figured they were little more than a vehicular anomaly—a hazard that would make a momentary fuss along the highway, then fade politely from the scene. But after a dozen or so occurrences—the sound of as many as four double-tandem logging trucks in a row, air brakes shrieking as they bore down on the Pass—I realized they were there to stay. I was a mere interloper from another land, caught unwittingly in a potentially violent, no-holds-barred game of King of the Mountain. That I managed to somehow survive their ruthless onslaught, all while driving alone on the left side of the road in an unfamiliar country, was one of the most resounding triumphs of my nineteen days in New Zealand.

As I worked my way up the Pass, the blazing sun receded and the temperatures began to cool. High above me, birds could be seen hitching rides on the gentle, early spring breeze—winged high-wire artists, carving their own traffic-free paths into the sky.

I'd already been on the ascent for three hours when I realized that the mountaintops everywhere around me were enveloped in fast-moving, rapidly darkening shadows. It was nearly dusk now, chilly enough to justify rolling up my windows. *This is spring?* I thought. *More like a New England November!* I slipped on my jacket, fed another CD into the player, and drove along to the tune of the Beatles' "Hard Day's Night"—the perfect anthem to accompany my trip into the ever higher, ever colder reaches of the nocturnal unknown.

Traffic had thinned, but I still couldn't afford to lessen my vigilance; the dwindling light made it increasingly difficult for me to see the lane markings. I gripped the steering wheel with ever greater intensity while negotiating the fragile, zigzag necklace of curves. My need to concentrate had begun to take its toll. I was exhausted by now, but nothing was going to stop me from enjoying the spectacular scenery.

Nothing, that is, but inclement weather.

Or more precisely, snow.

And a whole lot of it, too, right there in the subtropical splendor of springtime New Zealand! When I rolled down my window, a blast of wind carried a swirling vortex of snowflakes right into my van, where they assembled themselves neatly on the dashboard and refused to melt.

I suddenly remembered the sign at the base of the mountains and realized why it had been blabbering on so unseasonably about tire chains and personal responsibility. By the time I rolled my window up, brushed off the flakes, and continued maneuvering through the darkness, the flakes had turned into a full-blown blizzard.

I ought to have been frightened by my predicament, but I felt only exhilaration. Caught in a blizzard at the top of Arthur's Pass, with no hope of turning back and no idea what to do next? What more delicious development for the ardent adventurer in me!

The reality of my circumstances became even clearer when I began to see the ghostly outline of a uniformed authority figure just beyond my ice-encrusted windshield. Her pony tail bobbed as she waved her arms frantically and ordered me to pull off onto the side of the road.

"I'm sorry, sir," she shouted, "but you'll not be able to continue down the Pass tonight. It's just too dangerous for anyone to attempt the descent!"

I shouted back, asking her if I should plan to spend the night in my van. "Not necessarily," she said through what was fast becoming an impenetrable wall of heavy, wet snowflakes.

"You've three possible places where you might find lodging, all within walking distance from here. You might ask each in turn if they've accommodations for you for the evening."

I thanked her for her timely advice, got out of my van, and started down the road, dressed only in bluejeans, a T-shirt, and a lightweight summer jacket—clothing more appropriate for a vacation in the Bahamas than a night in the frozen tundra of Arthur's Pass.

About fifty yards down the road, I could see the warm glow of a single porch light ahead of me in the darkness. *Lookin' good!* I murmured to myself through the pair of half-frozen lips beneath my snow-caked mustache. I rang the bell, and a handsome young man with a single earring, a head as shiny as a cue ball, and a half-consumed bottle of Guinness cracked open the door and peered out at me. His eyes had that all-too-familiar look of a habitual imbiber. I could see a dozen party animals frolicking in the shadows behind him, laughing raucously while shaking their booties in front of a red-hot, crackling fire.

"Weather's really bad tonight!" I shivered. "I've been told I have to stay on the mountain until morning. This looks like just what I need!"

Mr. Clean took a deep swig from the bottle, then moved his bald head left to right.

"Sorry, chap! We've no extra beds tonight. There's another place across the road, 'bout a hundred yards down. You should give 'em a try!" He then smiled disingenuously, slammed the door tight against the elements, and went back to his mountaintop reveling.

I turned the collar of my jacket up around my neck, bent down against the swirling tempest, and struggled through the accumulating drifts toward a tiny clapboard building with a single light in one snow-glazed window. A woman with gnarled hands and a dried-apple complexion opened the door and peered out at me. "Don't even ask!" she said. "We got no extra beds for travelers caught in a blizzard—and you can bet we get a lot of 'em! Like the sign at the base o' the Pass says, if you got no tyre chains, you're on your own!"

By now I was as stiff as a candy cane and desperate for a place to stay. I then contributed my best abandoned-puppy expression to the cause of finding shelter.

"Nope, *sorry!*" she said, her face in the half-light of the cabin set in stone. "You've got one last chance, though! Just down from me, on the other side of the road, is a little place called Sanctuary. Either you go *there*, or you spend the night in your car—if you *got* one. I'd head down there right away if I was you."

I staggered on through the storm, little more than an apparition by now, barely able to see through my glasses. Just ahead of me, the place she'd described to me began to materialize in the falling snow. I stepped up to the door, rubbed the ice off my glasses, and squinted at a small, crudely lettered sign mounted

Fig. 39. Sanctuary Bunkhouse at the top of Arthur's Pass.

near the door of the cabin. I don't fully remember the words, but they went something like this:

> You've reached the Sanctuary at Arthur's Pass. No proprietor on the premises. For access, enter the code number on the key pad. To pay, use the honor system. Wi-Fi available. When you've finished your stay, leave your payment—Winter Rate, $18.00 per person—in the box just inside the door.

I entered the code number as directed, and the door creaked open. I stumbled over the threshold and into the vestibule, then forced the door shut against what had become a fierce, howling wind. Finally! I felt like Charlie Chaplin in *The Gold Rush*, and just the thought of its legendary dining scene made me ravenously hungry. At this point I'd have gladly eaten any shoe on the menu. Then I remembered having left a half-eaten granola bar in my knapsack, so the shoes stayed on my feet, right where they belonged.

Just to the left of the vestibule was a weatherbeaten, henhouse-like structure—what seemed little more than a quirky architectural afterthought. I pulled the chain on a single lightbulb dangling from the ceiling and found nearly a half dozen state-of-the-art computers—enough to serve a small-town library—lined up along one wall.

I wanted desperately to tear into that granola bar, park myself in front of a computer, and write to my friends back in the States, but I needed first to learn where I'd be sleeping for the night.

I worked my way down the hall and found a room on the left, lined on two sides with a series of gray, rough-hewn bunks worthy of a logging camp in the Klondike.

Now in full survival mode, I began to case the joint. In the storage bin under my bunk, I found a skimpy, army issue blanket and a wafer-thin pillow. Considering how cold it was inside the cabin, they were worth their weight in gold.

It was nearly pitch dark inside the cabin, and far too early for a man of my night-owl proclivities to turn in for the evening. It really didn't matter, though; I was so emotionally wired and breathtakingly cold by now that I doubted I'd be sleeping at all. I put my belongings on a chair beside my bunk, stomped the snow off my shoes, and headed back to the computer room with the blanket over my shoulders, thrilled to know that, thanks to the wonders of Wi-Fi, I'd at least have the pleasure of sharing my adventure with friends and family.

For the next three hours I sat hunched over my computer, wrapped tightly in my blanket and shaking like a leaf. I wrote

Fig. 40. The author's accommodations at the Bunkhouse.

and wrote, then wrote again to nearly everyone back home who meant something to me. The mere act of writing helped me keep my mind off the cold.

A tiny sign on the wall of the computer room admonished all users to leave $5.00 in a lock box for every hour of computer usage. I took NZ$50.00 from my wallet, stuffed it into the lock box, turned off the overhead light, and worked my way back to my bunk, frozen to the very marrow but grinning from ear to ear. I was thankful for the Wi-Fi, the bunk, and the adventure, so it was hardly the time to be tight with the dollar.

Once I'd managed to stretch out on my bunk, I wrapped one end of the blanket tightly around my shoes—it was much too cold for me to take them off—then pulled the other end up under my chin. Then I rolled myself into a cocoon-like configuration and made a concerted effort to fall asleep. I was the only one in the cabin, and it somehow made the cold even more bitter than usual.

Somewhere in the middle of the night I woke up, astounded that I'd managed to fall asleep at all. My knees were knocking like pins in a bowling alley, and puffs of crystallizing air were emerging dragon-like from my mouth. I realized I needed badly to go to the bathroom, but because of the bitter cold I fought the urge and tried my best to turn over and sleep through it.

Dumb idea. I finally gave in to reality, got up, and stumbled around in the darkness, and with the help of a flashlight I'd pulled from my knapsack, I found the bathroom. It was hilariously asymmetrical—little more than a closet-size cubby hole with one rickety toilet, a bear claw tub, and a tiny, triangular sink crammed into one corner.

I got down to business, then ran my hand along the wall, reached for the toilet paper, and came up empty. The Marriott this was not!

I got up, hobbled out into the hallway with my pants somewhere south of the border, reached high up on a shelf, and found one half-depleted roll of toilet paper with my name written all over it. Then, with mission accomplished, I groped my way back down the hallway, fell back into my bunk, and shivered my way through what could fairly be described as the poorest excuse for a good night's sleep I've ever endured.

There were moments during the night when, while half asleep and thrashing about in the cold, nothing seemed real. But I could hear myself breathing and feel myself shivering, and that was proof enough for me. I really wasn't having nightmares. I really hadn't been catapulted into a weather-induced psychosis. I actually was in the South Island of New Zealand and at the top of Arthur's Pass, marooned in a mountain cabin and toying with frostbite, and I couldn't have been happier. That night, in spite of the outrageous cold and the uncertainty of my circumstances, I don't think I've ever been more thankful to be alive, in good health, and able to feel the world around me.

Fig. 41. Sanctuary Bunkhouse, the morning after the blizzard.

I woke up the next morning with a shaft of sunlight cutting through the blanket I'd pulled over my face. My bones clacked like a sackful of castanets as I clamored out of my bunk—a stone-cold mummy, brought back from the dead.

I'd no need to put my clothes on; I'd worn all of them, including my hiking boots, straight through the night in an attempt to avoid freezing to death in my bunk. Though I was all alone in the cabin, I pulled a comb from my jeans pocket and wrestled my bed-head hair into compliance.

Once fully awake, I pulled back the curtains above my bunk and saw a living, breathing work of art just outside my window. It was immeasurably beautiful and achingly poetic, and I couldn't help wondering at that moment if I'd just died and gone to Heaven.

I pulled my little Olympus from my knapsack, pointed it out the window, and prayed that in spite of my technical incompetence as a photographer, the camera would do what it was built to do.

I needn't have worried. I'd learn later on, back in the States, that my camera—recommended to me by legendary New Hampshire photographer Barry Nation because of its portability and the quality of its lens—was more than up to the challenge.

My Improbable Journey to the Other Side of the World

I'd captured a priceless moment from my New Zealand journey, and my Olympus, with the welcome assistance of Arthur's Pass, had done all of the work for me.

Then a burst of post-adolescent laughter echoed down the hall opposite my bunk room.

Neighbors! I realized I hadn't been alone after all, and I felt more than a little violated. Who'd they think they *were*, anyway? This was my adventure and no one else's!

Still groggy from a night of wretched can't-sleep, I didn't really feel like being convivial. Nevertheless, I shrugged off my annoyance and headed down the hall toward the gathering.

I tapped gently on the door, and a lovely young woman with honey-blond hair and pale blue eyes welcomed me into the throng. The floor was covered with sleeping bags, and scattered about the room were shoes, knapsacks, half-eaten sandwiches, cameras still in their cases, and eight sleepy-eyed, college-age backpackers just in from the south of France.

A beat-up, camp-style teapot percolated on the stove, filling the room with sustained, high-pitched music. Next to it was a frying pan filled with scrambled eggs and sizzling bacon. An Arthur's Pass breakfast was about to be served, and I'd be a last-minute guest.

I couldn't speak even one tiny syllable of French—the typical monolingual American—so we communicated only marginally during our brief encounter. We were friendly aliens from two very different planets—a group of young Parisians on an overseas adventure and an aging American in a young man's jeans, working his way to Queenstown.

I had my tea and breakfast, said goodbye to the Parisians, and headed back to my bunk. Once I was fully awake and alert, I threw my belongings together and stepped out onto the road at the top of the Pass. The pavement was still covered with ice, but the sun was shining again, and I was assured the crews would arrive soon to clear the roads and make them safe for our descent.

I loaded my belongings into the van, then slipped in behind the steering wheel. While turning over the engine I noticed a large green and yellow bird walking straight toward me down the center of the road.

Clearly, he was a bird on a mission. To test his determination, I got out and walked down the road toward him, figuring it had to be a fluke. He couldn't possibly be coming to see me. But to my surprise he just kept on coming, walking steadily along an imaginary meridian line until he landed at my feet, stood fully at attention, and stared inquisitively up at me—a finely feathered puppy bird, waiting for his ball.

A man walking past me on the way to his car saw the look of wonderment on my face and joined us in the middle of the road. "Oh, that's not at all unusual for them!" he smiled. "He's an alpine parrot. They're among the smartest birds in the world. And he's not really looking to be fed. He's just interested in you and figured he'd come up and get acquainted."

I snapped a photo of my little friend, said goodbye to him across a spectacularly wide behavioral abyss, then got into my van and pulled out onto the main road. Through my rearview mirror I had one last, fond look at the Sanctuary, red and glistening in the snow, then headed happily down the mountain.

I learned later that I'd been kindred spirit to a kea, one proud ambassador for the world's only alpine parrot. They're unique to the South Island of New Zealand and renowned for their superior intelligence and natural curiosity—qualities essential to their survival in the harsh alpine winters. Researchers have found that keas can solve logical puzzles by pushing and pulling things in a certain sequence in order to get food. They're also known to work together as a species to achieve predetermined objectives.

As I slowly descended the Pass, I was once again surrounded by the invisible roar-and-screech of the logging trucks zigzagging their precious cargo down the mountain and into the doz-

Fig. 42. The author outside the Bunkhouse, waiting for the kea.

ens of cities and towns scattered across the lower extremities of the South Island.

Two hours into my downward journey, while gawking at snapshot after snapshot of spectacular scenery, I glanced down at the dashboard and discovered to my horror that the fuel indicator needle was on empty. Once again I was in crisis: alone in the mountains of New Zealand and dangerously close to running on empty, with no idea where the next gas station might be.

Where is Cranky, my Roadside Savior, when I need him most? I thought while forging ever downward, praying I'd not be stranded yet again in the mountains, and yet clearly, perversely savoring the possibility. Once again, I was having the time of my life being in trouble in a world lightyears away from my home in New England.

I eventually reached the base of the Pass, and straight ahead of me was the petroleum oasis I'd so fervently prayed for. I coasted into the station with the needle completely left of the red zone, filled up my tank with yet another $113 American, bought a large bottle of L&P and a Cadbury Wriggler, then headed down a long and winding road to what would be the last of my Kiwi adventures: Franz Josef Glacier, Doubtful Sound, and—finally—the bustling tourist mecca of Queenstown.

Franz Joseph Glacier: Cool Experience on a Warm Spring Day

The Franz Joseph Glacier—known as Ka Roimata o Hinehukatere by the Maoris—is a twelve-kilometer-long glacier located in Westland Tai Poutini National Park on the western coast of New Zealand's South Island.

At this point in my journey I was within driving distance, so I figured I had no excuse for not going there to bear witness to an astonishing but fast-disappearing natural phenomenon. After all, when would I ever get another opportunity to see a glacier?

Like the Fox Glacier twelve miles to the south, the Franz Josef descends from the Southern Alps to less than 980 feet above sea level, all amidst the lush greenery of what environmental scientists call a temperate rainforest. It finally terminates nineteen kilometers (twelve miles) from the Tasman Sea.

While glaciers appear to the casual observer to be frozen in time, the experts know they're actually a living, breathing entity, always on the move. Like other glaciers, the Franz Josef advances and retreats cyclically, driven by differences between the volume of meltwater at the foot of the glacier and the volume of snowfall feeding the névé—the vast blanket of compacted granular snow at the top of the glacier that has yet to become ice.

After retreating for several consecutive decades, the Franz Josef entered an advancing phase in 1984, and at times moved along at the rate of seventy centimeters a day—a phenomenal rate by glacial standards. In fact, the flow rate of the Franz Josef was nearly ten times that of the typical glacier. Over the longer term, it has been retreating steadily since the last Ice Age, and is believed to have extended into the sea some ten to fifteen thousand years ago.

The glacier was still advancing in 2008, but since then it has entered a very rapid phase of retreat. As is the case with most other New Zealand glaciers, mainly found on the eastern side of the southern Alps, the shrinking process is attributed to global warming.

For glaciers, for the experts who've devoted their lives to studying them, and for the very balance of nature itself, the news is not good. Scientists around the world generally concur that most of the planet's glaciers are on the decline, many of them significantly. If global warming continues unabated, they say, whether from natural cycles or human activity, many glaciers could literally melt out of existence.

To begin my rendezvous with the Franz Josef, I struck out on foot from a designated parking area in the midst of a chill, wind-whipped rainfall, having no idea how long it might actually take to reach the glacier itself.

Along the way, I needed the skill and focus of a mountain goat to negotiate the wide trail of stones and boulders left behind over tens of thousands of years in the wake of the retreating glacier. Finally, after nearly two hours of fancy footwork, I landed, soaking wet and a little winded, just where I wanted to be—smack on the perimeter of a massive superhighway of ice, around three hundred meters (nearly a thousand feet) thick in places and crawling steadily along at an imperceptible rate, unless you happen to be either a glaciologist or a human with unheard of visual acuity.

I never actually walked on the glacier. That would have involved a guided tour, and I hadn't sufficient time to take it. I had to be content to stand and stare in wonderment at the stunning vista ahead of me, moving snakelike through an unimaginably deep, V-shaped winding crevasse formed by sheer mountain cliffs hundreds of feet high and carpeted with lush, emerald-green subtropical vegetation. I'd seen my glacier, and one more fabulous Kiwi encounter could be checked off my list of must-see adventures.

Fig. 43. The author, happily windblown on the Doubtful Sound cruise.

Doubtful Sound: Call It Unforgettable

Doubtful Sound—a name replete with the sort of romance and mystery I've never been able to resist—is a huge fiord, three times longer than Milford Sound and with ten times the surface area, located in Fiordland in the far southwest of New Zealand. Like its smaller, more accessible neighbor, it has become a major destination for New Zealand tourists. While in the planning stage for my trip, I struggled to decide which of the two would be the better fit for me. In the end I chose Doubtful Sound not only because I was captivated by the evocative power of its name, but because I was heartened to learn that the boat I'd be taking would be less dense with tourists and therefore quieter and more serene than the one used for the Milford Sound excursion.

The marketers of Doubtful Sound tours have dubbed it the Sound of Silence for good reason. On the day I made the excursion, the only sounds we heard with any regularity were either the crash of the waterfalls tumbling into the fiord or the awestruck squeals and gasps of passengers from stem to stern of the boat.

Doubtful Sound was actually named Doubtful Harbour in 1770 by Captain Cook, who is credited by historians with having discovered the inlet. Since he was uncertain whether it was navigable under sail, he decided not to enter it. Only later was it renamed Doubtful Sound by whalers and sealers, though technically it's a fiord, not a sound.

On the day I took the Doubtful Sound tour, the scenery from start to finish could only be described as majestic, otherworldly, and in every respect truly breathtaking. The towering peaks were shrouded in a dense, poetically evocative mist, the wind at every turn was just one blow short of a tempest, and the lush green vegetation stood out like fine jewelry against the canopy of slate gray, silver-tinged clouds. There were several spectacular falls along the route, but Brown Falls—at 836 meters (2,740 feet) a roaring, liquid lion of a water drop—earned the trophy for most impressive plunge from mountaintop to Sound.

I'd hoped to see a great many bottlenose dolphins on the tour, but we were warned from the outset that because of their unique habitat in the Sound—exceedingly cold temperatures and freshwater overlay—their social grouping is much closer than those of bottlenose dolphins in other habitats. Scientists have also been increasingly concerned that the population of the Doubtful Sound dolphins appears to be in serious decline. Some environmental activists have argued that the decline can be attributed, at least in part, to the dramatic increase in tourists and the controversial freshwater discharge from the Manapouri Power Station.

Doubtful Sound is also host to many other wildlife species, including fur seals, penguins, whales, and an abundance of sea creatures, including many species of fish, starfish, sea anemones, and corals. The Sound is renowned for the presence of black coral trees—phenomena which occur in unusually shallow water for what is normally a deep-water species. And to top it off, Doubtful Sound has been identified as an Important Bird and Biodiversity Area by BirdLife International because of its status as a significant breeding site for Fiordland penguins.

Manapouri Hydroelectric Power Station: Underwater Marvel in Doubtful Sound

As a part of the Doubtful Sound tour, our boat made a side trip to the Manapouri Hydroelectric Power Station, a gigantic, state-of-the-art underground facility on the western arm of Lake Manapouri in Fiordland National Park. The station's machine hall, excavated from solid granite rock two hundred meters below the level of Lake Manapouri, is without question a technological marvel.

In the system, water is channeled through vertical penstocks into seven massive generators housed in the machine hall, taking advantage of the difference in the height of the mountains between Lake Manapouri and Doubtful Sound to act as a natural dam. The resulting electricity is used to power the Tiwai Point Aluminium Smelter (formerly the Comalco Aluminium Smelter) more than a hundred miles to the south.

It's the largest hydroelectric power station in New Zealand, but its size isn't the only reason it has garnered so much publicity since its completion in 1971. Not long after it was activated, it became the subject of protracted environmental protests by the Save Manapouri campaign, which alleged that modifications to it would wreak havoc on the all-important ecological balance of Lake Manapouri. And there were other reasons for the controversy. The plant's cost to New Zealand taxpayers, along with the dangers inherent in building it in the first place, engendered public anger and heated debate. The original Manapouri Station cost NZ$135.5 million (NZ$2.15 billion in 2013 dollars), required nearly eight million man-hours to construct, and took the lives of sixteen laborers in the course of its construction.

As impressed as I was with the Manapouri Station, I was eager to get back onto our boat for the return trip—including an ambitious excursion out into the Tasman Sea—then back to Doubtful Sound and the mainland. On the way home, we finally saw a school of frolicking dolphins and a playful gathering of fur seals.

Fig. 44. The TSS *Earnslaw*, Queenstown Harbor, South Island.

It was time now for me to get back on the road and make my bittersweet journey to the southernmost destination on my itinerary: Queenstown. No matter how exciting my stay in that city might be, I knew it would mark the end of my New Zealand adventure. It wasn't going to be an easy departure.

Queenstown: The Very Definition of "Tourist Mecca"

Queenstown would be my last stop in New Zealand, simply because, after nineteen days in the country, I'd scheduled myself to fly north from Queenstown to Auckland, then on to Boston and home to Maine.

Emotionally, I'd gotten to where author John Steinbeck of *Travels with Charley* fame must have been after he and his dog finished their ten-thousand-mile camper-van tour of America: I was still having fun, making discoveries, and collecting what would prove to be indelible memories, but I was also flirting with physical exhaustion and dreaming once again of home.

Queenstown, a product of the legendary gold rushes of the 1860s, has evolved rapidly into a world-class tourist destination, in part because it had the good fortune long ago to have established itself along the shores of Lake Wakatipu, ringed three quarters around by a truly spectacular mountain range, called with great irony and understatement the Remarkables.

People from Australia, Western Europe, Japan, China, the United States, and a host of other countries flock to Queenstown to take advantage of both its spectacular scenery and its innumerable opportunities for sports and outdoor adventuring. In the first few minutes of my very first day in town, I heard tourists talking together in at least a half-dozen languages as they strolled along Lake Wakatipu, then gathered along the boardwalk to watch the historic 1912 steamer TSS *Earnslaw*—known locally as the Lady of the Lake—make a regularly scheduled appearance at Steamer Wharf.

I ought to have been swept off my feet by this bustling city, but compared to the more leisurely pace of pretty much everywhere else in New Zealand but Auckland, Queenstown's circus-like atmosphere and frenetic tempo left me more exhausted than replenished.

To recover from my previous eighteen days of travel, I'd arranged to spend three leisurely days in Queenstown before flying home. Those three days would allow me the opportunity to explore at least one city in more depth than I'd been able to while hopscotching rapidly across the North and South Islands, tasting what little I could in each town along the way.

For me it was the people—not the relentlessly promoted tourist attractions—who made my visit to Queenstown so pleasurable. Queenstown is a delightfully cosmopolitan, multilingual mecca for the adventurous, sports-minded traveler. And yet, somehow, in spite of the town's sky-high metabolism, its inhabitants have managed to preserve that small-town, we're-all-in-this-together feeling that makes any city a more than worthwhile destination.

As soon as I'd settled into a Top 10 Holiday Park on the edge of town, I headed into the center of the city to have a look at its art galleries. There were plenty of them, too—the Queenstown Gallery of Fine Art, the David John Gallery, and Milford Galleries Queenstown, to name a few—and while they exhibited the works of many highly skilled artists from New Zealand and beyond, I found them in general to be a little too conservative and blatantly commercial for my tastes.

Not surprisingly, the one gallery that proved to be the most rewarding for me—an artist with a hearty appetite for the offbeat and playful—was the Queenstown Art Society gallery. I saw more spontaneous originality and artistic chance-taking there than in all of the downtown commercial galleries put together. Genuine imagination and technical mastery are, as I see it, two entirely different universes. Only rarely do the two come together in the mind of the same artist. When they do, it is pure magic.

It was at the Queenstown Art Society exhibit that I had the good fortune to meet Errol Bulling, an eighty-five-year-old retired business executive who'd taken up art as a hobby in his later years and gotten serious about his craft. Several of his landscapes were on display in the current QAS exhibit, and for the works of a late-in-life, self-taught artist, they were truly impressive.

When I'd finished touring the exhibit, I asked him to recommend a good place to eat.

"Fancy or plain?" he said. "Expensive or affordable?"

Fig. 45. Errol Bulling, the unofficial ambassador of Queenstown.

"Plain and affordable," I replied. "I'm on a strict budget, so I need to keep it simple."

"Then I've got just the place for you: Fergburger! And if you want some company, I'll go with you."

Fergburger? I expected to find some really outlandish items on their menu—barbecued wallaby, or perhaps chinchilla on a stick. Of course, if you happen to have watched more than one episode of Anthony Bourdain's popular food-and-travel show, *Parts Unknown*, you know there's really no creature on earth that won't eventually find its way onto a restaurant menu.

Outlandish food or not, I was delighted with Bulling's offer, and we immediately headed downtown to find Fergburger and have lunch.

From Berwick, Maine, to Queenstown, South Island: what a difference! I'd spent the last forty years of my life in northern New England, a dramatically different cultural environment from what I'd been experiencing for the past two weeks in New Zealand. The temperament of the people in Maine and New Hampshire—famously laconic, parochial, and taciturn—has been known to add the chill of winter to an August afternoon. So here in New Zealand, Errol Bulling—naturally gregarious, eager to please, and almost aggressively friendly—was an enormous breath of fresh air. He was also typical of the people I'd met in nearly every town I'd visited, from Auckland and Tauranga in the North Island to the South Island cities of New Plymouth, Christchurch, and now, of course, Queenstown.

When Errol called Fergburger a prized destination, he wasn't exaggerating. The line of people waiting for their sandwiches was half a block long, and the aroma of burgers-in-progress wafting out onto the street was tantalizing—an olfactory assault on the senses.

I ordered my burger on a sesame bun, topped off with sweet onions, swiss cheese, and portobello mushrooms. It turned out to be more authentically American in concept than many of the burgers available to me in the southern Maine / Seacoast New Hampshire region—with the notable exception of our Wild Willy's, which to the tastebuds of the hamburger aficionado is an equally impressive piece of culinary wizardry.

When we'd finished our burgers, I thanked Errol for sending me to Fergburger and prepared to go off on my own and explore more of the downtown area.

"Oh, we're just getting started!" he laughed. "I've some great things to show you. Wanna see a really big tree?" He spread his arms out as far as possible from his sides. "There's one overlooking the city, just down from my home."

I was suffering from a minor bout of travel fatigue, but I didn't have the heart to say no to him, so off we went to see the tree, with Errol doing the driving. We got there in ten minutes, and it really was a whopper. "A giant sequoia," he said. "The kauri tree has had a rough go of it here in New Zealand, so the sequoia has been brought here as part of the country's reforestation effort."

I'd seen a sequoia at the Christchurch Botanic Gardens, but this one was even more massive—a full eighty feet in circumference, and tall enough to reach out and touch the clouds over Queenstown Harbor.

"Impressive, huh!" he said. Then he pointed to a distant outcropping on the sprawling necklace of hills overlooking the city. "But I've got something even more exciting to show you!"

We hopped back into his car and worked our way up a steep incline to a place where the view overlooking the harbor was pure Hollywood spectacular. While I gaped at the stunning panorama, he walked back and forth on the wide expanse of grass overlooking the city. "See?" he shouted. "This is where it all happened!"

"Where what happened?"

"Where Peter Jackson filmed a scene from his movie *The Hobbit: An Unexpected Journey*!" He beamed with pride as he related the event. "I was an extra!"

Errol was filled to overflowing, not just with the energy and enthusiasm of a twenty-year-old, but with delightful, heartwarming surprises. He promised me a still photograph of the filming of the *Hobbit* scene he'd taken part in, then asked me if I'd mind coming with him to a nearby cemetery. I saw no reason to say no, and a few minutes later we were strolling through a memorial garden with dozens of crumbling, moss-covered tombstones tumbling down an incline toward the heart of the city.

"Many important New Zealanders are buried here," he said wistfully, "including my wife. I come here regularly to pay my respects to her. Could never allow myself to forget what she meant to me."

"And what a beautiful final resting place, overlooking the Harbor," I said.

He spent a few minutes alone at her grave, then headed back to his car. "Going to my place now," he said. "Come along! I've got more stuff to show you—and we'll have dessert, too."

When we reached his home, Errol prepared the dessert while I took an informal tour of the place, beginning with the living room. Not surprisingly, it was crammed full of multicultural stimuli—the treasured artifacts of a well-lived existence. Photos of friends and relatives were tacked up in every available space between items he'd acquired from years of world travel. On the walls were elaborately carved figures, a Hawaiian ceremonial skirt, a collection of precious geodes from several continents—Bulling is a lifetime member of the Mineralogical Society of America—and a wide array of Bulling's own meticulously rendered landscapes, including evocative paintings of lily pads, all painted skillfully in oil on canvas. I learned later that his paintings are nearly as well-traveled as he is: they're also in homes in Japan, Canada, Australia, England, and the United States.

The visual cornucopia that is Errol's place was only the beginning. In one corner of the living room was a piano, and on it was a looseleaf notebook with the titles of more than a thousand pop tunes and old standards scrawled on page after page of the book.

"Name a song," he crowed, "*any* song—and I can almost guarantee it's in this book. Nothing in it but the titles, but that's all I need to get me going." He then sat down and banged out nearly a dozen tunes, investing every ounce of his *joie de vivre* into every one of them. By then, the Bulling residence was really rocking, and I wondered if the man ever sat in a chair and rested.

While he was whaling away at the piano, I noticed a group of three small, multicolored balls sitting on a chair near the coffee table. They looked remarkably like miniature beach balls, but were enclosed in fabric.

"What are these for?" I asked when he'd finished his last song.

"Those? Oh, *those!*" He jumped up from the piano, grabbed the three balls in one hand, then dashed over to his turntable and set an LP spinning.

On came a raucous, high-octane version of "The Bluebells of Scotland," and then the balls I'd seen sitting on the table were in the air.

He leapt and teetered around the living room, juggling with perfect timing to the song's festive, hard-driving rhythms. Every once in a while he'd drop the balls, then dart around the room, scoop them up, and jump back into action. When the accordion had registered its last grand flourish, the song

Fig. 46. Errol's juggling balls at the ready.

was over and Errol flopped down onto the couch, laughing like a teenager as he caught his breath.

"Stunning!" I laughed, genuinely impressed with the diversity of his skills. "Artist, piano player, movie extra," I marveled. "And a damn good juggler to boot!"

His chest was still heaving from the exertion. "A fella needs to have a good time in life," he said, chuckling. "The way I see it, there's very little we can't accomplish, if only we put our minds to it."

Sadly, my time with Errol Bulling—multi-talented Kiwi and the perfect ambassador for Queenstown's irrepressible, intercontinental exuberance—had come to an end. Errol, a man of uncommon warmth and extraordinary abilities, had shared with me an entire day of his high-spirited, action-packed life, and I couldn't have been happier about the encounter. I went to bed that night (actually slumped over in the passenger seat of my JUCY van) feeling both contented and fulfilled. It was hands down the best sleep I'd had since arriving in New Zealand three weeks before.

I decided my last day on New Zealand soil would be devoted entirely to my own solitary, low-key adventuring. I'd need to take it easy before getting back on the plane for what would be another grueling, eighteen-hour flight from Queenstown to Auckland, then home to Boston.

The next morning I got up early, walked into town, and read the morning edition of the *New Zealand Herald* over a leisurely breakfast at a tiny side-street cafe. I'd begun to get emotional about my departure, so before actually eating my meal I carefully arranged the plate of food, the cup of tea, and the newspaper, then photographed them to take home with me as a remembrance.

I had the entire day to myself now, but still didn't know how I wanted to spend the time. I knew I wouldn't be going skydiving, hang gliding, or bungee jumping—wildly popular activities in the sports-obsessed city of Queenstown, but clearly not meant for me. I paid my bill, put my copy of the *Herald* in my backpack, then struck out toward the center of Queenstown in search of one last New Zealand adventure.

Several times over the past two days, while in the downtown area, I'd walked past Skyline Gondola, perched a heart-stopping 1,476 feet above Brecon Street. An interesting choice, to be sure; I'd read about it in my *Eyewitness Travel Guide*. But I'd decided long before my arrival in Queenstown that under no circumstances would I ever set foot in one of those pathetically fragile, precariously dangling cars.

Even if I overcame my terror of heights and agreed to take a ride, I'd have been the one tourist most likely to crawl into a dysfunctional car. I preferred to get back to America in one recognizable piece instead of a bucketful of splats. I looked wistfully up at the string of gondolas gliding upward into the clouds, then kept moving.

I spent the next several hours exploring the lively network of streets and shops clustered along the northeast shore of Lake Wakatipu, backed by the towering, snow-capped Remarkables range; the Queenstown Gardens, a quiet oasis in an otherwise high-velocity tourist town; and Kiwi Birdlife Park, replete with alpine parrots, owls, parakeets, and the rare wading black stilt. Altogether, they were just the kind of low-key adventures I'd been looking for.

By early afternoon I was hungry and in need of a rest from my trampings, so I stopped at the legendary Cow Restaurant in Cow Lane and enjoyed a slice of hand-rolled pizza, washed down by a tumbler of fresh-squeezed lemonade.

It was time to work my way back to the Top 10 Holiday Park and gather up my belongs for the trip home, but I really wasn't in a hurry. By now I was consciously dragging my heels, doing my best to slow down my inevitable departure from a country I'd fallen in love with and didn't want to leave.

I headed back down Brecon Street, trying my best to avoid looking at Skyline Gondola. Then, right next to it, I noticed a steep staircase leading up to what appeared to be an elementary school, with children playing together in an enclosed area.

The sound of their joyful yelps and screeches triggered long-dormant memories and presented an intriguing opportunity. *Maybe I could stop by and play for them!* I thought to myself.

It wouldn't be the first time. I'd stopped unannounced at a school while vacationing in Pittsburg, New Hampshire, a few years ago—Moose Country, near the Canadian border—and ended up conducting an ad hoc flute clinic for the band director and his students. It was an imaginative way for me to connect with the community while simultaneously sharing my expertise. I was a one-man, on-the-road cultural exchange, and I was sure it could work here, too.

I trudged up the staircase, rang the security buzzer, introduced myself to the school secretary, and pleaded my case. "Good idea!" she beamed. "I'll check with the band director and see what we can do for you." Ten minutes later, she came back and announced that while the director would have loved having me in, it couldn't be worked into the schedule. School would soon be done for the day, and he was still in rehearsals.

I thanked her for her trouble, then trod down the staircase and back out onto the street. To the left of me I could hear the rhythmic hum of that ever-ascending string of gondolas, winging its way with fluid, clockwork precision up to Bob's Peak and back down again.

I stood fast at the bottom of the hill, impressed with the courage of the passengers but wondering why I hadn't the nerve to be up there with them, taking in the sights.

Then the shrill sound of a bell pierced the serenity of the afternoon, and down the staircase came a long line of smiling children in identical blue-and-white uniforms, just released from their school day and moving single file toward a waiting school bus.

As the line moved past me down the steps, one small girl, no more than six years old, abruptly stepped out of the line and stood transfixed before me.

"You're *Santa Claus*, aren't you?" she said. "*I* know you!"

I'd grown accustomed to being identified as either St. Nicholas or Jerry Garcia wherever I happened to be, so her assertion really didn't surprise me. But in New Zealand, too?

"No, I'm not Santa!" I said. "But what an honor to know you think I look like him!"

"Well, I *still* think you're Santa," she said.

"The *real* Santa will come by at Christmas," I assured her. "I'm sure you'll know him when you see him!"

Just then, the string of gondolas next to us finished its trip down the mountain and came to a halt.

"Betcha you've never been up in one o' *those*!" I said, pointing to the gondola closest to street level. At this point, I needed badly not to be the only person in all of Queenstown who'd never taken a ride on a gondola.

"Oh, yes I have!" she chimed. "I go up there with my friends *all* summer long!"

I praised her for her courage, and as she fell back in line with her classmates and skipped off with them toward the bus, I looked up at the string of gondolas and remembered what Nelson Mandela said long ago, after having spent twenty-seven years in various prisons as punishment for his anti-apartheid views: "I learned that courage is not the absence of fear," he said, "but the triumph over it. The brave man is not he who does not feel afraid, but he who conquers that fear."

Could I really afford to allow Santa Claus—the very symbol of courage for his ability to climb rooftops around the world, then come down safely every time—become known as a coward?

Saying no didn't make sense. To get to New Zealand, I'd spent eighteen hours stuffed into an airplane packed with more than four hundred travelers, nearly six miles up into the stratosphere. I'd driven several miles up into Arthur's Pass in a raging blizzard, maneuvering along treacherous mountain roads choked with bumper-to-bumper logging trucks. And then, for nearly three weeks, I'd slept while sitting up like a store dummy in my cramped and suffocating travel van, unwilling to put together the portable bedding provided to me by the JUCY company.

Fig. 47. The Flute Guy playing at Queenstown Harbor on his last day in New Zealand.

I'd survived every one of those ordeals and more. I figured that if she could do it, then so could I. And so, come to think of it, could Santa, even if he wasn't really Santa after all.

It was still only 3:00 p.m., and I had several hours to myself to spend any way I pleased. I headed straight to the Skyline ticket booth, bought a two-way pass, fell in line behind dozens of smiling tourists, and climbed into a waiting gondola.

It was a sleek, aerodynamically designed, one-room dwelling place—a temporary condo in the sky with beautifully upholstered benches and tall, wraparound windows that afforded a panoramic view of the Remarkables range, Lake Wakatipu, and all of Queenstown.

The interior was squeaky clean and surprisingly spacious. The ride to the top was remarkably smooth—no lurching, no swaying, no precipitous rocking to and fro. As we climbed methodically up the side of the mountain, I watched transfixed as the lights far below me twinkled, the cars moved slowly along the streets, and tourists scurried about like happy ants in a lakeside utopia. From the observation deck at the top of Bob's Peak, the TSS *Earnslaw* could be seen chugging back into Main Town Pier, chock full of tourists waving ecstatically to the people on shore.

In the time it took to complete the journey from ground level to Bob's Peak and back again—and in spite of the incomparable beauty of my surroundings—I relived the most memorable highlights of my three weeks in New Zealand: my life-changing performance in Tauranga; my rain-soaked encounter with a policeman after being caught driving too slowly in the Coromandel Peninsula; my heartwarming time with Cranky, the roadside savior; the climb to Arthur's Pass in a raging blizzard, topped off by an overnight stay in a mountainside cabin; and only yesterday, my multifaceted adventure with Errol Bulling—ambassador to Queenstown and juggler extraordinaire.

By the time I'd disembarked from my gondola and rejoined the throngs of tourists along Brecon Street, the sun had begun to set. I decided to pay one last visit to Steamer Wharf, where I'd be able to watch the TSS *Earnslaw* make yet another journey out onto Lake Wakatipu beneath a breathtaking canopy of stars illuminating the Remarkables.

As a paean to the city of Queenstown—and to all of what I'd experienced in New Zealand for the past three weeks—I pulled my flute from my backpack, cut through the crowd lining the shore, and played "Dance of the Blessed Spirits" one more time.

Fig. 48. Streetside diner Eifion W. Thomas, wishing the author well on the eve of his departure.

The last poignant notes of Gluck's melody floated out over the water and joined the smoke from the stack of the *Earnslaw* as it maneuvered gracefully into harbor. For me—a ramblin' man from Maine with an insatiable appetite for adventuring—it was a fitting way to end my all-too-brief stay in the spectacular, endlessly fascinating land of the Kiwi.

Afterward, as I strolled one last time along the wharf and past a street-side cabaret, a smiling, plentifully bearded man—Walt Whitman incarnate, plucked from Civil War America and deposited felicitously onto the streets of twenty-first-century Queenstown—smiled his unsolicited approval of me, a man he'd never seen before and would never see again. Then I made my way back to the park for one last night in New Zealand—a country I never thought I'd set foot in and will never be able to forget.

Chapter 8

Franklin Case and the Loan

Don't ever let anyone tell you that he or she is "just a teacher," or that teaching, from preschool to post-graduate level, isn't among the highest callings a person can aspire to—equivalent in power and nobility to that of doctor, scientist, or philosopher. Anyone who takes the time to read the news or listen to the blathering of extreme right-wing politicians knows that the profession continues to take an unjust, mean-spirited beating from every corner of our often ungrateful, pitifully uninformed society.

When a really good teacher makes his or her mark on even one student of any ability, the concentric circles of appreciation build not just for a day or for a year, but for a lifetime. I know, because it's happened to me on more than one occasion, at every level of my matriculation. This is the story of one teacher's enormous influence on my conduct, character, and values. It's a cause for celebration, and I've been celebrating, quietly but appreciatively, ever since the day I first stepped into his classroom more than fifty years ago.

Incoming freshmen at American colleges and universities must inevitably sign up for some version of freshman composition, the course that purports to separate the literate from the illiterate and sends an ironclad warning to any students who think they can get through year one without improving their skills as writers.

On registration day in 1962 I stood in the bowels of a cavernous field house, in what seemed like unending lines, hoping to find a composition class that would fit nicely into my schedule. And, like any normal eighteen-year-old, I crossed my fingers that I'd have the good fortune to land with an instructor as lenient as he was likable. I'd entered school as a music major, but freshman comp was a gauntlet that all incoming students, no matter what their academic specialty, were required to pass through.

The course catalogue was intimidating. It consisted of page after page of esoteric course descriptions, room numbers, schedules, and the names of the instructors—all in small print with closely packed sentences. The lack of illustration anywhere in the catalogue made it feel like a small-town phone book, or perhaps the parts list in an auto repair shop. For me, already a confirmed lover of music, art, and the written word, the sheer impersonality of it made the blood freeze in my veins.

How could I possibly hope to make a wise choice? There were only two ways for me to choose from the blur of names: I could either trust in a word-of-mouth recommendation or take a wild gamble that a name alone could somehow predict the kind of star I was about to hitch my wagon to.

After going through a formidably long and uninspiring list of instructors for freshman composition—forgettable names like Peters, Carpenter, and Ainsley—I settled on the only name that in any way piqued my interest: Franklin Case. Here, I thought, was a name swaddled in romantic cachet and emblematic of adventure. It had both an appealing professorial aura and a beguilingly musical rhythm that to my raw and callow ears exuded an almost piratical playfulness.

He's my man! I thought as I completed the necessary forms and secured a place in his three-days-a-week, 8:00 a.m. class.

On the following Friday, with my registration complete and my textbooks at the ready, I reported to Welch Hall, a stately edifice with an arched entryway and the smell of floor wax, old books, and freshly sharpened pencils. Welch, as people called it, was something of an architectural icon at the University, with a storied past of some sort (everyone said that, but no one really knew what it was) and a timeworn elegance that made one think of wire-rimmed glasses, meerschaum pipes, and herringbone sport coats with dark chocolate elbow patches.

I'd loved reading and writing as a high schooler, so the reality that I was about to step into an actual university writing class filled me with a sense of unabashed pride and the most delicious anticipation.

The first morning of freshman comp—my very first taste of university-level instruction—didn't disappoint me. Outside, the sun was shining down on a beautifully manicured campus, and optimism was everywhere in the air. To an eighteen-year-old who'd grown up stranded between the industrial city of Jackson, Michigan (billed as the birthplace of the Republican Party), and the Bible-thumping village of Rives Junction, this could easily have been the courtyard at Oxford or Yale. The freshly mowed, emerald green lawns were carpeted with freshly fallen leaves, providing the perfect playground for a small army of squirrels foraging for food in advance of the coming winter.

Waiting for class to begin was for me, a young man full of anticipation and bursting with idealism, a lot like waiting for the curtain to rise on act 1 of a play. Soon the show would open, and I'd finally have a modest role in a great academic drama unfolding not just on the Ypsilanti campus but at colleges and universities around the country.

At precisely 8:00 a.m., Franklin Case slipped through the entranceway, closed the door behind him, and walked to the front of the room. A good twenty to twenty-five students waited quietly at their desks, their clothes neatly pressed, their hair carefully combed, and a look of mild foreboding in their eyes. The year 1962 was still very much in the grip of the Eisenhower era, so in both appearance and temperament we were more the Nelsons than the Beatles, blissfully unaware of the cultural tidal wave that would soon sweep us up, throw us into the maelstrom, and change us forever. We were in the full, tumultuous flowering of our late adolescence, with all of the fears and insecurities that come with the package. But, for now at least, we were officially in college, and all was right with the world.

"Good morning!" said the instructor with a voice that sang of scholarly sophistication and the search for truth. "If you're not registered for freshman comp, or if your schedule doesn't list Franklin Case as the instructor, then you have the wrong class!"

One blushing student got up and left the room; the rest stayed right where they were.

Case moved a shock of straight, walnut-colored hair back from his forehead, then leaned against his desk and surveyed the room full of students. He had the smile of a camp counselor and the hands of a poet.

Once he'd gotten through the more perfunctory first-day chores—the semester schedule, the required textbooks, and his expectations for his students—he adopted a more serious demeanor.

"If there's just one thing you learn in my class this semester," he said, "I'd like it to be the meaning of the word *hubris*." He gave to it an almost cryptic emphasis, and while I had no idea what he was talking about, I figured it must be a very important word.

"Hubris!" he said again. "The word has its roots in ancient Greece, but it's really a timeless concept. It has profound relevance in every succeeding generation, including, of course, the one we're living in right now."

As a teenager I'd grown accustomed to the sound of my father's voice saying, "Put down that book and come with me. We've got *work* to do!" So the arrival of a well-dressed, well-informed, benevolent-sounding male in my life was both a shock to my system and a priceless gift to the aspiring intellectual in me.

He recited the definition with the caring intensity of an Episcopal priest. "Hubris!" he repeated. "Extreme pride or arrogance, often indicating a loss of contact with reality and an overestimation of one's own competence or capabilities, especially when the person exhibiting it is in a position of power."

He was onto something, all right. I'd known a few people like that, and I was only eighteen when Franklin Case and his message of arrogance—the intellectual kind, anyway—came into my life.

For the next few minutes he challenged us to identify historical figures whose names had become synonymous with the idea of hubris. Among the candidates were Genghis Khan, Adolf Hitler, and Emperor Hirohito. The list, disturbingly long and intimidating, made my skin crawl. If it was indeed hubris that made these and other like-minded people the monsters we read about in our high school textbooks, then I was glad the historians would never have reason to add my own humble name to the list.

Once we'd absorbed the meaning of the word and were sufficiently impressed with the decency and good intentions of Mr. Franklin Case, we turned to more prosaic matters. Every week, for sixteen consecutive weeks, we'd be required to produce a five-hundred-word essay based on a subject to be announced, and we'd be graded solely on the basis of the sophistication of our thinking and our demonstrated allegiance to the universal rules of grammar.

I fell for Case hook, line, and sinker, and for all the right reasons. From the moment he finished his inaugural lecture, I'd have done pretty much anything for him.

I got right down to the business of being an ideal student. I'd outline my essay on the very day he assigned the topic, then finish it that night—a week ahead of time—often while feeding quarters into my dormitory's washer and dryer. This allowed me to devote the rest of the week to required reading in other courses and rehearsing as a music student. More importantly, it was my respect for the instructor that drove me to complete my assignments earlier rather than later. I was now deeply immersed in university life, bursting with pride, and driven to excel, and I had Franklin Case to thank for igniting a passion for higher learning in me.

Writing the required five-hundred-word essays was relatively easy for me because I loved to write and wanted very much to please and impress my instructor. Finding my muse wasn't always so easy, though. On one late-night occasion I had to enlist the services of a bottle of cheap wine to bring one of my harder-to-write essays to life. The result was a truly sophomoric, painfully extended metaphor having to do with my idea of hot, steamy sex. My recollection is that it barely slipped in under the wire, earning me a lowly B- and causing me lingering guilt for weeks afterward.

My first year in college was in nearly every respect a personal triumph. As a student of music, my grades were sky-high. I'd also earned a B+ in freshman comp. While I would undoubtedly have been happier with an A, it didn't really matter. I considered a B+ from Franklin Case a singular accomplishment.

Then, somewhere in the second semester of my sophomore year, personal issues began to wedge their way into my classwork, and the once-tranquil waters of academia turned noticeably choppy. I missed my high school girlfriend, but at the same time I'd begun to suffer enormous guilt for having fallen in love with a music department classmate—an accomplished pianist named Karen Gonda who'd been assigned to accompany me in a performance of composer Albert Périlhou's *Ballade*. That composition—a beloved staple of the flutist's repertoire—was a song certain to plunge the lethal knife of passion into the hearts of two young and libidinous musicians. For me at least, the knife went deep and stayed there for months, causing both exhilaration and pain in equal portions.

Simultaneously, my relationship with my parents had begun to come apart at the seams. They'd grown increasingly unhappy with the changes in my appearance, behavior, and attitudes, and I was equally disenchanted with their intolerance and insensitivity. We hardly knew each other anymore, and to make matters worse, I'd begun to get into financial trouble. When my next semester's tuition came due, I hadn't the funds to cover it.

Determined to pay my bills and stay in school, but too proud and too stubborn to turn to my disapproving parents for financial help, I grew desperate and decided to approach someone and ask for a short-term loan to get me over the hump.

I ran through the list of music department faculty and decided on Mitchell Osadchuk, the Department of Music's portly, immaculately groomed trumpet instructor and brass ensemble coach. He seemed the most likely professor to hear my plea and grant me a loan. The next morning I approached him, full of apprehension but reasonably certain that here was a man of decency and compassion who respected me as a musician and would help pull me out of the financial pit I'd dug for myself.

I soon learned the hard way that his unquestioned faith in me was more my delusion than reality.

"Look at you!" he said with pursed lips and a look just short of revulsion. "Your shoes aren't polished. Your hair is uncombed. Your clothes aren't pressed. No, I will *not* help you." And then the distinguished professor Mitchell Osadchuk—the man with the perfectly tailored suit, the impeccably manicured hands, and the demeanor of a man righteously certain of himself—pivoted around and headed smugly down the hall to his office.

I stood there for a moment, feeling ashamed and humiliated, then gathered up what was left of my crumbling self-esteem and left the building. Of course, Mitchell Osadchuk owed me nothing beyond his services as an instructor, but at the time I was too naive and too self-absorbed to understand that. I had classes to attend, papers to write, and rehearsing to do, but looming over me was the specter of almost certain expulsion from school. My mood was increasingly, unbearably dark.

That night, lying alone in my dorm room and staring at the ceiling, I searched with quiet desperation for a solution. *Which would be worse*, I thought, *crawling home to my parents, who'll be in no mood to deal with my self-inflicted crisis, or approaching another professor who might be more inclined than Mr. Osadchuk to come to my rescue?*

Suddenly I remembered Franklin Case. The image of him on that very first day of freshman comp—his look of imperturbability, his wry, professorial demeanor, and the sort of kindly expression every young boy yearns to see in his father—came to me with almost biblical force. As I lay in the deafening silence of my dorm room, something told me to go to him, leave my shame behind me, and ask for his help.

I found my way to a pay phone early the next morning, and with shaking hands and quivering lip, dialed him up. He answered on the third ring, then listened patiently as I spun my tale of familial angst and financial crisis.

"All right, Mr. Bachelder," he said with the same soothing voice that had so ingratiated me to him on the first day of classes. "No need to tell me the details. I want you to meet me in the parking lot of Ypsilanti Savings Bank this coming Saturday at 9:00 a.m. See you there!"

I didn't really know what he had in mind, but I must have blubbered into the phone my heartfelt appreciation for his kindness. I suspect I also had tears in my eyes at that moment—a response not altogether unusual for me when confronted with objects of beauty or acts of supreme kindness.

Bright and early Saturday morning, I drove to the bank as instructed, parked my car, and saw Franklin Case waiting for me. He greeted me with a warm smile and a remark or two about the weather—it was a lovely, blue-sky-with-clouds kind of day—then handed me a sealed envelope he'd just gotten from the bank. I accepted it with a combination of embarrassment and deep appreciation, then slipped it into the inside pocket of my jacket without looking to see what he'd loaned me.

"Is a hundred dollars enough?" he asked.

A hundred dollars? I was dumbfounded. But I also knew it wasn't enough to rescue me from my sinking ship, so I gathered up my courage and told him the truth. "The fact is that I owe nearly three hundred in tuition, due three weeks from today."

He looked at me with a look of extraordinary empathy and understanding, swept the shock of hair back from his forehead in the usual way, then said, "Meet me this coming Saturday, and the Saturday after that, and I'll loan you one hundred additional dollars on each of those days."

I was now a nineteen-year-old and still wet around the ears, so other than issuing a polite thank you, I said nothing. I knew he could tell how embarrassed I was to have asked him for money, and I felt like an absolute fool.

"You know," he said, "one day several years ago, a friend of mine came to me and asked for a sizable amount of money to tide him over in a crisis. I was strapped for cash at the time. I thought about it, hesitated, then told him I really wasn't in a position to lend that amount of money to him. I learned later that he'd committed suicide, and I vowed I'd never again say no to someone in such obvious need."

I met Case on each of the next two Saturdays, accepted the additional installments of his loan, paid my tuition the day before it was due, then returned to my academic routine and finished the semester, filled to overflowing with appreciation for the gift of a second chance.

Many things, both entirely predictable and genuinely unexpected, happened to me over the next few months. Unable to find peace of mind in my faltering relationship with my parents, I did the unthinkable and, in spite of Franklin Case's help with my expenses, dropped out of school in the middle of my sophomore year. My favorite music teacher, Dr. William "Bill" Fitch—a man who'd championed me as a capable, highly motivated student of music—was visibly and vocally upset. He couldn't understand why I'd chosen to leave school, and I was just as confused as he was about my reasons for leaving.

Franklin Case and the Loan

Out of school and back in my hometown again, I reconnected with my high school girlfriend and married her, but when the marriage ended in divorce, I took a position as a construction site accountant in New Baltimore, Michigan. It was the last occupation I could ever have imagined pursuing, and I detested the work. For me—a wildly idealistic young man with artistic sensibilities that no one in my family appeared to understand—the work of an accountant, stranded in a mobile-home headquarters on the far edge of nowhere, was both appallingly mind-numbing and spiritually debilitating.

It took only a few weeks for me to realize that the work site in New Baltimore, a God-forsaken expanse of treeless land laced with a never-ending labyrinth of gas pipes, was not for me. And it wasn't just the topography that made the assignment so undesirable: I had a crude, grossly overweight boss named Vernon Buttles, and I was forced every day to go out into the field and deal with a surly ragtag army of itinerant welders—men with reprehensible ideas about women and life in general. I knew in my heart that the classroom was where I really belonged. A few days later I said my perfunctory goodbye to Mr. Buttles, borrowed additional money for tuition—this time from my hometown bank—and was back in school the next September.

I remarried in graduate school, systematically repaid Case's loan while finishing a degree in music, and then, having fallen head-over-heels in love with English and American literature, accepted a teaching fellowship in freshman composition. Ironically, I found myself teaching at the very same university where I'd signed up for freshman comp only seven years earlier.

Through nearly five additional decades of living since that encounter, I had never forgotten Franklin Case. In 2012 I decided to track him down, but I needed first to learn whether he was still alive, and if so, how I might get in touch with him and express my appreciation for both the loan and the gift of his exemplary kindness and compassion.

With the help of the investigative gifts and computer savvy of my daughter in Cincinnati, I finally learned that he was still living with his wife in Ypsilanti, the town where a decade or so ago he'd finished a distinguished career as university professor, author, and playwright.

I wrote a long, rambling note of appreciation to him, and in a few weeks he responded with characteristic warmth and generosity: Would I like to go out for a meal with him the next time I was in Ypsilanti, where I could regale him with tales of my many adventures over the years?

Happy Dawg Walks the Sad Man

Fig. 49. Franklin Case at Haab's Restaurant, Ypsilanti, Michigan, on the day of our reunion (March 2013).

The answer—a resounding yes—could not have been otherwise. I was already scheduled to visit my then eighty-eight-year-old father in nearby Jackson, so a visit with Case would be easy to arrange.

Early in March of 2013 I showed up at Haab's Restaurant in downtown Ypsilanti, a legendary establishment I'd often spent time in while an undergraduate. To kill time until his arrival, I photographed both the restaurant's colorful facade and portions of the adjacent shops along West Michigan Avenue.

At the appointed time I stepped into the lobby, and moments later, Case strode past the window and into the restaurant. Though nearly fifty years had passed since I first saw him, I recognized him instantly.

Other than the snowy white of his carefully combed hair, I could see no discernible difference in the man. His posture was still ramrod straight, perhaps emblematic of his time as a Korean War veteran. He had the physique of a thirty-year-old, putting my growing asymmetrical plumpness to shame, and in his eyes I saw the same unmistakeable kindness and high character that defined him for me on that long-ago first day in his classroom.

We had a warm and poignant reunion that day, touching on the handful of experiences that offered proof of our shared place in time. To my astonishment, Case remembered that in my sophomore year I'd published an essay in *Cellar Roots*, the campus literary magazine he'd founded and nourished in the early '60s.

We also discovered our mutual disdain for a brash, ultra-conservative grad student named Joe Sobran, the darling of a small handful of faculty members for his arrogant self-assurance and his near-encyclopedic knowledge of Shakespearian literature.

Sobran, along with a dozen others (including me), was a graduate teaching fellow in the Department of English at EMU in 1969. At the time, it would have been nearly impossible to find anyone who didn't agree that Sobran was the most insufferably narcissistic young academic on campus.

Ever the contrarian, Sobran took great pride in his membership in a hidebound, curmudgeonly group of Shakespearean scholars who, in spite of a plenitude of evidence to the contrary, insisted that Shakespeare never wrote the plays ascribed to him. The author, they were certain, was the Renaissance English poet Edward de Vere, the 17th Earl of Oxford.

During our reunion I learned that Sobran, newly arrived on campus and oozing with the same repulsive hubris Case had warned us about on the first day of classes, met Case inadvertently one day in the faculty lounge, then haughtily rebuffed Case's generous offer of advice about how best to navigate the political waters of the English department.

"Why would I care what you think?" he said, "You don't have a doctorate, do you?"

When in 1971 the university invited arch-conservative William F. Buckley to appear on campus, a great many professors opposed the idea of playing host to such a controversial figure—but not Sobran. He wrote a letter to the school's newspaper voicing his unqualified support for the Buckley appearance, and when Buckley saw and read the letter, he fell for Sobran's unctuous, snake-oil self-promotion, invited him to New York for an interview, and hired him shortly afterward as a cub writer / reporter for the fabled *National Review*.

Many years later, the two came to philosophical blows in the wake of a remark Sobran made that Buckley construed to be anti-Semitic. Sobran had accused Buckley of being "jumpy about Jews," and Buckley, his feathers famously ruffled over the incident, fired his one-time protégé.

In 2010, to my great surprise, I came across Joe Sobran's obituary in the *New York Times*. This maddeningly obdurate man, so certain of his brilliance and the righteousness of his thinking, died at the age of only sixty-four from kidney failure related to diabetes.

"My friend Joe Sobran died last Thursday," wrote ultra-conservative axe-thrower Ann Coulter, "and [with his passing] the world lost its greatest writer." Coulter was a fierce defender of Sobran's political views, and in her tribute she credited him with having had an enormous influence on her own writing style. She also revealed to the world, perhaps unwittingly, that she has what can only be called an astonishing gift for hyperbole.

One is tempted to conjecture that in the end, Joe Sobran became the author of his very own Shakespearean tragedy when his admittedly reckless remark caused Buckley to relieve him of his post at the *National Review*. The mordant, high-octane hubris that defined him on so many occasions may finally have caught up with him.

Sobran will always represent for me the polar opposite of the values that Case embodied: decency, humility, compassion, and an uncompromising devotion to both intellectual inquiry and the sometimes precarious business of living a life truly worth living.

Franklin Case is to my way of thinking the very prototype of the effective teacher—a man who on that very first day in the classroom, with one carefully chosen word and a warm glow of humanity in his eyes, managed to etch a place of honor in my memory that has remained there, unspoiled, for more than half a century. He stands as a powerful reminder to all of us that erudition alone does not make a teacher. To be worthy of the title, one must also have two absolutely essential qualities—palpable warmth and genuine humility. No teacher has ever been truly beloved without them.

Franklin Case and the Loan

It was my great good fortune, fifty years ago, that the man whose name I'd chosen entirely at random from a nearly unreadable course catalogue (simply because it had within its mellifluous rhythms a hint of adventure) had both warmth and humility in happy abundance. I can't help think that if there were more teachers at every academic level like Franklin Case, the world we live in would be a very different, infinitely more rewarding place.

Fig. 50. *Gargoyle Goat and the Swamp Dwellers* by Ross Bachelder.

※ Tiny Novelette 4 ※

Gargoyle Goat and the Swamp Dwellers

For countless years, Gargoyle Goat had lived alone in the West African country of what is now Guinea-Bissau, in a thatch-roofed cottage overlooking the mighty Atlantic. His home in the seaside village of Tombali was flanked on the east by mangrove swamps teeming with exotic wildlife and flora of unimaginable beauty.

His friends called him Goat for short because of the one great horn protruding inexplicably from his skull. Some said he was a distant relative of the manatees who've lurked for centuries in the canals and estuaries, lunching on seagrass and basking in warm, shallow waters beneath the irresistible sunlight of a summer afternoon. Others thought he was simply an unusually diminutive unicorn, or perhaps a genetic aberration yet to be identified and doomed to extinction.

Whatever he was, for as long as anyone could remember, Goat would drape the harness of his calabash over one shoulder each morning, then take the blowfish taxi to the aqua pasture, where he'd stop at the Lily Pad Diner, have a late breakfast of pan-fried yam fufu sprinkled with grains of paradise, then kick back and treat himself to a steaming cup of warga mixed with fresh, native palm wine. Afterward he'd set himself up in the town square and make driving, virtuoso rhythms on his calabash as the Tombalians happily danced their afternoons away.

What the residents of Tombali *didn't* know was that after the dancers finished dancing and went home for the evening, Goat would move his operation to the far side of the swamps, then serenade the legions of swamp dwellers—creatures for whom he quite understandably had a far greater affinity—beneath the warm yellow light of the Guinea-Bissau moon.

He loved jamming with the jabirus, flinging with the flamingos, fiddling with the crabs, and grooving with the mangrove monitors. Even the spoonbills, wallabies, and mudskippers would join in the fun, until one night, when the poisonous

Sea Snake and his henchman, Flying Fox, who hated noise and loved to make trouble, decided they'd had it with the late-night revelries.

To put a stop to the swampland cacophonies, they sneaked up on Goat while he wasn't looking, impaled his beloved calabash on the end of his horn, and tied his tail in knots so tight that he lost his balance and tumbled headfirst into the swamp.

His horn was stuck deep into the mud, and unless he managed somehow to pull it out, and fast, he would surely drown. Then the rhythmic thrum of the calabash would be forever silenced, and the dancing of the swamp dwellers would be no more.

But the jabirus and mudskippers—and indeed all of the other loyal swamp dwellers—weren't about to let either their sacred ritual or their dear friend Goat come to an unhappy end.

And so, with only seconds to spare, they pulled Goat up from the mud, administered CPR, presented him with a new and even more elegant calabash with which to pound out his driving rhythms, and banished Sea Snake and Flying Fox forever from the pomp and splendor of the mangrove swamps. Gargoyle Goat was back in charge of the swamp dwellers—and the dancers of Tombali, too—and once again, all was right with the world.

Chapter 9

A Tale of Three Commissions

The Harbor-Scene Saw, Bernie and the King, and Shapes from Deep within Me

Commissions are not for the faint of heart. I've accepted a few in my nearly twenty years as a visual artist, and many memorable tales—some triumphant, others cautionary—emerged from those experiences. Three of my commissions were colorful enough to have carved themselves indelibly into my consciousness, and for better or worse, after many years of hibernation, the stories behind them have come out, begging to be told.

The Harbor-Scene Saw

In the world of music, the most notorious cliché is probably the jug band, complete with washboard percussion and washtub bass—the perfect Ma and Pa Kettle ensemble. In television, the most notorious cliché was, for all but a few diehard enthusiasts (including me), *The Benny Hill Show*. And in the visual arts community, what could be more hopelessly cliché than—God help us—a painting on a saw?

And yet that is precisely what I was asked nearly twenty years ago to create. It was my very first commission as a fledgling artist.

My commissioner was a fellow I'll call Lennie—an affable, homespun New Hampshirite with a cutting-edge saw-sharpening business and a propensity for hanging interminably over my table at breakfast places, wherever in the Seacoast area we happened to cross paths on a given morning.

For the proprietor of a saw-maintenance enterprise, he didn't appear to be especially sharp. And because he inevitably overstayed his welcome, he became for me the very archetype of the hapless boor. Nevertheless, I liked him. He was friendly, polite, and good-natured, and so I did my best to be both courteous and patient with him when he approached my table. I figured there had to be far worse things in the world than being dull, even in the world of saw sharpening.

One morning, after a good twenty minutes of hanging like a bat in a cave over my languishing breakfast—chit-chatting away, oblivious to the fact that I was trying my damnedest to read the morning paper—he went silent for nearly half a minute, then hit me up with a question.

"I see you do some drawin,'" he said, making note of the art books and drawing supplies I always had with me in the morning. "I was wonderin' if you could paint somethin' for me." He looked nervously down at the floor. The only thing missing was a solitary stalk of wheat dangling down from between his choppers.

"Possibly," I said, "but I'd need to know what you have in mind."

"A harbor scene. You know, boats and shoreline and stuff. On a saw."

"*On a saw?*" I gasped a little too audibly. "A *saw-scape?*" I sat there squirming, trying to imagine what my artist friends would say if they were to learn I'd agreed to paint a goddamn harbor scene on a saw. It would be a moment of supreme humiliation, and my career as an artist would be over in less time than it takes to trim off the end of a two-by-four.

"Well, you're pretty good at art," he said, cracking his knuckles as he shifted back and forth like a good ol' boy at a NASCAR event. Lennie really was a good man, and as I looked up at him from my unread newspaper and my breakfast-gone-cold, I couldn't help myself: I was flattered.

"I betcha you can do it!" he said. "I'd hang it up in my office. It'd be good for my business—and I'd pay you a hundred dollars to paint it for me."

Suddenly there were dollar signs where my retinas used to be. Finally, a project with some real *teeth* in it! I was hooked, and I hoped the souls of Picasso and Renoir would eventually forgive me for the blasphemy I was about to commit in the name of the almighty dollar.

"Okay," I said. "I'll do it for you." I shuddered inwardly while mouthing the words, and felt a knot of apprehension forming in my belly. "I'll come up with something, but give me a month or two. I'll have to do some fancy research to prepare for this one!"

"Great!" he said, but not one word more, and then he was gone.

A Tale of Three Commissions

The next morning I went straight to Baldface Books, across the border in Dover, New Hampshire, and thirty minutes later I walked out with a half-dozen secondhand coffee-table books full of pumped up, excessively romanticized photos of well-known coastlines and harbors in Maine and New Hampshire. Since I'd never painted a harbor scene—not on a canvas, not on a toilet seat, and certainly not on a saw—I had my work cut out for me and would need every visual aid I could come up with.

Later that afternoon I chose a dozen or so photographs from the books, laid them out tentatively on my worktable, identified the most desirable details from the lot of them, then pieced them together into a composition that I prayed would somehow manage to look authentic while strung out along the unlikely contours of a handsaw.

Throughout the process I fought off a terrifying vision of me as the very incarnation of that infamous New Hampshire farmer who sold his soul to the devil in return for immortality. And the way I was feeling, I knew that once my multi-toothed abomination made it into the public arena, I'd gladly pay a hefty fee to hire Daniel Webster as my defense attorney.

I bought a handsaw at Rocky's Ace Hardware in Dover, brought it home, and painted it storm-cloud gray. My plan was to play the more vibrant colors of my saw-scape against the neutral background, injecting as much energy into the scene as I could possibly muster.

If as an artist you've ever painted a sailboat, you'll know that capturing its proportions convincingly on canvas—the elegant triangulations of the jib and mainsail, the majestic sweep of the hull, the exact height and position of the mast—is among the most daunting challenges in all of nautical painting. It is next to impossible to slip even the most minute inaccuracies past the eagle-eye scrutiny of the sailboat aficionado. I figured I'd sweat blood—or perhaps unfiltered saltwater—while struggling to get a small armada of little boats correctly rendered against the water. At the same time I prayed that Lennie, my commissioner, knew even less than I did, either about sailboats or how to paint a credible schooner on a handsaw.

An equally daunting challenge was to paint anything close to accurate proportions onto the trapezoidal expanse of a typical handsaw, minus the handle—a substrate so ridiculously ill-suited for the rendering of a seascape—uh, *saw-scape*—that it was beyond laughable. It soon became painfully obvious to me that, in the matter of painting a harbor scene on a saw, I was clearly in over my head. My very first commission was not going at all swimmingly, and I knew with terrible certainty that

I'd never be satisfied with my effort. Instead of being thought of as a cut above the average saw painter, I was destined to become a notorious, inglorious hack.

In spite of the nauseating wave of foreboding washing over me—a growing fear that I was about to paint the worst damn harbor scene you ever saw—I forged ahead with the project. I laid in a distant stand of pine trees along the far shore of the harbor, interspersing them here and there with harbor-side cottages of various sizes and colors, then paused to consider what the weather might be like in my painting.

At a moment like this, an artist realizes that, for better or worse, he's suddenly in a position to play god. He's been blessed—some would say cursed—with the terrible, Thor-like power to do whatever suits his fancy with the elements. Will he dish out blistering, unrelenting sunlight; a roaring, house-flattening wind; or perhaps a fusillade of grapefruit-size hail? Standing there before his easel, he's about learn what it would be like to have unlimited, life-threatening power.

Whipping up a storm of the century sounded intriguing—and in a diabolical sort of way, downright fun—but considering what I remembered of Lennie's tepid personality and easygoing ways, I turned my back on the idea of a tempest and settled for tranquillity.

In my saw-scape, the boats would be bobbing in a harbor as gentle as a toddler's bath, and the trees would be still as a Buddhist temple. I'd chosen a palette more temperate than a Morandi still life, determined not to rock the boat, either in my sawtooth harbor or in the milk-warm mind of Lennie.

When the day of delivery arrived, I was prepared for anything from silent disapproval to caterwauling contempt. Would he merely sniff contemptuously at my effort, or get down and dirty and tell me it was crap?

We met in the parking lot of Ben Franklin Crafts in Somersworth, New Hampshire. Lennie saw me parked under a stand of pines, eased out of his pickup, and came loping toward me like a ranch hand in a horse opera.

"Got that *saw* painted?" he asked.

They'd probably not put it quite like that at Sotheby's, I thought while ceremoniously removing the saw from my Subaru. I was tempted to yank it out of the bag, prop it up on my knee, and play a tune or two on it before handing it over to him, but I knew better: it would crack the paint.

"All set!" I said, trying to put a smiley face on a potential fiasco. But as I waited for Lennie's response—at this point, even a modest grunt or groan would suffice—my mood was anything but sunny.

What came next was an eerie, disconcerting silence. People invariably exaggerate when relating what they've experienced in a crisis, but I swear Lennie stood as motionless as a tombstone for a good three minutes while trying to decide how he felt about my painting. I decided to hang tough and say nothing in response to his absurdly protracted pondering. He'd eventually tell me what he thought, and I'd eventually learn to live with his verdict.

"Well," he said, "it really isn't what I was looking for." I saw it coming, but I wasn't about to budge.

He continued to stand there with his hands in his pockets, looking for all the world as if he were deeply depressed and about to ask if I happened to know a good psychiatrist. It was shortly after 2:00 p.m. now, and the gulls circling above the parking lot, looking for discarded French fries from "school's out" teenagers, may as well have been buzzards preparing to swoop down and help themselves to the disintegrating carcass of my painterly roadkill.

"Okay," he murmured. "I guess I'll take it."

Not exactly a ringing endorsement, I thought as I folded up the bag I'd transported the painting in and headed for my car.

"Y'did whatcha could," he sighed, then slowly shook his head—a mournful hound dog on a failed hunt—and handed over my hundred dollars.

I watched him pull out into traffic with my painting next to him on the passenger seat, then got into my own car and drove back to Berwick, proud that I'd not demeaned myself by begging for his approval.

Did I permanently harm my reputation as an artist by agreeing to paint a harbor scene on a saw? I don't think so. What mattered most to me was not my reputation, but my integrity. Of course, one might fairly argue that it was reckless of me to take on a project whose very idea—painting on a handsaw instead of a high-quality canvas—was so deeply repugnant to the vast majority of "serious" artists.

For me, it was a different matter altogether. I knew I'd most likely lose the respect of a handful of fellow artists by agreeing to take on what they'd consider an unforgivably low-brow project. Indeed, some had already registered their disenchantment with me simply by virtue of the disdainful, nose-in-the-air expressions on their faces. But by coming across, for better or worse, with what Lennie needed—a simple picture on a humble saw—

I'd tested my mettle and learned both my serious limitations as an artist and the harsh realities of the marketplace.

I ought to have known it was going to be next to impossible for me—an artist blissfully untethered to the academic community—to please a conventional, college-trained mind. On top of that, the wild child in me relished the undeniable absurdity of it all—not just the idea of cramming an entire harbor onto a saw, but of the ludicrous circumstances I'd walked into as an artist. My funny bone had been tickled to distraction by Lenny's request, and there was no way I could bring myself to walk away from such a challenge.

By floating a battalion of miniature sailboats on the surface of a saw, I was thumbing my nose at the almost comic uptightness of those academics, so brilliantly lampooned in the film *Art School Confidential*. For one brief interlude I'd been the bad boy of the Seacoast arts scene, and it felt perversely, outrageously, Monty Python delicious.

After suffering through the escapade of Lennie and the handsaw, I was now in the market for a more uplifting experience. I'd soon be asked to complete yet another commission, and this time I prayed fervently that it wouldn't be on a saw.

Bernie and the King

I met Bernie Severance more than twenty years ago somewhere on the breakfast circuit in southern Maine and Seacoast New Hampshire. I'd been going out alone for breakfast for years, always less for the pleasure of eating than for the time alone to read, write, and savor those treasured pockets of serenity that make the rest of our frenzied lives more tolerable.

While some mornings were painfully monotonous—lacking that romance-of-the-road mindset that makes us eager to bound out of bed and get on with our lives—others were delightfully unpredictable and, on occasion, full of unexpected adventure. On mornings like that, I couldn't imagine wanting to be anywhere else but tucked into my favorite booth in some out-of-the-way diner, still half asleep but alert enough to sip my coffee while dreaming, however foolishly, of literary triumph and occupational bliss.

The first time I saw Bernie—early one morning in a Burger King restaurant in Somersworth—he was so quiet and so apparently diffident that he seemed more like a promotional cardboard cutout than a real, live diner, half-asleep and in for his daily fix of pancakes and coffee.

I don't think he spoke more than two dozen words altogether in the times I saw him around the area. He'd become the "Silent Cal" of the Seacoast, addicted to breakfast and IHOPping from restaurant to restaurant in search of the perfect omelet.

And then one day he showed up at Ben Franklin Crafts in Rochester, where I managed the frame shop and Franklin Gallery.

"Got a question for you," he said, employing more words in that one sentence than I was accustomed to hearing from him in a ten-minute chat. "I know you told me once you're an artist. Any chance you could paint a portrait for me?"

"Well, sure!" I said. "Of course, it depends a whole lot on what sort of portrait you're looking for."

"Oh, just an old Army buddy and me," he said, getting more and more loquacious with each additional utterance. "It was in Germany, in the '50s."

"Sounds like something I can handle," I said, licking my chops at the prospect of yet another lucrative commission. "But I'll need reference photos—as many as you can come up with—before I agree to this."

"Yup. I can do that," he said with more understatement than a French mime with a throat ailment.

The next day he dropped by the frame shop, left me a manila folder stuffed with the reference photos I'd requested, then turned around, tipped his cap, and tossed a gushing, monosyllabic "Bye!" over his shoulder as he headed for the exit. *A very nice man*, I thought (and a study in prolixity if there ever was one).

Once he was gone, I opened the folder and pulled out the stack of photos. Clearly, they'd not been well taken care of. Many of them had cracks in the emulsion, and nearly all of them were severely faded from having been exposed over the years to excessive amounts of light. They had the crenellated borders so characteristic of '50s-era snapshots. *Probably from a Brownie Hawkeye*, I thought. They also had a *Leave It to Beaver* innocence about them that would have put a smile on Ward Cleaver's face.

I sifted through the stack of photos, snapping them down onto the counter one at a time like cards in a game of solitaire. The first dozen or so were of Bernie, dressed in Army fatigues and hanging around with his bunkmates. He looked comfortable in the shoes of a soldier, and right at home with the boys.

The next three photos in the stack, of a handsome young man standing with one lanky arm slung over Bernie's shoulder, stopped me in my tracks. Beneath the man's army-issue cap was a smile worthy of a Hollywood star, and yet he had a homespun, boy-next-door quality about him. *Such a pretty face for just another average joe in the Army,* I thought. *There has to be a story here.*

And then it all started to make sense: '50s-era, non-combat assignment in Germany, face like a movie-industry hunk. I began to look more carefully, and all the information I needed—the toothy, country boy smile, the trademark snarl of the upper lip, the Adonis-like perfection of the face—was right there in those photos. By God, it was *Elvis*!

I called Bernie the next morning. "Bernie!" I said. "Are you telling me you were actually buddies with *Elvis Presley* while in the Army, or are those photos just doctored up?"

"No doctoring," he said. "They're the real thing." His voice held all the excitement of a man who'd just been told his shirts are done at the cleaners.

I was still in shock. "Well," I said, "did you do all sorts of off-duty stuff with him? I mean, were you really close?"

"Nah, he was just kinda there a lot. Anyway, I was hoping you'd do a portrait of him and me together."

"You're asking *me* to paint a portrait of you and *Elvis*?" I said. "I don't know if I could pull that off!"

Everybody knows what Elvis Presley looked like! I thought. How could I possibly convince Bernie—or anyone else, for that matter—that the man next to him in the portrait I'd painted was actually Elvis?

"Oh, I think you can do it," he said. "Besides, I don't know any other artists. Look, I'll pay you five hundred dollars. Would that be enough?"

He needn't have asked. I said yes, then wiped the drool off my face and patted my billfold.

"Good," he said, "that's good. I'll come by in a day or two and settle with you."

The next morning he showed up bright and early at the frame shop, reached for his wallet, pulled out a fistful of Andy Jacksons, and handed me my five hundred on the spot. "Just call me when the painting's ready, and I'll come down and pick it up. There's no hurry."

For the next several nights I barely slept. Every few hours I'd sit bolt upright in bed, breaking out in a cold sweat at the prospect of trying to capture a convincing likeness of what was then the most publicized face on the planet. Then, each day after work, I'd race home and pull dozens of Presley photos off the internet—images I badly needed in order to fill in the details that were either barely legible or completely obliterated in the snapshots Bernie had given me.

When those weren't enough to reassure me, I headed down to Barnes & Noble and purchased not one but three profusely illustrated books about Presley's time in Germany with Priscilla, with his bunkmates, and with women from around the world who could never get enough news about his every grin and grimace while in uniform.

Once I'd chosen the snapshot with the most favorable pose, I had it enlarged and printed, then transferred the image to my canvas, employing the usual grid method. It was time to get down to business, so I tackled the project with an unsettling combination of let's-get-it-done gusto and a grim determination to wrestle it into compliance with the one and only photo I had to go on. If I were to fail to capture even a tolerable likeness of the King, Bernie would never forgive me, and neither—bless his dear, departed soul—would Elvis.

From the moment I first touched my brush to the canvas, I felt as if I'd been sent down into the painterly bowels of Hell—a Dante's *Inferno* of high expectations, just for artists. I can't begin to tell you how many times I repainted the most telling portions of Presley's one-of-a-kind facial anatomy. The nose, the lips, the eyes, the eyebrows, the cheekbones—every feature was unlike those of any other human, and nearly impossible to render with enough accuracy to convince me that the man I'd just painted was really Elvis.

The worst challenge by far was that inimitable snarl. Was he smiling or sneering? Perhaps he was just flirting into the camera, knowing full well that even the most minute and fleeting movements of his famous lip would be sent around the world within hours for all to see and learn cold. Capturing the essence of the man who would one day become the world's hunka hunka burnin' love was going to be harder than scaling Mt. Everest in knickers and flip-flops.

And getting Elvis right wasn't my only daunting challenge. I was also being paid big bucks to nail down Bernie's distinctive countenance. His last name—Severance—was quintessentially British, and with his rosy cheeks, creamy complexion, and unassuming demeanor, so was he. To me, Bernie was the Pillsbury Doughboy in Army fatigues, and somehow I'd have to find a way to capture the wonderful, little-boy innocence he'd managed to carry with him into adulthood, working from reference photos so grainy and ill-focused as to be indecipherable.

To achieve anything like accuracy in my depiction of the uniforms, which were hopelessly faded in the reference photo, I was forced to track down and then study a book devoted entirely to the history of military uniforms. And given my undeniable weakness in rendering fabric of any kind, I worried that simply by having agreed to paint those uniforms, I was headed for a monumental aesthetic train wreck—a painterly catastrophe from which I might never recover.

When the portrait was finally done, I called Bernie and arranged to meet him the next morning in the parking lot at Ben Franklin Crafts. After all, I knew from experience that a parking lot is the best possible place to hand over a commission. This way, I figured no one else would be able to see the result of my labors.

When I pulled into the parking lot, Bernie was waiting for me, slumped down in the driver's seat of his car and staring vacantly through the windshield. By the time I'd gotten the painting out of my car, he was standing next to me, ready to claim his portrait.

"Well, here it is!" I said. "I really enjoyed doing this for you!" (*Liar, liar, pants on fire!*) At this point, I was prepared to say anything to save face and complete the transaction.

I then waited eagerly for his response. Would seeing my portrait unleash a torrent of pent-up emotions—poignant memories of his privileged time in Germany with the very man who'd one day become the king of rock 'n' roll?

Apparently it didn't.

His only response was "Yup." One word, three letters, no discernible pulse.

He smiled faintly at me, took *Bernie and the King* out of my hands, held it gingerly in front of him without really looking at it, then walked over to his car and slipped the painting down onto the floor behind the driver's seat. Then, in less time than it takes to swat a fly or flick a booger, Bernie Severance was gone. I drove back to Berwick under a cloud of ineffable sadness tempered by an enormous sense of relief that I was finally out from under the pressure of turning a two-dimensional canvas into a three-dimensional Elvis.

Thousands of artists had tried it before me, but few had really succeeded. What made me think I could ever succeed at such an insurmountable task?

The answer lay deep within me. For as long as I can remember, I've harbored an enormous appetite for attempting to do the undoable. It may have come from a childhood in which my parents seldom if ever told me that with a little hard work and a whole lot of self-assurance, I could achieve anything I set out to do.

It was also the era of Wernher von Braun and the race for Cold War supremacy, and one way or another, members of the younger generation were being told by pretty much everyone around them—parents, space-race enthusiasts, politicians, and the press—that if we weren't in the sciences, we probably weren't very intelligent.

It wasn't until I was well into grad school—after years of being stereotyped as an intellectual lightweight with touchy-feely tendencies—that I learned an invaluable lesson: people in the sciences really aren't inherently more intelligent than everyone else.

Was my portrait of Bernie and Elvis really all that bad? In some ways, perhaps it was; in other ways, I'm not buying it. Part of being a true professional is having the courage to admit your weaknesses while simultaneously working to overcome them. That's where the stubborn streak in me came into play. No one was going to tell me I shouldn't at least try to capture the face of Elvis—or Adolf Hitler or Marilyn Monroe, for that matter—on a blank, thirsty canvas.

Did I have all of the technical competence I needed to pull off the assignment when I so blithely agreed to do it? Absolutely not! But there has always been a part of me that learns best not from within the stultifying atmosphere of a classroom, but by the liberating, exhilarating seat of my pants.

Bernie and Elvis may at times have been a torment to paint, but for a time, at least, they'd become my two best friends, simply by reminding me of both my obvious strengths and my glaring weaknesses. Then, without needing to say more than a *Yup* and a *Thank you, Ma'am*, they challenged me to get down to work, correct my deficiencies, and get on with the business of making art and believing in myself.

Shapes from Deep within Me

Bill Daughtry, who lives in Gonic, New Hampshire, and has been active for many years in a round-robin group of French-language enthusiasts in nearby Berwick, Maine, is a handsomely dressed, fastidiously groomed man—articulate, personable, and remarkably well informed about history and politics.

Shapes from Deep within Me came about when Daughtry approached me one day on the recommendation of a friend and asked if I might be willing to create a work of art to add to the remarkably diverse collection in his apartment. I'd admired him from a distance but had never been social with him, so the mere fact that he asked me to create a work of art for his home meant a lot to me.

"What sort of artwork are you looking for?" I asked him after he'd finished marching me around his home to see his collection.

"Well, I'm not really sure," he said. "Right now, I just know I'd like to have you create a drawing. I don't have many of them, and I'd like to solve that problem. And I know that what you're going to draw for me has to be just the right size, when framed, to fit comfortably into a particular space."

He escorted me to a place near one corner of his dining room, then pointed at a gap between two framed artworks. "Right here, between these two paintings," he said. "You see, I like the art in my home to blend into my decor and be well positioned in relation to the other works."

I asked him for a yardstick, and together we measured what would be the exact size of the work he needed. He declared that it would need to be vertical in configuration and precisely 6" x 23". "No more and no less," he said with a stern expression on his wise, patrician face.

I couldn't help but be a little intimidated by both his requirement that the commissioned work be exactly one size and one size only, and by the disarming ambiguity of his taste in art. "I like abstract stuff," he said, "but not *too* abstract. Know what I mean?"

I did not know what he meant, but I agreed to come up with an artwork that would be exactly 6" x 23". Then I promised to submit the finished piece for his approval within a month or two. In effect, I'd just agreed to create a work on spec and take the consequences if he didn't like it enough to purchase it.

Once we'd determined the size of the piece, we began to talk about compensation—the fair market value of the work I was about to create. I was in no position to ask for an exorbitant amount. The truth is that I was hungry more for another commission to add to my résumé than for the money I'd get for completing the project. Bill agreed to pay me a hundred dollars for the finished work—but only if it met his approval.

That night, at home in my studio, I spent a lot of time trying to decide what to draw, wondering all the while where on earth I'd found the audacity to tell Mr. William Daughtry, appreciator of fine art, that I was sure I could create a piece he'd be proud to own.

In at least one respect I knew just what I was doing, simply because I'd done it many times before. I've always loved throwing myself into what seemed like impossible challenges, and then, after much sweating and worrying, managing to reach deep within myself and come up with the goods.

A Tale of Three Commissions

My appetite for derring-do can be insatiable. I decided right then and there to create not one piece but *three*. That way, I figured, Daughtry could choose his favorite drawing from the three, I'd have a greater chance of making a sale, and the two he didn't choose would be all set for future exhibits. *Not a bad strategy*, I thought to myself as the ideas began to form themselves in my subconscious like Jell-O in a mold.

The first piece I created, *Like an Egyptian*, was nearly entirely abstract and highly stylized—a kind of Art Deco construction featuring beige-tinted line work, hints of Egyptian monumentalism, and a light sprinkling of Paul Klee. I labored mightily over it, making many adjustments along the way until I was reasonably certain that as a composition it was both balanced and dynamic.

The second piece—a complex, interlocking accumulation of faces, trees, and flowers, entitled *Up from the Medieval*—was purely figurative. It began as a kind of Middle Ages fantasy, then evolved into what could only be described as a crazy aesthetic salad prepared in the kitchen of a madcap chef.

As I got deeper into the project, an indefinable narrative of sorts began to emerge. The faces—some frowning, some tearful, all floating in a tangle of delicately flowered bushes and finely tentacled trees—had a certain messianic urgency about them, tinged with either simple regret or intolerable sadness.

Along the left-side perimeter was a nude whose hands and legs grew directly from the branches of a tree and were poetically intertwined with them. Portions of my rendering of her didn't come out especially well, so I camouflaged her with additional tree limbs, making it difficult for anyone to see her on first inspection. She became my beautiful mystery woman, and the fact that she was difficult to pin down as a figure contributed significantly to the melancholy aura of my drawing.

Two down and one to go. Things were going smoothly enough, but as I prepared to create a third drawing, identical in size and configuration to the others but with its own unique personality, I realized I had a daunting task ahead of me.

I'd also begun to feel the pressure of the deadline for the project, so it made sense for me to cut a panel of mat board, then carry it and my drawing supplies with me each day. That way, I could work on the third drawing wherever I happened to be, both before and after work—usually in a restaurant, over tea. Each morning, for a good two weeks, I'd lay the panel on the table at my booth, assemble my supplies, stare off into the void, and wait for some fragmentary idea that would light the fuse of creativity for a third time and send me on my way.

Fig. 51. *Shapes from Deep within Me* by Ross Bachelder.

I started in the upper left-hand corner of the panel, sketching a tiny, purely abstract image, then laid in another very different image—also abstract—next to it. Suddenly, a plan for the panel emerged. I'd systematically lay in a complex network of tiny abstract images, one at a time but in line with certain basic rules: each new image had to be utterly unlike the one before, and yet clearly in spatial and emotional rapport with it.

Over more than two weeks I added image after image using gel pen, chalk, hard and soft leads, and white pencil, until the entire 6" x 23" panel had become a tapestry of interlocking shapes, each with what I hoped was its own unassailable integrity, and yet all working harmoniously together—a kind of chamber recital for the eye, performed by dozens of tiny instruments, each with their very own visual "sound."

It remains to this day my favorite of all the works I've done, and I doubt I'll ever be able to make another quite as successful—as true both to itself and to me—as this one. Were it possible, I'd be content to learn, long after my death, that *Shapes from Deep within Me* had emerged as my signature accomplishment as an artist.

When I'd completed *Shapes from Deep within Me*, it was time to call Bill Daughtry and arrange to show him the results of my labor. On the appointed day I drove to Gonic, lined the three framed drawings up on his kitchen table, and waited to see which one he'd choose—or whether he'd choose one at all.

He finally settled on *Like an Egyptian*, the very first one I did. My second effort, *Up from the Medieval*, clearly failed to impress him.

I was at first a little surprised that Daughtry chose *Like an Egyptian* over the others, then greatly relieved that he passed over *Shapes from Deep within Me*. It meant that, until the piece was either sold or pulled out of circulation, I'd have the pleasure of watching *Shapes* travel from exhibit to exhibit and back again—a piece with an uncertain future, but with its own unique personality, ready and willing to speak to any who might wish to experience its peculiar charms. Of course, I'll be proud if it finally sells, but it's been with me long enough now that I feel it's a bit like a seventeen-year-old on the verge of adulthood: I'll wish it well, but I will hate to see it go.

Chapter 10
Philadelphia Story
My Intoxicating Brush with Bucky

As a child growing up near the sleepy village of Rives Junction, Michigan, I had only a parochial, small-town perspective. It was in some ways an idyllic existence, with fields of swaying corn; country lanes that invited long days of safe, Tom Sawyer roaming; trees with plump black cherries; and bushes with unimaginably delicious red raspberries.

I attended a series of quaint one-room schools from kindergarten through grade six, and while the warm, familial experiences there contributed significantly to the empathetic part of me, they did little to encourage big-city aspirations. Nor did my parents—who'd lived through World War II and were now just thankful to have washed their hands of Hitler and settled into a more placid existence—ever really speak to me of soaring dreams and lofty ambitions.

It was up to me, with the help of a handful of caring teachers, to ignite the fires of intellectual inquiry in my belly and send myself off to college. I earned degrees in music and English literature, finished a graduate teaching fellowship, married, and started a family. Then—just two weeks after Richard Nixon resigned the presidency and went home to California with his tail between his legs and his place in history irretrievably tarnished—we moved to Maine. Just five years later, I'd embark on a Boston-to-Philly adventure that would have enormous impact on both my future and my feelings about myself. This is the story of that adventure.

In the summer of 1979 I traveled with a friend from my home in southern Maine to the City of Brotherly Love to interview R. Buckminster Fuller, the world-renowned philosopher, inventor, architect, and visionary, hoping to write and publish a magazine article about him. I'd harbored a longtime passion for the man—his unconventional ways of thinking, his genius as an inventor and philosopher, and his lineal and philosophical connections to his grandaunt, the early feminist and New England Transcendentalist Margaret Fuller.

I had little money then. Only five years before, at the age of thirty, I'd moved with my wife and daughter from Michigan to Maine. While my wife, Marilyn, had secured a position as a public school music teacher, I was less occupationally settled, writing as a freelancer, performing as a musician, and speaking publicly on occasion about everything from New England Transcendentalism and the music of Charles Ives to active fatherhood and the fair distribution of labor within the traditional family.

It was the era of Germaine Greer, Bella Abzug, and Gloria Steinem and her earthshaking brainchild, *Ms.* magazine. As a deeply committed husband and father, I found myself listening intently to what the feminists were telling men and women about their roles in childrearing. For reasons both scholarly and practical, I became motivated enough to appear on the public television show *Woman*, hosted by Sandra Elkin and aired on station WNED in Buffalo; on *The Tom Larson Show* at WSBK Television (Channel 38) in Boston; and on the Maine Public Broadcasting Network in Orono, Maine—all well-established forums in which I was asked to talk about what it was like to be a "house husband" while my wife was serving as the official breadwinner. I felt certain I could make a lasting contribution, however modest, to the debate about active fatherhood and smart parenting.

At the time I was especially keen on the idea of becoming a freelance magazine writer. Penning articles for regional and national magazines, I reasoned, would give me yet another important pulpit from which to preach, not only about male feminism but about any other issues that struck me as worthy of my time and energy. I'd already published articles in two magazines—*Sepia* (out of Chicago) and *New Hampshire Profiles* (based in the capital city of Concord). It was time now to make a bold move and add an even more significant article to my growing list of publishing credits.

To that end I wrote to Lloyd Shearer, the writer of "Walter Scott's Personality Parade"—a weekly question-and-answer column in *Parade* magazine—and asked him what I might do to jump-start my career as a magazine writer. He sent my letter back to me a few weeks later with some brief but sage advice—apparently born of harsh experience—scrawled hurriedly across one corner. "You'll never make any money at magazine writing!" he raged. "I'd get out of it fast if I were you."

What Mr. Shearer couldn't have known was that I've always been stubborn as a mule in any endeavor, willing to ignore common sense and sail exuberantly and fool-heartedly into uncharted waters to achieve my goal of the moment. I was hell-bent on becoming a magazine writer, and nothing short of forgetting how to type or losing my memory altogether was about to stop me.

I compiled a list of the people who in recent years had engendered the most passion in me for their accomplishments. Near the top of the list were two of my favorite original thinkers: Nathaniel Hawthorne, the father of the modern American novel and author of *The Scarlet Letter* and *The Marble Faun*, and sex educator and birth control champion Margaret Sanger, founder of America's first birth control clinic. I knew these and dozens of other men and woman of historical significance would be superb subjects for profiles.

And then I remembered Bucky. He'd engaged me intellectually more than anyone I could think of since I'd left grad school, and not only would he make a terrific magazine profile, he was very much alive and, I hoped, available.

The next morning I sat down and wrote an impassioned letter to Bucky. I'd written a lot of persuasive letters and essays over the years, so I was reasonably certain my letter would net me an interview with Fuller, the inventor of the geodesic dome and author of *Operating Manual for Spaceship Earth* and other highly praised, groundbreaking books. If I managed to land the interview, it would undoubtedly be my best journalistic catch so far. Full of optimism, I began in earnest to plan for the trip to Philly.

Two months later, a response arrived in the mail.

"Thank you for writing, Mr. Bachelder," wrote his executive secretary, "but Mr. Fuller is much too busy right now to agree to an interview. He did appreciate hearing from you, though."

I was still young enough and brash enough not to allow a simple rejection letter to shut me down. I immediately went to my desk and wrote another letter to Fuller.

"I really want very much to meet with you, Mr. Fuller!" I wrote. "I do hope you'll reconsider my proposal. And I feel sure you won't regret having agreed to an interview."

This time, I didn't have to wait long for a response.

"Dear Mr. Bachelder," wrote the same woman who'd so emphatically said no to my first entreaty. "Mr. Fuller would be happy to meet with you in his Penn State University office on Wednesday, July 18 at 11:00 a.m. Thank you for your interest in his important work. We'll see you on the eighteenth."

Bingo! My devil-may-care persistence had paid off, and I'd soon be on my way to Philadelphia.

To fund the trip, I took on the odious task of sanding, planing, and refinishing three old apartment house doors belonging to friend and restaurateur Mike Plumer, all for the impecunious sum of fifty dollars. To my surprise, once I'd finished the doors and pocketed the cash, Mike cheerfully agreed to my last-minute proposal that he go with me to Philly.

Our motives for such an ambitious trip were clear enough. I wanted badly to come home with the makings of a publication-worthy article; Mike just wanted to have a good look at the city, embark on an adventure or two, then get back to his work as the owner and chef of the Colonial Restaurant in Berwick, the town we both lived in. I figured that Mike, who was fearless in traffic and good at problem-solving, would make a terrific navigator for my voyage to Philly.

Early on Wednesday, July 17, we put our affairs in order, said goodbye to northern New England, and shot off down the Spaulding Turnpike, tucked into the bucket seats of Mike's little red MG Midget convertible. By noon we were somewhere in Connecticut, with the top rolled back like the lid of a tuna can and the radio spewing out an endless ribbon of pulsing rock anthems. We'd become two carefree road warriors heading gleefully into the urban jungle and preparing for battle.

By late afternoon we'd arrived on the outskirts of Philadelphia, and twenty minutes later we were in the heart of the city, weaving chaotically through a dense forest of skyscrapers, determined to pay our respects to the profusion of Cradle-of-Liberty landmarks all around us. Accompanied by a big-city symphony of honking horns, screeching tires, and the bellowing of traffic cops, we managed to catch drive-by glimpses of the Liberty Bell, the iconic statue of Benjamin Franklin, and—as the final leg of our self-made patriotic tour—Independence Hall, birthplace of the Declaration of Independence and the United States Constitution.

We then set off to find the downtown offices of Penn State University—the site of my interview with Fuller. (I wanted to wake up the next morning knowing precisely where I'd be going.) Once we'd located the place, we planned to find a motel and settle in for the night.

Downtown Philly was the Indy 500 redux—an asphalt labyrinth teeming with half-crazed, work-bound locals, along with a madcap flow of recently arrived tourists, including the two of us, who hadn't a clue either where they were going or how to get there.

Mike, always the daredevil, was at the wheel. He plunged into the gas-guzzling maelstrom without a moment's hesitation, and we were off to the races. I was assigned the task of navigator, and with the help of a tiny-print map, I began to shout out the street names.

"Left on Chestnut!" I shouted over the din of rush-hour traffic. He popped the clutch and roared past a trio of slow-moving buses, provoking a frenzy of blaring horns and indignant drivers half a block long.

"Jesus, what a nightmare!" Mike bellowed. "What next? Gimme a goddamn street!"

"Take a left onto Broad!" I snapped. "It'll take us right into Penn Square, and then we'll be within easy walking distance of Bucky's place!"

He made the left turn as directed, and everything was copacetic until we noticed a spinning blue light atop the car behind us.

"The cops!" I yelled.

We were trapped. I'd sent us the wrong way down a one-way street, and in a few seconds we were surrounded by a terrifying posse of angry commuters, screaming in concert out their car windows while simultaneously extending us a warm Philadelphia welcome with the aid of their middle fingers.

The policeman waved us frantically to the side of the road, then pulled up behind us, leaving the lights of his squad car flashing crazily in the sunlight.

When the driver's-side door finally opened, out stepped a giant of a man. He must have been six feet, six inches—a modern-day, black-leather Paul Bunyan with lemon-yellow, one-way sunglasses; knee-length, Gestapo-style leather boots; and a sinister, Darth Vader smirk on his pockmarked face.

I went silent while folding my map and watching Mike's knuckles turn white as he gripped the steering wheel of the MG. I'd read somewhere in the *Philadelphia Inquirer* that the cops in Philly were notorious for stopping and ticketing you just for sport—troopers on a power trip, with the ubiquitous badge and pistol their tools of intimidation.

Officer Bunyan strode over to our car—suddenly more wind-up toy than MG—then leaned an available elbow on the sill and cocked his hat insolently up toward the back of his head.

"You two realize what yer *doin'*?" he sneered. "You got *any* idea?"

"Not really, officer," said Mike, putting on his most blatantly manufactured smile of innocence for the occasion. "Sorry!" he said sheepishly. "This is the first time we've ever driven in Philly, and the signs are confusing."

"He's right," I chimed in. "We're brand-new to the area, and ..."

"My God!" said the cop, shouting over the roar of the bumper-to-bumper traffic and moving his immense head back and forth in utter disbelief.

"You're goin' the *wrong* goddamn way down a *bus lane*! I ought to hit you up with a hundred-dollar fine!" In 1979, a hundred dollars was a whole lot of money.

He flapped his ticket pad rhythmically against his thigh, pulled a ballpoint pen out of his shirt pocket, pointed it menacingly toward the two of us, then ambled back in slow, John Wayne motion to his squad car.

"We're about to get nailed for double what it cost us to drive down to Philly in the first place!" I lamented.

Mike looked at me and chuckled malevolently. "I've got three more doors for you to do when we get back to Maine," he said. "You're gonna owe me *big time* for this one!"

By the time the cop came back to our car, his smirk had softened into a sardonic, bemused half-smile. "Well, I see your record's clean," he said. "That's *one* thing your favor. And besides, I like your little red car. Sweet little machines, these MGs!" He moved his hat back where it belonged, then transformed himself abruptly from mafia don to high school buddy.

"So whatcha doin' in Philly?" he purred.

"We're here on business," I said, enormously relieved at his change in tone. "I've come down to interview Buckminster Fuller, and my friend Mike here agreed to do the driving."

"Never heard of him," he barked. "Fuller, I mean. And what the hell's he done that would make you drive all the way down to Philly just to talk with him?"

"Well, the tetrahedral truss, for one thing," I said with a hint of smug self-congratulation in my voice. "It revolutionized the construction industry! And then there's the Dymaxion car. You'd love it here in Philly; it can move sideways into a parallel parking slot!"

"Sounds like a swell fella," he sneered. "A real *intellectual*." Then he abandoned the good-guy image and stepped back into his black leather, Stormtrooper persona.

"Look, I'll let you go this time, but you'd better turn this tin puppy around—he tapped the hood of the MG with his nightstick—and get the hell out o' this one-way 'fore I change my mind!"

As he walked with giant, Jack-and-the-beanstalk steps back to his cruiser, I shouted, "Thank you, Officer!" but my words were lost on him as he pulled out into traffic, turned off his spinning blue light, and moved on to other, more financially rewarding encounters than ours.

We needed next to find a place to stay. After driving past a half-dozen tantalizing luxury hotels—between us we had less than a hundred dollars in our pockets—we came to our senses, drove back to the outskirts, and pulled up in front of the cheapest motel we could find, parked like a rusted-out Chevy in one of the seediest parts of town. As long as it had two beds and a toilet, we figured, we'd manage to survive the experience.

The exterior of the place looked like the facade of an abandoned funhouse, with shattered windows, drooping shutters, half-eaten fast food on the lawn, and a clock above the main entrance that had no hands and hadn't told time in decades. We stepped into the lobby, walked across a threadbare, whiskey-stained carpet, and arranged with the desk clerk to stay for the night. The place smelled like a holding pen for unwashed felons and hardcore drunks. The elevator—a classic 1930s film-noir model with crumbling Art Nouveau wall trim, lacquered metal accordion doors, and badly scarred, dark-wood panelling—rumbled ominously as we rose to the fifth floor. The operator said nothing, but looked us over suspiciously from head to toe before dropping us off.

When we stepped off the elevator and into the hallway, we were greeted with a chorus of sinister, deep-throated dog barks—not from one dog, but several. The dogs snarled like guard dogs in a maximum-security prison.

The unusually wide hallway leading to our room featured strips of wallpaper drooping down toward what smelled suspiciously like urine-soaked carpeting. A fire hose hung flaccidly from the wall next to the door of our room, its protective window shattered, the housing caked with dust from decades of inattention.

"Nice digs!" said Mike.

"Absolutely four-star!" I responded. "AAA approved!"

We popped open the door, dropped our suitcases on the floor, and had a look around. One bare lightbulb illuminated the area surrounding the beds, which sloped surreally downward toward the headboard. The curtains on the window facing the alley were actually two half-shredded panels of what looked like shower curtain material, one red, the other blue—patched-together substitutes for the original equipment. In the bathroom was a cast iron bathtub that would have been charming but for the months-old buildup of soap scum along its rim and the mildew underneath it, looking remarkably like the fetid moat of some long-abandoned castle.

The theme song from *Happy Days* screamed idiotically from the room next door. A cloud of low-grade marijuana hung like a

Beijing smog bank over every inch of the surroundings. A woman moaned repeatedly from within the room across from ours, in remarkably precise rhythm with the squeak-squeak-squeak of bedsprings. It was still only early afternoon.

We decided to get the hell out of the place. When the elevator rumbled back up to the fifth floor, we scrambled onto it, dragging our suitcases behind us. The operator stood silent as a stone, not bothering to ask us why we were leaving. It was more than likely he'd watched this very scenario countless times.

Once back in the lobby, I gave the desk clerk a feeble excuse—something about realizing we were simply too far from our appointment—and together Mike and I bid adieu to the place, jumping over a trio of half-eaten apples swarming with fruit flies as we crossed the lobby and stepped out onto the street.

The next morning, after having found a more tolerable place to hang our hats, we left the MG in an underground parking garage, had breakfast at a local diner, then walked the five blocks to the Penn State offices of Bucky Fuller. It was 10:45 now, just fifteen minutes before the scheduled interview. Mike headed off toward the downtown area to do some exploring while I introduced myself to a doorman who was likely doubling as a security guard.

"Hello!" I said with a blast of just-got-here gusto. "I'm here to interview Buckminster Fuller."

"Yeah, I'm sure he can't wait t' see ya!" he cracked. "You're only the fourth guy to come here this morning, and it ain't even eleven o'clock!" Clearly, he was accustomed to a never-ending stream of Bucky lovers in town to pay homage to the guru. "Go right ahead," he said, gesturing to the staircase just inside the entrance. "Elevator's not in service. Anyway, it's only twelve floors up. You'll get yourself a good workout."

I huffed and puffed my way to the twelfth floor, found Fuller's office, and was greeted by a cheerful, middle-aged woman in a flower print dress with matching scarf. She pointed me toward a row of brightly upholstered chairs opposite her desk, then said, "You must be Mr. Bachelder. Please have a seat. Mr. Fuller will be with you shortly."

She was right. In less than five minutes, Mr. R. Buckminster Fuller, world-renowned inventor, poet, and intellectual rock star, stepped through a door just off the waiting room and ushered me into his office.

He was solidly built and diminutive, with a well-tailored suit, prominent, black-rimmed spectacles, and an air of absolute but unpretentious authority. I figured I was only one of a dozen journalists he'd met with this week alone, and yet he immediately put me at ease, making me feel just as important as the movers and shakers he dealt with every day.

As he stepped up and shook my hand, I looked down at my scuffed-up shoes and wrinkled dress slacks—the result of hours on the road, stuffed uncomfortably into Mike's tuna-can Midget—and felt more like a hapless slob than a serious journalist.

"Welcome to Philadelphia!" he smiled. "You're the writer from Maine, then? I've an hour or so for the interview. Glad to see you. I've a home up in Maine myself!"

We both settled into our respective chairs, and what had seemed only a few months ago like an impossible dream—me, an unknown freelancer from a tiny Maine village, interviewing Bucky Fuller, world traveler on Spaceship Earth—was now a reality. Though I'd labored mightily in advance of the interview, I suddenly felt utterly unprepared for the encounter, and my mood switched from wild-eyed optimism to deep insecurity.

It was a do-or-die moment. *You didn't come down here to suffer a meltdown!* I howled inwardly, praying that Fuller couldn't see through my trembling, tissue-paper psyche.

By now Bucky had gone completely silent, waiting politely to hear what I had on my mind. I'd written my questions and comments on a stack of 3 x 5 cards and arranged them in the order of their planned delivery. I removed the elastic, peeled the first card off the stack, and dove headlong into the interview. Right away, I learned that, while my first few questions seemed embarrassingly ho-hum and perfunctory, his responses, one after the other, were breathtakingly incisive, imaginative, and well-informed—the polar opposite of predictable. Somehow, his unabashed exuberance gave me the psychological lift I was looking for, and off we went with the interview.

"It's obvious from reading the newspapers," I said, "that cities like Detroit and Boston—and Philadelphia, too—are struggling to make improvements in housing, transportation, and other issues that affect the quality of life. And yet nothing ever really seems to get done. It makes me wonder if the politicians in charge of improving our cities are consulting the right people."

"Anything the politicians can do is what we call ameliorative," said Fuller. "It's not a curing action; it's a matter of reducing the pain for a moment. The city as we know it is obsolete! Eventually, when we have the right equipment, we'll experience a very different way of living. When, for example, we finally stop sending armaments around the world—and we'll gradually do just that—then all of the high-level scientific capability to produce technology will be turned on the improvement of our cities. We'll be able to produce dwellings wherever we want them, in just one day, then remove them when we're done with them. Cities will serve us, not the other way around."

Then I switched to a very different topic. "What can we as a society do to discourage class distinctions and bring about racial equality?"

"We all know that Karl Marx was saying we'd better do away with class distinctions," he said. "But the nobles were saying we have to preserve them! The concepts of class and race are no longer valid. A child pays *no attention* to color. And as a culture, we've finally arrived at a stage in which people in any occupation you can think of can be either black-skinned or white-skinned. There is no such thing as a 'race' of people!"

Fig. 52. R. Buckminster Fuller U.S. postage stamp.

So much for the question of racial equality; now I wanted to know what Fuller would have to say about America's schools.

"The educational establishment seems eternally to be floundering in its mission to make enlightened, well-informed citizens of this nation's children," I said. "Where and how do we begin to make truly lasting improvements in our schools?"

"Education occurs in the real world," he said, "and they don't teach that in schools. Our entire school system in this country has an enormous momentum behind it, and a political structure built into it. The fact is that people get education *themselves*. The really great education is self-education. When you learn by reading alone, then get experimental evidence from your television or other sources, you avoid having to learn in front of kids in the classroom, where you can easily develop an inferiority complex. It is nearly always the best thinkers—usually the brightest people—who take the longest to think things over. It isn't logical to assume that people who take longer than others to learn are dull. More often than not, what they really are is *persistent*!"

It was a spectacular performance. Clearly, Fuller was going to have cogent, near-infallible answers for any question I could ask him.

"What can the airline industry around the world do to bring about improvements in the safety, comfort, and affordability of air travel?" I asked.

"The airlines should not tell people where they can and cannot go," he said. "Instead of *exploiting* humanity in its policies and programs, the airlines should *accommodate* humanity. Right now, the airlines are trying to find out how many people they can fit inside their planes. It's the profit motive at work. They have us sitting in the torture seat—the middle seat of the three-seat section of airplanes—with our elbows in someone else's belly. What right have they to treat human beings that way? The safety of air travel doesn't worry me; we've made enormous advances in that realm. But there are no laws about comfort!"

The interview was humming along beautifully. My questions were tolerably well-informed, and not surprisingly, his answers—always brilliant, always startlingly unconventional—were beyond spectacular.

And then the plane to perfection took an abrupt nosedive.

"How," I asked, "will the rapid evolution of the microcomputer actually affect people—including me—who hardly ever use a computer?"

"Well," Fuller responded, "I'm sure that our brains *are* computers, so anyone with a brain is using a computer right this moment."

I gasped. It was a bona fide intellectual sucker punch, and I was immediately down for the count. Bereft of anything like an intelligent response to his observation, I shrank into insignificance, hoping against hope that the chair I was sitting in would swallow me up, then spit me out somewhere—anywhere—north of Philadelphia.

To compound my trauma, I discovered that I'd managed somehow to get the remaining 3 x 5 cards hopelessly out of order. I wasn't about to sit there like an imbecile, shuffling that pitiful stack of cards in front of a man known around the world for his intimidatingly precise, brilliantly mathematical mind, so I decided to wing it.

And then I began to panic. What on earth was I thinking three months ago, back in Maine? I'd just driven nearly four hundred miles to Philadelphia to interview Bucky Fuller, and now, at the worst possible time, I'd begun to doubt my ability to pull off the most electrifying caper of my life. I knew I was about as scientific as a Vegas pole dancer, and by now, so did he.

I thumbed through my mental Rolodex for whatever intellectually probing questions I could find, humbly recorded his answers to them in my notebook, then threw in the towel. I'd just managed to establish myself in Fuller's presence as more starstruck road groupie than serious magazine writer, and with no remaining hope of impressing him with my erudition, I gave up all pretense and asked for his autograph.

"I'd love to give it to my daughter," I said, but really wanted it as much for myself as for Amy. I'd no doubt he saw through my ruse with laser-beam acuity.

"Of course!" he smiled, and with that smile came a revelation. Bucky Fuller wasn't loved the world over merely because of his wide-ranging intelligence. He was also loved because, beneath the coat of many intellectual colors that fit him so well, he was really just a regular guy. This man called Bucky was the neighbor you always wish you had—the guy you could come to without reservation to share your most urgent questions about the riddle of the universe or how to purge your lawn of those pesky dandelions.

Fig. 53. "Once in love with Amy, always in love with Amy—that's me!" (Drawing by R. Buckminster Fuller for the author's daughter).

Without another word, he reached into his desk drawer, pulled out a sheet of lined notebook paper and three ballpoint pens—one red, one blue, and one black—and laid them down in front of him. Then he leaned forward and began without hesitation to pour line after line onto the sheet.

Before long I realized what he was drawing. It was a geodesic dome—a spherical network of triangles that by now had become instantly recognizable in nearly every teeming metropolis and quaint village on the planet. The drawing he was doing just for my daughter—and in reality for me as well—represented what many historians consider his signature accomplishment as an inventor and a scientist. Soon I'd take possession of that drawing, then deliver it proudly to Amy. For one sweet moment, I forgot altogether why I'd come down to Philly in the first place.

He finished the drawing, then laid the three pens down side by side on his desk, fussing with them until they were perfectly

aligned. It was just what I might have expected from Bucky, a man so incomparably brilliant and yet so endearingly human.
"What did you say your daughter's name was?"
"Amy," I said. "Amy Alice."
He picked up the black pen and dashed a message across the bottom of the sheet:

> Once in love with Amy, always in love with Amy.
> That's me! —Bucky Fuller

Then he shuffled his papers like a network reporter, stood up without fanfare, and said, "Well, Mr. Bachelder, this interview is over. I've got to pee!"
I made my way down the staircase and out onto the street, relieved to be done with the interview but glowing with pride at my accomplishment. Mike was waiting for me outside. He'd had the pleasure of exploring downtown Philly, a living museum of American history. I'd had the pleasure of knowing that, while talking with one of the greatest thinkers of the twentieth century, I'd managed to avoid making a complete fool of myself. For the son of a blue-collar worker, plagued by years of self-doubt and yet burning with late-blooming ambition, I'd come a long way.
A few months after my return to Maine, I learned to my delight that Fuller was scheduled to speak publicly at the Bull and Claw, a popular restaurant north of downtown Kennebunk. Since the place was only a few miles from my home, I arranged immediately to take Amy with me to the event—an informal, lecture-and-banquet affair—and introduce her to Bucky.
We attended the lecture, ate our dinner, then waited in line to meet Mr. Fuller. When I introduced Amy to him—a man of enormous accomplishment, reaching out to a very young girl in possession of what he loved most, an inquiring mind—he couldn't have been more gracious. The two of them shook hands, then chatted for a moment about her school and the paper she'd written about him for Mrs. Crandall's sixth-grade class.
How wonderful it has been for me, after all of these years, to remember that this world-renowned man of ideas, the very R. Buckminster Fuller of tetrahedral brilliance and Dymaxion fame, had the decency and class to thank our daughter—an eleven-year-old girl from a tiny village in Maine—for coming to Kennebunk to hear him talk about issues of supreme importance to the survival of the species. As we made our way back to Berwick, I wondered if even Kurt Vonnegut, who in his own

way was both the kindred spirit and intellectual equal of Bucky, could have spun a more heartwarming tale than this.

It didn't take long for me to find a publisher for my article—a new and ambitious Maine-focused magazine north of Portland. Since Fuller had spent a considerable portion of his younger years on Bear Island in Maine's Penobscot Bay, it was a good fit. And then, just one month before my article was scheduled for publication, the magazine folded, and the piece I'd worked so hard to bring to life crept sorrowfully back into its manila folder, never to make it into print. The actual contents of the interview are preserved on one prehistoric cassette tape languishing somewhere in a desk drawer in my home office.

I suppose I ought to have been upset that my article never made it into a magazine, but I really wasn't. I simply put a checkmark next to another life-changing adventure, then moved on with my life as husband, father, and aspiring writer, comforted by the knowledge that I'd actually managed to land an unlikely audience with one of the great entrepreneurial thinkers of the twentieth century.

What meant the most to me was the simple fact that I'd had the thirty-something audacity to ask for the encounter in the first place. It was an event of major significance in the development of both my understanding of the world and my belief in myself. I'd rid myself of the worst of my many years of self-doubt, and thanks to Bucky Fuller I was finally on the road to becoming my very own keeper.

Fig. 54. *Weeping Wilma Saves the Lake* by Ross Bachelder.

❀ Tiny Novelette 5 ❀

Weeping Wilma Saves the Lake

Wilma Myklebust, a Norwegian immigrant living in Sleepy Eye, Minnesota, in the '50s, was normal in every way but one: she suffered from a rare and untreatable disease called crylomania—bedlam of the tear ducts—that caused her to cry not just once in a while, but around the clock.

Now, most babies cry the moment they're born—a natural reaction to their sudden expulsion into an utterly unfamiliar environment, along with the traditional slap on the bum that gets them breathing. But Wilma Myklebust began shedding tears right in the womb, and even after sliding triumphantly down the chute and into the sunlight, then getting on with her life, she never managed to turn off the faucet.

By the time she'd reached adolescence—reason enough for the average girl to cry at the drop of a Harlequin romance—Mikkelsen's Corner Grocery could never keep enough tissues in stock for Weeping Wilma. Because of it, Marit and Johannes, her parents, ordered them in bundles the size of hay bales, then had them delivered by rail each month from Sappi Fine Paper in Cloquet, 250 miles northeast of Sleepy Eye.

That Wilma was so hopelessly waterlogged was truly ironic, given that the town was in the throes of its worst drought in decades. But there was no shortage of water at the Myklebust house. The chairs and couches made an embarrassing crinkling sound whenever guests would sit on them, because they had to be covered with plastic to protect them from the endless onslaught of tears. Wilma lost her job at McDonald's because the fries and burgers were always soggy when she handed them out at the drive-through. Even worse, no one invited her to the senior prom, knowing she'd appear to be sad on what ought to be the happiest night of the year. Instead, she stayed home and cried her heart out, not just because she was home alone, but because she couldn't have stopped crying if she wanted to.

Still, there were a few good things about living with crylomania. When Wilma's waterbed needed replenishing, she could fill it in less than an hour from just one good cry about nothing. And when the flowers needed watering, Johannes would simply send her outdoors to do her crying, with the result that the Myklebusts had the most spectacular garden in all of Sleepy Eye.

Tears or not, life has a habit of moving inexorably along. Wilma's tears continued to flow unabated well into her later years, and, not surprisingly, she began to wonder if she would ever experience happiness minus her tears. Then, one night, while lying in bed and crying her eyes out, she got an emergency call from the Sleepy Eye Chamber of Commerce. Thanks to the drought, the renowned Sleepy Eye Lake was now little more than a toddler's play pool, and the tourists had stopped coming. Would Miss Myklebust be willing to come down right away and cry the lake back to its former glory? Elated, she filled Sleepy Eye Lake to the brim in less than a day, and soon there was a gold plaque in the Town Square that read, "This beloved lake was brought back from certain extinction by the tears of Miss Wilma Myklebust, the hero of Sleepy Eye, Minnesota." And next Sunday at church, there wasn't a dry eye in the house, including Wilma's.

Chapter 11

The Precarious World of Arts Criticism
Dishing It Out and Taking It on the Chin

Arts criticism is a rough-and-tumble world, replete with glamour but fraught with aesthetic and temperamental land mines. Writers and actors, dancers and producers, artists and composers—all swear they can't do without it, but when the hammer comes down on their creations, the critic is suddenly more beast than benefactor. Whether you're working in Hollywood or Hoboken, Davenport or Des Moines, if you're a critic, you're both pundit and punching bag, and to succeed in the profession, you'd better have two absolutely essential qualities: the courage of your convictions and the mindset of a five-star general.

Writing for Deadline: Tale of a Small-Town Reviewer

In the '90s, I spent one season writing arts criticism for the Biddeford, Maine, *Journal Tribune*—primarily reviews of productions at Hackmatack Playhouse in Berwick. Then, a few years later, I spent two seasons as a freelancer for *Spotlight*, at the time the *Portsmouth Herald*'s weekly arts magazine, where I regularly reviewed plays, art exhibits, and live musical performances.

For the *Journal Tribune*—my very first gig as an arts reviewer—I'd often have less than two days' notice to attend an opening night performance. Worse, the reviews I'd be assigned to write would be due on the editor's desk by no later than 10:00 a.m. on the day after the performance.

I'd had experience meeting deadlines as a columnist and book reviewer for the onetime *Somersworth/Berwick Free Press* in the mid-'70s, under the guidance of its esteemed editor, Leola

Peppler, so I was accustomed to working under pressure. But never had I faced deadlines as severe as those required of me at the *Journal Tribune*. It meant that the quicker I managed to get home and start writing my review, the earlier I'd be able to collapse into bed, knowing I'd have just enough time to drive to Biddeford the next morning and hand-deliver my review to the *Journal Tribune*'s branch office in Sanford.

Given the heat I was under to write fast as hell and deliver even faster, it was fortunate for me that I lived just four miles from Hackmatack. With a little planning and a whole lot of hustle, I could always count on getting home only a few minutes after the play had ended. To facilitate my rapid evacuation from the premises, I'd always ask for a seat on stage right of the theater, and in a row as near as possible to the parking lot. Once the show was done, I'd dash out the door, race to my waiting car, and drive cannonball style along Diamond Hill—more cowpath than road at the time—and straight to my home off Little River Road. I'd then explode out of my car and into the kitchen, climb the stairs to my unfinished attic, toting my Olympia portable and a jar of Wite-Out, and begin immediately to write my review.

There was undoubtedly a certain struggling-artist romance in the situation I'd created for myself. I'd hung a trouble light from the rafters to illuminate the wobbly legged card table that doubled as my office, all nicely centered on a faded blue rug and warmed by a cup of coffee whose sole purpose was to keep me awake long enough to finish my review, tighten the prose, and stuff it into an envelope for next-day delivery.

Occasionally, a wasp would buzz over my head, likely sent by the editor to make sure I was doing what I was being paid to do. It was on those moonlit opening nights, while working feverishly at my typewriter and rubbing my hands together in the late-night chill, that the attic became my garret and I became a small-town Hemingway, swept up in the fierce nocturnal exhilaration that comes with being a writer, on assignment and in demand.

At the *Herald*, things were more organized, more bureaucratic, and much more competitive. I was one of a stable of three freelance arts writers, working beside Jeanne McCartin (at this writing, still reviewing plays and writing a weekly column for the *Herald*) and another woman whose name has been lost to freelance history. They come and they go, as I would soon learn firsthand.

During my tenure at the *Herald*, I contributed, every fourth week, to a round-robin column I'd proposed to the editor when

I first signed on as a reviewer. We called it "Critic's Corner," and it was a hit.

My editor at the time was a quiet, thoughtful young woman, fresh out of college, with the fetchingly colorful name of Holly Beaverstock. Because Holly liked my writing and was at all times both highly professional and endearingly personable, she was an absolute joy to work with—the kind of editor every writer wishes he or she would have the good fortune to work with. But when Holly left the *Herald* to take a job in another state, the assignments abruptly stopped coming. The new editor was no longer interested in my services, the other freelancers were more than happy to take the assignments I was no longer getting, and no matter how much the public liked and applauded my work as a reviewer, my time with the *Herald* was over.

I wrote dozens of reviews during my two years with the *Herald*, and while the majority of my encounters with area creatives haven't managed to fix themselves permanently in my mind, a few of them stand out as having been truly memorable assignments worth sharing.

Gallery at 100 Market: Four Floors of Art, Commission-Free

In 1999 I reviewed the inaugural exhibit of the Gallery at 100 Market in Portsmouth—artworks in several media on four of the five floors of a stylish office building down by the Portsmouth Harbor tugs. Along the way, I learned just how generous and enterprising a CEO can be, but that was just the beginning. The chance to review 100 Market quickly proved to be an invaluable gateway into the world of the visual arts: how things work behind the scenes; how galleries, like artists, have to sell their services to the public; and how people at every level of the visual arts community must conduct themselves if they're going to survive and prosper.

Rye, New Hampshire, developer/investor Michael Simchik, the man behind 100 Market, decided early on that having serious artworks by local and regional artists on the walls of his building—without charging a commission from the sale of any exhibited works—would be a cost-effective way for him to decorate the facility while stimulating the economy and enriching the cultural climate of Portsmouth.

As an exhibit venue, it was an immediate hit. For artists, it was a place to showcase their juried artworks without the additional financial burden of a commission. The relatively high ceilings were also a big draw, providing local artists for the first time with a rare opportunity to have their large-scale works exhibited close by, right in the Seacoast region.

The Gallery at 100 Market quickly became a major cultural gathering place, an urban oasis where both the locals and tourists from around the world could come and immerse themselves in the Seacoast region's thriving visual arts community.

I also learned on the night of the opening just how hungry some artists are for favorable publicity. As I was pulling quotes for my exhibit review from Roger Goldenberg, an artist whose flamboyant, jazz-influenced abstracts had caught my attention, I realized that a veritable conga line of artists had begun to form just down the hall from where we were standing. It then dawned on me that they were waiting for me.

Word must have spread like wildfire that a reporter was on the premises. One by one, they climbed up the gangplank to talk with the skipper of the good ship *Spotlight*. I listened to what each artist had to say, then bade them all farewell, finished my tour of the exhibit, and went home to Berwick, knowing that only a handful of publicity-hungry aspirants would ever make it into print. Without irresistible creative gifts, special favors, or plain luck, only a few fortunate artists ever manage to survive the cut.

At the 100 Market opening, I saw many beautiful, emotionally charged works. Others were to my thinking only marginally successful (a category I was always content to be in when, as an artist, I had my own works juried into the gallery on several later occasions). Finally, I saw paintings that struck me as embarrassingly narcissistic, copycat statements—works technically competent but lacking in any real emotional fire. And yet all of them, no matter how naive or sophisticated, had managed to find an appreciative audience, and they'd come from a place within the artist that cares more about beauty and sensitivity than cruelty and violence. When artists are painting or drawing, dancing or making music, they're not harming people—they're simply nurturing them.

Fifteen years after its premiere exhibit, the Gallery at 100 Market is still actively serving the Seacoast. In spite of an up-and-down economy, it continues to be an intrepid force for good in and well beyond the Seacoast region. That I'd been tapped to review the gallery's premiere exhibit gave me equal servings of pride, pleasure, and a sense of forward motion as a writer.

Reviewing the Leddy: Certain Rules Apply

One night, while working as a writer for the *Herald*, I got a last-minute call from Holly, the *Spotlight* editor. "Would you like to review *H.M.S. Pinafore* at the Leddy Center for the Performing Arts this coming Friday evening?" she said.

The Leddy, as the locals were fond of calling it, was in the quaint village of Epping, New Hampshire, not far from Manchester. "Nobody else wants to do this review," she said, "because they're predicting bad weather, and there are a lot of kids in the production."

"Sure!" I said. "I love Gilbert and Sullivan!" (And it didn't hurt that I'd also spent seven years running my own teen theater. For me, this was the perfect assignment.)

I called the Leddy Center box office the night before the performance and explained that I was a *Portsmouth Herald* reviewer and needed to reserve a complimentary ticket for the Friday evening performance. Surprisingly, there was a pause at the other end of the phone, and I wondered if the line had suddenly gone dead.

"Uhh, I'm sorry," said the voice, "but the Leddy Center doesn't allow reviews of its productions when a lot of the actors are children."

"*Really!*" I said. "I should think you'd welcome them! I've run my own teen theater, and I can promise you the kids dearly love being reviewed. It's good for them to stand up against the judgment of reviewers, too. Toughens 'em up!"

"I really am sorry," said the voice. "But thank you for your interest in the Leddy Center. We do hope you'll come and review our other shows. They're always well staged and well received."

What a crock! I thought to myself. I hung up the phone, resigned to the enormous difficulty of changing the opinion of anyone who's decided unilaterally that children's theater isn't real theater.

I called Holly to tell her I'd been turned down, and she urged me not to worry about it. "I'll have another assignment for you early next week," she said. "With or without the Leddy, there's always plenty of good theater to review around here."

I went to bed that night grumbling to myself about the unfair hand the youngsters, the *Herald*, and I had just been dealt. I knew from experience with my own company just how good young actors can be when given strong direction, constant encouragement, a truly challenging script, and—when they've worked hard at their craft and shown real growth as actors—abundant praise.

The next morning I went to work, still brooding about the slight and regretting the loss of an opportunity to review the play and convince both the Leddy and the theater-going public that it's okay to have constructive opinions about the stage work of young people.

On the way home that afternoon, a vast army of dark, angry clouds fell into formation over the Seacoast region, preparing for meteorological battle. Soon afterward a heavy, wet snow began to fall, and traffic slowed to a crawl. As I fought for enough traction to make it up an incline, I began to think about an even more difficult scenario playing itself out right then at the Leddy: a wildly enthusiastic troupe of young actors, dying to get onstage but terrified that yet another nor'easter would shut down the theater and keep the *H.M.S. Pinafore* from ever pulling up anchor and leaving harbor.

I decided to skip going home for supper and drive straight to the Leddy Center instead, without telling Holly. The weather might let them down; the theater might think they were better off not being reviewed; but I couldn't forget the drive and determination of my own actors as they rehearsed and rehearsed for their performances. I knew that among young people everywhere—especially kids with a heightened sense of purpose and the means to achieve their dream—a stubborn refusal to quit was a nearly universal trait. I wasn't about to let them down by being an inexcusable no-show.

As I worked my way to the outskirts of Rochester and merged onto Route 125, the density of the snow doubled and visibility was near zero. My wiper blades were repeatedly caked with ice, forcing me to stop every ten minutes and employ my frozen fingertips to clear them. A mile or two down the road I saw a car plunged over an embankment and lodged in the rapidly growing blanket of snow. Shortly after that, on the other side of the road, I saw three more cars in the same predicament, one of them upside down in the median, its roof crushed and its tires spinning helplessly in the storm.

While navigating the twenty miles between Rochester and Epping, I counted altogether twenty-two vehicles stranded in the blizzard. *There's no way in the world the Leddy's gonna be open for business!* I lamented. At least I knew I'd be able to write and tell the children later on that I'd tried to be there for them.

Because I'd left much earlier than usual for the trip to Epping, I managed in spite of the storm to make it to the theater with a good twenty minutes to spare. Only a handful of cars were parked outside the theater, barely visible in the falling snow. *Must be Leddy Center staff, shutting down the place*, I thought.

I kept my car heater on while jotting down a note to the actors. "Sorry the weather shut you down!" I wrote. "I wanted at least for you to know that I came down with every intention of reviewing your performance." I stuffed the note into a spare envelope, found a pushpin in the glove compartment, then plodded through a good eighteen inches of drifting snow and posted my note on the front door.

As I headed back to my car, the door creaked open against the wind, and a warm, yellow light glowed from within the theater. With it came the sound of pre-curtain chatter and recorded music—songs from *H.M.S. Pinafore* being pumped into the lobby. The Leddy was open for business.

I pulled my note off the door, stomped the snow off my feet, went inside, and bought a ticket, saying nothing about my affiliation with the *Herald*. My review notebook would stay in the car; it would have been a dead giveaway for the real purpose of my visit. I knew the play program would give me the essential information I'd need to write the review.

The show was even better than I'd hoped it would be. The set was magnificent. The actors were well cast and uniformly in control of their characters. They knew their lines cold, and delivered them with professional-level timing, indicating strong, thoroughly committed direction. The music was rousing and expertly performed, and the costumes were spectacular.

After the show I crawled back home through the still-raging blizzard, listening to the musical hum of my car heater in close harmony with the clickity-snap of my windshield wipers. I needed to write my review that night, so I knew it would be many hours before I'd be allowed to lay my song-filled head on the pillow and call it a day.

The next morning I fired off my review to Holly, and two days later it appeared, complete and unedited, in the *Herald*:

March 16th, 2000

Dear Spotlight readers:

I regularly write reviews for the *Portsmouth Herald*, but when I called the Leddy Center last week to arrange for a complimentary ticket, I was told I wouldn't be allowed to review the Leddy's performance of *H.M.S. Pinafore*, one of my all-time favorite musicals.

Why? Because the management apparently forbids reviews of Leddy Center productions if several of the actors are children.

I ran my own teen theater for seven years, so the chance to see a production featuring young people had great appeal to me.

I don't easily take no for an answer when it comes my creative work, so despite the threat of a major nor'easter, I came down to Epping and saw the show anyway.

Since I really liked the production, it seems a pity that I wasn't allowed to review it!

Just think: if it weren't for that pesky rule, I could have told you that the costumes, the lighting, and the set were terrific.

I could have waxed poetic about the quality of the acting, singing, and dancing, too! But because this production was primarily the work of young people, I wasn't allowed to write even one little word of praise about it in the papers.

I can assure you I'd have been proud to see my name on the program as the director—it was that good! But thanks to that granite-hard ban against reviewing child actors at the Leddy, I had to zip my lips and be content with merely having *seen* the production. After all, telling everyone in the Seacoast how good it really was would have been a lapse in professional judgment, and I would have lost my credibility as a reviewer.

And on and on I went, to the very end of the review. My nefarious little scheme had worked! I'd snuck in undetected and reviewed a play I was told I'd not be allowed under any circumstances to review. A few days later I heard from Elaine Gatchell, who with her husband Bruce founded and continues to run the Center:

> March 21st, 2000
>
> Thank you so much for your wonderful review of *H.M.S. Pinafore*! I and all of the actors—and especially the high schoolers—really appreciated your kind words.
>
> Sincerely,
>
> Elaine Gatchell

Along with the letter was a photo of the entire cast of *Pinafore*, and every one of the actors had signed his or her name at the bottom.

I was reasonably certain I'd made a difference in the lives of the younger actors in the production, simply by taking them seriously as theater professionals. In my book, anyone, young or old, who's working really hard in a given endeavor and cares deeply about that endeavor, can be considered a professional. The Leddy's production of *H.M.S. Pinafore* reinforced my long-held conviction that good work is good work, no matter who you are, how old you might be, or what (if any) formal training you've had.

Fancy credentials not required! Just go out onstage and, to the best of your ability, show me what you can do. That's *professionalism*, and it never goes out of style.

Seacoast Repertory Theatre

I've crossed paths with producer Roy Rogosin only a few times over the years, mostly during a period in the early '90s when I was unemployed and approached him about the possibility of working for Seacoast Repertory Theatre.

Rogosin has really been around. His many accomplishments include acting as the personal conductor for Johnny Mathis and Michel Legrand. He's conducted in London, on Broadway, at the Kennedy Center, and at the White House. He's written for television and motion pictures, and when I interviewed with him for employment, he was the artistic director at Seacoast Rep—sometimes also called the SRT.

In 1999 he went on to replace the legendary John Lane as the producer at Ogunquit Playhouse, another storied theater just over the border on Route 1 in Maine. He remained in that position until 2005.

On top of all that, Rogosin can always impress us with the fact that he's married to Eileen Diamond Rogosin, one of the second-season Mouseketeers. (I watched her and her fellow *Mickey Mouse Club* members every afternoon as a child growing up in Michigan, so I remember her well.) And Rogosin can lay it on even thicker by reminding us that his wife was once a dancer with the New York City Ballet under George Balanchine. Talk about connections!

Roy's now an artist in residence on the Santa Fe campus of St. John's College, which boasts on its web site that "there's no other college quite like St. John's." Eileen is there, too, teaching acting and performance. (Once you've gotten the bug, it never goes away.)

In my encounters with Rogosin, I learned quickly that there's no other theater guy quite like Roy Rogosin. Like other prominent people who've worked with or who've otherwise been in close proximity to the big-name people of the world, he exuded an aura of absolute certainty about his gifts every time I sat across a table from him.

Roy knew I'd had considerable experience in the fine and performing arts as a marketer and publicist, so he was at least marginally interested in having me on the staff of Seacoast Rep. He also knew I was looking for work and would be more than pleased to find a home in his theater. I'd be able to put my marketing and publicity skills to work for him, and I figured I'd also be available on call as both pit orchestra musician and bit part actor. As I saw it, if I were to wear not one but several hats while working for Roy, I'd save Seacoast Rep some serious money.

The problem was the money. He wanted to pay me a meager five dollars per hour for forty hours per week of labor, but I wanted better than that. In one of our several interviews, we went around and around about the reasons he thought I should be satisfied with his rate, and I followed with the reasons I wasn't.

"There's not as much discretionary money around here as you think," he said. "Do you have any idea how much it costs to run this place? And besides, my theater could be your playground! You can work in any area of SRT, have access to all of our resources, and make things happen for yourself every day."

"But to be really successful here," I argued, "I'd undoubtedly have to work more than forty hours per week—especially if I were tapped on occasion to be a bit part actor or pit orchestra musician. I could do all of that for you in addition to my work as publicist."

"We can't afford any more than the two hundred dollars per week I'm offering you," he said. "That's the reality I'm facing."

"But I've tons of experience as an arts publicist!" I countered. "I'm a thoroughly experienced writer. And an accomplished musician!"

"Accomplished?" he said. "What do you mean by *accomplished*?" I shed my usual diffidence and became noticeably bellicose.

"I mean I'm a damn good flute player!" I said. "And if I were paid a decent salary as your employee—better than the five-per you're offering—I'd do pit work for you without additional compensation. I know what I'm doing in whole lot of areas, and I can save you a whole lot of money doing it!"

"We're at an impasse, then," he said. "I can't afford you, and you're unwilling to work at the rate I'm offering you. Let's call it a draw for now. But of course, if you change your mind, you know where to reach me."

I saw Rogosin only a few times after that series of interviews: once when he was onstage at the Music Hall in Portsmouth, accepting an award on behalf of the cast and crew of a Seacoast Repertory production, and again when I picked up a freelance assignment building flats for an upcoming SRT musical.

I crossed paths with him again in 1991, not in person but from a distance. Holly Beaverstock, then the editor of *Spotlight*, had assigned me to review an ambitious musical Rogosin had only recently written. Called *Minding the Store*, it was a true-to-life musical fable based on a book of the same name by none other than Stanley Marcus, the man pegged to be in charge of the operations of Nieman Marcus after Herbert Marcus—a co-founder of Neiman Marcus and its chief executive officer—died in 1950.

Rogosin's play—a collaboration between him and his brother Joel Rogosin, a Hollywood producer and screenwriter—focused on the mercantile and familial machinations of the Neiman Marcus dynasty. The performance at SRT would be its world premiere, and in keeping with Roy's preternatural gift for flamboyant marketing strategies, he saw to it that Stanley Marcus—then the spry, eighty-six-year-old patriarch of the Neiman Marcus chain—would be the guest of honor at the premiere. The lyrics for *Minding the Store* were penned by Bruce Belland, lead singer of the '60s pop vocal sensation the Four Preps.

I ought to have been intimidated at the prospect of reviewing Rogosin's play, but after having reviewed dozens of plays for the *Herald* and other newspapers—reviews whose carefully constructed candor always managed to offend at least someone on- or offstage—I'd grown the thick skin that's essential equipment for any serious critic. And since I'd always written from a posture not of arrogance but of compassion and diplomacy, I figured Roy, who surely had grown the hide of a rhinoceros by now, would be able to handle any negative comments I might feel compelled to share with my readers.

Still, on the night before the premiere, I suffered more than my share of cold-sweat trepidations at the thought of what might happen to me, not to mention my fledgling career as arts journalist and critic, if I discovered I couldn't really find anything good to say about the play. I'd then have felt duty-bound to let it rip for everyone in the Seacoast—including Roy Rogosin and Stanley Marcus—to read.

As it turned out, I had nothing to fear. *Minding the Store* was by any measure a good, solid effort—a musical replete with well-crafted dialogue; believable characters; a compelling story line; clever, eminently singable lyrics; and enough energy and emotion to capture the hearts of anyone who saw the performance and listened carefully to the underlying messages.

I wrote my review late on the night of the opening, and on the following Thursday it appeared as scheduled in *Spotlight*. A few days later, a crisp, white envelope with the SRT logo on it arrived in my mailbox at home.

It was a letter from Roy.

> The Seacoast Repertory Theatre
> 125 Bow Street
> Portsmouth, New Hampshire 03801
>
> Dear Ross,
>
> I am not in the habit of corresponding with critics, for obvious reasons. Gratitude for good reviews can seem sycophantic, and response to negative reviews, merely petulant.
>
> However, I must take exception to my own rule to comment on your last two reviews of our work: *The Complete History of America (Abridged)* and *Minding the Store*.
>
> *Complete History* is a piece easy to mistake for mere slapstick. Your thoughtful analysis of it, and your astute perceptions of its underlying value, were a good source of appreciation. Things are not what they seem, and even something as entertaining as *Complete History* has substance some do not take the trouble to see. So thank you for your scrutiny.
>
> *Minding the Store* is, for me, obviously, a more personal project. It is born over many years of consideration and reconsideration. As you did with *Complete History*, you seem to really go to the heart of what I wrote—recognizing the superficial pleasures, but also remarking on the underlying questions of family loyalties and the price of dreams. It was particularly gratifying to me to find that, however flawed it may be, my work was clear.
>
> In a region where the level of critical writing is often wanting, yours is a penetrating eye and an articulate voice.

Thank you for coming to see our work, and for the continued excellence of yours.

Sincerely,

Roy M. Rogosin
Artistic Director
Seacoast Repertory Theatre

Given our earlier failure to forge an occupational alliance at SRT, the letter truly surprised me. More importantly, it provided me with some invaluable insights into the often mysterious, beneath-the-surface ways of the theater world.

Those who inhabit that universe can appear to be maddeningly parochial and self-absorbed, in part because they're so deeply immersed in the less-than-glamorous chores that help hold a struggling theater together. The actors, the directors, the producers, the stage managers; the costume builders, the set designers, the publicists: in theaters everywhere, it is the grueling, often thankless work they do that makes possible the onstage magic that so many others—the multitudes of theater lovers outside the tightly sealed doors of the acting community—tend to take for granted.

The Roy Rogosin I knew was a classic example of the fanatically devoted artistic director. He put in astronomically long hours to make SRT work. He wore countless hats in order to fulfill his daily responsibilities. Like any responsible CEO, he knew he had to be careful not to delegate authority to people who might prove to be incapable of meeting his standard for excellence. He endured the relentless pressure that comes from living always on the edge of financial collapse in a world where money is notoriously hard to come by and the possibility of failure is always waiting in the wings.

All of these things had to be weighing heavily on Rogosin's mind as he relinquished his valuable work time to talk with yet another job seeker convinced of his abilities and begging for employment. When he didn't hire me at SRT, I figured he'd seen nothing in me worth more than the two hundred dollars per week he was willing to pay me as a condition of employment. I went away thinking that in a few weeks he'd likely forget he'd ever sat down with me to hear me plead my case.

When the letter came, it was a cogent reminder of the fallibility of first impressions. I learned that Rogosin was far more than the man who'd locked horns with me in our negotiations, dismissing me with what seemed at the time like an unforgivably smug, oddly nonchalant dose of obduracy. Did he really have reason to believe I was the accomplished musician I claimed I was? Could a man who'd been the personal conductor for Johnny Mathis—a man who'd conducted at the Kennedy Center and the White House—be expected to be impressed with anything that I, a far less celebrated transplant from a Michigan factory town, had to say about myself?

Until I read his letter, I'd failed to understand that, like other highly driven people, Rogosin was simply too deeply immersed in his administrative work to worry about my insecurities. Like any prospective employer, he didn't owe me a job. Nor did he owe me anything more than the amount of time he'd allotted to me to tell my story. His first concern that day was not me; it was making decisions—personal, professional, and financial—that were best for his theater. SRT was Roy Rogosin's baby, and like any proud and loving parent, he was going to do what he thought best for his baby, regardless of the opinions of others.

By choosing to ignore convention; to scale the invisible, inviolable wall between performer and critic; then to praise my insights and abilities as a writer, Rogosin gave me a gift far greater than the job I'd wanted so fervently to land only a short time before. He saw from the form and substance of my review that I cared as much about the quality of my writing as he did about the quality of his theater. In any endeavor, there is no praise more coveted than the praise of a peer.

At the same time, through the decency and eloquence of his letter, he revealed himself to me not merely as a hard-driving, high-achieving professional but as a man of emotional depth and intellectual substance—the kind of man who can make the difference between an endeavor that flourishes from hard work and idealism and one that fails from the lack of either quality. It's those two priceless qualities—hard work and idealism—that keep the performing arts such a vital, life-affirming force in our otherwise prosaic lives.

A Measure of Makem, a Dose of Dunn: Light and Dark in the City of Portsmouth

What a difference the character of just one artist can make within the larger world of the arts! Like any city with a thriving fine and performing arts community, Portsmouth is home to an occasionally combustible blend of both the charitable and the churlish—gifted artists who conduct themselves with warmth and humility, and equally gifted artists who, thanks to an almost comically inflated sense of their worth to the world, choose to sting when others choose to nurture.

First, the charitable.

When in the early '90s the world-renowned Irish folk singer Tommy Makem, a Dover resident, was scheduled to appear first at the Manchester, New Hampshire, Dana Center for the Humanities, then at the University of New Hampshire in Durham, I got the nod from my editor, Holly Beaverstock, to do the cover story for *Spotlight*.

Makem, long thought by fans and critics alike to be the godfather of Irish music, was second only to philosopher/inventor R. Buckminster Fuller in the list of truly illustrious personages I'd had the pleasure of interviewing as a freelancer. For that reason, I might have expected Mr. Makem to be aloof, protective of his privacy, and even hard to handle while being interviewed by yet another obscure, nameless journalist from a small New England town.

What happened was quite the opposite. In our meeting at the Bagel Works in downtown Portsmouth, Makem was warm, gracious, polite, and disarmingly eager to cooperate with me to make the article a success for all concerned. In demeanor he was courtly and professorial; in conversation he was colorful and direct. He had a captivating country doctor twinkle in his eye, and because he dispensed wisdom with the ease and authority of an armchair philosopher, I found myself wanting to put away my pencil, drop my required persona as a journalist, and just be with the man.

My interview with Makem was one of my shining moments as an arts journalist. With boundless enthusiasm, unspoiled by even one little snippet of self-importance, he showered me with both his memorable exploits as a musician and his obvious affection for friends, neighbors, family, and anyone else whose path he happened to cross. I nearly forgot I was interviewing a man who'd long ago established himself as a legendary figure in the world of music.

As I shook his hand, thanked him profusely for his time, and headed home to write my cover story, I found myself wishing a few of my other interview subjects could have been even half as kind and cooperative as Makem was with me. With his uncommon grace and humility, he gave me renewed hope for a change into a kinder, gentler world—one in which the rich, the famous, and the highly accomplished people of the world actually remembered their roots and lived their lives not from an attitude of superiority but from a posture of humility.

And now, the churlish.

Robert Dunn, an irascible, brooding figure who'd haunted the streets of Portsmouth and the pages of poetry anthologies for several decades in the Seacoast region, was another Holly Beaverstock assignment that made me rub my hands together in gleeful anticipation. I thought, *Wow—the poet laureate of Portsmouth! This should be a plum assignment!*

I'd always enjoyed interviewing people whose reputation preceded them, but whom I'd never had the pleasure of meeting. Because of it, the Dunn gig promised to be a memorable encounter—an intriguing mystery waiting to be solved. Would Mr. Dunn live up to my enduring vision of what a poet laureate should look like and how he should behave? I'd soon find out, because our meeting was scheduled for the next Monday morning, and my story was due on Holly's desk by noon of the next day.

We met downtown at the legendary Portsmouth Athenaeum. Incorporated in 1817, the Portsmouth Athenaeum is one of only twenty athenaeums still operating in America and committed, according to its mission statement, to "facilitating convivial interchange and intellectual discourse." My kind of institution! I figured it would be the perfect place for a poet laureate to step out of the sunlight on a quiet afternoon, sit pensively in the shadows thrown by stacks of sagely tomes, and ply his venerable craft in deference to the gods.

Once inside the Athenaeum, away from the interminable honk-and-roar of vehicles along Islington Street, one could easily imagine Hawthorne, Emerson, Margaret Fuller, and other members of the elite group of Concord intellectuals, up from the manse in a very different era, huddling over the Athenaeum's modest collection of precious books and priceless artifacts. It was that kind of place.

While preparing for the interview, I learned that Dunn and his poetry had accumulated a great many admirers over the years. When the poet died in 2008, J. Dennis Robinson wrote with obvious affection that Robert—dubbed the "Penny Poet" because of his habit of selling his hand-sewn booklets of poetry while walking the streets and alleys of Portsmouth—was "unique, idiosyncratic, singular, gentle, peculiar ... an outsider, a philosopher, an eccentric, a *mensch*. He was the love child, if such a thing were possible, of Gandhi, R. Crumb, William Blake, Ichabod Crane, and Stephen Hawking."

It was more than likely that Dunn had come across all of those historical figures in his studies, and if I had learned in the interview that he admired their brilliance and eccentricity as much as I did, I'd have been on the verge of discovering a literary soulmate—a man who might just make as ideal a neighbor as Tommy Makem.

Dunn was already waiting for me as I walked through the door of the Athenaeum, notebook in hand, and I extended my other hand in greeting. He sat slumped in a chair near the window, a distant, desultory ghost of a man, oddly materialized and yet grudgingly on display in downtown Portsmouth on an otherwise ordinary, late-winter day.

I waited for him to reciprocate, but got nothing in return. No smile, no gesture, and neither visible nor audible acknowledgement that we were about to engage in a conversation. He sat like a stone, still clad in his trademark rumpled trench coat, and peering, mantis-like, from behind large, horn-rimmed glasses.

"Well, Mr. Dunn!" I began. "I'm glad to have the chance to interview you. I've heard many good things about you and your poetry! Now that I've been assigned to write a feature story, I need to ask some questions about your work."

"Okay," he muttered. "Go ahead and ask."

"First, how long have you been writing poetry?" It was my first volley, and clearly it did not impress him.

"Look," he said, "I thought we were going to have a *serious* interview!" He glowered, shifted nervously in his chair, then for the first time showed signs of something like a corporeal presence. He'd gotten me off balance, and he knew it.

"And so did I!" I replied. "I have many serious questions to ask you, but to put together a credible story, I have to ask the more prosaic questions, too."

"Perhaps so," he snapped, "but I came down here to talk about poetry, not myself."

Swell! I thought. *So warm and cuddly, these laureates.* I turned to him, steeled my resolve to do the work I'd been assigned to do, and plowed through the series of questions I'd so meticulously prepared for our encounter. As I look back on the experience, it was like trying to have a meaningful conversation with a box of corn flakes long past their fresh date.

Not surprisingly, our exchange was mercifully short, and, for a conversation with a widely admired poet laureate, appallingly unfeeling and unemotional. The entire struggle lasted less than half an hour—I made sure of that, and so did he—and I was more than pleased to leave him slumped over in his chair and get back out onto Islington Street, where the air was fresh and the living was easier.

In his dress and demeanor, Robert Dunn lived up to all of my expectations of how a poet laureate might be: charmingly frumpy, blissfully indifferent to fashion, allergic to the usual social amenities. In his conduct—the brusqueness, the snarly disposition, the impatience, the outright rudeness—he failed to impress me in any way.

It's a curious thing that we as a society appear to have granted a very special status to people who describe themselves as poets, often with no questions asked. Did he think that as a poet he was inherently superior to me, a mere arts journalist and critic? Did being tapped as the poet laureate of Portsmouth make him feel even more important than the legions of poets who toil without reward in the vineyards of the average? And perhaps most importantly, is there something in poets that makes them certain they have a higher calling than do writers in any other genre?

Charles Dickens, Mark Twain, Ernest Hemingway, H. L. Mencken: all were journalists at one time or another, and all were superb writers in other genres. Dorothy Parker—another universally admired journalist—was an enormously gifted critic, short story writer, satirist, and poet, able to switch from genre to genre with little apparent effort. And yet the public is much less likely to issue them a halo than they are to put that same halo over the head of someone who's chosen to be known exclusively as a poet.

People tend to think of poets as inherently superior in wisdom, insight, and writerly skill, but anyone who reads the works of a wide range of poets knows that, like writers in any genre, they have within their ranks every level of competence, from the spectacular (Sylvia Plath) to the abominable (William Topaz McGonagall).

It's also worthwhile, I think, to point out that all poets were writers before they were poets. They didn't pick up a pencil while still in elementary school and begin spewing astonishing couplets and breathtaking cantos before nap time. The great majority of them didn't add poetry to their bag of writerly tricks until later in their lives. Writing is writing, and it's either well crafted or it isn't.

And apropos of my encounter with Mr. Dunn, manners are manners, no matter who has the opportunity, if not the obligation, to employ them while in the company of others.

For one of privilege and accomplishment to pull rank on another—someone he's earmarked on first meeting, and without sufficient evidence, as having gifts and accomplishments inferior to his own—is to violate the very premise of what it means to be a poet. Walt Whitman, whose epic narrative *Leaves of Grass* shook the world of poetry to its foundations and forever changed the course of modern literature, would understand precisely where I'm coming from in this matter. In my book, genuine poets—at least those worthy of the distinction—have room in their hearts for all of the well-meaning people around them, regardless of their social status, their chosen occupation, or the level of their accomplishments. That's where, in civil society, good manners ought without reservation to come into play.

Of course, Robert Dunn was hardly alone in his propensity to pull rank and choose rudeness over civility. It can happen anywhere, including the world of the visual arts, and not surprisingly, it has happened to me. After all, there's not a person on the planet it *hasn't* happened to.

When I submitted several works to the jurors at the New Hampshire Art Association several years ago, I decided to write and present an optional defense of my work along with my submittal. I'd spent the last year creating a series of more than forty unconventional drawings, each intended to explore the idea of the doodle as the fundamental vocabulary of all artists from the time they were toddlers with a crayon in their hand to full-blown adulthood. Whether the tools are simple or sophisticated, all artworks since recorded time—and before—have inevitably begun with a single line on the wall of a cave, on a block of granite, on a blank sheet of paper, or on some other surface.

I also pointed out that no less an artist than Pablo Picasso had great respect for the doodle—a simple, viscerally created line or series of lines—as the beginning point of any work of art. He loved the cartoon, a genre that depends entirely on imaginative, playful line work, and well into old age he was proud to draw not like an academically trained artist but like a child. In 2010, the Metropolitan Museum of Art mounted an exhibit of his works that included an astonishingly inventive array of late-in-life cartoons. In that same year, Tim Burton, another artist who understands the expressive power of cartoons, was featured in an exhibit of more than seven hundred works in multiple media at the Museum of Modern Art. His featured works included brilliantly imaginative doodles scrawled in the margins of his notebooks during junior high study hall.

I might have been wiser to skip the optional defense and just turn my works over to the jury for their scrutiny. My submittal, along with the defense, netted the following acerbic, mean-spirited rejection, scrawled dismissively across the bottom of the submittal form: "They're nothing but doodles—have no clear meaning."

My anger came not from having had my artworks rejected. After all, I'd endured many rejections as an artist over the years, and during the many years I managed my own gallery, I had to dish them out, too. The anger came from my realization that I'd been unnecessarily insulted in the course of being rejected. A person in a position to say no to me with dignity and compassion chose instead to drive the hot knife of disapproval into the heart of a project which, while meaningless to the juror, had enormous meaning for me. Even the rainy-day doodles of a toddler have meaning; just ask the toddler, and then his parents.

How to find fault with or say no to a given work in any discipline is a matter of both style and substance. Anyone with common sense and a beating heart knows it's poor form to kick somebody while he's down. It's precisely at the difficult moment of rejection that a critic or juror must choose to carry out his or her responsibilities with either a heavy hammer or a caring hug.

In the matter of style, Robert Dunn and the anonymous juror who thought my drawings had "no clear meaning" appear to have had a great deal in common. But it's not the sort of style that deserves to be celebrated.

As for substance, they and others like them ought to have known that the task of anyone in a position to judge—including the arts journalist or reviewer—is not to make an artist, a musician, or an actor feel like a failure. It's to inform him or her that, at least this time around, the work in question either didn't fit the needs of the jury or failed to impress a reviewer. Saying no or "not a good fit for this show" is often both necessary and wise—the best thing for everyone concerned. But it ought never to be seen as an opportunity to condemn the maker.

Chapter 12

The Art of the Assemblage
An Elegant Chaos, Joyfully Conceived

Found objects: they're a whole lot cheaper than oils, and a whole lot harder to find. But it's that very difficulty—the need to walk long distances and search the roadsides, gutters, and alleyways with microscopic precision and an unfettered imagination—that makes the art of the assemblage such a joyful endeavor. If you don't like littering your house with rusty, soiled, broken, timeworn oddities, you'd best avoid the life of an assemblage-maker. If, on the other hand, the word junk *isn't in your vocabulary—if everything you encounter is beautiful in its own inimitable way—then you've just risen to found-object heaven, and you'll have trouble saying no to nearly everything you stumble across while in the heat of discovery.*

The found-object assemblage appeals to my sense of adventure in a way that strictly two-dimensional artworks cannot. As an artist I've a passionate interest in both—I frequently paint, draw and photograph—but creating an assemblage is an entirely different world.

Joseph Cornell was one of the early makers of assemblages, and his mastery of the genre has motivated countless artists to try their hand at it. I learned early on, though, that when conceiving an assemblage, there's a clear and present danger of being seen as having taken the easy path as an artist—of being only superficially clever, lacking in painterly skill, or being downright lazy as an artist.

To bring a memorable assemblage into the world requires travel, exploration, an unbridled imagination, and a sense of the absurd. The process speaks eloquently to the compulsive, devil-may-care, wanderer/tinkerer in me.

When I set about to create an assemblage, I seldom walk the streets or enter a store with a set idea. For me, it's more productive to approach the project blindly, then wait until I stumble upon just one unpretentious item that sparks an idea. The hunt for that one inspiring object—something that fires up my creative engines—is the most rewarding part of the process. Once that happens, I go into high gear, traveling wherever my intuition takes me and adding one object after another until a concept is born.

Here, then, are the stories behind the creation of four of my favorite assemblages. If the process intrigues you, give it a try. Take a walk in your neighborhood, climb up into your attic, or drive to the nearest antique and collectibles store. With plenty of persistence and a little bit of luck, it's likely you'll find that one deceptively useless piece that will inspire you to create an assemblage of your own.

The Ghost of Emin Bey

One of my earliest assemblages came about nearly a decade ago because of my need to meet a deadline. I'd heard about an intriguing exhibit at the now defunct Experimental Gallery in Salem, Massachusetts, and decided to whip something up and submit it to the jury. I had only two weeks to make it happen.

Philosopher/inventor Bucky Fuller liked to say that deadlines tend to mortify, but for me, at least, they have quite the opposite effect. For some reason, they're a powerful stimulant to action, often leading to a more imaginative solution than would have been possible for me when creating without time constrictions.

I also like knowing that with an assemblage I'll not have to deal with paints and brushes and all the preparatory work they entail. I just trade them in for another, entirely different set of technical challenges having to do with how to go about mounting and integrating the objects I find.

The morning after seeing Experimental Gallery's call for art, I headed down to Route 1 in Wells, an area known in and well beyond southern Maine as "Antique Row." From Ogunquit to Arundel, one can explore the greatest concentration of shops, both high-end and affordable, that a compulsive picker ever could hope to find.

I began my search at Bo-Mar Hall antiques in Wells—one of my favorite treasure hunting destinations. After burrowing through dozens of neatly arranged booths, each belonging to a different collector, I stumbled across a rusty, baby-blue metal box with a handle at the top and a lockable clasp. It was just the sort of eccentric but serviceable container that appeals to me, so without bothering to open it, I bought it on the spot.

The proprietor explained that it was designed for 1930s-era doll collectors who needed a safe way to store and transport their valuable, hand-crafted dolls from show to show in the collectible doll circuit.

At home in my studio, I put the box up on my work table and popped open the door. Inside was what appeared to be a miniature stage, with a platform at the bottom and a small crosspiece at the top. I half-expected to see a solitary actor step out from under imaginary lights, move downstage to the apron, take a bow, and begin to tap dance.

Curiously, the interior of the box was lined with faded yellow newspaper articles. One in particular—an article about the search for missing world traveler Emin Bey—immediately caught my eye. In a matter of seconds an idea began to form, and I was off to the races.

While I enjoy a good story from any historical era, I'm no historian. After reading what was left of the article, I decided to enlist Mr. Bey merely as a springboard to an imaginary, multimedia adventure-in-a-box—a siren call to the romantic world traveler in all of us and a look at the ways in which the bubble of human perfection can be burst, often with tragic consequences. A considerable portion of my narrative would be historically accurate; the rest would be a literary flight of fancy—a romp through history, but with playful, evocative embellishments.

To set the stage for the story, I wired four miniature, multicolored lights into the panel at the top of the box, then carved a block of basswood into a fantastical, wildly grinning mask—an evocation of what I imagined to be the spirit of Emin Bey. The mask took up nearly all of the available space within the box. That fact alone helped establish him as an outsize world figure, capable of dominating a room and showing up anywhere on earth at any time, in the most unlikely of places. He'd be like the peripatetic time traveler in Virginia Woolf's picaresque novel, *Orlando*.

To add spice to the adventure, I decided to give Bey a mistress—a woman named Abhilasha Shishekli. She'd be passionately in love with him, but deeply distressed because of the distance between them and waiting anxiously for his return to Constantinople and into her arms.

Next, I composed a short pamphlet, including a letter from Abhilasha to her lover, bound it to look as if it had been around for years, wallpapered the interior of the box, then attached the pamphlet to the inside with a cord. I decorated the exterior of the box with stamps and images that defined it as having traveled the world, then added a miniature poster that invited visitors to open the box and see what mysteries lay within it. My hope was that once they'd gotten inside, they'd be sufficiently curious to open up the letter and read it. The pamphlet read as follows:

The Central Library
Oppeln, Prussia
December 17th, 1905

To the Reader: Below is a complete and unedited letter from the beautiful and sophisticated Abhilasha Shishekli to Mehemet

Fig. 55. *The Ghost of Emin Bey* (assemblage, front and side view).

Emin Pasha, the celebrated doctor, naturalist, and world traveler. The letter, touchingly perfumed and beribboned, was found in the winter of 1901 along with other personal effects in a dresser drawer in the author's room in Constantinople, where she lived with her father, subsisting on a small academic stipend while teaching drawing to the local schoolchildren. It is thought to be the last letter she wrote to Pasha before his departure to distant lands.

Born Eduard Carl Oscar Theodor Schnitzer in 1840 in Oppeln, Prussia, Pasha studied at several German universities, qualifying as a doctor in 1864. After abruptly being disqualified from medical practice, he left Germany for Constantinople, where he fell in love with the daughter of a local professor who helped him reenter the medical profession. Then, after adding Turkish, Albanian, and Greek to his already extensive repertoire of European lan-

Fig. 56. *The Ghost of Emin Bey* (assemblage, interior view).

guages, he toured the world, conducting scientific research and eventually winning an important appointment as the Governor of Equatoria in Africa. It is then that he became known around the world as Emin Bey.

Scholars know little about the passionate liaison between Emin Bey and Abhilasha Shishekli. It is known, however, that their love affair persisted in spite of the great distance between them, brought about by Pasha's world travels for the purpose of scientific research. The aforementioned letter offers incontestable proof of Abhilasha's passion for Emin.

Constantinople: April 20th, 1891

My Dear Emin,

Where have you BEEN, my Faithful One? Since your hasty departure for Wadelai I have longed for the sound of your mellifluous voice, the touch of your strong but tender hand, the heavenly twinkle in your celestial eyes.

And yet, my beloved Pasha, though I have penned more than twenty letters to you since the first snow fell in the mountains above Constantinople, you have not written! My darling, you are breaking my heart! Do you not KNOW that?

They say in the local newspapers (and what beautiful illustrations I saw there) that your trip to Cairo was even more memorable than Khartoum and Buganda. Can it be true? If so, it is simply not fair, my handsome Governor!

How I wish I could have been at your side as you rode that proud, brocaded camel to the hotel—though I've heard those strange beasts are not nearly as sweet of breath as they are of temperament! I would have lounged with you on your luxurious, lantern-lit balcony, surrounded by splendidly manicured, tantalizingly aromatic gardens, dining on rice pilaf and stuffed cucumbers while the stars shone above you in the dark Egyptian nights.

How jealous your exploits have made me! Just think: me here at home, alone and dejected in my spare little room on the edge of a sleepy university, with nothing more than my day-old bread, a flask of cheap wine, and these forbidden, unrequited thoughts of you in my arms! What would my students think if they knew about the wine— and YOU?

The Art of the Assemblage

I've heard, too, that the women of Cairo are as ravishingly beautiful as they are noble—full to overflowing with grace and liquidity. I must ask you quite honestly, my dear: in spite of all their natural charms and PURCHASED elegance, can they still hope to compete with ME for your priceless affections? I pray, my dear Pasha, that you have seen fit to behave yourself as you crossed the great, dark continent of Africa! I shall not forgive you if you even so much as GLIMPSE at the unclothed ankles of the local beauties! That will be as far as your hungry eyes are allowed to travel. After all, you know that your appetite will be properly fed here at home, where you belong—with ME!

To think that you, my very own Mehemet Emin Pasha, have been the subject of an impassioned rescue across this vast and teeming globe, and that the venerated Henry Morton Stanley would lead the search! Here in Turkey they're calling his quest "The Emin Pasha Relief Expedition," no less!

As you might imagine, I am eternally grateful that Dr. Stanley found you in such high spirits and—thank God—all in one piece! At first I feared for your safety because of those hordes of roaming mercenaries—cutthroats and knaves, every last one of them! But I have since come to my senses, and have every faith that the brave Captain Stairs, with the help of your precious friend Wilhelm Junker, will shield you from harm and bring you home to me and the city where we first fell in love. Of course, I've always known of your worth to humanity, but I didn't realize, my dear Schnitzer, that I would be sharing your blazing accomplishments with all the peoples of the earth!

Until we meet again, my darling Emin, I pledge to you my heart, my undying loyalty, and the full depth and breadth of my affections. May our great, All-knowing God protect you as you complete your journey from Cairo to my waiting arms. And now I shall return to bed, comforted by the knowledge of your imminent return.

All my love,

*Your devoted
Abhilasha*

Editor's Note: In 1881, the feared general Muhammad Ahmad began a revolt against the local army, and by 1883, Equatoria, along with Emin Bey and his meager band of soldiers, was cut off from the civilized world. Soon, with world opinion on his side, Dr. Stanley organized the Emin Pasha Relief Expedition, traveling up the Congo River and through the Ituri Forest—a difficult route that resulted in the loss of two-thirds of the expedition.

Stanley finally met Emin Bey in Lado in April of 1888. After a year of argument and indecision, Stanley persuaded him to leave for the coast. Tired and hungry, Emin and his troops arrived in Bagamoyo in 1890. He then entered German military service and led an expedition to the lakes of the interior. After fierce and courageous battle, Emin Bey was killed by slave traders at Kinene.

Abhilasha Shishekli died alone in 1893 in a remote Turkish village, despondent after learning of the death of her beloved Pasha. Her final letter to him—the last, irrefutable evidence of her affections—is on permanent display under sealed glass at the Museum of Military History in Constantinople. Historians may read the letter by appointment throughout the year during regularly scheduled hours; the general public may read it only on special occasions, under strict supervision, as determined by a select committee of museum curators.

Gerhardt Schleider

Chief of Military Research
The Central Library
Oppeln, Prussia

I know of only one or two people who ever took the time to open up my assemblage, study its contents, and read the letter attached to it. And yet, somehow, it didn't matter. For me, the act of creating the project in the first place was the only really important thing.

However foolishly, I found myself even liking the idea that only a tiny number of people would ever come into contact with *The Ghost of Emin Bey*. That they'd be willing to devote even a moment to the study of my assemblage became an unspoken, unheralded gift to me: a sign of approval that means more to an artist than any large but less attentive audience could ever mean. My feelings about this have undoubtedly evolved from my time in the theater, where a small but responsive audience is infinitely more valuable to actors than a hall full of people snoozing in their loges or talking on their cell phones.

I once performed a solo flute recital at the Unitarian Church in Portsmouth, New Hampshire, before an audience of five. Two of the five were friends—one working as my sound engineer, the other as my ticket taker. The other three wandered in off the street to see what the noise was all about. It's not the size of the crowd that makes an event worthwhile, it's that there is anyone at all to make the all-important connection between the artist, the viewer, and the art. Thanks to *The Ghost of Emin Bey*, I had the pleasure, however small, of completing that circuit.

Little Girl, Little Girl, What Will the Future Bring?

The idea for *Little Girl, Little Girl* evolved quite spontaneously from my purchase of yet another set of baby shoes (as an assemblage artist I've harbored a longtime fascination for them), entirely for the purpose of integrating them into a yet-to-be-created work of art.

There's a certain understated majesty in a simple pair of shoes. These centuries-old, always-evolving devices facilitate our ever more ambitious perambulations into foot-unfriendly territory. They're also an emotionally powerful repository for the storage of our own very personal history.

Within the close, leathery confines of a shoe rests the always endearing, sometimes disturbing story of the one unique person who occupied them. Just where, we inevitably wonder, has the wearer of those empty shoes been? What town or city did she call home? How did she dress above shoe-level? What, or whom, did she love? What triumphs did she celebrate, and what indignities did she endure while tucked so tightly and purposefully into her shoes?

Our senses are stimulated by the distinctive appearance and physical properties of a timeworn shoe. The plain leathery perfume of a long-ago-manufactured shoe can be an unmistakable footprint from a life either well lived or marked by tragedy. Even the rough, asymmetrical sole of a heavily traveled shoe has within it a poignant melodrama, either tenderly ingratiating or disturbingly sinister, begging to be told.

These were the feelings I carried within me when I headed down again to Antique Row, the Arundel-to-Ogunquit corridor, to see where one particular pair of shoes might take me.

My first stop was at Bo-Mar Hall antiques.[1] I've become a familiar face there, and the employees often ask me what proj-

---

[1] Author's note: Sadly, Bowmar Hall Antiques closed its doors forever only a few months before *Happy Dawg Walks the Sad Man* was published—a victim of changing times and a landlord who had other plans for this and other, similar

ect I'm working on. Seeing nothing workable there—one can't strike it rich on every occasion—I headed to another prime destination for the assemblage artist on the hunt: Blacksmiths' Mall in Ogunquit, only a few miles from Bo-Mar. Blacksmiths' is near the heart of downtown, only a five-minute walk from the Atlantic.

I needed only ten minutes to stumble across just the pair of shoes I'd hoped to find. Beneath the richly bronzed exterior, they were remarkably well preserved—tiny, scarred, and weather-beaten, with threadbare laces and tongues twisted like potato chips from being stuffed over and over again into the shoes.

The baby who wore those shoes long ago—I'll call her Millicent—must now be either dead or well into her nineties. I sniffed the shoes' interior, imagining I might smell some lingering evidence of the beguiling perfume of a baby's feet. I peered into their shadowy openings and wondered for a moment if, like Alice, I might tumble chaotically downward into an exotic Wonderland of multicolored little people and leaping, otherworldly creatures. The allure of an anonymous pair of baby shoes presents us with a rare opportunity to imagine starting over again with our lives—of rewriting the story of ourselves into a more appealing, more rewarding tale of triumph over adversity.

So I had my pair of shoes, but what next? I couldn't just plop them down on a tabletop and call them art.

And yet, why not? Marcel Duchamp did just that with a battle-weary, out-of-service urinal, sparking the ready-made movement that dramatically expanded the idea of what is and isn't art. But this was a pair of shoes, not a urinal, and I wanted them to be the visual starting point for an implied narrative about the formative years of one tiny child who, like the rest of us, was born with an empty slate—a budding Existentialist—but would soon have a story as worthwhile as any other to share with the world. I looked for a way to display the shoes that would evoke that long-ago time when Millicent woke up each morning to a warm and welcoming sun, the smell of fresh flowers on the nightstand near her crib, and the proud smiles of two adoring parents.

As I continued searching for add-ons, I saw leaning against a shelf full of tattered cookbooks a gray cardboard photo frame—a triptych with cathedral-like archways at the top of each opening—decorated all around with a delicate, silvery border and

---

facilities along Route 1 in Wells. It was a great and irreplaceable loss to the artist community—and to anyone else who cherishes antiques and collectibles and understands both their emotional power and their historical significance.

punctuated here and there with tiny, pale pink roses cradled in moss-green leaves. It was the Victorian era personified.

Each of the frame's openings featured a faded black-and-white photograph of a different 1930s girl, standing alone, wearing a frilly white dress, and smiling shyly into the camera. They varied noticeably in height, but their facial features were strikingly similar, so it was likely they were sisters. *So young, so innocent, and so full of possibilities!* I thought, and suddenly, the concept for my assemblage found its voice and came to life.

I decided on the spot to call my assemblage *Little Girl, Little Girl, What Will the Future Bring*? An evocative title was all I needed to set my creative machinery in motion.

I knew somehow that simply leaving those photos in their frame wouldn't suffice. I needed a fresh, idiosyncratic approach to this project. What, I wondered, might I put in each of those openings that would carry the weight and substance of my sentiment?

Then, across the aisle from where I'd discovered the triptych, I saw a display of early American dolls. One of them was unusually tiny, dwarfed by the larger dolls standing in a row behind her. *That's it!* I thought. *Actual dolls!*

I picked up Millicent and held her up against the triptych. She fit perfectly into the center opening, and to my delight her eyes fluttered, making her come eerily alive in my hands. She became a shy, inquisitive creature, freshly arrived in the universe and unselfconsciously consuming the world around her.

I found the clerk, made my purchases, and headed toward the car with a smile of victory on my face.

The doll and the triptych were beside me on the car seat as I pulled out onto Route 1 south and turned on the radio. Astonishingly, Merle Travis's legendary "Won'tcha Be My Baby" blared out from the dashboard. The creative adrenaline was now pumping with even greater urgency through my aesthetic veins.

As I worked my way south through Ogunquit and then York, fighting the ever-growing tourist traffic, I suddenly remembered Dover Doll Clinic, a place I'd driven by countless times on my way to Portsmouth. I made a U-turn and headed there on the double. *I'll put dolls in the openings to the left and right of Millicent!* With that decision, *Little Girl, Little Girl* was quickly gaining momentum.

I arrived in Dover, drove down Central Avenue past the sprawling, tree-lined Pine Hill Cemetery, and pulled left into the DDC parking lot. Out stepped Patricia Aveni, a sprightly, diminutive woman with a warm smile and an easygoing demeanor.

Fig. 57. *Little Girl, Little Girl, What Does the Future Bring?* (assemblage).

"I'm looking for dolls' heads," I said, "not the rest of the doll, just the head." She gave me a bemused, sideways glance—*how macabre: a headhunter*—then ushered me into the workshop attached to the rear of her home. "Dolls' heads we have," she said, smiling. "You bet! And arms and eyes and hair and feet, too. You've come to the right place. Come see!"

On the rear wall of the workshop was a series of cabinets containing an astonishing array of doll parts stored by category in dozens of meticulously labeled pull-out drawers. Here was evidence of a woman with a passion for dolls that rivaled and perhaps even exceeded my own passion for art. With the establishment of her business, she'd acted on a longstanding reverence for dolls of every imaginable kind, painstakingly designed and packed with emotion. Dover Doll Clinic was home to a museum-quality collection of dolls from around the world, chronicling more than a century of human ingenuity and expert craftsmanship.

I showed her the doll I'd purchased in Wells, explained the concept I was working on, then began pulling out drawer after drawer to find something that would click for me. I picked up one beautifully crafted head, studied its features, and realized that, like the doll I'd purchased in Wells, this head featured eyes that fluttered.

"Perfect!" I said. "If you had another just like it, I could put one on each side of the full-bodied doll and make a trio—three pair of eyes, all aflutter!"

A ten-minute search paid off. At the bottom of a basket brimming with heads of every imaginable kind, I found another head exactly like the first one. I thanked Aveni profusely, popped the heads into a sack, and headed home to begin turning my found objects into what I hoped would be a credible assemblage. *Better not get stopped for speeding*, I thought to myself. *I wouldn't want the cops to see I've got two heads in a sack.*

Several days later, after numerous tweaks, touchups, and conceptual shifts, *Little Girl, Little Girl, What Will the Future Bring?* was a reality. Each of the two dolls' heads ended up being cradled in the openings of the shoes I'd found in the early stages of the project, then enthroned proudly on either side of the tiny, full-bodied doll at center stage. Whenever I tipped the entire assemblage forward and then back again, the three pairs of eyes would flutter in unison. Altogether they were eerie, evocative, and remarkably lifelike. I felt sure they'd be a hit in an exhibit, though I fully expected that some people would be spooked by the fluttering of those eyes.

Little Girl, Little Girl entered the marketplace, found a home in three consecutive Seacoast New Hampshire exhibits, and was finally sold to Anne Strout, a friend and fellow artist from Falmouth, Maine. Its purchase helped fund my then-imminent trip to New Zealand, and gave three pairs of fluttering, emotion-packed eyes a warm and caring home in which to dream their little doll dreams.

Incantation

Incantation, like *Little Girl, Little Girl*, started with a shoe. It had no mate when I discovered it at Blacksmiths' Mall in Ogunquit, buried in an antique barrel filled with nostalgic, long-ago discarded domestic items. There may have been a colorful story behind its disappearance—perhaps it was torn off during some long-ago playground scuffle, and never retrieved—but it's more likely it was orphaned when the other shoe was bronzed as a keepsake.

Once I'd bought the shoe, I began to search for an object that might function as a backdrop—a stage on which the story of the shoe and its wearer might best be told. Twenty minutes later, I found an object whose size, shape, vintage, texture, and colors made it an ideal candidate for the job. It took me a few minutes to decide what it was: a beautifully designed wicker basket that could easily have been either a magazine rack or a vehicle for transporting logs from woodpile to hearth.

I had the shoe and the basket, but now I needed to find a platform of some sort to support the shoe and showcase it against the backdrop. The textural match between the shoe and the basket was so strong that the design ante was raised dramatically. I had to find a third item with the same vintage look, and with a shape that would fully harmonize it with the other items.

Finding the right platform turned out to be considerably more challenging than finding the backdrop. Finally, high on a shelf in the back of the store, I found precisely what I'd been trying to envision: a rectangular, chestnut-brown wooden box whose scratches, stains, and square-head nails branded it as yet another century-old object with some sort of utilitarian purpose—probably a piece of kitchen equipment. The front of the box was covered with wire mesh, and at the top was a lid which, when opened, would allow the user to fill the box with something.

That something clearly couldn't have been liquid, so by the process of elimination, I was on to the scent. I learned from one of the store clerks that it was a late-Colonial-era grain sifter. While it was crudely constructed, it was nevertheless fully capable of serving as the platform I needed.

The shoe fit perfectly atop the sifter, but my design work was far from over. There had to be something to put inside that sifter that would heighten the mystery of my evolving assemblage. It would have to fit nicely into the sifter, but it would also have to have an air of the inexplicable about it. I dug and dug in every nook and cranny of the shop, then found a tall, pencil-thin metal sculpture of an emaciated, buddha-like figure, somewhere in spirit and concept between the eerily elongated religious figures of El Greco and the long-limbed, Twiggy-like creations of surrealist sculptor Alberto Giacometti.

Whatever its derivations, the sculpture now lives a solitary life inside the grain sifter, cloaked in shadows and barely visible unless the light where it's exhibited is positioned in such a way that it can penetrate the mesh. That the sculpture can't easily be seen only adds to the inscrutability of the piece, and that's just the effect I was looking for.

My assemblage—a kind of grandmother's-attic echinoderm—now had its skeletal casing; a shoe from some toddler who we can only hope led a happy, productive existence as an adult; a quirky but functional platform for the shoe; and a chimerical bronze figure dwelling uneasily within it.

But something was missing. So far, it appeared to be little more than a box within a box, interesting but not arresting. To bring it fully to life, I needed to add lively colors and textural accents—materials that would energize it while simultaneously contributing to the underlying enigma of the piece.

I could never have predicted the solution. While rifling through a bin full of vintage clothing and accessories, including old hats, doilies, and scarves that Aunt Bee would have worn proudly down in Mayberry, I caught a flash of color that I instantly knew would complement what I'd created so far. It looked a little like a discarded tangle of autumn leaves, or perhaps some creepy-crawly thing that had stopped crawling long ago in the moisture-filled darkness of a fruit cellar. I held it up against the unfinished assemblage, and without even knowing what it was, asked myself how I might put it to work for me.

One is wise to suspend all logic—and perhaps even common sense—when creating a found-object assemblage. Spontaneity is an essential tool when working in the genre. With too much planning, design solutions often come across as facile and slick. Better to think as a child, abandon fastidiousness as an ideal, and seek a more playful, less predictable design.

My creepy-crawly thing was both curvilinear and elastic. When I stretched it, then let it go, it snapped back like a pincer into its original, hemispherical shape. Because of its warm colors and appealing textures, it was quaint and yet remarkably architectural in a futuristic sort of way—reminiscent of one of Bucky Fuller's geodesic domes, but without the triangles.

I locked it around the top of the magazine rack, but realized it not only looked ridiculous in that position but would have competed unfairly for attention with the shoe, whose job was to dominate the assemblage. Applying it to the back of the rack didn't work, either: 90 percent of it would have been hidden from view.

The only option left to me was the bottom, so I snapped it into place from underneath, and *presto*! It instantly fell into place within the evolving configuration of my assemblage, echoing the semicircular contours of the rack and nicely counterbalancing the shoe at its opposite end. It was almost organically attached now, as if the entire creation had been conceived as one, manufactured, marketed, and sold in the novelties section of some long-ago department store.

I had nearly all I needed now to make this a successful assemblage, so I headed to the front of the shop and laid my findings out on the counter. The employees at Blacksmiths' Mall knew me well as "that man who makes assemblages," so I showed them the items I'd found and explained what I planned to do to unite them.

Fig. 58. *Incantation* (assemblage).

"By the way," I said, pointing at the creepy-crawly thing. "What on earth *is* this? I haven't the foggiest!"

"Oh, that's easy!" said Joan, who was nearly always working when I was out object-hunting at Blacksmiths' Mall. "It's a pineapple hat! My neighbor always liked them. She had several of 'em lined up neatly on a shelf in her closet, and on Sundays she would choose one and wear it proudly in the church she attended up in Millinocket."

I paid for my little closet of curiosities, bagged everything up, and headed back to Berwick, happy to have found all of what I needed to complete my project. Over the next two days the piece came together just as I'd conceived it. I cross-wired it at the top, behind the platform where the shoe would be showcased, then hung it on the wall in my studio, stepped back, and studied it.

I was still not happy. Something was missing. Annoyed, I left the assemblage on the wall, went about my affairs, then retired for the evening, optimistic that the bud of the concept of my assemblage would soon find sunlight, become a flower, and take root in an exhibit somewhere.

The next morning I jumped into my car and drove off toward an unknown destination, determined to find that one magical object that would lend final authority to my assemblage.

I found that object in the most unlikely of places—an upscale gift shop in downtown Newburyport, Massachusetts. I generally avoid the self-consciously trendy gift shops, which seem motivated less by good taste and imagination than by the siren song of tourist dollars. The object I found was a tiny, Buddha-like figure, held still in the midst of a karate-like kick and wearing a warm, ingratiating smile that made my heart melt and my wallet open for business. I had to have that Buddha!

I'd needed only my little high-kicking sage, along with another last-minute find—a pearl-inlaid, gold-trimmed medallion I positioned just above the pineapple hat—to bring my assemblage fully to life. I decided to call it *Incantation*, and I hoped that it might someday find a home with someone who would learn to treasure its mystical, playful aura.

Considering how much I had needed to travel to find the components of my assemblage, it's ironic that it was finally purchased in October of 2014 by Macpage LLC—a corporate accounting firm and art gallery in South Portland, Maine, where the assemblage had been on exhibit—then donated to the Maine Better Transportation Association in Augusta. I can now rightfully claim that *Incantation* has really been around.

Waste Not Thy Time on This Good Earth

Not surprisingly, around the time I turned sixty I began to reflect more frequently on the impermanence of life—on the inescapable reality of our mortality. Then, one night while I was struggling to fall asleep and wondering just what lay ahead for me, the words "waste not thy time on this good earth" came to me. I immediately liked the sound and substance of them—their inherent musicality, their biblical tone—and it didn't take long for them to become both compelling aphorism and motivational whip. Now that I've entered the seventh decade of my life, that mildly sinister admonition has taken on an even greater urgency. Welcome, my friends, to Septuagenarian City.

It was that memorable aphorism, along with a magnificent pair of century-old shoes I'd found in an antique shop in Northwood, New Hampshire—shoes worn happily into disrepair by some exuberant toddler of unknown circumstances—that provided both the spark and the impetus for an assemblage. I found them, fell in love with them, and knew there'd be no turning back. I was prepared to do whatever necessary to give them their due. I had no idea how they were going to be integrated into an assemblage, but that didn't worry me. It is the *not knowing*, followed by the inevitable challenge of solving a long series of technical problems, that are together an integral part of both the artistry and the pleasure of creating a found-object assemblage.

To begin this assemblage, I headed straight down School Street in Berwick, Maine, to Nick Zerbinopoulos's Curiosity Shop, a proud, longstanding repository for generations of once-loved, discarded items of every imaginable kind. The Curiosity Shop is next to the fire station and just down from the local bank.

Nick, a colorful New Englander of Greek extraction, now well into his eighties, has been at the helm of the Curiosity Shop since 1976. A born raconteur and people magnet, he's worked over the years as a car salesman, auctioneer, and door-to-door bread peddler. For the addicted assemblage maker, Nick and his shop are an invaluable resource.

I knew from innumerable visits over the years that a large portion of the place is crammed full of a wildly disparate array of things—everything from tools and furniture to glassware, books, and unidentifiable somethings—objects divorced long ago from their original purposes, then tossed helter-skelter into bins and made available to anyone with either a practical need or a passion for repurposing.

I needed first to find a way to suspend those shoes against a backdrop of some sort, and after a great deal of digging, I found just what I needed: a heavy-duty cast iron hook soldered into the center of a small, square plate with screw holes in each of its four corners. It was as old and weather-beaten as the shoes, and therefore a good aesthetic match for them.

The Art of the Assemblage

The plate was too rugged to be mounted onto the surface of a canvas panel, so I chose a square slab of quarter-inch plywood as the backdrop, then mounted the plate onto it, off-center and just above the bottom edge of the panel, allowing half an inch of surface space between the bottom of the plate and the beginning of a yet-to-be-chosen picture frame.

What next? I wondered, *and where will I find it?* I was tired that day, not at all interested in driving down to the coast and stomping through the antique stores, so I headed down to my basement instead and began rummaging around in various boxes, looking for an object that would fire me up and get me started.

When creating a found-object assemblage, it is best to avoid feeling discouraged. It's far more productive to be patient and to adopt an attitude of playfulness. Incubation is also critically important when working in this genre. Whenever I begin work on an assemblage, I inevitably turn to daydreaming, which for an artist leads naturally to what behavioral scientists call free association.

I found a stack of old *Life* magazines on a shelf near the workbench, and they immediately struck me as having potential. *Life* and other vintage magazines have proven over time to be a rich source of inspiration for me as an artist. Because I've snipped countless images from them over several years of making collages and assemblages, many them have shards of paper dangling from what's left of their pages.

I pulled a late-1930s issue from the stack, flipped through the pages, and found a well-illustrated article about a German army attack on an Italian army encampment. In the most prominent image, a battle-weary soldier could be seen staring despairingly at the aftermath of the attack—burned out tanks, overturned jeeps, and dead fellow soldiers strewn gruesomely about the ground. The photograph—a square, uncompromising, black-and-white record of the ravages of war—was directly proportional to the plywood panel, so with no clear purpose in mind, I went upstairs to my studio and mounted it dead-center on the panel.

Finally, a narrative, fully in harmony with the design of the assemblage, had begun to emerge. War: a terrible waste of time, global resources, and human potential. Why does the human species so readily engage in battle? Why can we not find more peaceful ways to coexist while sharing the beauty and riches of this world? I scanned the rest of the article and absorbed the terrifying details of the battle, made even more powerful by the inescapable truths contained in the images.

It was time again to put the project aside to incubate. Remembering Bucky Fuller's famous assertion that napping often leads to creative solutions for intractable problems, I went upstairs, lay down on my bed, pulled my favorite quilt up to my chin, and fell asleep.

The next morning, while poring over my bookshelves for a good book to read over tea and toast, I found the worn and tattered copy of Omar Khayyám's *The Rubaiyat* that I'd purchased long ago at a used bookstore in London while visiting England to write about the theater. Like the victims of that tragic battle in Italy, the book had obviously been through battles of a different sort, unintentionally scarred and disfigured at the loving hands of appreciative readers in England, or perhaps in other, nearby countries.

I liked its evocative, ruby-red color, the beautiful gold embossments of the title, and the dramatic, asymmetrical tear in its cover. I also realized that its rectilinear shape would nicely complement the shape of both the frame and the photograph, so with no small amount of guilt, I tore the cover off the book and mounted it at the lower, left-hand corner of the assemblage. The contrast between the rich, red cover and the faded cream color of the panel added considerable energy to the piece.

I picked up the remaining pages of the book, now in a heap on the floor and quite beyond repair, then searched through them for a quatrain that might supplement and then elucidate the emerging narrative.

What quatrain would work best? I wondered. I read through several more quatrains, dismissed them as unworkable, then continued leafing through the book until I reached quatrain seven:

> Come, fill the Cup, and in the Fire of Spring
> The Winter Garment of Repentance fling:
> The Bird of Time has but a little way
> To fly—and Lo! The Bird is on the Wing.

I snipped the quatrain from the page, found a box of matches in a kitchen drawer, struck one up, and systematically moved the flame around the perimeter of the square of paper, being careful not to burn too far into the actual text. It was nicely singed all around, now—antiqued enough to be added to the interlocking pieces of my assemblage. I centered and overlapped the quatrain at the top of the photograph, locking words and image together in one concise, poignant assertion about the absurdity of wasting our precious hours of existence by turning to violence to resolve our philosophical and political differences.

I was moving rapidly now, grabbing and examining anything around the house that might work itself harmoniously into the assemblage. In a side drawer of my desk, I found a tiny button of ceramic, then mounted it just beneath the quatrain, adding a colorful touch of much-needed optimism to what had quickly become a rather lugubrious work of art.

The assemblage now looked weak at the very top. I needed an item directly above the quatrain—something that would counter the shoes at the bottom of the assemblage and play into the text of the quatrain. In the desk drawer where I kept smaller items that might eventually find a home in my assemblages, I found a long-ago purchased pair of earrings, each one a tiny, intricately carved wooden bird. I removed the clasp from the back of each earring, then added a touch of glue to each and perched them directly above the quatrain, facing each other where they would complement Khayyám's poetry while speaking to each other in their very own melodious, peace-loving language.

In the same drawer I found a scrap of blank film strip, then mounted it over the upper body of the soldier standing at the upper left of the photograph—a young man who could easily have been fighting on either side of the conflict, and who, like all the others, had only a slim chance of surviving the rigors of battle and going home with limbs and emotions fully intact. The scrap of film contributed greatly to the sense of immediacy. Here, on a simple, stage-like square of plywood, a flesh-and-blood, real-time drama had just played itself out on a far-away battlefield that could have been anywhere on our fractious, war-torn planet.

It now spoke of peace versus war—time well spent versus time foolishly squandered. So far, so good, but the project was still not speaking loudly and clearly enough to me and its potential audience. What could I add to my assemblage, I wondered, that would increase a sense of *urgency*—of humanity's need to come to its senses and choose peaceful solutions instead of death and destruction?

Remembering once again Fuller's assertion that one must break away from a problem in order to solve it, I went downstairs to start a load of laundry and think about what might come next. As I reached for the box of soap, I noticed a half-assembled mantle clock—French Rococo in style and covered with several years of dust—perched silently on top of the water heater.

That's what was missing: *time*! Clocks have become the indispensable way we measure the precious commodity of time, whether wisely used or foolishly spent. I grabbed a screwdriver off the workbench, loosened the screws on the clock face, and took it back upstairs to my studio with the works still attached and fully functional. Painted at the center of the clock face was a beautiful spray of antique red-and-pink roses tied with a ribbon and set against a creamy yellow background.

In less than an hour, I'd mounted the clock face at the lower left corner of the assemblage, aligning it precisely with the embossment lines on the cover of Khayyam's *Rubaiyat*. For the assemblage artist, it was a match made in heaven: the rich antique reds of both the flowers and the book cover; the way the two rectilinear objects played together in perfect harmony, like two cellos in an eighteenth-century concerto; and the way the clock spoke almost organically to the author of that quatrain, sharing his profound awareness of the sweet-and-sour evanescence of our lives. In the space just above the clock face and to the left of the book cover, I mounted a tarnished medallion that looked remarkably like an ancient coin. It nicely filled the space while contributing to the antique feeling of the assemblage as a whole.

I was almost finished now, and yet what I'd done with the clock, no matter how aesthetically appealing, had created an imbalance, disturbing the unity and serenity I'd worked so hard to achieve.

The creation of a work of art seldom goes smoothly, and because of that, the process can be both physically and emotionally draining. I was tired from several hours of labor, so I put the unfinished assemblage on a shelf in my studio and prepared for bed, determined to incubate for the night, then get up and look for one final addition to the piece that would give it the balance it needed. The inspiration, I figured, would come either from a dream or from one more session of treasure hunting early the next morning before work.

Several hours later, after a night of fitful sleeping, I woke without any fresh ideas about how to put a wrap on the project. I didn't have to report to work until 3:00 p.m., so I drove back to Antique Row and spent a good two hours walking through shops in Ogunquit, Wells, and Arundel, trying without success to find the elusive item.

Just before 3:00 p.m. I pulled into the parking lot at work, grumbling to myself that this assemblage had demanded more time, more incubation, and more gas money than any other I'd created. I'd begun seriously to wonder whether all of what I'd gone through to breathe life into this piece really had been worth the effort.

I walked toward the store entrance with my assemblage still in my car, my laptop hanging from my shoulder, and a grow-

The Art of the Assemblage

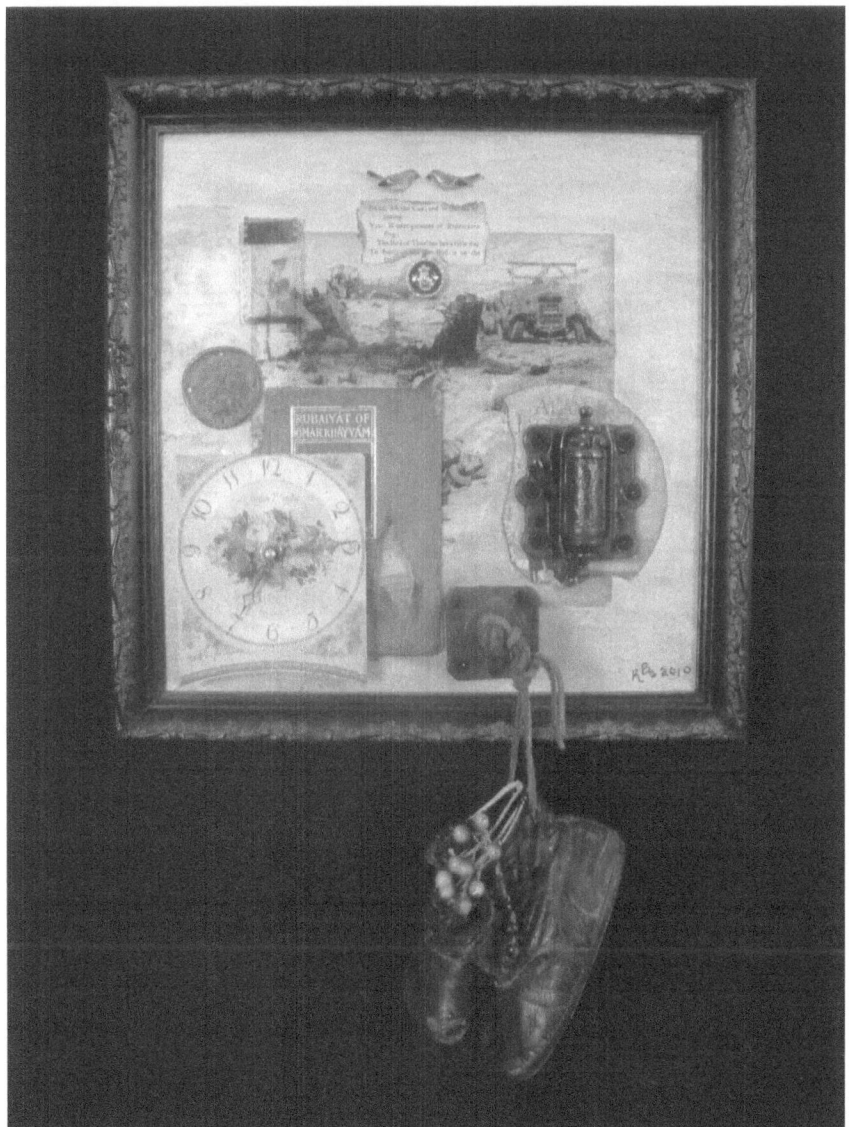

Fig. 59. *Waste Not Thy Time on This Good Earth* (assemblage).

ing cloud of despondency hanging over my head. Just before I reached the door, my foot slipped on a small piece of trash someone had tossed out of his car and onto the macadam. "People are such pigs!" I mumbled, then bent down to pick up the offending item.

It was a jagged, grime-covered crescent of plastic—part of an old CD that had lost its allure for whomever had decided unceremoniously to divest himself of it. I flipped it over to see what musician was featured on it. It turned out to be Alan Jackson—someone of no interest to me—but both the shape of the object and the colors of the label struck me like a miniature bolt of aesthetic lightning.

Its shape—a onetime perfect circle that would now play in delightful opposition to the concave bottom of the clock—was a perfect foil for the twin rectangles of the clock and the *Rubaiyat*. The warm cream and ruby red of the label couldn't have been more perfectly synchronized with the colors of the assemblage. The fact that the once-treasured CD was now as broken and lifeless as a soldier lying dead on a battlefield made it another ideal metaphor for the wanton destruction and utter futility of war.

I tucked the crescent into my shirt pocket and reported to work, wearing for the first time in several days a broad smile of victory and carrying a heady feeling of accomplishment.

After work I came home and applied glue to the back of the CD, then mounted it above and to the right of the hooked bracket that held the suspended pair of baby shoes. It now overlapped nicely with the Life magazine clipping of that Italian battle. The color and shape were perfect, but I realized I still wasn't done: it wasn't dark enough to counter-balance the clock, the book cover, the suspended shoes, and the frame I already knew I'd be using for the assemblage.

There just had to be something in the wood shop that would finish off that CD! I dashed downstairs, and in a bucket underneath the basement staircase I found a rusty Victorian era door hinge. Strong candidate! I raced upstairs, huffing and puffing, and dropped it down onto the surface of the CD. Not only did it fit perfectly; it also echoed the shape of the book cover and clock face to the left of it. As I saw it, that hinge could easily have been taken from a bedroom door in the home of the very child who wore those shoes as a toddler. I screwed the hinge down through the CD and into the plywood panel, then set the clock to current time, cross-wired the back, hung it on the wall, and studied it carefully for flaws or inconsistencies. Finally, the piece was aesthetically balanced, trouble-free, full of emotion, and ready for exhibit.

As I look back on the four assemblages I created—*The Ghost of Emin Bey*; *Little Girl, Little Girl*; *Incantation*; and *Waste Not Thy Time on This Good Earth*—I realize that three of the four were built quite unintentionally around a roughly similar theme or leitmotif: worry, often leading to loss and followed inevitably by sadness.

The Art of the Assemblage

In *The Ghost of Emin Bey*, Abhilasha was certain Emin, her lover, would return safe and sound to Constantinople, but then she was crushed after learning he'd been killed in battle. I like to think the toddler in *Little Girl, Little Girl* had no reason to worry about her future, but it is the job of parents to worry about their children, and I've no doubt they did just that. As *Waste Not Thy Time on This Good Earth* slowly came together, it proved to be a lament about the horror and absurdity of military conflict and a heartfelt tribute to the legions of soldiers who for countless centuries have answered the call for service with a mixture of patriotic devotion and genuine trepidation.

Of the four assemblages, only *Incantation* was full of optimism. The little Buddha atop the toddler's shoe had a wise and benevolent smile on his face, as if he were certain that the sun would always shine down on humankind and all would be well. Of course, we know that life is never really that simple. There will always be a challenging blend of the Happy Dawg and the Sad Man in every living being. The human condition—that ominous grey cloud of uncertainty that's at the heart of our mortality—demands that we learn to live with the unsettling fragility of our lives. Our most enduring hope is that, more often than not, the Happy Dawg will walk the Sad Man—not the other way around.

The slow and steady evolution of an assemblage, inevitably marked by complications and setbacks, is remarkably like the building of our own lives. In the beginning, we're awash with optimism and eager to experiment, making our choices and learning to live with our mistakes. In art as in life, to have a satisfactory result, one must be burning with desire to create something lasting and beautiful. Without that burning, there's a good chance that the dreams we dream—like the assemblages we build—will never quite come to fruition.

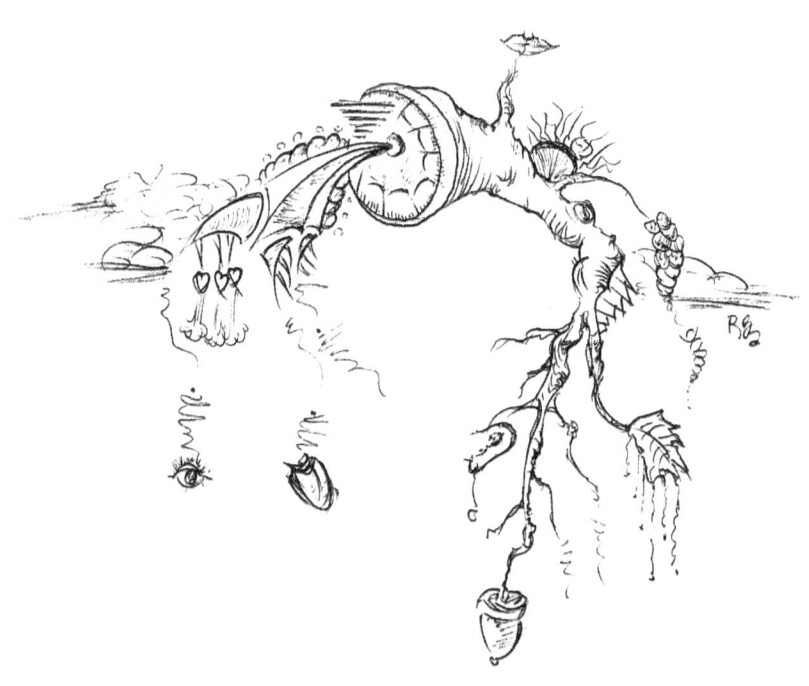

Fig. 60. *Barnaby Rupert's Obsession* by Ross Bachelder.

🌸 Tiny Novelette 6 🌸

Barnaby Rupert's Obsession

Barnaby Rupert, an avid reader who lived with his pet sugar glider, Icarus, in an abandoned school bus on the outskirts of Bowbells, North Dakota, had wondered for years about the origins of the universe.

Before he was barely out of kindergarten, he began asking himself, *Where could this thing called life possibly have begun?* So profound were his questions that his teachers couldn't help wondering if he might be an idiot savant, a smart-mouthed little eccentric, or a flat-out lunatic-in-embryo.

But now he was nearly thirty and still didn't have the answer. Then he remembered his friend Gaylord McFlickers, who operated Let It Rip, a chain of wildly successful, inflation-proof whoopee cushion retail outlets down in Karlsruhe, and paid him a visit.

"You're a smart fellow, Gaylord!" he said. "Where do you think I should begin?" Gaylord thought for a moment, finished the day's cushion quota of five hundred—a real blowout, even by Let It Rip standards—then said, "Ol' Doc Seuss knows more than all the politicians in Washington—and the leading academics, too. Time to read up, boy! Start with *The Cat in the Hat*, move on to *Bartholomew and the Ooblek*, then go straight to *Oh, the Places You'll Go!*

That night, back in his school bus in Bowbells and tucked into seat number seventeen, where he always messed with Lulu Threshnik on the way to school, Barnaby read all three of Seuss's books, then topped them off with Heinlein's *Stranger in a Strange Land* and Lawson's *McWhinney's Jaunt*. (McWhinney, for those who may not know it, was the proud possessor of the world's only levitating bicycle.) Then he dozed off and slept like a baby, with dreams of flower-strewn meadows and cliffs of pure chalcedony dancing in his head.

When he woke up the next morning, he had his answer. "*Greece!*" he bellowed. "I don't know why I didn't think of it!" Then he made himself a peanut butter and pickle sandwich, filled his thermos with leftover chocolate cupuaçu juice, stuffed volume 2 of Pashley's *Travels in Crete* in his rucksack, and headed on foot to the nearest airport.

Less than a minute out of Karlsruhe he saw tethered to a quaking aspen a fluorescent pink and green bicycle hovering just inches above the sidewalk, with the words *Suessmobile* and *Heraklion or Bust* draped across the handlebars.

"Just like McWhinney's bicycle!" he shouted. "It floats!" He cut the contraption loose from the tree, tucked Icarus into the accessories box, honked the horn, and headed to the taxidermy in Anamoose to load up on Z-Gas (the very same fuel that propelled McWhinney's two-wheel contraption). Then, with the wind at his back and a whoopie cushion roaring neath his bum, he soared buoyantly across the Atlantic at lightning speed, landing with a bump in a mysterious garden on the outskirts of Heraklion, just down from Nikos Kazantzakis's grave.

At the very center of the garden was a magnificent tree swaying rhythmically in the wind and laden with the most extraordinary fruit: beating hearts, moistened lips, listening ears, and lapping tongues.

A sign above the entrance read, "Thanks to the genius of McWhinney, the wisdom of Seuss, and the incomparable power of the whoopee cushion, you've discovered the Humanitree—the One True Source of every living creature since the beginning of time." Barnaby had finally discovered the origins of the universe, and at that moment he knew with certainty that he and the town of Bowbells would never again be the same.

Chapter 13

Theater in Small-Town New England
I've Done a Lot, and Loved Nearly All of It

Can the lives we lead and the plays we see really be separated? The one is for the most part unscripted and, on occasion, alarmingly chaotic; the other is carefully plotted, fully rehearsed, and vigorously marketed. And yet both worlds have a beginning, a middle, and an end. They're both replete with stories begging to be told, and it is the very human compulsion to tell them, whether onstage or on the streets of daily experience, that makes a life.

What happens onstage and under the lights, in front of a paying audience, has the power to affect profoundly that other, offstage life we lead. Theater informs, teaches, inspires, and reveals. It also exhilarates, disturbs, and disappoints.

I may not have been on or near a stage for the past several years, but I don't really feel as if I've ever left the theater. It's an inextinguishable part of me. Every one of our days is another performance, waiting to be seen, to be praised or panned, or to be blithely ignored. We climb onto a stage of one kind or another, do the best we possibly can in the role we've been given, then step aside and make room for the endless parade of actors destined to fill our shoes. It's been a damn good show, and I'm thankful to have been in it this long. And who knows: the run may just be more extended than I'd even hoped for. That would be nice, I think.

I've done a lot of theater in my life. I've labored mightily in that world, logging countless hours as bit part actor, set designer and builder, pit orchestra musician, theater manager, publicist, playwright, songwriter, and play reviewer.

In Maine I've worked under John Lane as the publicity director at Ogunquit Playhouse; under S. Carleton Guptill as actor, publicist, pit orchestra musician, and set builder at Hackmatack

Fig. 61. The author in one of his earliest onstage assignments, as a traveling minstrel in Moliére's *The Doctor in Spite of Himself* (Portsmouth, New Hampshire, 1977).

Playhouse; as the founder and director of the Berwick Young People's Theater, where I wrote, produced, and directed musical comedies for seven summers; as a pit orchestra musician at both

Biddeford City Theater and the Portland Players; and as an actor at the one-time Embassy Players in Portland.

In New Hampshire, I worked as the marketer, publicist, and newsletter editor under John Hallowell at Liberty Stage Company in Portsmouth, and I reviewed art exhibits, concerts, and plays for the *Portsmouth Herald*. In Dover, I worked as actor and general manager under Edouard Langlois at the Edwin Booth Theater, acted at Side Street Theatre under director Dona Masi, and played in the pit orchestra at Garrison Players and the one-time Bell Center for Music & the Arts.

From this accounting, one might think I had an actual career in the theater, but that hasn't really been the case. I simply managed, somehow, to find the time to weave a remarkably wide range of theatrical experiences into the fabric of an even more complex existence as writer, artist, and musician.

Until 1997, when my work in those disciplines began to demand more and more of my time, the theater was a nearly constant presence in my life—a multidisciplinary stage on which I could act out my love affair with the fine and performing arts. That universe, which for thousands of years has had its very own inimitable language and arcane rituals, has always been a powerful magnet for anyone with a passion for more than one creative endeavor within the realm of the fine and performing arts. I was drawn to it like a moth to a porch light, and it has provided me with innumerable heart-stopping hours of pure pleasure and creative fulfillment. Theater, like life itself, has offered moments of both supreme triumph and deep disappointment, and altogether it has had a significant influence on my writing, my music, my multimedia artworks, and my outlook on life.

Tent Theater in Mount Clemens: Testing the Waters in Michigan

My very first theatrical adventure was in 1965 in Mt. Clemens, Michigan, where I found work playing flute in a summertime tent theater production of Rogers and Hammerstein's beloved musical *The King and I*. I remember little about the experience other than the warm summer weather, a breeze that kept blowing the music off my stand, and an onstage incident that introduced to me in the most dramatic way the tragicomic vicissitudes of live theater.

Essential to any credible production of *The King and I* has always been a dog—live onstage—whose ostensible purpose is to underscore the steamy virility and political clout of King Mongkut of Siam. Of course, the real purpose of the dog, as anyone who spends time in either the green room or the box office of a theater knows, is to sell tickets and cover the exorbitant, always escalating cost of producing and performing a play.

In the Mt. Clemens production—a mere two-week, fourteen-show run, including the matinees—the dog of choice was a brawny, statuesque German shepherd, named Pete when he was out of costume and lounging on the lawn behind the tent, gnawing on a bone while waiting to rehearse.

On opening night—my first-ever performance as a pit orchestra musician—Pete was the very model of heart-stopping good looks and thespian propriety. He'd been trained rigorously to follow the King's commands at every critical moment without disrupting the flow of onstage dialogue. The moment he hit the stage, the audience fell instantly in love with him.

He was doing just fine, but like countless other actors before him, both animal and human, he suffered an unscripted moment of onstage panic. Being a dog, he reacted just as a dog who also happens to be an actor might be expected to act: he bolted, then tumbled chaotically off the proscenium and dangled at the end of his leash while sending an earsplitting medley of yelps into the audience.

Fortunately, two techies standing just off stage left came to the rescue. Pete was settled down and lifted back up onto the stage, and the show, as we've always been told it would, managed to go on without further incident.

That terrifying moment of canine calamity, leading to a complete loss of decorum in full public view, has come to symbolize my deepest feelings and forebodings about live theater and the many major and minor roles I've played in it, both on- and offstage, over several decades. Things can go astonishingly well one night, then terribly wrong the next. That's the nature of things in drama, as in life, and to find happiness in either world, one must first understand and then accept that reality.

Hackmatack Playhouse

The vast majority of my work in professional theater has been right here in northern New England, where I moved in 1974, three years after finishing graduate school in Michigan. I soon learned that the southern Maine / Seacoast New Hampshire region was a tourist-driven hotbed for the dramatic arts.

Happily, we landed in a town with what was then a fledgling barn theater just down the road from our newly rented apart-

Fig. 62. Hackmatack Playhouse, still operating on the grounds of the Guptill Homestead in Berwick, Maine, after more than forty years.

ment. It didn't take long for Hackmatack Playhouse, founded in 1972 by S. Carleton Guptill, to become the most important place in Berwick for me. I discovered that three of the shows in Hackmatack's five-show summer season were popular Broadway musicals, designed to draw tourists from all over northern New England and beyond. It meant I could make money on occasion as a pit orchestra musician, and I began to get calls for gigs.

One of my earliest memories while playing shows at Hackmatack was the theater's ever-present house dog, Doofus. He was to the Playhouse what a cat is to a bookstore—a thoroughly spoiled animal magnet for visitors of every stripe. On any day, visitors to the homestead could see him loping around the grounds or basking in the sun, chasing his burr-infested tail or dreaming his midsummer dreams. During daytime rehearsals, he'd jog from actor to actor, looking for either a midday snack or a pat on the head. He was *family*, and he could never get enough of the TLC the actors and support staff showered on him.

At night, when the lights were lit and the curtain was raised, Doofus loved to hang out in the storage area beneath the stage, oblivious to the pounding of the actors' feet and the wailings of the tiny, three-piece orchestra crammed into the cubby-hole to the left of the stage. Every once in a while, during an especially poignant scene, he'd scratch furiously at himself, declaring war on the fleas that used him, brazenly, as their homestead taxi. And when Doofus wasn't stealing scenes from the actors during performances, the Playhouse bats were always happy to take over where he left off. They loved to cruise round and round the house, then swoop down across the stage, narrowly missing the heads of actors while daring them not to break character.

A memorable incident at Hackmatack occurred when I was in the pit orchestra for a three-week run of *The Sound of Music*. My daughter, Amy, then just eight years old, had landed the role of Gretl, the youngest daughter of the von Trapp family, and because I'd been tapped to play in the pit orchestra, I was privileged to have a front row seat for all fourteen of her performances.

Amy sang her modest cameo role beautifully each night, and right on cue, the audiences could be counted on to gush their approval at the sweetness of both the character and the girl. But one night, smack in the middle of "So Long, Farewell" (the tenderest of melodies), she stepped too close to the edge of the stage and tumbled into the audience. Fortunately, an alert audience member saw her coming, caught her in his lap, and put her back onstage, where she completed her scene to ripples of benign laughter and smiles of relief.

By then I'd come to love the Playhouse so much that I wanted to share its story with anyone in Maine and the rest of New England who might appreciate it. I decided to explore the possibility of writing a profile of Hackmatack Playhouse, then finding a home for it in a magazine.

I'd already had success as a magazine freelancer, publishing an article about karate black-belt John Mason for *Sepia* magazine (based in Chicago) and a profile of Manchester artist Corrine Trippetti for *New Hampshire Profiles*, so I went ahead with my plans to write an article about Hackmatack, confident that getting it published in yet another high-quality magazine would be an important stepping stone for me as a freelancer.

I looked around and decided that *Down East* magazine, with a devoted readership in and far beyond the borders of the Pine Tree State, would be the perfect fit for a double profile—the story of both the Playhouse and the homestead. I queried the editors, and after dozens of hours of interviewing and researching, wrote the article on spec. Half a year later, I learned that my profile, complete with photographs of both the Playhouse and the grounds of the Guptill family home, had been accepted for publication.

I was ecstatic. Then began the wait—that agonizing period between acceptance and publication with which writers are all too familiar—to see how the article would look once the magazine was printed and distributed. The editor was a friendly young fellow, both in writing and over the telephone, so I was fairly bubbling over with optimism, certain that the profile, to which I'd devoted countless hours, would be reproduced with little if any editing.

When my complimentary copy of *Down East* magazine arrived in the mail, I eagerly tore the wrapper off, full to overflowing with pride that I'd added yet another article to my growing list of magazine credits. *This will be glorious!* I thought to myself.

I should have known. That friendly young fellow—the one with the warm telephone demeanor and dripping sincerity—had dismembered and eviscerated my article so completely that I hardly recognized it. Gone was the entire second half of my profile—the proud story of the Guptill homestead. Gone was the dignified title I'd so meticulously crafted. In its place, screaming audaciously from the top of the article, was a headline so tasteless that I instantly became sick to my stomach:

Hijinks in a Cow Barn!
The Story of Hackmatack Playhouse

Not *my* story! Not the story I'd written with such energy and idealism. And in place of the photos I'd hired a professional photographer to take was a truly horrendous black-and-white image—two actors with goony, Vaudevillian leers on their faces—that failed in every respect to capture either the tone or the substance of my article. And for all that work, I made only a hundred dollars—barely enough to cover the cost of creating it.

I was angry, humiliated, and disillusioned. I spent the next year or two praying that no one who mattered to me, including the people in that photograph, had ever picked up the magazine and stumbled across that article.

And yet, in spite of it, I continued to immerse myself in the theater. I went on to do pit work in neighboring southern Maine playhouses, including Biddeford City Theater and the Portland Players in South Portland. I also decided I wanted to be an actor, and I promised myself to take pretty much any role, however small, to achieve my goal. With a lot of hard work, I began to flesh out my résumé with minor roles in theaters in Seacoast New Hampshire and southern Maine.

Ogunquit Square Theater

My very first full-fledged acting assignment was at Ogunquit Square Theater, just twenty minutes from my home in Berwick. S. Carleton Guptill, the founder and artistic director of Hackmatack Playhouse, occasionally jobbed out his theatrical skills to area theaters. After he was hired to direct Neil Simon's *The Odd Couple* at OST, he cast me in the role of Roy, the card player.

I soon found out that memorizing lines didn't come naturally to me. I had to run my lines over and over again until I finally got control of them, but that wasn't enough for the role of Roy. I needed also to master the craft of playing poker in live performance while delivering those lines.

The problem was that I knew absolutely nothing about poker, while the actors around me knew the game cold. On top of that, the role of Roy required that I smoke onstage. It ought to have been easy, but because I'd stopped smoking several years before, I was out of practice—as lousy at smoking as I was at playing poker. I knew with alarming certainty that both our audiences and my fellow actors would see right through my ineptitude with the weed and wonder how I ever landed the role of Roy in the first place.

In spite of all of the negatives, I managed to get through the rehearsals and ready myself for what I hoped would be at least a tolerable performance.

On opening night I was pumped full of adrenaline and ready for action. I'd invited my parents, who were in town from Michigan to visit with us, to come down from the nearby Norseman Inn and Motel to attend the performance. That a hurricane was brewing that weekend added yet another layer of excitement to my very first ambitious assignment as an actor.

The curtain went up, the lines began to fly, the cards were dealt, and the cigarettes were smoked. The audience laughed and applauded in all the right places. I made it through the play without dropping a line, took my bows with the rest of the cast, changed into my street clothes, then walked down into the auditorium to greet my parents and accept what I was certain would be effusive praise for my onstage work.

Things didn't go as planned.

First, my father: "Why didn't you tell us you were going to smoke on stage?" he raged. "You *know* your mother has asthma!"

Then, my mother: "The smoke nearly *killed* me!" she wheezed, full of anger because of my insensitivity. "I wish we hadn't come."

So much for family unity, I thought as they left me standing in the theater and headed out to their car.

Actors deserve both respect and applause for their remarkable ability to perform with great skill, night after night, in the most volatile imaginable circumstances. Those hard-earned skills are all the more impressive when one considers an actor's uncanny ability to leave his personal life in the dressing room and step out onto the stage each night as an utterly different person. The ability of an actor to compartmentalize is no less impressive than that of the successful athlete, concert pianist, or surgeon.

As hard as it was to be Roy, the experience turned out to be a precious gift—a modest accomplishment that gave me the courage I'd need to go onstage again and continue to grow as an actor. That I was able, in spite of my inner demons, to lock my long-standing familial troubles in a closet, get onto that stage, and deliver a credible performance gave me a small but powerful dose of self-respect.

Side Street Theater

I continued to audition for roles, and before long I landed the role of Doctor Chasuble, playing opposite Miss Laetitia Prism in an outdoor, Side Street Theater production of Oscar Wilde's comedy *The Importance of Being Earnest*. The play would be staged around a very British trellis on the lawn of the elegant Kennebunkport Inn, not far from then-President George Herbert Walker Bush's oceanside home at Walker's Point. I was still in my late thirties at the time, so to be taken seriously as a pompous, aging cleric, I had to whiten my hair, age my complexion, and stuff a pillow into my pants to prepare for each performance.

I've long ago forgotten the name of the woman who played Miss Prism, but for our purposes we'll call her Ariana.

The name fits what I remember of her like a contessa's glove. She was a resident of the Port—shorthand for Kennebunkport, the only city in the world with that name. The Port has always been disturbingly top-heavy with people certain of their town's superiority over every other village within fifty miles of their home.

One night, after yet another arduous rehearsal of Wilde's play, Ariana learned that my car was in the repair shop, then kindly agreed to give me a ride to my home in Berwick. I accepted her offer with a mixture of gratitude and foreboding, since in the course of our rehearsals she'd begun to reveal the very attitudes for which the more uppity residents of Kennebunkport are so well known.

Everything was fine until we reached the outskirts of town. The stretch of road on Route 9 between Hackmatack Playhouse

Fig. 63. Miss Letitia Prism, Dr. Frederick Chasuble, and the Honorable Gwendolen Fairfax in Side Street Theater's production of Oscar Wilde's *The Importance of Being Earnest* (c. 1978).

and the center of Berwick was still observably down on its luck in the '70s, with several homes badly in need of repair.

Suddenly, it was Miss Prism, not Ariana, sitting next to me in the car. "Oh, dear!" she gasped, her eyes rolling and her nose brushing the grey plush roof of her BMW. "I don't see how *anyone* could choose to live *here*!"

I might easily have shrugged off the arrogance of her assertion were it not for the unpleasant fact that as Dr. Chasuble I was required each night to plant a kiss on Miss Prism's powdered and privileged cheek, then declare my undying love for her. Determined to conduct myself as a professional, I sucked it up and behaved myself for the rest of the run, giving the role of Doctor Chasuble all I had in me as an actor in development. Once we'd completed the run, we went our separate ways, and I never saw Miss Prism again.

Dover Repertory Theater

My next stage opportunity popped up right in my own backyard. S. Carleton Guptill, the man who founded Hackmatack Playhouse in 1972, decided in the late '80s to open a second company—first called Hackmatack at Cocheco Falls, then Hackmatack Repertory Theater, and then, finally, Dover Repertory Theater—across the border in New Hampshire. He knew that if he established the theater in a larger, more culturally sophisticated town, he'd be able to produce more serious drama than the tourist-friendly shows he was forced to do at Hackmatack to survive financially.

In 1994 I approached Carl about employment with DRT and landed what seemed at the time like a golden opportunity—a chance to be paid a weekly salary to market the theater, write the publicity, and act in several of its plays.

As a condition of my hiring, Guptill privately asked me to fulfill a truly difficult mission: I was to do whatever was necessary to help bring peace and a spirit of cooperation to a company that was riddled with jealously, rancor, and distrust. Such conditions are not uncommon in the world of theater, but at DRT they were hopelessly entrenched and fast nearing the boiling point. Guptill knew that unless he could bring about a truce in his theater's bloody war of egos, the company that meant so much to him might very well be forced to close.

On my very first day at the theater, one of the more seasoned actors warned me that I ought not to have anything to do with a certain handful of DRT members. I had to wonder how that was possible, since I'd be working with them anyway, virtually every day of the week.

Clearly, the picture was even worse than the one Carl had painted for me on the day he hired me. Nevertheless, proud to have been tapped for the assignment, I resolved to do what Carl had asked me to do. I felt sure that my gentler, more diplomatic approach to things would begin to melt the frozen tundra that was keeping the theater in psychological bondage and sabotaging Guptill's lifelong mission to bring top-quality, life-changing drama to a city ripe for its arrival.

Dover Repertory had put together an ambitious season, including *The Prime of Miss Jean Brodie* (the 1968 stage play based on a novel by Muriel Spark). I decided early on that, when I wasn't tending to the theater's publicity, I'd audition for considerably more ambitious roles than I was accustomed to seeking. After several tries, I was cast in what for me were two really challenging assignments.

The first role was as one of four madrigal singers in a musical adaptation of Charles Dickens's *A Christmas Carol*, directed by Carol Davenport and featuring fourteen four-part madrigals woven into the narrative. My chances of landing the role had been greatly enhanced when Davenport remembered that I was an experienced musician and occasional singer who could handle either tenor or baritone in all fourteen madrigals.

The second role was as Uncle Billy in a stage adaptation of Frank Capra's *It's a Wonderful Life* (based on the short story "The Greatest Gift" by Philip Van Doren Stern). It was a big responsibility, and I blossomed as an actor because of what it took to pull the role off.

The hardest part of playing Uncle Billy was that I had to work intimately onstage with DRT's artistic director, James Darling—a thoroughly seasoned actor who'd been cast in the critical role of the tyrannical, thoroughly loathsome slumlord, Mr. Henry F. Potter. Darling was a fine, hard-working actor, deadly serious about his craft, but surly and brooding in a Heathcliff sort of way when offstage—not unlike the character he'd been chosen to play. Unless one had earned Darling's trust, both on- and offstage, he was difficult to work with, even under the best of circumstances. He had no patience for actors less experienced and less skilled than he, and he could smell my thespian insecurities from a mile away. He was unfailingly loyal to seasoned actors whose work he respected, but dismissive and—on all too many occasions—contemptuous of those still finding their way in the theater world.

The most important scene in the entire play—central to the plot line because of the way it elucidated the story and propelled the action toward its inevitable ending—was the one in which Uncle Billy, a kindly but absent-minded old man, hands a folded newspaper over to Potter. Unfortunately, inside that newspaper was the money that George Bailey had entrusted to Uncle Billy for safekeeping—money that would have saved Bailey Building and Loan Association from financial collapse, had he not so carelessly put it in the worst possible hands.

In every rehearsal, I dreaded the moment when we ran the money-in-the-newspaper scene. Not only was I aware that Darling didn't trust me to time the handoff with skill and precision, I got the distinct feeling that he didn't really like me. Unable to leave his antipathy for me in the dressing room, he brought it onstage with him in every rehearsal.

Before long I began to detect an icy, impenetrable wall between me and several of the more established actors—an early and ominous sign that I wasn't going to be welcomed easily into the circle as a true theater professional.

My most persistent memory of this phenomenon happened one afternoon between the acts of a matinee performance of *Petticoat Fever*—a farce about life in the Klondike, directed by

Carl Guptill—in which we were required each day to change rapidly from heavy wintertime clothing into shirts and pants more suitable for the dog days of August than the dead of winter.

There were at least a half dozen of us in the dressing room that afternoon, including James Darling, Carol Davenport, Jason Bolduc, and me.

As Bolduc removed his pants in the midst of a lightning-fast costume change, Davenport unleashed a stagey, bloodcurdling shriek. Once the pants were off, all that was left were the remnants of a timeworn pair of Fruit of the Looms. Only a half dozen strands of cotton were holding up the waistband.

"Jason!" she shouted. "That's little more than a *G-string!*"

Darling chuckled from across the room. Jason, a happy-go-lucky young man, blushed and then shrugged his shoulders. The rest of the troupe went silent, with the notable exception of me.

"G-string?" I said. "I think we're talking F-sharp at best!"

I thought the F-sharp one-liner was surely one of my finer moments as an amateur humorist, but Davenport clearly didn't think so and made sure I knew it.

"That's really dumb!" she said.

What ought to have been a moment of thespian camaraderie had turned abruptly into something between a reprimand and a warning: *Don't somehow get the idea that you're going to be a true-blue member of this company!*

In spite of that and other unsettling moments—incidents that altogether felt more like a fraternity hazing than a welcome into the fold—I dug in, maintained my professionalism, and delivered a credible performance. By the time we'd reached the final weekend of the play, the chilly temperatures in the Klondike had begun to warm.

We finished the DRT season with a triumphant, two-week run of *It's a Wonderful Life*. By then, things had begun to mellow throughout the company, perhaps because we were now in the thick of the holiday season and a spirit of goodwill had begun to assert itself in opposition to the pettiness that had defined the theater for so many weeks.

To build on that spirit and top off the season, Darling and his partner, Leslie, decided to throw a New Year's Eve party at their home in nearby Somersworth, New Hampshire, high up on what the locals call "the Hill."

In spite of the sudden improvement in the climate of the theater, I didn't really want to be there. I'd grown increasingly cynical about my chances of ever being warmly welcomed into the theater, and to make matters worse, I and the other members of DRT were mourning the loss of its founder and beloved captain,

Carl Guptill, who died of cancer on November 27, in the midst of the theater's run of *It's a Wonderful Life*. Guptill cared deeply for James Darling—enough to have chosen him to take over the theater after his passing—so Darling was especially distraught and, understandably, full of anxiety.

Nevertheless, I decided to play the good soldier, rid myself of my cynicism for one night, and report for active duty. It was only fair: Carl Guptill had taken a chance on me, and I knew I wouldn't sleep well that night if I were let him down—to disrespect his memory by going AWOL.

In spite of the sadness everywhere around us, the mood inside the Darling residence was both festive and cathartic. We'd put the cap on an ambitious, tension-filled season, and it was time now for all of us, regardless of our philosophical and temperamental differences, to remember what brought us together in the first place—the pursuit of excellence, born of a passion for the arts—and seek common ground.

Multicolored holiday lights, intertwined with pine boughs and holly, were glowing everywhere around me as I strode into a living room filled with exhausted but jubilant actors. They were finally and exultantly offstage—though some actors never really are—and in full party mode.

Across the room was Darling, deep in conversation with Jim Sears, Carol Davenport, and other members of the tightly knit group of veteran actors who were together the core of Dover Repertory. Knowing how difficult it would be for me even to attempt to join them, I gave up on the idea and headed straight to a table off the kitchen, resplendent with the usual holiday cuisine, including hors d'oeuvres, freshly baked pastries, and a virtual standing army of fine wines and whiskies.

It's no secret that a great many theater people like to drink—perhaps especially after an arduous rehearsal or triumphant performance. Not only can time in a pub help them relax after long hours of emotionally demanding labor, it often has the power to unite them as a troupe and reinforce their common purposes as a company.

For various reasons, I didn't share their enthusiasm for social drinking, and that, more often than not, made me the odd man out at DRT. I've never liked the longstanding presumption that, to have a good time, one must drink—even at a cast party—so I grabbed a bottle of spring water and walked back into the living room, looking for someone with whom I could engage in tolerable smalltalk.

Darling must have seen that I was packing not booze but spring water, because I remember watching him work his way toward me through the crowd with a full shot glass in each hand. It was the first time he'd approached me that evening, and other than onstage and in performance, the first time in many weeks that he'd acknowledged my presence at all. When he'd managed to position himself directly in front of me, he stopped and looked me straight in the eyes.

"Have a drink!" he bellowed, banging one of the glasses down on the mantle next to us and sloshing a portion of its contents onto the polished mahogany surface.

"No, thank you," I said. "I'm fine with what I have."

The shot glass stayed on the mantle. Darling may have been extending an olive branch, but I was in no mood to return the favor. He then did an abrupt about-face and disappeared into the crowd of celebrating actors. I found my jacket, and then, shortly after midnight, slipped quietly out of the party and into the early morning moonlight of a brand new year. Since I'd no longer be working at the theater, there would be no need to think again about how I might make peace with either Darling or the theater Guptill had wanted so badly to save. Another chapter of my life in the theater had been written, and new and challenging adventures lay ahead of me, there for the taking.

In at least one respect, James Darling did me an immense favor by being so impatient with me over the course of the season. Not only did he toughen me up as an actor, he also revealed, to anyone who took the time to see through his thick but vulnerable skin, the depths of his own onstage and offstage insecurities. He, like everyone else in the company, was fully human.

To be an actor requires a very special kind of toughness. Darling had it in abundance, and though he couldn't see it in me at the time, I knew I had no small amount of it myself—more than Uncle Billy and more than I ever knew I had until I was forced to put it to work onstage, surrounded by more seasoned actors than me.

After Guptill died, Darling purchased Dover Repertory from Sandy Guptill—Carl's widow—more determined than ever to honor Carl's memory by keeping the theater alive. And now, as both owner and artistic director of his very own theater, he would need all of the toughness he could muster, and more.

I'd managed to make it through the DRT season with only a few minor lumps and bruises on my ego to show for it. The final performance had been a gem, but the cast party, for me at least, had been a disaster. And yet I went home from that house on the Hill in Somersworth full of New Year optimism and thinking that, on balance, the life of an actor really can be a wonderful thing.

Life at the Edwin Booth: Out of the Frying Pan and into the Fire

The Edwin Booth Theater, named after the brother of the man who assassinated Abraham Lincoln, was for a time the love of Edouard Langlois's life. He could pour his formidable multidisciplinary talents into show after show, then sit back and listen to the incomparable music of exultant, five-star reviews.

I knew of Langlois's achievements long before the Booth became a reality. Edouard was known throughout the Seacoast region of New Hampshire as an actor, director, set designer, and costumier with impressive New York City chops. And though few people knew it, he was also a visual artist of extraordinary power and originality. His eerily poetic multimedia artworks—unapologetically dark and melancholy—were influenced by his Catholic upbringing, his longtime love affair with the Mexican Day of the Dead culture, and his own seldom-articulated struggle to come to terms with the inner demons that plague us all, in one way or another, from the cradle to the grave.

My first exposure to Langlois's trenchant humor and lacerating, off-the-cuff critiquing was in the late '70s at the Beaver Dam Grange in North Berwick, Maine, home to a wide range of social events, including political meetings, bean suppers, and, on occasion, live theatrical performances. Berwick's grange had all of the unique architectural qualities that made granges throughout New England such a beloved part of New England history. The floors creaked back at the stomping of feet of both actors and audiences, the windows rattled ominously in the brisk winter winds, and the sprawling, dust-covered furnace, whose tentacles reached into all corners of the basement, wheezed and groaned under the labor of pumping badly needed heat into the leak-infested facility.

Though I'd acted with Edouard once in an outdoor performance in downtown Portsmouth, New Hampshire, I didn't really know him very well. (I *do* remember that, for the entire run of the show, we were nearly asphyxiated each day by rows of Greyhound buses idling along Congress Street.)

I also had a bit part in a locally produced movie directed by Edouard and shot at the home of legendary Seacoast area actor Mert Rogers. (Mert, a hilarious, often irascible woman, acted frequently in Lake Side Players productions, staged in the grange hall in Bow Lake, New Hampshire. Rogers, who aged with great dignity into the role of grand dame of the local theater commu-

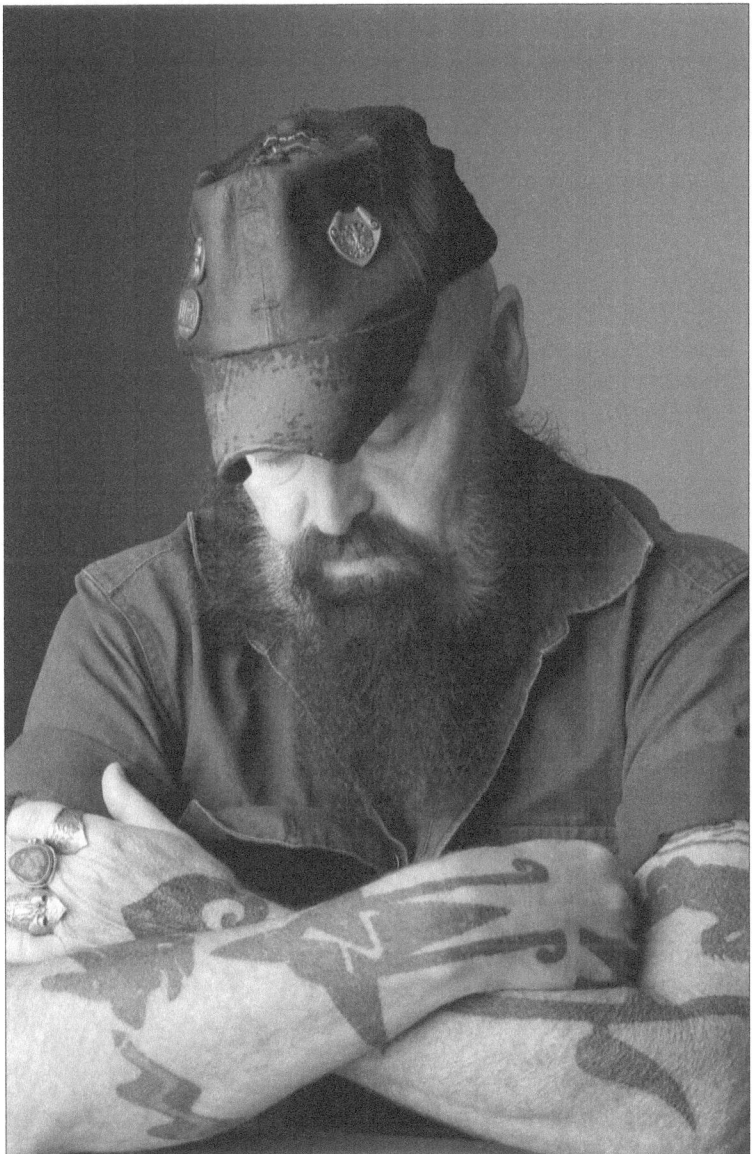

Fig. 64. An award-winning portrait of actor, director, costumier, and set designer Edouard Langlois by portrait photographer Michael Penney.

nity, had a talking toilet in her Stagecoach Road home that was all the rage with her friends.) I was cast as one of several mourners in the opening scene of the movie, kneeling before a coffin borrowed from a local funeral home.

Getting to know Edouard—whose closest friends called him Eddie—in any meaningful way was hard work. One was admitted into his private world only by making it through the fierce, unforgiving gauntlet of his rush-to-judgment moments. "Oh, that's *so middle class!*" he'd say, always with an unsettling mixture of pity and contempt.

At the grange, we'd just seen a performance of Frank D. Gilroy's Pulitzer award–winning play *The Subject Was Roses*, a wry and poignant drama whose movie version helped make Patricia Neal and Jack Albertson famous. Afterward, it was time to go downstairs and mingle with members of the audience.

As I worked my way down the narrow, rickety stairs, Eddie stopped me and looked me straight in the eyes.

"What'd you think of the show?" he asked with a devilish twinkle in his jet-black eyes.

"I thought it was *wonderful*," I said, "a truly beautiful story. And well acted, too!"

"*Really?*" he said. "So you didn't think it was a *kiss-ass piece of shit?*"

I remembered that incident vividly more than thirty years later, when, for some inexplicable reason, I agreed to be the general manager of Eddie's new Dover-based repertory company, the Edwin Booth. And given the growing list of outrageous anecdotes about Eddie being passed around within the acting community, I should have known what I was getting into. *Why*, I ought to have asked myself, *would anyone want to work with a man who, while the artistic director of the Durham Stage Company, refused to accept a bouquet of congratulatory flowers from his own cast after the final performance of the season?*

To my great surprise, I discovered early in the season that Eddie was easy to work with: respectful, sociable, and generous with the time we needed to brainstorm together about how best to publicize the Booth's ambitious roster of plays. I relished the opportunity to get to know Eddie—a tattooed and bewhiskered maverick, indifferent to fashion and known for both his trenchant humor and wide-ranging intellect.

Eddie had no tolerance for fluff, either in or out of the theater world. The only plays he'd ever agree to bring to the stage were plays of *substance*—works penned by renowned playwrights, certain to be dense with emotion and oozing with intellectuality. He'd produced Henrik Ibsen's celebrated play *Hedda Gabler* on more than one occasion, with his sister Deborah Langlois—herself a formidably talented actor—in the title role.

For the season in which I was general manager, he produced a stage adaptation of F. W. Murnau's *Nosferatu*, an unauthorized

1922 German Expressionist vampire film based on Bram Stoker's *Dracula*. Another was Tony Kushner's award-winning *Angels in America*, which treated the subject of homosexuality and AIDS with great sensitivity and unassailable integrity. Eddie really had no peers, either within or beyond the Seacoast region, for his mastery of stage direction, costume building, and set design. Both plays were enormously successful, and I had the satisfaction of knowing that my behind-the-scenes work as publicist had contributed modestly to the continuing success of the Edwin Booth.

The worst part of my job as GM was the unending struggle to wring essential, time-sensitive information out of a troupe of actors too self-absorbed and too hopelessly unorganized to deliver the information I needed to publicize their plays. Eddie wasn't very well organized, either; like his actors, he loathed the business end of the theater and prayed fervently that someone else—anyone but him—could be counted on to grapple with the less-than-inspiring administrative underbelly of his company.

That someone else was me. And while marketing and publicizing the Edwin Booth was by its very nature a daunting challenge, it was a dream assignment compared to dealing with the more temperamental actors in the troupe.

The trouble began when I was unexpectedly drawn into the Booth's production of Arthur Miller's *Death of a Salesman* as an actor. Langlois, who knew I was a professional musician with acting experience, created the onstage role of Grandfather / Flute Player especially for his production, then gave the role to me.

The addition of music, played by the grandfather and performed live onstage, was a wise and daring move—the sort of move for which Eddie was known and even revered. Sound plays an essential role in any production of *Death of a Salesman*, establishing mood and reinforcing the storyline. In Langlois's production, it helped to define the onstage character of the grandfather and contributed importantly to the psychological makeup of all of the characters in the play. For Eddie, who was always looking for fresh, innovative ways to stage a production, having me merely play a familiar piece from the wings, invisible to the audience, wouldn't have been enough.

He asked me to compose three distinct, scene-specific melodies for his production of *Salesman*, then built a strikingly morose, Lincolnesque costume for me, complete with stovepipe hat and cravat. Next, he choreographed me to move across the stage in three dreamlike cameo appearances, all while simultaneously playing the flute and struggling to keep the hat on my head. It was an exciting challenge for any actor, and Eddie was especially proud of the way he'd conceived and designed the important, mood-setting role.

Unfortunately, some of the principals in the production weren't as appreciative. A niggling, self-righteous knot of them, full of their usual galloping stage hubris, began privately to carp at Langlois for having inserted me into what they saw as their very own thespian turf—territory that belonged entirely to them and didn't need any intrusions from outsiders. Once I got wind of their feelings, the role of Grandfather / Flute Player became more albatross than asset for me as an actor, and I was rattled.

The next night, half an hour before curtain, I went to Eddie, ill-focused and bubbling over with performance anxiety, and told him what some of his actors—people he'd worked with for years and cared deeply for—were saying about me and the character I'd been asked to portray.

"If they don't like it, that's tough!" he said. "I conceived this role. I like your flute music. I like the character just the way I envisioned him. And I like what you're doing with him onstage. You're staying in this production!"

It was just what I needed, and precisely what a truly professional director needs to do when one of his actors is having an offstage moment of insecurity that's bound to affect both his own performance and the integrity of the production as a whole.

No matter how ill-timed and abrasive Eddie's behavior might be in the course of producing and directing, in my dealings with him I could always count on him to be thoroughly professional in the service of art. When we weren't performing up to his standards, he'd tell us so. When we did our work and did it well, he'd praise us and defend us against the worst of what theater people, who can be appallingly narcissistic, are known to do to each other when their fragile egos are tampered with.

Langlois, like many theater people I've known and worked with, proved time and again that he could be temperamental, boorishly certain of the rectitude of his opinions, and almost comically smug. And yet, because of his artistic integrity, his boundless creativity, and his refusal to conform to anyone else's reality, Edouard Langlois—the most original artist I've ever had the pleasure of knowing and working with—earned my deepest admiration and unqualified support.

In a very real sense, Eddie is the perfect archetype for theater people everywhere, who in spite of their obvious vanities and raging insecurities are passionately in love with the world and viscerally, artfully involved in all of what it means to be human. Their blood burns hot and flows freely, both on- and offstage. They can behave as spoiled little children, then surprise everyone with the depth of their wisdom and caring.

Actors suffer no biases against people because of their race, their age, their physical characteristics, or their sexual orientation. They've a sacred mission to give their fellow humans a spot-on vision of themselves, with all of their superior gifts and maddening imperfections on parade. Eddie Langlois has done that with more consummate skill, blazing passion, and incomparable artistry than any other theater professional I know.

In the spring of 2014, Eddie, then fast approaching seventy, moved to Oregon to be near his relatives. It was a shock to see him go; I don't think there was anyone in Seacoast New Hampshire who ever thought he'd leave New England.

Before he'd even had a chance to settle into his new home, Langlois—who had been passionately in love with opera for many years—visited the Opera Theater Oregon and explored with them the possibility of producing a puppet opera he'd been working on with friends for the past several years.

Eddie Langlois was gone, and the state of New Hampshire had lost a titan of the arts.

Back at the Hack: A Rough-and-Tumble Summer

My work as an actor at Hackmatack Playhouse, confined to one arduous but exhilarating summer in 1995, was both challenging and rewarding in ways that only the smaller roles in a production can be.

As is often the case with bit part actors, especially in smaller theaters, I'd been hired to do much more than acting. Between twice-a-day, three-hour rehearsals for each show, I worked six days a week as a set-building crew member, then went home late at night—often after fourteen hours of labor—and worked on the season's publicity. Several times a day I'd be pulled off my hands and knees without warning, then told to put down my backstage hammer, take off my tool belt, and rush up onto the stage to be plugged abruptly into a scene. As soon as the director had taken me where he wanted me to go in my character, I'd leap off the stage, cut through the dressing room, scurry around to the backstage area, and resume my work on the set for the play I'd soon be performing in.

I'd turned fifty-one that year, so it's fair to say the grueling physical labor took a lot out of me. Still, after the fiasco of working that spring as the clerk in a nearby Little Professor bookstore, I was so happy to be doing what I was doing that I refused to allow myself to slow down. I'd arrive at 9:00 a.m., work until well past the supper hour, then drive home along Diamond Hill Road, exhausted from the relentless labor of set-building. Then, after attending to publicity and correspondence, I'd fall asleep each night filled to overflowing with the intoxicating magic of live theater.

I had bit part roles in three of the five shows that summer: as Mr. Beckman in *Gypsy*, the story of dancer Gypsy Rose Lee; as a run-of-the-mill sailor in *Mr. Roberts*, a paean to love and valor in the South Pacific during WWII; and as someone's much-abused lover in the wildly popular, season-ending *La Cage aux Folles* (*The Bird Cage*). Sam Scalamoni, the artistic director, gave us a real workout in all three productions. For his high standards and powerful work ethic, he earned the unqualified respect of everyone in the company.

In *Gypsy* I had the pleasure of being lifted up into the air each night on a chair while puffing proudly on a phony cigar and beaming to an audience ripe for the play's ending and laughing uproariously at my aerial antics. It was the tiniest of cameos, but a delight to play and a welcome break from the intense labor of set building and publicity deadlines.

In *Mr. Roberts* I had a much more ambitious role as a sailor assigned to a battleship in the South Pacific. As part of my assignment, I was required to appear each night in an on-board attack scene calling for hair-trigger timing and artfully feigned stress under imaginary fire. As is usual for a bit part actor, I was surrounded by thoroughly experienced principals with formidable stage chops—people like Blaine Pickett, one of the funniest and most endearing actors I've ever worked with, and David Kaye, a Brandeis graduate and a stickler for onstage perfection who went on to become professor and chair of the Department of Theatre and Dance at the University of New Hampshire in Durham. Working with such talent was intimidating, but I gathered up my courage and accepted the role of proud novitiate to a group of actors almost religiously devoted to their craft.

My character was responsible for opening the entire play while coming up from the ship's hold—actually a trap door cut into the stage to facilitate my scene-opening cameo—all in the most inky imaginable darkness. I'd rehearsed that crucial, mood-setting scene countless times, but one night, after failing to pick up a critically important sound cue, I came up a tad early from the deep, in full view of the audience and looking more like a bewildered prairie dog than a serious actor.

Jim Murphy—a well-known Seacoast area actor who was working the light board that evening but often had major roles in area productions—was enraged. From that moment on, whenever we crossed paths, he was so cold to me that I felt as if I'd just stepped into a meat locker to hold court with a side of beef. It was for me another bleak, cautionary tale—an unsettling reminder that the typical bit part actor must be prepared to incur the wrath of his more seasoned onstage brethren while working his way up the ladder to respectability.

In *La Cage aux Folles*, I had a modest walk-on role as the much-maligned lover who appears onstage three times—first with a blood-soaked bandage on his forehead, next with his left arm in a sling, and then with a bum leg and a crutch. On the third and final cameo, I was whipped each night across the stage and into submission, eliciting an obscenely spirited roar of approval from the audience. The more banged up I was with each appearance, the more they laughed and cheered.

La Cage aux Folles was the sort of show that quickly revealed its remarkable power to unleash all of our most passionate yearnings as a culture. With a surefire blend of decadent flamboyance and heartwarming *joie de vivre*, it invited us to declare our freedom from stifling conventions and find our bliss, no matter what form that bliss might take. At a crucial moment in our country's understanding of what it means to be in love, this deceptively lighthearted comedy found an artful, entertaining way to challenge our parochial thinking and move us toward a more fully integrated culture, built not of hatred and distrust but of all-embracing love and mutual respect for the different ways we choose to live our lives.

Embassy Players of Portland: A Secular Humanist Gets Religion

I few years ago, I landed what for me—an actor with a long history of bit part roles—turned out to be a major assignment: acting, singing, and dancing in the role of Caiaphas in *A Remarkable Mary*, a Biblical musical produced at Embassy Players of Portland, Maine. How I managed to land that role is a story that speaks eloquently to the hair-raising unpredictability of the theater world.

I didn't set out to act at Embassy Players. I'd finally decided to get serious about being an actor, so I began to look beyond my own immediate community for opportunities to audition. The *Portland Press Herald* listed a city-wide, multi-theater audition —a cattle-call affair with directors from play companies all over Portland in attendance. It was just what I was looking for, and I jumped at the chance to prepare as I'd never prepared before, then put myself to the test.

The requirement for the call was the usual: prepare two contrasting monologues—one warm and upbeat, the other high-minded and serious.

I don't remember which two I chose, but what I do remember is that over the next three weeks I drove myself mercilessly to prepare for the audition. I ran my lines before work, during work, and late at night while lying alone in my darkened bedroom, staring at the ceiling and visualizing my audition in progress. I was determined to learn my lines so thoroughly that they'd be certain to pour forth from me effortlessly on audition day. Knowing my lines cold, I figured, would allow me to concentrate entirely on the emotional content, technical nuances, and inward motivations of my character. Because of my thorough preparation, I'd astound the directors with the pinpoint accuracy of my lines and the chest-thumping authority of my performance.

On the day of the audition, while driving the forty-five minutes from Berwick to Portland along I-95 north, I continued to drill myself without cease—a throat-singing Tibetan monk in blue jeans, chanting my mantras into the Maine woods as if my very life depended on it. Once in downtown Portland, I parked my car, walked nervously into a ground-floor auditorium, and claimed one of the few folding chairs available in a gathering of more than fifty actors and a small army of producers and directors.

My turn came twenty minutes into the event—twenty minutes in which I sat there and ran my lines so relentlessly that I can remember nothing of the actors who preceded me. When it was my turn to audition, a stone-faced young man with a red-orange beard and wire-rimmed glasses nodded toward me, then announced me to the crowd with not a flicker of emotion in his voice. His ice-cold demeanor disarmed me and froze the very blood that until that moment had been coursing wildly in my veins.

I cheerfully identified myself to the assemblage, then dove headlong into my audition.

But to my shock and dismay, nothing came out. I failed on first attempt to deliver even one word of the first monologue.

I tried again, not once but twice, to shrug off the misfire and pull up something—anything—from the reservoir of lines I'd labored so hard to learn. When I finally realized the well was truly dry, I pulled myself together, apologized for having failed to deliver my monologue, tipped my imaginary hat, and slunk back to Berwick, wondering along the way if this was destined to go down in my personal history as my very last audition.

The next evening, while skulking around at home and licking my wounds, I heard the telephone ring.

"Mr. Bachelder?" said a robust, wholesome-sounding male voice at the end of the phone. "Embassy Players calling. I was at the auditions in Portland on Thursday and saw you there, delivering your monologue."

"Monologue?" I wondered why anyone would have reason to call me after my onstage disintegration. "*What* monologue?" I said. "I never uttered one word of it!"

"We've *all* had moments like that!" he said. "The fact that you lost your focus that one time is not any sort of proof of your ability as an actor. Actually, we really liked what we saw of you! You have good, solid stage presence, and just the kind of energy we're looking for in the show we're producing. We'd like you to come up for an audition."

Dumbfounded didn't begin to describe how I felt at that moment. I said yes, hung up the phone, and allowed myself a precious moment or two to savor my unlikely transformation from ruined thespian to aspiring actor, all in a matter of hours.

Less than a week later, I walked into Embassy Players, read lines with a small group of fellow actors, sang portions of a song accompanied by the company's founder and musical director, Hank Beebe, and got in line for a group assessment of our ability to move rhythmically to music.

Once we'd completed the audition, we were instructed to wait in an adjoining room, where we'd soon learn who, if anyone, was cast in the play.

Ten minutes later, Beebe strode into the room with a smile on his face and a checklist in his hand. "Before we tell you whether any of you have been cast," he said, "I want to tell you about the play. It's a musical called *A Remarkable Mary*, but it's also a serious religious drama, with comic relief in several scenes and a great many challenging roles. If there are any among you who can't see yourselves in a religious musical, now's the time to say so."

Me, in a *religious* musical? Couldn't they see I was a raging secular humanist? "This ain't gonna work," I mumbled to myself.

I decided it was best to wait and see what, if any role I'd be offered. And if I did manage to land a role—*fat chance!*—I figured I'd just thank the producers for their faith in me, cut my losses, and go back to Berwick.

A man nearly young enough to be my grandson spoke up first. "Thanks for the audition," he said, "but I'm not really a Christian. I think it would be dishonest of me to take a role in a religious play." He handed his script to one of Beebe's assistants, then slipped quietly out the side entrance of the theater.

I was next in line for Judgment Day, and I was really feeling the heat. *Would it really matter*, I asked myself, *if I'm not a Christian? And what would Beebe think if I also gave him a flat-out no?*

Beebe then turned to me. "And you, Ross? We think you'd make a terrific Caiaphas. We're offering you the part. It's a demanding role for any actor," he said, "but we feel certain you'll be up for the challenge!"

A toxic blend of intellectual dishonesty and outright shame spread over me, and my face turned bright red. I wanted badly to hand my script back to the director and walk out the door, but began to have second thoughts.

Was I really so weighed down by my own precious intellectual convictions that I couldn't imagine taking what I considered a less than ideal role? And was I a serious, committed actor or not?

I turned to the director and said, "Yes. I'll do it!"

For the next several weeks I worked long and hard to prepare for my assignment. I did some basic research into the life of Caiaphas and learned he was the Jewish high priest who played a major role in the trial of Jesus, accusing him of blasphemy for claiming to be the Messiah. I learned my lines cold and never missed them in performance, I sang each song with borrowed religious conviction but tolerable authority, and I grew exponentially as an actor.

As I look back on it, playing a major role in a religious drama taught me many invaluable lessons. The producers who attended the cattle-call audition in Portland months before had looked beyond my failure to deliver my monologue and seen something of value in me as an actor. They'd trusted me—a man who'd failed to utter even one word of his required monologues at the audition—to learn the role of Caiaphas thoroughly, then come across with the goods, live and onstage, in a musical that meant a great deal to them both theatrically and spiritually. Thanks to them, I learned something about tolerance, open-mindedness, and the true meaning of professionalism.

I never mentioned to them that I wasn't formally religious—that other than working as the paid musician for a Sunday service, or attending a wedding or funeral, I hadn't been inside a church in nearly half a century. Nor, to their everlasting credit, did they choose to quiz me about my religious convictions.

Near the end of the run of *A Remarkable Mary*, Beebe announced that Embassy Players would be taking the play down to New York City for a three-show run at a theater that often reciprocated by bringing their own productions north to Portland.

I ought to have jumped at the chance to add a New York City appearance to my actor's résumé, but something inside me said no. As often happens in the theater world, the bloom had finally come off the rose in my relationship with the producers. As we piled on the performances, they'd become noticeably more impatient with the actors. And, however unfairly, I'd begun to think there was a righteous tone in their criticisms. My aversion to anything sanctimonious brought the ordinarily hidden cynical part of me straight to the surface.

Fig. 65. The author as Caiaphas in the Embassy Players' production of *A Remarkable Mary*, Portland, Maine.

The day after our final performance, I mailed Beebe a letter of resignation, explaining that I was far too busy in other areas of my life to continue in the role of Caiaphas and would not be going to New York City with the rest of the troupe. A week later I showed up at the theater, thanked Hank and his wife for their faith in me as an actor, turned in my costume, and left the city of Portland, ashamed for having abandoned the role they'd invested so heavily in. I then headed home to Berwick to contemplate my next move as a theater professional.

I wondered if anyone could have asked more of a company of actors. They'd shown me their professional integrity, and to the best of my ability I'd shown them mine. It was in some ways an even exchange. I'd grown considerably, both personally and professionally, during my brief time with Embassy Players. And after our unlikely collaboration, I went away hoping they'd been even half as pleased with my performance as I was for having been entrusted with the role of Caiaphas in the first place.

The Berwick Young People's Theater: Doing It All, Seven Days a Week

In the mid 1980s, near the end of my seven years as a public school music teacher, I founded the Berwick Young People's Theater, a tuition summer theater for teens. My goal was to give area youngsters a chance to work in a more challenging theatrical environment than young people traditionally have available to them. I was convinced that, by offering them sophisticated scripts, ambitious sets, and higher than usual expectations for production and performance, I'd be giving them a chance to show the theater-going public—and themselves—just how remarkably skilled they can be when challenged to work at a higher level than they are accustomed to.

I also knew that children who are active in the fine and performing arts tend to do better in the classroom in all subjects and feel better about themselves than those who aren't active in the arts.

The theater had no permanent home, so each season we'd scramble for a suitable place in which to stage our productions. Over the seven seasons of our existence, we staged productions in three venues: the basement of Our Lady of Peace, a Catholic church in Berwick; a well-worn grange hall in the nearby town of South Lebanon; and, thanks to the generosity of founder S. Carleton Guptill, in a combination storage barn and rehearsal facility on the property of Hackmatack Playhouse in Berwick.

I knew from painful experience that many plays for young actors were merely dumbed-down versions of the classics, designed to be easier for students to learn, teachers to teach, and publishers to market. Things have gotten much better since then, but at the time there was relatively little to offer the serious producer of plays for young people. I wanted more substantive, more challenging material for my actors, and when the market didn't offer me what I was looking for, I decided to take a stab at writing the plays myself.

I quickly realized that I was more interested in creating musical comedies than straight dramas. I also knew from years of experience with young people that my actors would love the chance both to act and to sing. And since I had done so much writing in other genres and had been active for years as a musician, I felt reasonably certain I could write both the stories and the music.

Altogether, over seven seasons, I wrote and produced eight musicals and the nearly seventy songs that went with them. Among the shows were *Digby's Folly*; *The Taming of Max Pettigrew*; *The Shortwave Radio Connection*; *Felicity, Maine—The Town That Forgot to Laugh*; and *Sweet and Sour Dreams: A Nightlife of the Young*.

Among the most enthusiastic and highly motivated actors in the company were Jordan Pike, now in his mid-thirties and the founder of Two Toad Farm in Lebanon, Maine, and Amy Laviolette, a natural-born actor of great skill and sensitivity who dearly loved her time onstage but died tragically in her early thirties, a victim of anorexia.

Thanks to my lifelong fascination with words and my insatiable appetite for anything even remotely funny, all of the plays I wrote were stuffed to the gills with humor and laced with high-level vocabulary and abundant wordplay, tempered by what I hoped were typical moments of teenage poignancy. I wanted my actors to discover the joys of learning new words and mastering complex dialogue, so I held back nothing while constructing my characters and giving them words to deliver onstage. In nearly every season, the actors met and often exceeded both their own expectations and mine. The result was that many adults had their very first opportunity to see their children working at a very high level and succeeding in ways few might have expected.

My longtime friend Mike Plumer, a successful restaurateur and master of pretty much anything mechanical, stepped in and built not only a set of theater lights from scratch but also a light board to operate them. He worked out the lighting cues and ran the board whenever he could get away from his work as owner-operator of Jake's City Kitchen, at the time a wildly popular restaurant in downtown Dover, New Hampshire. Mike brought his own high expectations as a restaurant professional to his work as lighting designer, and the quality of his lighting plans contributed enormously to the success of our performances.

I enlisted the help of my wife, Marilyn—a highly successful music educator and pit orchestra musician—to arrange my songs, assemble an orchestra made up of exceptionally talented young musicians from her own public school music program, then conduct that orchestra live in our performances. She often played electric bass while conducting, and on more than one occasion our daughter, Amy, a middle school student at the time, sat in on electric piano.

I knew that children love to dance, so I hired a local movement coach and choreographer, Tia Almeida Pike—Jordan's mother—to choreograph our dance routines.

We had many moments of laughter and creative fulfillment in our onstage and offstage work, but two of those moments continue to stand out for me after all these years.

The first moment—a shamelessly corny, Vaudevillian sight gag—enjoyed only a brief time onstage each night but managed in every single performance to elicit laughter and contribute importantly to the flavor and spirit of the play. In *The Shortwave Radio Connection*, I created a group called the Curiosity Club, knowing that such a device would allow me as playwright to unite my characters around a common goal—the achievement of excellence in everything they set out to do. Since the members of the Curiosity Club as I conceived them were as unconventional as they were precocious, I wanted anything they'd invented—anything our audiences would see—to be unlike anything a typical theater goer would expect to see in a musical.

The clubhouse needed a telephone, but I couldn't allow us to put just any old phone on the set, so I headed down to Nick Zerbinopoulos's Curiosity Shop in Berwick, bought a beat-up wooden toilet seat, painted it a bright, iridescent gold, and mounted it at upstage center on the set. I then hid a conventional, wall-mounted phone behind it, recessed into the flat.

In live performance, just after the Curiosity Club members were introduced to their new clubhouse, one of the actors would say, "How will we be able to call home? My parents will want to know where I am!"

"Easy," said another club member, beaming at the audience as he lifted up the lid of the toilet seat. "You can just call 'em on the toile-phone!"

The success of that humble sight gag became both a tribute to the magic of theater and a lesson for everyone in the company about the power of imagination in any setting. One of the actors liked it so much, he claimed it after the final performance of *The Shortwave Radio Connection*, then mounted it permanently in the door of his bedroom.

One of live theater's greatest strengths lies in its ability to live night after night in a playful, make-believe land of its very own manufacture. Hand in hand with that strength is the exceptional power of a play to bring people from many walks of life together, and, while they're away from their real-life worries for a few

Fig. 66. Skywave, created by restaurateur Mike Plumer for the Berwick Young People's Theater production of *The Shortwave Radio Connection*.

hours, remind them of their common humanity. *The Shortwave Radio Connection* accomplished that with more success than any other play I wrote during our seven years of producing musicals.

The second moment I recall had to do with Skywave, a prop I conceived as the centerpiece for our production of the same play. I enlisted Mike Plumer, the man who'd built our lights and light board, to come up with a one-of-a-kind radio with imaginary powers. In the script, its function would be to allow the intellectually precocious members of the Curiosity Club to talk again with Maria, a member of their club who'd passed away at a painfully young age. I knew that a stage prop of such critical importance to the storyline would have to be a visual tour de force.

He managed somehow to build it in less than three days, then delivered it to the actors in time for our next rehearsal. It was an unqualified triumph as a stage prop. The actors loved working with it, and each night the audiences responded with warmth and appreciation as the lights came up slowly and mysteriously on the radio.

My seven years producing plays for teens was really my very first opportunity to bring together all of my creative preoccupations—writing, music, and art—in one inspiring, labor-intensive endeavor. It had an enormous, lasting impact on my future as an arts multiple, revealing over time its profound influence on my writing, my studio art, my work as a musician, and my thinking in general about the nature of creativity as I've experienced it over the past forty years. And if any of the actors in BYPT found inspiration, increased self-esteem, and intellectual growth from their work in our plays, then the value of my countless hours of work on the project will have been immeasurably more than I could have hoped for.

Liberty Stage Company: *A Sleep of Prisoners* Comes to Life

In the mid-'70s, not long after moving with my family from south central Michigan to northern New England, I landed a position as marketer and publicist for Liberty Stage Company in Portsmouth, New Hampshire. Liberty Stage, tucked inauspiciously into a cluttered, second-floor room in the old post office building on Pleasant Street, was the brainchild of John Hallowell, a Harvard graduate who for some inexplicable reason refused over and over again to admit that he'd ever matriculated there.

Hallowell, who was strikingly tall and always spoke slowly with a *basso profundo* voice, was instantly identifiable as he strode around town in his London Fog trench coat, brooding as he walked in his familiar, hunched-over way. He appeared on most days to be absurdly, even comically cerebral, as if he'd been locked long ago into an academic think tank by the dean, then forced to stay there until he'd solved all of the world's problems.

As a callow graduate of a far less prestigious Midwestern college—still just over thirty years old and struggling to find myself—I couldn't help being at least initially proud of my affiliation with Liberty Stage Company. It was as if I'd prayed, however foolishly, that some of Hallowell's self-conscious intellectuality would rub off on me and accelerate my entry into a higher level of inspired creativity. It didn't take long for me to be thoroughly disillusioned by the reality of my circumstances.

Right away, I was pegged to be the editor and chief writer for *IN BRIEF*, the company's marketing newsletter. *IN BRIEF*—almost embarrassingly erudite in tone and content—was expected to double as both the voice of Liberty Stage Company and a critically essential money-making machine.

When not breathing life into quarterly editions of *IN BRIEF*, I spent several hours a day at a tiny desk next to Hallowell's, cold-calling churches in Maine, New Hampshire, and Massachusetts in an attempt to persuade them to book *A Sleep of Prisoners*—Christopher Fry's poignant drama about four prisoners of war trapped in a church in enemy territory. If we managed to secure a booking, Hallowell expected the play to be performed not in a conventional theater but in the church itself. It made good sense: performing there would eliminate the need to build a set and save Liberty Stage Company a great deal of money. The church would be the set, and on paper, at least, there couldn't have been a more fortuitous arrangement for everyone involved.

On the days when John scheduled me to do the cold-calling, I dreaded coming to work. For only fifty dollars a week, I'd be required to talk for several hours each day on the telephone, in full view of John and his fellow actors. While they and other unidentified hangers-on walked into the room whenever they felt like it and loitered for hours, engaging in small-talk and generally making fools of themselves with their intellectual posturing, I was tethered to the telephone like a circus elephant to a stake.

We concentrated on Catholic and Episcopal churches because John thought they were the most likely to empathize with the tone and content of *A Sleep of Prisoners*, but there were days when my cold-calling garnered not even one mouse-worthy nibble of interest in our services. If a marketer goes to market and comes home with nothing to show for it, how long can he or she be expected to be employed? I waited every day for Hallowell to hand me my pink slip, but the moment of severance never seemed to come.

The cultural and political backdrop at Liberty Stage was built on wild-eyed aesthetic idealism and radical politics. Though I neither asked for nor was ever given the details, I finally gleaned from casual listening that one of Hallowell's friends—a man named Snick—was an avowed anti-nuclear activist who, along with his friends, was bent on shutting down the Seabrook Nuclear Power Plant just south of Portsmouth.

Snick, whose full name I never managed to learn, was for me hardly more than a second-tier shadow puppet in the Liberty Stage drama. He'd hang around the office several days a week, clad melodramatically in a black trench coat and combat boots—the obligatory cloak-and-dagger uniform of the times—with his hair in comical disarray and a cigarette dangling from his mouth. He was the classic post-hippie-era rebel, but with a clear and controversial cause. It was all very entertaining, but when Snick was with his friends and in performance mode at Liberty Stage, I was never invited to be a part of the show.

Creating *IN BRIEF* every three months, entirely from scratch, was for me a powerful opportunity—the newsletter was a blank, thirsty canvas onto which I could paint my thoughts and convictions with near perfect freedom of expression. Hallowell always insisted on reviewing the final draft of my articles, but I needn't have worried: he green-lighted nearly everything I wrote.

We published and distributed three well-received issues of *IN BRIEF* during my year with Liberty Stage, but our struggle to book *A Sleep of Prisoners* into area churches yielded less than a half dozen play dates.

I remember attending a late-November performance—the last of the season—staged in a handsome but poorly heated gray-stone church on Main Street in Durham, New Hampshire. The architecture had a certain medieval character that worked in harmony with the dark, brooding mood of the play.

Fewer than ten people were huddled together in the audience. With their winter coats pulled tightly up to their chins, they looked remarkably like a mournful gathering of London gargoyles, brought down from their skyward perches and ushered in mercifully from the cold. In spite of the inhospitable weather and poor attendance, the actors in *A Sleep of Prisoners* performed superbly, filling every corner of the church with their hyper-intellectual dialogue. While I can't claim to have fully understood the play's message, I was glad I went. I also knew instinctively that I'd just seen a beautifully written play, performed by actors at the top of their game and passionate about their craft.

Long after I'd left the employ of Liberty Stage, I saw John walking across the Sarah Mildred Long Bridge in Portsmouth one winter morning, looking remarkably like George Bailey in *It's a Wonderful Life* just before his guardian angel, Clarence Oddbody, comes down from the Pearly Gates and saves him from a watery death. I'd lost touch entirely with the company by then, but the striking image of its long-ago founder, walking dejectedly along that bridge with his shoulders hunched against the wind, gave me reason to wonder about the fate of Hallowell and his grand experiment in culturally relevant, cutting-edge theater.

It's likely that John Hallowell's uncompromising fidelity to an ideal—a theater for the people, lovingly conceived and beautifully executed—spelled certain doom for his company. When I look back on my Liberty Stage experience, beyond the swaggering, trench-coated Snick and the suffocating intellectual pretensions that hung over the company like a toxic cloud as I hustled for bookings, I realize that John had genuinely preferred artistic triumph over financial success.

Was Liberty Stage Company a success? Perhaps, in many ways, it wasn't. But in the ways that count—late at night, when after a triumphant performance the actors and the director know for certain they'd hit their mark onstage—the answer was an unequivocal yes.

His unyielding allegiance to a principle—excellence at all costs, including box office failure—is both a cautionary tale and a beacon of hope for anyone who sets out to put on a play, then discovers just how difficult it is to balance idealism with the need for a paycheck. The trick for any acting troupe is to be so good at the less romantic, offstage functions of play production that the onstage work can move merrily along, show after show, without one painful moment of compromise in the quality of its productions.

Liberty Stage Company went broke in part because of an almost maniacal devotion to *A Sleep of Prisoners*—a play whose deadly serious, highly cerebral message was almost certain to appeal only to a tiny segment of the theater-going public. Ironically, the play's actors were no less imprisoned by their idealism than the characters they portrayed, trapped as they were in an unfamiliar church in enemy territory. In that sense, Liberty Stage Company was itself a powerful, mesmerizing play within a play—a noble experiment that may have failed financially, but managed in spite of that to bring to the stage a play of profound social significance, then perform it with consummate skill and unassailable integrity. What theater, anywhere in the world, wouldn't be proud to have done that?

The Cliff House: Forty Nights on the Shores of the Atlantic

In the late '70s I teamed up with Seacoast-area theater professionals Sharon Hilton and Jeff Starbird to form a small itinerant theater troupe. We called ourselves Starbird, Hilton, and Carlin, and we were out to make steady money as actors.

Sharon, who at a young age was already remarkably experienced in play directing and production, was automatically tagged to be the director. We conceived our production as a fast-moving theatrical oleo of vocal and instrumental solos, stand-up comedy, and a one-act play, all designed to appeal to busloads of starry-eyed tourists up from southern New England for a few days of pleasure along the Atlantic.

I replaced my own last name with the name Carlin because it sounded terrific in the press releases, and because, silly as it seems in retrospect, I was determined not to use my last name, Bachelder, as an actor. I knew from painful experience, while growing up in Michigan, that no one ever seemed to know how to pronounce it.

Less than a month after founding our troupe, we landed a six-week, forty-performance gig at the renowned Cliff House Resort & Spa in Ogunquit and went straight into rehearsals.

Hilton tolerated no nonsense in her role as director. If we clowned around during scene rehearsals, she'd order us to cease and desist, then immediately get us back on track. Finally, after nearly three months of hard work, the time for opening night had arrived.

Being onstage night after night—the featured entertainment in an elegant resort overlooking the Atlantic—was for all of us a heady experience. Our audiences were nearly always dominated by wave upon wave of what some theater people callously describe as the Blue Hairs—older women in flower-print dresses, lined up like off-duty soldiers in the matinees of theaters across America. Beside them would be their grudging, dutiful husbands, all decked out in cream-colored polyester pants hitched up well north of their often bulging waistlines. Of course we were young then, and from our naive, *A Star Is Born* perspective, we couldn't imagine that one day we'd appear to be just as old and out of touch as the people actors like to joke about in the green room while waiting to go onstage.

Jeff, a twenty-something free spirit who lived alone in a self-made geodesic dome in the woods near Ogunquit, fancied himself as a classic crooner in the mold of Como and Sinatra. He was tapped to sing several old standards—songs like "Bewitched, Bothered and Bewildered" and "That Old Black Magic." While in performance he had a booming baritone voice and a concupiscent twinkle in his eyes, and because of it the women loved him to distraction.

Because I'd had years of experience as a "serious" musician, I was booked to play the musical heavy. I performed "Sentimentale" from Claude Bolling's *Suite for Flute and Jazz Piano* each night, hoping to bring a touch of high-minded classicism to what was mostly an upbeat, feel-good string of matinee-style entertainments.

I'd also been chosen to sing one old standard with piano accompaniment at each performance. The hope was that if I could deliver a tolerable performance of "On the Sunny Side of the Street" each night, I'd relieve Starbird of the burden of singing so many vocal numbers. After less than a week into the forty-show run, I listened one night to a tape of myself as a jazz vocalist, then immediately applied the hook and removed my song from the show.

To liven things up each night, Hilton and I performed an outrageously corny skit called "The Fishing Hat" that made Dagwood and Blondie seem almost avant-garde by comparison. In spite of a hopelessly antiquated plot, it managed to bring down the house nearly every night.

After forty nights of performing—a gig that netted each of us just over a thousand dollars—it was time to move on to other things.

Sharon went on to found Renaissance Stage Company, and shortly after that, yet another theatrical endeavor—InterPlay Productions—devoted to touring Seacoast-area schools with plays about values and self-esteem.

Jeff went back to his hut in the woods to live his unconventional lifestyle, breaking away on only one occasion to take a lucrative acting and singing role in upstate New York. Then, only a few months after the Cliff House run, Sharon and I learned that he'd died of AIDS. We attended his funeral and wept at the memory of the good times we'd had while performing together.

I continued to take freelance writing assignments and gigs as a flute player, but I'd also begun to look for steady employment in theater publicity. After a dozen or so inquiries, I answered a classified ad in the *Boston Globe*, and within a few weeks I'd landed the job of director of publicity for "America's Foremost Summer Theatre," Ogunquit Playhouse. John Lane, who'd been coming up from New York City for years to oversee the summer season, would be my boss for the 1979 season. I'd be writing the publicity for big-name actors from all over the country, and I couldn't help wondering what I'd done to deserve such good fortune.

John Lane of Ogunquit Playhouse: The Man, the Theater, and the Lessons I Learned

My first chore as director of publicity—under direct orders from Mr. Lane—was to buy a black suit and matching black shoes to wear on the all-important opening nights, when I'd be the very public liaison between the Playhouse, the audience, and the ever-present theater critics.

The local reviewers weren't about to intimidate me, but the ones up from the *Globe* or the *Times*? I had to be ready for them, and Lane—a man of sartorial splendor, with every hair in place and nails filed to perfection—would be making a list and checking it twice to make sure I was honoring his dress code.

The easy part was the suit. After hours of pounding the pavement in southern Maine stores, I found a suit for just under a hundred dollars—in 1979, a tolerably good price. It was ebony black, slicker than the ice on a Maine winter road, and positively funereal in appearance. I could have moonlighted as a pallbearer to augment my two-hundred-a-week salary as PR man, and I would have been a credit to the deceased.

And then there were the shoes. I would never have gotten away with the footwear I favored at the time—brown leather work shoes which, in combination with my jet black suit, would have made me a *bon vivant* in clod-hoppers. In John's world, such an ensemble would have been grounds for immediate dismissal.

I finally settled on wingtips, a style of shoe designed long ago by the Scots—though the Irish have also been known to claim that distinction—and featuring perforations that allowed water to drain from them when the wearer was crossing bogs on the Isle of Skye. Since the wingtip had long ago moved on from its more practical origins and become the very symbol of business-world sophistication, I figured I needed to put nothing less than my best foot forward. And since Lane was reputed to have two hundred pairs of shoes from around the world in a barn behind the Playhouse, I felt an even greater urgency to impress him with my good taste in footwear.

I first wore my wingtips when the *Herald American*'s Elliot Norton—known as the dean of American theater critics—came up from Boston to review a show. The Harvard-educated Norton, a man of prodigious erudition and writerly elegance, was the very definition of *patrician*. He was immaculately groomed and meticulously dressed—a Boston Brahmin with wavy, perfectly combed white hair, a lanky, easy-going demeanor, and impeccable manners.

With my black silk tie, Van Heusen shirt, and spit-shined shoes, I figured I'd manage to pass muster with John as a representative of the Playhouse. I remember nothing of the conversation that transpired between Mr. Norton and me, but those shoes, glowing like two twin ocean liners beneath the lobby lights, provided me with the confidence I needed to perform my duties as PR man with tolerable dignity and professionalism.

The '79 season included an odd mixture of lesser-known Broadway tryout plays (like *Same Time, Next Year*) and proven box-office hits (including *Camelot*, *Deathtrap*, and *The Man of La Mancha*). *La Mancha* starred fabled actor/singer John Raitt—the proud father of award-winning entertainer Bonnie Raitt—as the tender-hearted, impossibly dreaming Don Quixote.

John Raitt's booming baritone voice, dashing good looks, and powerful stage presence made him a perennial favorite in the country's summer-season circuit. He drew rave reviews in Ogunquit, making the women swoon and the men feel inadequate as he delivered each night an inspiring, roof-shaking performance of "The Impossible Dream (The Quest)."

Well, *almost* every night. During one matinee performance of *La Mancha*, the wind outside began to howl, and torrents of rain, blown in from the Atlantic, pummeled mercilessly against the Playhouse roof. The stage lights flickered several times, then went dark.

It would take more than a summertime tempest to stop Mr. Raitt. Known throughout the country for his many decades of devotion to musical theater as an art form, he rallied the entire cast and instructed them to sit down along the apron of the stage. Then crew members moved in and lit candles to illuminate the actors, and as the storm continued to lash the Playhouse, the entire company sang more than a dozen songs from *La Mancha* and other well known musicals, culminating in Raitt's heartrending performance of "The Impossible Dream."

Later, he set up a card table in the lobby and spent well over an hour autographing the play programs of his adoring fans—a ritual he'd gladly performed for many decades in theaters across the country.

One of my first missteps as publicity director was to violate what I learned later was an unwritten law of the professional theater world: administrators were expected never to interact in any personal way with the actors while a play was in production. I'd always been highly gregarious, so it never dawned on me that my Midwestern, puppy dog demeanor might prove on occasion to be a workplace liability.

One day John asked me to post a rehearsal schedule on the actors' call board, so I walked across the lawn to the dressing room and posted the schedule as directed. As I was leaving, Charles Kimbrough—a well-known stage actor who from 1988 to 1998 went on to play the veteran news anchor Jim Dial on television opposite Candace Bergen in *Murphy Brown*—nodded hello to me in the hallway.

Kimbrough, who was starring that summer in *Same Time, Next Year* at the Playhouse, was warm, witty, and highly approachable in a way that the other actors that summer—with the notable exceptions of Betsy Palmer, Anne Jackson, and a couple of others—were not.

I remember making what was meant to be an amusing quip of some sort, and Kimbrough responded with one of his own. I was so touched by his humanity—his utter lack of stage hubris—that I went back to my office, penned a limerick to honor the occasion, then strode back to the dressing room and posted it on the call board with his name prominently written at the top. Later that afternoon, Lane called me into his office, handed me the confiscated limerick, and with a chillingly acerbic smile admonished me never again to set foot in the actors' quarters.

My office at the Playhouse featured only a battle-scarred desk, an aging swivel chair, and a beat-up corkboard with a small army of pushpins on it, waiting to be called up and pressed into action.

To keep up with the incessant flow of deadlines, I carpeted both the corkboard and the surface of my desk with notes to myself—reminders of what I must do and when I must do it. It was my time-tested way of maintaining order and assuring the boss that I could be counted on to deliver all phases of the season's publicity on time and free of errors.

One July morning, Lane stopped by my office, moved toward my desk, then stood silently behind me with a bemused smile on his thoroughly tanned, meticulously shaved face. I went uneasily about my business while wondering just what he had on his mind.

"All of these *notes!*" he said, breaking the silence with an unmistakeable tone of distaste and disapproval in his carefully chosen, precisely articulated words. "It's not *professional*! Please remove them. Surely there are other ways for you to keep track of your duties!" He then glided out the door and moved with Gene Kelly ease into his own charmed and privileged life as the producer of—we were never allowed to forget it—America's Foremost Summer Theatre.

Lane really did make an effort to bring me into the fold as an employee of the Playhouse, but as I saw it, always with conditions—spoken or unspoken, real or imagined—attached. One day at work, entirely without warning, he asked me to join him for lunch at Barnacle Billy's, a popular seafood restaurant in nearby Perkins Cove. The invitation simultaneously warmed my heart and froze my blood. I'd never really expected to be in a social situation with John Lane, and I wasn't emotionally prepared to make meaningful conversation with him.

We drove down to the Cove right away and settled in to an outdoor table. The sky, cloudless and dazzlingly blue, overlooked a harbor embellished with soaring gulls and bobbing sailboats. Lane did his best to engage me in conversation as we munched politely on fresh-from-the-Atlantic lobster, washed down with tumblers of fresh-squeezed lemonade.

We were a study in contrasts: he a well-traveled, unimaginably rich theatrical producer, and I a man of humble, working-class origins who'd done very little traveling and had seldom if ever crossed paths with the highly successful people of the world. He said nothing to offend me during our time together, and yet, as we returned to our respective offices at the Playhouse, I couldn't rid myself of the feeling that I was disappointing him at every turn and would never manage to meet his expectations as an employee.

Yoga at Lunchtime: Mind, Body, and Allegiance

In spite of his moments of withering disapproval, Lane could be disarmingly gracious and warm of heart. "Have I told you that each Wednesday we have a lunch-hour yoga session in the lobby?" he said one day shortly before noon. "It's really a very good way to release the tensions of the workplace. You're not obligated to attend, but you're certainly welcome to join us!"

I've never been a fan of yoga, which to me seems cult-like, pretentious, and inimical to my hard-wired, get-it-done way of burning through existence. My idea of relaxation nearly always includes books. On my lunch hours I'd break open my brown-bag cuisine and read myself into a condition of serenity. I harbored no ambition to be a contortionist, but as a gesture of respect for John, I decided to give yoga a try.

The instructor—let's call him Sebastian—was a dashing fellow with tousled, sandy-blond hair and a willowy, fat-free body of the sort that's required equipment for anyone teaching yoga. While it's nowhere written in the rules, one can't help believe that being a sumo wrestler—or perhaps the bouncer in a bar—wouldn't cut it in Yoga Land.

When I arrived for my first lunch-hour session, the lights had already been dimmed, and a sweet, feather-like cloud of music, Asian in flavor and coming from a small portable radio in one corner of the lobby, had begun to envelop the participants like a morning fog from the nearby Atlantic.

Then Sebastian, with impressive skill and fluidity, began to take us through a series of moves. While the others responded to his guidance with an almost spiritual glow of reverence, breathing and twisting their limbs with refined, balletic precision, I rubbed my aching calves and yearned to be in my usual lunchtime cocoon, reclining on the Playhouse lawn and flipping through the pages of my current read—a tattered, dog-eared edition of Fyodor Dostoevsky's novel *Crime and Punishment*. The fate of my muscles was of no concern to me that summer; it was my mind—not my glutes—that I wanted most to exercise. I vowed never to return to the sessions, comforted with the knowledge that, after all, they were completely optional. *How kind of Lane to offer*, I thought, *and with no strings attached!*

Over the next three weeks, as we broke for lunch, I'd sneak past the lobby full of yoga lovers pretzeling reverently on the carpet, then slip out onto the lawn to devour my novel, polish off my sandwich, and seek my own, ever-elusive peace of mind. It wasn't yoga, but it was heaven to me.

A few days later, John approached me as I settled into my office and prepared to crank out a press release for *Same Time, Next Year*.

"Good morning, Mr. Bachelder!" he said with unctuous solicitude, his patented, sunbaked smile illuminating the room. "We missed you at the yoga session! Perhaps we shall see you there again on Wednesday."

The smile was warm enough, but the eyes—two menacing, glacially cold daggers—were pointed directly at my heart. *No strings attached?* I was not a natural joiner, and John Lane had finally realized that about me. Clearly, he intended to strike a death-blow to my lone-wolf propensities, then draw me inexorably into compliance with his vision of how the director of publicity ought to conduct himself. I couldn't help wondering if I'd just driven the last, long nail into my own self-made coffin as an employee of Ogunquit Playhouse.

The Voice-Over Incident

Early in the season, I was informed that I'd be doing the voice-over for a television advertisement to be aired on channel six in Portland, Maine. I was excited at the prospect of carrying out such an important assignment, knowing the advertisement would play a critical role in generating box office revenue.

It would be my job to write the script, then tape the voice-over live in the studios of Atlantic Video in nearby Kittery, Maine. *Kitt*ry, as the locals like to call it, is a quaint seaside village—the oldest town in Maine—just across the border from Portsmouth, New Hampshire. It's populated with a mixture of blue collar workers, Portsmouth Naval Shipyard employees, and people migrating to northern New England with money to burn—lots and lots of money. I figured that, on the day I was scheduled to tape the voice-over, there was a good chance I'd be rubbing shoulders with the privileged elite of the Pine Tree State.

To my surprise, I learned that John Lane and the theater's general manager, Henry J. Weller Jr., would be accompanying me on my journey. We met at the Playhouse, then drove to Kittery in Lane's car, which had sleek lines and enough gadgetry on the dashboard to guide a 747. Wedged between Lane and Weller in the front seat of the four-wheel luxury liner, I felt like a slice of cheap baloney trapped in a sandwich only the Queen of England could afford to eat.

We made our way down the Spaulding Turnpike and arrived promptly at 9:00 a.m. After several hours of taping and re-taping, we wrapped up the project, said our goodbyes to Atlantic Video, and headed out of Kittery, weaving our way along an idyllic sliver of land with storybook houses tucked into the coastline at every turn. The area was lined with dense outcroppings of pine trees that played their familiar summertime music while swaying gracefully in brisk ocean winds. To an inlander from the small, tannery-dominated town of Berwick, the scene was more theater set than neighborhood.

I sat in the back seat on the return trip, a young and ambitious college graduate, one generation removed from my blue collar roots but still painfully aware of my origins and what they said about my hopes for the future. *How wonderful it would be to live in one of those storybook cottages by the sea!* I thought while smelling the sweet salt air from my open window.

The men in the front seat saw things differently. "Such a shame, what's happening here in Maine," Lane said. "These shacks are an *eyesore!*"

Weller shook his head and voiced his approval of the boss's remark. "It really is a pity. One has to wonder what this region is *coming* to."

I shrank into one corner of the back seat and stared out the window at the beautiful homes and soaring pines rushing past us with cinematic splendor. I wanted badly to get out of the car at the next intersection, thank Lane and Weller for their trouble, then catch a ride with someone—anyone, really—who might have a better understanding of the real world than these two men appeared to have. Unfortunately, I knew with maddening certainty that it wasn't going to happen. I needed a job, and I'd finish my work as publicity director as promised—with dignity and professionalism—then begin to look for more suitable employment.

We deposited Weller somewhere between Kittery and Dover, then headed farther inland, where John had promised to drop me off at my home. As we crossed the bridge between Somersworth, New Hampshire, and Berwick, Maine, the all-too-familiar Prime Tanning smokestack loomed ahead of us, belching its toxic fumes into the unhappy sky over the Salmon Falls River.

When we arrived at 2 River Street, I decided for some reason—either manners or masochism—to invite John into our home. If I hadn't, I'd have been angry with myself for keeping him away from the truth about my life apart from the Playhouse.

Our home—a tiny, two-story apartment-like house attached to a white Victorian four times as large and ten times as beautiful—was easily more shack-like than the million-dollar cottages Lane had so imperiously ridiculed in Kittery. The ceilings were low, the wallpaper was water-stained and peeling in places, and the furniture—half college dorm and half thrift shop in origin—was almost comically mismatched. In spite of its many quirks and decrepitudes, we loved the place.

John Lane, the storied impresario and dashing *bon vivant*, made his way up the rickety stairs, stepped ahead of me into our tiny living room, and stood on the ornate, turn-of-the-century furnace grate at its center. Then, with a bemused smile on his tanned and patrician face, he looked politely around him. "Nice place!" he said, but it was hard for me to believe he really meant it. I thanked him for bringing me home, then escorted him to his car and assured him that I'd be back to work the next morning as scheduled.

I went to bed that night wondering, along with Lane and Weller, what the world was coming to, but from a dramatically different perspective. When million-dollar seaside cottages along the Atlantic—homes I and my contemporaries could inhabit only in our dreams—are to the monied upper crust only shacks to be sneered at, one has genuine cause to be alarmed at this country's precipitous decline in both common sense and plain human decency. That I was earning my weekly paycheck from a man with such elitist, otherworldly sensibilities caused me no small amount of discomfort, supplemented with an unhealthy dose of angst. I couldn't see very far into my future, but I knew with certainty that my path to fulfillment would have to change, and the sooner the better.

The Potted Palm Incident

On opening nights, the Playhouse lobby had the look and feel of a scene from *Sunset Boulevard*, with garish, in-your-face colors straight from the early days of CinemaScope. I half expected to see Norma Desmond come gliding down a spectacular winding staircase, her skirts dusting the plush green carpet as she moved with cloud-like delicacy into the lobby of the theater. (It didn't really matter that there was no staircase at the Playhouse; one can do miracles with the gift of imagination.)

The Playhouse lobby couldn't hide the painful reality that it had seen better days and was badly in need of a facelift. While always clean and tidy, it was obvious to the careful observer that it had gradually become a little frayed around the edges. The photos of the many stage luminaries who'd appeared at the Playhouse over the years were noticeably dated, just enough to give visitors the sense that time was standing still at America's Foremost Summer Theatre.

By now, the opening nights had become almost routine. I'd bring my required costume with me on a hanger in the morning, remembering always to stash the essential wingtips carefully in the trunk of my car to avoid scuffing them. After finishing my eight hours of work at the theater, I'd drive into downtown Ogunquit, enjoy a leisurely supper, then drive back to the theater and report for opening-night duty.

One night, I'd gotten back nearly an hour earlier than I needed to, so I took my usual position in the lobby and settled in for an interlude of people-watching. We had a full house—Thursdays were the most popular nights to see a play—so the lobby was even more crowded than usual.

As I made note of the elegant costumes and shameless posturing of the guests, I noticed a group of Golden Years urban sophisticates—fancy folk, out for a night at the theater—standing near one of the lobby's potted palms and talking loudly amongst themselves.

One moment they were laughing about Mrs. Jorgensen's hat, which looked for all the world, they thought, like a nest of newly hatched robins. The next moment, I and others near me could hear one member of the group lamenting what he considered the dramatic change in the makeup of audiences in American theaters. "So many Negroes and Jews now!" said one silk-tied gentleman. "It's not like it used to be!" A woman next to him, dressed in pale aqua chiffon and draped with jewels, nodded in agreement. "Amen to that!" she said with Waspish enthusiasm. "Why, *I* remember when ..."

That was enough for me. Not long after they'd finished their glib opening night exchange, I knew I'd not be asking to come back for another season. I was finished with Ogunquit Playhouse. Knowing I'd no longer have to compromise my values in return for boasting that I was an employee of America's Foremost Summer Theatre came as an enormous relief and felt like a personal victory.

With the final performance of the summer only a week away, the Playhouse season was effectively over. I'd finished my work as publicist, so other than laying the groundwork for another summer season, there was little left to accomplish. Since I knew I wouldn't be a part of the next season, I spent those two glacially slow weeks preparing an elaborate plan—a detailed description of the work I'd been required to do—for the man or woman destined to replace me.

Lane, who continued to be enthroned in his office around the corner from me, never approached me again. My guess is that he was either too busy to worry about me or had himself decided I'd not be back again as the director of publicity, and consequently I was not worth talking to. Each day I'd come into work, sit down in the silence of my office, and add to the plan, hoping to salvage some small portion of professional dignity before leaving the premises forever.

A gentle rain was falling in Ogunquit on my final day of employment at the Playhouse. The actors were long gone, and with them nearly all of the support staff. Summer was nearly over, darkness was coming earlier and earlier, and the evening temperatures had begun to turn chilly.

When the clock finally reached 5:00 p.m., I sealed up the plan, wrote the words, "To My Replacement as Publicity Director" on the front of the envelope, walked quietly through a side door and into the empty parking lot, and drove the twenty miles inland to a more welcoming place—my simple, unpretentious home on a quiet side street in Berwick. A life-changing adventure had now come to an end.

I've no doubt that Ogunquit Playhouse and similar professional theaters across the country have long ago outgrown such reprehensible attitudes—the unsavory ghosts of a bygone era. When John Lane had hired me as his publicity director that summer, he made me feel like a million dollars. Then, in just a few short weeks, I had more than ample reason to wonder just what alien subculture I'd gotten myself into.

Ironically, there are times when the people who've done us the greatest favors turn out to be the authors of our most crushing disappointments. John continued his proud stewardship of the Playhouse, and after hanging up my funeral suit and chucking my wingtips—they found a new and more appreciative home at Goodwill Industries—I went on to other, less prestigious but more rewarding pursuits as a freelancer in the arts.

Mr. Lane and Mr. Bachelder: we were two highly unlikely workmates—one a shrewd and wizened operator from the world of privilege, the other an idealistic young man, newly arrived from the Midwest and struggling to free himself from the more negative aspects of his blue-collar heritage and seek upward mobility. Neither of us got all of what we were looking for from the collaboration. Still, for one sun-drenched, exhilarating summer, John Lane was my reluctant and perhaps unwitting mentor. More through guarded proximity than meaningful interaction, I learned a great deal about the rarified world he inhabited.

Without his many-colored influences that summer, I'd not be the man I am today. And yet I can't help but be amused at the thought that only a week or two after I'd packed up and left the Playhouse for good, John Lane had probably forgotten he'd ever hired me.

Chapter 14

The Friendly Toast
Second Home for the Nonconformist Diner

Some people dine at restaurants just for the food, but for me that's never been sufficient reason to eat out. It's the proximity to the people that I crave, not the cuisine. I don't need necessarily to interact with them; in fact, I nearly always choose to dine alone. I only need to be near people, over piping hot tea and a suitable nibble, in order to free myself inwardly to read and write and draw and dream with a clear head, an open heart, and a powerful sense of self-renewal.

If you've found a restaurant that can do all of that for you and more, then you're more than likely the happiest of diners. I've found mine, and for more than two decades now—nearly always over a cup of no. 12 almond tea and a slab of cheyenne cheddar toast—this restaurant has been my oasis, my muse, and my morning-time nirvana.

Ahh, the Toast. The *Friendly* Toast. When I first discovered the place more than twenty years ago—it was then in Dover, New Hampshire, and is now in nearby Portsmouth—it was more playfully counterculture in feeling and appearance than any other restaurant north of Boston I'd ever been to.

For starters, the menu included Drunkard's French Toast, Guy Scramble, Hansel & Gretel Waffles, and a killer Sklarmageddon omelet with bacon, sausage, ham, red-chile pecans, jalapeño jack and Swiss cheeses, and a zesty, maple/sour cream topping—enough on one outsized plate to feed a pair of breakfast-deprived Marines.

Or how about these delectable, fabulously nuanced offerings, some of which are still proudly on the menu:

- **Kitchen Sink Quesadilla:** four coconut-fried shrimp and quesadilla wedges with spicy pecans, jalapeño jack and cheddar, sautéed spinach, fried red onions, and sweet potato fries, topped with mango sour cream and a balsamic glaze.

- **Guinness-Battered Onion Rings:** double-dunked for a real beer flavor (with cilantro-caper dip).

- **Le Petit Monstre:** a chicken burrito made with marinated breast meat, tabasco, cream cheese, roasted corn salsa, green olives, lettuce, and plum tomatoes.

- **The Red Neck:** warm (but still pink) roast beef on a kaiser roll, with your choice of Jack Daniel's barbecue sauce or horseradish mayonnaise.

I've frequented this marvelously offbeat restaurant ever since its unheralded appearance on Broadway Street in Dover in the '80s. With Reagan in the White House and corporate conformity awash in the land, the Toast became an indispensable haven for blue-collar folks with left-wing sensibilities, artists looking for any restaurant in the area that didn't have flower baskets and sunbonnets on its walls, and that loyal but dwindling army of disciples of Kerouac—anyone out on the road and desperate to sit down in front of an imaginative plate of food in overwhelmingly white-bread America.

Back then, the Toast was a pleasantly ramshackle building, hardly bigger than a bread truck, with a tiny handful of oddly mismatched tables, a charmingly claustrophobic bathroom, and just two servers to handle what was then only a polite trickle of regulars seasoned with a few idiosyncratic, drop-by diners.

One of the servers was Deb Murray, a friendly, plain-talking young woman with playful mix-and-match clothing, an array of colorful tattoos, and a lively, counterculture aura that contributed enormously to the Toast's ambiance. Everything about Deb and the Toast seemed to be saying "We ain't like the others, and we're proud of it!"

The other server was Melissa Jasper, the self-effacing founder of the Friendly Toast and the brains behind the endeavor. Only a fine mind could conceive a project as colorful, playfully unorthodox, and intelligently designed as the Toast. I learned only later that, while utterly lacking in the pretentiousness that so often comes with the package, she has a master of arts in English literature from the University of New Hampshire.

Those who've come to love the Toast—and by now they may very well number in the tens of thousands—should be thankful

Fig. 67. Interior of the Friendly Toast, Portsmouth, New Hampshire (before the renovation).

that she chose to apply her entrepreneurial gifts to the restaurant industry instead of to academia, where it would have been next to impossible for her to make her own unique and invaluable contribution to life in Seacoast New Hampshire. And since people from all over the world have dined at and continue to flock to the Friendly Toast, her influence as a restaurant professional has been the polar opposite of provincial, contributing significantly to the cosmopolitan aura of the once down-on-its-heels, now flourishing city of Portsmouth.

Her manner of dress—an eccentric mix of flea-market finds and hand-me-downs, enhanced by assorted rings and necklaces—made having her as my waitress a thoroughly thespian event. She never wore the same costume twice in a row, and her flamboyant, post-hippie-era couture, like the unpredictable appearance of her restaurant's walls, was both the source and the evidence of her savvy as a proprietor. In the formative years of the Toast, Jasper was her very own two-legged marketing plan, and with the help of her irrepressible sidekick, Deb Murray, her strategy worked like a charm.

I wasn't alone in my appreciation for Melissa's ways. More than one middle-aged male diner, trapped in some tedious occupation and yearning for something more colorful than the life he was living, fell in love with her—or at least the idea of her—but knew better than to say so. And yet, in spite of her innocent, country-girl charm and undeniable sex appeal, she always kept her professional distance from her diners while greeting them with a warm smile and engaging them in playful conversation.

When Jasper wasn't winning her customers over with her personality, she was busy in the tiny kitchen at the rear of the restaurant, creating the other, not-so-secret secret of her success—one-of-a-kind, imaginatively seasoned, environmentally sensitive entrees.

The Friendly Toast

Why have I been so deeply, inextricably in love with the Toast for so many years? I can rattle off many good reasons, starting with the playful decor, the colorful employees, and the delicious foods and beverages.

- **The music:** Dining at the Toast has always meant hearing a great many songs that seldom if ever get played on conventional radio stations. The Toast never inflicts elevator music on its customers. One day you're apt to hear Johnny Cash singing "I Walk the Line," followed by a medley of classic Beatles tunes and the velvet tones of a Frank Sinatra ballad. Another day you're just as likely to be treated to obscure hard-rock music, and, on occasion, songs so far out of the mainstream that you're tempted to think they might have come from some faraway, yet-to-be-discovered planet. The Toast's musical offerings are also refreshing because they're never pre-packaged. And since they're nearly always chosen by the Friendly Toast employees, they're delightfully free of corporate influence.

- **The decor:** If you've ever watched *American Pickers* on television or simply harbored a lifelong urge to sort through other people's junk in hopes of finding treasure, then the Toast will be the perfect destination for you.

    Quite by happenstance, the Friendly Toast has a philosophical ally in the Museum of Bad Art. MOBA, with branches in the Massachusetts cities of Somerville, Brookline, and—until it was kicked out of its bathroom gallery in December 2012, when the theater decided to convert it into a screening room—Dedham. MOBA is famous for having gone out of its way to showcase what the typical academic would consider banal, appallingly unskilled and uninformed artworks. And without really trying, the Friendly Toast is just as successful at thumbing its nose at the idea of what is good and proper within the realm of the visual arts.

    The kind of artworks found on the walls of the Toast, often described by art historians as "outsider art," are altogether a badly needed antidote to the preciosity of works turned out by university art school graduates—students conditioned by their professors to turn out formulaic works with the greatest likelihood of being accepted by conventional galleries.

    The artworks at the Toast might best be described as a goofy visual potpourri—a rollicking accumulation of two- and three-dimensional objects plucked from unknown sources and displayed, without apology, wherever they can be made to fit. If they were music, they'd be a medley worthy of "Weird Al" Yankovic, Peter Schickele, and Spike Jones. As a longtime Toast regular, I've enjoyed having a front-row seat from which I can watch the jaws of tourists drop when they see for the first time the astounding menagerie of *objets d'art* populating the restaurant.

There's the larger-than-life smiling toddler, rising into the upper atmosphere of the restaurant in KR99, his red and white, ocarina-shaped helicopter; the snow-white fairyland deer prancing gayly above the dining room, just ahead of the neon "Beer and Lunch" sign; and a four-foot tall bottle of Liquid Ivory soap. And who could fail to see the seven-foot tall, brick-red sea horse, swimming nonchalantly across the higher reaches of the restaurant?

- **The servers:** The young men and women who wait tables at the Toast have been a critically important part of the restaurant's success. Some of them, including long-timer Kristen Goss, have been employed at the Toast for a decade and more—a rare commitment in what is usually the revolving-door subculture of the average restaurant. Goss and her workmates have made an enormous contribution to the restaurant's one-of-a-kind persona; the place wouldn't be the same without them.

  You'll find no mindless regimentation and cookie-cutter uniforms at the Toast. The unabashed, street-theater eccentricity of the Toast's employees is what gives the place its invaluable, inimitable mystique. A restaurant whose frontline employees are left alone, within reason, to be entirely themselves—trusted to connect meaningfully and genuinely with their customers, regardless of how they choose to dress and groom themselves—is an increasingly rare phenomenon anywhere in America.

  To fully appreciate the difference, one might visit a Starbucks or Panera, then dine at the Toast immediately afterward, on the same day. No matter how warm and polite are the employees of the corporately owned and managed restaurants, and no matter how well-prepared the food, one cannot help but see just how robotic they've become under the influence of their employee-conduct manuals, their corporate image-makers, and the relentless scrutiny of their quality control supervisors. Over time, the corporate stranglehold on employee appearance and conduct becomes either subtly or overtly dehumanizing.

The restaurant industry is remarkably similar to the world of live theater. The chefs are the playwrights; the servers are the directors; the plates of well-prepared, artfully presented food are the actors; and the men and women who fork over serious money for their meals are the legions of at-large critics with the collective power either to sink a performance or send it to off to Broadway.

In the same way that otherwise conventional people love to see irreverent, norm-challenging plays, like *Hair* or *The Full Monty*, diners of every stripe enjoy a culinary night on the town in a setting utterly unlike the one they inhabit, day in and day out, at home and at work.

The problem, more and more, is where to find that setting. Travel anywhere in America, and you'll see that establishments like the Friendly Toast have become the Alamos of the restaurant world, holding on for dear life in the battle against land-grabbing corporate franchises—the Applebee's, Outbacks, and Olive Gardens of the world, bent on pursuing the almighty dollar at the expense of anything like genuine originality. All too often, the result of such wholesale regimentation is a string of restaurants whose architecture and cuisine are mind-numbingly similar and achingly predictable. While such restaurants may be cost-effective for management and profitable for the owners—people who seldom if ever set foot in the restaurants they've invested in—they're ultimately soul-killing for the once-proud personalities of the cities forced to play host to them.

That the Toast, under the wise guidance of its founder, Melissa Jasper, managed to survive the coast-to-coast assault on individuality for so many years bears witness to both her exceptional business savvy and the courage and integrity with which she conducted herself within the restaurant industry. So successful was her formula that in 2009 she opened a second, strategically positioned Friendly Toast on Kendall Square in Cambridge, Massachusetts—the home of Harvard University, MIT, and Le Cordon Bleu college of culinary arts.

And then, in 2013, the wheels of change began to turn. The Seacoast community learned that both the Portsmouth and Cambridge locations of the Toast had been sold to out-of-town investors Eric Goodwin and Scott Pulver. Melissa and her husband Robert had fled the city of Portsmouth to become urban homesteaders in the long-suffering metropolis of Detroit. Shortly after their arrival, they opened another spectacular restaurant—the Zenith at the Fisher—housed in the iconic, Art Deco-style Fisher Building on West Grand Boulevard and featuring southern and Mexican cuisine. The Jaspers' unexpected move to the Midwest was undoubtedly northern New England's loss and Detroit's gain—the Zenith was welcomed enthusiastically into a city desperate for revitalization.[1]

Meanwhile, back in northern New England, the House that Melissa Built appeared to be in danger of collapsing, not as a physical structure but as the one remaining temple of individuality in Portsmouth—a city that in the last decade or so has unwittingly divested itself of many of its most endearing charms and idiosyncrasies.

Since the Jaspers' departure, I've watched the new owners—well-meaning, number-crunching men with what I imagine to be little if any countercultural blood in their veins—begin to make both procedural adjustments and cosmetic alterations to their new restaurant. All fine and good: the place got itself a new floor, new booths, a good corner-to-corner scrubbing, dramatically improved bathrooms, and a much-needed tightening of monetary procedures. All were badly needed, warmly welcomed changes.

In the beginning, everyone quietly rejoiced at the news that, under new management, the Toast's unique decor—the wildly eclectic assemblage of found objects and memorabilia that make the place a one-of-a-kind dining experience—would not be tampered with.

It didn't take long, though, for the bubble of continuity to burst.

One of the most endearing features of the Friendly Toast had always been the haphazard arrangement of the artworks on

---

[1] In July 2015, the entire Fisher Building was suddenly purchased by a development group, and the leases of many of the building's business tenants—whose employees dined regularly at the Zenith and were an important source of revenue—were not renewed. Zenith couldn't survive either the sudden loss of business or the dramatic increase in rent, and in spite of the Jaspers' valiant struggle to make the restaurant work, Zenith at the Fisher closed its doors in August.

And then, only a few short weeks after they'd left the Fisher Building, the Jaspers found a new home for the Zenith on West Forest Avenue in midtown Detroit—in the heart of Wayne State University—and opened their doors again in September. The magic that Melissa had worked to such great advantage on the Friendly Toast—and again on Zenith at the Fisher—would now be applied to the new Zenith on West Forest Avenue, and once again Detroit area diners with a taste for fine cuisine in an unconventional setting had reason to rejoice.

its walls. Flea market–quality paintings and oddball posters of every conceivable size, shape, and configuration were mounted chaotically from floor to ceiling of the place, silently jockeying for position in a kind of King of the Mountain battle for low-art supremacy. Even the most frequent diners, including me, wondered if they'd actually managed to see every one of them.

But then the fun—if one would choose to call it that—began. One day the walls of the Toast were crammed full of artworks arranged in helter-skelter fashion, and the next, the collection had been dramatically thinned out. Whatever works survived the cut were then rearranged with fanatical, quasi-military attention to tidiness.

- **Gone:** the Chinchilla Ranch sign. Like so many other items on the walls of the Toast, the presence of that sign in the restaurant made no sense whatsoever—which is one of the reasons it was a treasure for all who saw and laughed at it while dining at the Toast.

- **Gone:** the Guinness-Battered Onion Rings and Drunkard's French Toast—perhaps removed from the menu in response to the unfortunate reality that Portsmouth, especially on weekends, has become a notorious liquid oasis for beer-guzzling college students within and well beyond the Seacoast.

- **Gone:** the Salvation Army sign saying "A man may be down, but he's never out." That slogan had become a proud if unintended mission statement for the Toast, which from the very beginning had prided itself on caring as much for the downtrodden as it did for the affluent.

- **Gone:** Deb Murray, who along with Jasper and Goss was one of the pioneering members of the Friendly Toast. Murray helped establish the counterculture persona of the restaurant from its earliest beginnings.

Overnight, it was as if Martha Stewart had broken into Picasso's atelier, tossed out anything in the least bit askew or asymmetrical, then replaced it with precisely aligned groupings of ceiling tile. Many of the original artworks had survived the onslaught, but some of the ripe, red blood of spontaneity had been drained from the wall itself.

Then, the Toast's menu—for so many years the visual gateway and pop art emblem of the Toast—was unceremoniously stripped of some of its most distinctive graphics and moments of hilarious word-play. It was to the most passionate Toast regulars a small but ominous sign of things to come—the opening volley in an all-out war against the unusual. The Friendly Toast, a restaurant long cherished for its unique persona, its concern for the environment, its offbeat sense of humor, and its reputation as the proud purveyor of imaginative, health-conscious foods and beverages, appeared to be in danger of dumbing itself down in the name of middle-class propriety, institutional conformity, and the worship of money.

The behavior of some of the waitstaff had begun to change, too—and, as I saw it, not always for the better. A certain Red Lobster rhetoric was creeping into the on-the-job vocabulary of the newer employees—hospitality industry lingo like "Good morning, and welcome to the Friendly Toast," and "Is there anything else I can do for you, sir?" It was as if the Toast's longtime waitstaff—competent, caring, laid-back employees with blue-green hair, nose rings, and tattoos—had suddenly forgotten how to speak plain English. Because of it, I half-expected to see long-time Red Lobster favorites like popcorn shrimp and Cheddar Bay biscuits come tumbling out of my servers' aprons and onto my table.

The abrupt change in the employees' speech patterns could be chalked up to managerial expectations, so I wasn't about to hold the frontline employees responsible for their new way of talking. They were still the same friendly, helpful people I'd come to know and care for, but I was already yearning for their speedy return to a more natural, more indigenous way of speaking. The way I figured it, if I'd wanted artificial intelligence for supper, I'd have dined at a robotics factory.

Perhaps the most striking thing about today's Friendly Toast is the way in which the loyal frontline workers from the Jasper era—people, including Kristen Goss, who've been cheerfully serving customers for many years—have managed somehow to hold on to their precious individuality while simultaneously honoring the expectations of a new management team and taking good care of their customers, just the way they always have.

Many of the most successful restaurants in Portsmouth, from the quaintly pretentious (the Dolphin Striker) to the proudly blue collar (Gilley's Diner), have been successful because they've achieved a harmonious balance between a carefully calculated personality, an imaginative menu, and smart business practices. When any restaurant is blessed with those qualities, it will be hard for anyone or anything, short of a severe economic downturn, to derail the culinary train.

If, on the other hand, any one of those qualities—the style, the substance, the business practices—is allowed to go into decline, the result can be disastrous.

Why, the new owners of the Toast ought to ask themselves, *were the lines always so long and the booths so fully occupied when Melissa was in charge?* The answers, I think, are clear and unequivocal.

- **Style:** The Toast according to Jasper had a decor and a feel unlike any other restaurant in northern New England—playful, unorthodox, and proudly, visibly anti-establishment. And at the heart of the Friendly Toast style were its servers—young men and women of warmth, humor, and the most remarkable professionalism. Without their unique personalities and finely honed skills, the Toast as we know it today would have quickly ceased to exist. And thanks to their collective style as servers, the Friendly Toast established itself as both an indispensable local treasure and a powerful tourist magnet.

- **Substance:** Under Melissa's always resourceful, highly imaginative direction, the chefs and line cooks consistently offered foods and beverages of the highest quality—food with enormous personality, lovingly prepared and artfully presented by caring, colorful servers. We can only hope that the new owners of the Toast take the time to learn what worked so well in the past, then incorporate the best of the Jasper-era practices into their own philosophy as restaurateurs. If they do, then the city of Portsmouth can continue to expect the same high culinary standards and devotion to service to continue unabated.

- **Business practices:** Whatever one might have to say about the Toast's way of doing business—like many establishments, it had its struggles on occasion with code enforcement officials, then moved quickly to make adjustments and comply with the rules—one cannot deny its staying power as a restaurant. It has hung tough for more than twenty years in a highly competitive, rules-obsessed industry while other less attentive and less compliant eateries fell by the wayside, one by one, like pins in a bowling alley.

It's important to remember that a *good* restaurant is never really just a restaurant. It's also a gathering place for the dreaming of dreams, the promulgation of ideas, and the celebration

Fig. 68. "Greetings from the Friendly Toast" (promotional postcard distributed gratis by the new owners after Melissa Jasper sold the Toast in 2013).

of life. French writer and philosopher Albert Camus—a major contributor to the school of thought called absurdism—once said, "All great deeds and all great thoughts have a ridiculous beginning. Great works are often born on a street corner or in a restaurant's revolving door."

I know from experience just what Camus meant. I've never found an environment more suitable for the business of writing, the dreaming of dreams, or positive engagement with the world than the Toast. I invariably feel better about myself and my circumstances when I'm there.

Early in 2015, the Friendly Toast added a small but beautifully appointed bar to its facility. While for business reasons it probably made good sense to have a bar at the Toast, it altered the persona of the place in yet another way that was bound to erode its original, counterculture ambiance. Overnight, the Friendly Toast became—for me at least—yet another ho-hum, cookie-cutter watering hole for the swarms of college students and other good-time people making their weekend pilgrimage to late-night, happy-hour Portsmouth.

Did the city really need yet another bar? I hardly think so. But everyone knows that liquor is a proven moneymaker, and since a great many people appear to have forgotten how to have a good time without it, the presence of a bar at the back of the Friendly Toast is good news for both its new owners and the growing number of people who never seem to have enough choices for drinking on a Saturday night.

Liquor or not, the Toast is still authentically, endearingly *friendly*. It's a happy place to be in, alone or with friends. It has been for me the most fertile imaginable soil for the planting of my own little garden of possibilities. My thoughts may never be perceived as great; my deeds may never prove to have changed the world in any lasting way; but at the Friendly Toast I've experienced my greatest creative epiphanies—my finest moments of inspiration about pretty much anything you can think of.

The Friendly Toast—a maverick institution with a personality unlike any other—has made an enormous difference in my life. Had it not been there when I migrated to New England so many years ago, I doubt that today I'd even recognize who I would have become in its absence.

Thanks to wise management, inventive cooking, smart hiring practices, and no small amount of imagination, the Friendly Toast in the Jasper years established itself as a force to be reckoned with in the north-of-Boston restaurant industry. It improved the quality of life for countless men and women by consistently serving up moments of warmth and levity along with damn good food—all while providing a home away from home for people from every walk of life or part of the world, regardless of their age, race, sexual orientation, social status, religious and political persuasion, or appearance.

Now, the legacy of the Toast has been passed to a new generation. I and others in the Friendly Toast community hope the new owners will show us they have the wisdom to preserve the unique personality of their restaurant while honoring Melissa Jasper's commitment to quality food and superlative service. And most importantly, may they show us they have the courage to be unmistakably, exhilaratingly *different* in all the ways that the corporate franchises can never hope to be—ways that really matter in a restaurant that's actually worth preserving.

Fig. 69. The Unstoppable Thought by Ross Bachelder (illustration for "Penelope Brood's Dilemma").

※ Tiny Novelette 7 ※

Penelope Brood's Dilemma

Penelope Brood was a thinker, but not the kind of thinker Rodin had in mind. She was tall, athletic, and strikingly beautiful—a woman in every conventional sense of the word. But beauty and athleticism were not her only strong suits. She was also highly intelligent—so brilliant that men found her intimidating and women were jealous. *How is it possible*, they'd ask themselves late at night, *that such a beautiful, athletically gifted woman can also be so deeply intelligent?* She had it all, and it hardly seemed fair.

And it wasn't just her formidable intelligence that made others uncomfortable. It was the white hot *intensity* of her thinking—about everything from dark energy and the black hole controversy to the Riemann hypothesis and the Fermi paradox. People who spent time with her would inevitably come away swearing they'd seen a halo of pure contemplation hovering over her glowing, patrician countenance.

Experts from around the world called her day and night, begging for solutions to problems that had plagued humankind for centuries. It became next to impossible for her to have a good night's sleep, so to escape the avalanche of requests, she finally cut the cord on her landline, tossed her electronic media into the nearest trash bin, and moved from the suburbs of Chicago to a cabin nestled in the mountains of Possum Trot, Kentucky, with only her thousand-volume library and her beloved feline, Heraclitus, as her loyal companions.

And yet the thoughts kept coming. To ease her relentless cerebrations, she'd put an ice pack on her forehead at night, then take a double dose of Don't Even *Think* It—the miracle drug invented for excessive ruminators and only recently approved by the FDA—in the morning. Having such a powerful mind might seem a wonderful thing to some, but for Penelope Brood, it was a waking nightmare.

Then, one morning, she woke up with just one wildly improbable idea roaring like a waterfall in her head: *What if, in just one marathon evening of thinking, I could solve not just a handful of the world's problems—the scourge of cancer, the human propensity for vio-*

lence, the quest for immortality—but all of them? She figured it was worth a shot. If she succeeded, she'd have single-mindedly taken the world to a higher place, the experts would finally stop their relentless calling, and in a new and better world she'd once again be able to experience what it feels like to sleep like a baby.

The very next night, Penelope locked her cabin door, shut the windows, brewed a pot of coffee strong enough to strip the pavement off the Los Angeles freeway, then lit her lantern and got down to the business of thinking away all of the world's most intractable problems.

So intense was her thinking that sparks began to fly and a dark, tremulous cloud of urgent thinking filled the cabin. By then she felt she must surely be wrestling with the devil himself. Then, after nearly ten hours of wild-eyed cogitating, she glanced across the room and saw the hair on the neck of Heraclitus—a cat usually more even-tempered than a Tibetan monk on a mountain retreat—stand up suddenly like the bristles on a warthog.

Soon the dishes began to rattle, the lantern swayed and went dark, and the walls began to tremble. Outside, a stunning display of fireworks brightened the sky over Possum Trot, and one by one, the windows of the cabin blew out, spewing shards of molten glass out onto the land around the cabin.

Then, as Penelope watched in amazement, Heraclitus abruptly stood up on his hind legs, strode with scholarly panache to Penelope's bookshelf, donned his cat-friendly bifocals, and pored over book after book until the entire library had been devoured like some vast, epicurean meal of the mind.

Once Heraclitus had finished his reading, he thought and thought and thought again, and in less than the time it takes to wash a sink full of dishes, he'd solved all of the world's problems. The dark of night gave way to a glorious sunrise, and peace descended on every corner of the globe. For the first time in her life, Penelope Brood went to bed that night knowing she would never again need to think about *anything* unless she damn well felt like it. From then on, whenever she needed to rest her mind, her friend Heraclitus—one smart feline by any measure—would do her thinking for her. The experts no longer had a reason to call Penelope, and all was well with the world.

Chapter 15

The Story of Three Paintings
The Lobstermen's Lament, Rocky and Ellie May, and *Vito Ciccotelli*

When as artists we can lose ourselves in a painting—when we can leave our workaday lives behind us and become one with the line work, the brushstrokes, and the smell and movement of the paint—it is then that we know we were meant to do just what we're doing at that moment, and nothing else. It's the same for musicians and dancers, scientists and explorers, writers and architects. That overwhelming feeling of passionate immersion just can't be beat. It's not easy to achieve, but I had it at one time or another while painting Lobstermen's Lament, Rocky and Ellie Mae, *and* Vito Ciccotelli—*artworks which for one reason or another have played critically important roles in my evolution as a visual artist.*

The Lobstermen's Lament: A Way of Life under Siege

The idea for *The Lobstermen's Lament* came about a few years ago while I was walking along an isolated beach at the end of Wild Rose Lane in Portsmouth, New Hampshire, enjoying the fresh, bracing air and pungent aroma of the Atlantic. Along the way I stumbled across what turned out to be the weather-beaten door from a lobster trap, washed up onto the shore and left to slumber in the tangle of shells and seaweed that rides in like clockwork with the ebb and flow of the tides.

To me, at least, the door—pastel red and green and scarred from being repeatedly tossed off a lobster boat and left to lie in wait in shallow waters—was beautiful. I hoped it would one day play a major role in a yet-to-be-conceived assemblage, but I wasn't in the market for assemblages at the time, so when I got home, I went upstairs to my studio, tossed the door into a crate filled with items that might find a home in future projects, then forgot about it altogether.

Two years later, on a hot and steamy afternoon in July, I began work on a three-foot-square abstract for an upcoming exhibit at the Newburyport Art Association in Massachusetts, where I was a member. At the time, I'd been immersed in writings about abstract expressionist painter Jackson Pollock, and I decided to try Pollock's then-controversial method of applying standard house paint to a canvas laid out on the floor of his studio—sometimes directly from a can, other times from hardened brushes, sticks, and even basting syringes—in the form of dynamic, serendipitously applied drips and loops.

I was home alone at the time, clad only in boxers and a T-shirt to avoid getting the notoriously hard-to-remove acrylic on my clothing. Before long, I was hopping around like a toddler on a trampoline, an action painter lost in the exhilarating business of dripping exotic ropes and droplets of paint onto the canvas in all-over fashion.

Artists usually discover early on that their inevitable mistakes—sudden wrong turns in the process of painting—more often than not have a happy ending. My first mistake while working on *Lobstermen's Lament* was a failure of efficiency: I'd gotten so caught up in the joy of dripping paint onto my canvas that I'd begun to splash it onto both the floor and a nearby area rug. To put a stop to that, I picked up the painting, complete with freshly applied streaks of both acrylic and India ink, then darted down the stairs, through the kitchen, and out into the backyard, struggling like Charlie Chaplin in a street chase to hold the painting parallel to the ground and prevent the rivulets of paint from traveling into undesirable places on the canvas.

I was now in the side yard of my home, still clad in my underwear and in full view of my neighbors, but at this point, like Rhett Butler in *Gone with the Wind*, I really didn't give a damn. The painting was the thing, and any oglers would have to figure out how to cope with the sight of an underdressed artist romping around in his boxers, bereft of his modesty.

The first thing I noticed while standing there on the lawn, besides a vast army of ominous, inky black clouds marching in suddenly from the Atlantic, was that some errant streaks of black paint had begun to travel down in parallel lines from one side of the painting to its opposite. "Damn!" I squealed. "I've just ruined my abstract!"

Then I realized I'd just been handed not a disaster but an opportunity—a chance to turn an unfortunate error into a felicitous event. I tipped the canvas perpendicular to the ground, then allowed the parallel streaks of paint to travel as far down across the canvas as they felt like going. Then I methodically revolved the painting, still in perpendicular configuration, until I'd managed to guide the still-wet paint down from all four sides toward their opposites, forming a grid that ran counter to the drips and splashes everywhere on the surface of the canvas. The contrast between the grid and the splashes added enormous energy to my composition.

But something was missing. The piece now had a certain in-your-face harshness about it, quite the opposite of the more finely calibrated effect I was looking for. It needed to be tamed, but the question was how to domesticate it without robbing it of the swirling, multicolored intensity I'd achieved. By now I wondered if I should just go ahead and sound the death knell for another dying work of art.

Then, as the wind picked up noticeably and the clouds grew more threatening, I came up with a radical solution. To save my painting, I decided to go for broke.

I left my abstract on the lawn, ran back into the house, pulled a can of vanilla-colored spray paint from a welter of art supplies in the basement, then dashed back outdoors and applied a delicate mist of acrylic to the entire surface of the painting. Meanwhile, the skies continued to darken, and the grove of towering pine trees behind our house began to sway symmetrically in the wind, as precisely choreographed as dancers at the Bolshoi.

Then the rain began to fall, not politely but in torrents. As it pounded down onto the canvas, it began to dissolve the acrylic, causing the various colors and design elements to blend unintentionally into each other. I picked up the painting, then dashed across the lawn, holding it ahead of me in the wind as I might have held a card table. Once inside the house, I laid it on the kitchen floor, then stood there for a good five minutes, still dripping wet, and studied it.

Still something missing!

And then I was struck with an epiphany, easily as powerful as the thunder and lightning animating the skies just outside my kitchen.

The lobster trap door! I immediately made a note to myself never to throw away a found object for fear it might somehow have outgrown its usefulness.

I raced upstairs two steps at a time, pulled the door from the crate I'd left it in, and rushed downstairs. When I held it carefully over the still-wet canvas, my earlier intuition was confirmed: it was the perfect complement to the grid that had evolved so

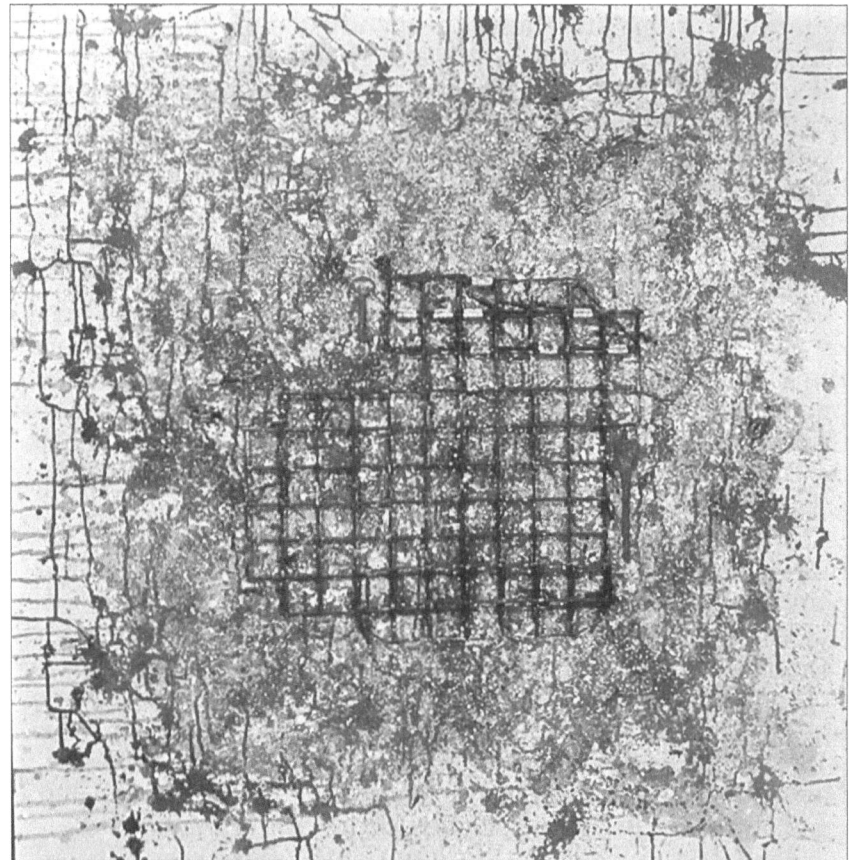

Fig. 70. *The Lobstermen's Lament: A Way of Life under Siege* by Ross Bachelder.

unpredictably from the movement of acrylic rivulets on my canvas only a few minutes before.

I dried my painting using the hair dryer I keep in my studio—essential equipment for many acrylic painters—then laid the door down on the center of the canvas. Then I set up two kitchen chairs facing each other, perched the abstract between them, crawled under the resulting bridge, and with the help of an awl and four garden-strength Twist-Ems, tied the door permanently to the canvas from underneath. My drip painting, a pure abstract until the moment when I attached the door to it, was now a multimedia assemblage with an implied narrative. I named it *The Lobstermen's Lament: A Way of Life under Siege*.

It took only three unrelated incidents—a lobster trap door washed up on the shores of the Atlantic, a raging midsummer thunderstorm, and one ultimately fortuitous mistake as an artist—to turn *The Lobstermen's Lament* into the unique, socially relevant work of art it is today.

Of course, being unique and socially relevant hardly guarantees that an artwork will appeal to the public. *Lobstermen's Lament* has been exhibited in several Seacoast New Hampshire and southern Maine galleries—including, in the summer of 2014, the Sarah Orne Jewett House Museum and Visitor Center in South Berwick, in its inaugural exhibit, *Here by the Sea: Contemporary Art of the Piscataqua*.

The Lobstermen's Lament may one day find a home with someone who loves abstract art and found-object assemblages as much as I do. Until then, I'll be content to have it near me in my studio as a cogent reminder of the power of one little act of derring-do to turn a failed painting into an artistic triumph.

Rocky and Ellie May: The Two-Dog Commission

For as long as I can remember, I've been going out in the morning for breakfast at any one of an ever-expanding list of favorite restaurants, choosing according to my mood.

One of my favorites was Weeks Backstreet Kitchen, a popular gathering place at the corner of Washington and Locust in Dover, New Hampshire, just down the street from Dover Public Library. I'd check a book or two out of the library, then go down to Backstreet Kitchen and read, usually over tea and toast. And then, afterward, I'd draw.

One morning in the fall of 2008, while settled into my favorite corner table at Weeks and working up a sketch of Rembrandt van Rijn, I sensed someone standing just behind me, looking over my shoulder.

"Look at *that*!" she said. "I didn't know you were an artist, too!"

The woman turned out to be Linda Skvirsky, my favorite Backstreet Kitchen waitress and by far the most consistently professional one of the bunch.

"Well, I do draw and paint on occasion," I said, "but the writing takes up most of my time."

"*Nice work* on that face!" she said, looking first at the sketch, then me. "Any chance you could do a drawing for me? I'm looking for a more creative gift than usual for my husband. He's tired of shirts and ties, and I'm tired of shopping for them."

"Depends on what you have in mind," I said. I didn't want to take on a project I couldn't handle.

"A *dog*!" she said. His name is Rocky. "Just a simple sketch—that's all I'm looking for! It would make a fantastic gift for him."

I'd never drawn a dog in my life, but I was also in the market for fresh subjects to nurse my growing passion for portraiture. And as always, I needed money. So I took a chance and agreed on the spot to draw a portrait of Rocky, sight unseen.

"Wonderful!" she said. "How much would you need to charge me?"

I had absolutely no idea what the going price might be for a drawing of a dog, but I took a stab. "Uhh, fifty? One hundred?" I said. "Would that be too much?"

"No, that's perfect!" she said. "And take your time. It'll be a Christmas gift, so you've got weeks and weeks to prepare."

I arranged to come to Linda's home the following week and take whatever reference photos I'd need in order to pull off the project. My Rocky, I realized, would need to look like her Rocky, and neither she nor I would be willing to settle for less than perfection. I finished my breakfast, thanked her for her trust in me, then worked my way through rush hour traffic to Berwick, wondering if I'd temporarily lost my mind. "Me, painting a dog portrait?" I muttered. What on earth was I thinking? I'd never *had* a dog and I'd never *drawn* a dog!

I slept poorly that night, tossing and turning while struggling to envision Linda's precious Rocky coming to life on my humble sketch pad. I was selling myself short again, and needed to cut it out. "Better get a grip," I grumbled into the darkness.

The next morning, as often happens with the disappearance of demons and the arrival of sunlight, I rallied. "You can do it," I gurgled into the bathroom mirror while brushing my teeth. Oddly, two matching rivulets of Sensodyne trickled down from the corners of my mouth, making me look like a sleepy bloodhound with a bushy beard. "You can *do* it!" I said again for good measure.

I fed the cats, poured fresh hot tea into my travel cup, and dashed off to work with a touch of newfound optimism, pleading with my inner Rembrandt for even one little moment of divine guidance to set me on the path to painterly success.

That night I called my artist friend Lisa Toole—a dog lover with a deeper understanding of canine behavior than I, a cat lover, could ever hope to have—and asked her to come with me to the photo session and coax Rocky into compliance. Lisa had been a classmate of Linda's many years ago. She agreed, and the next morning we met at the Skvirsky residence and knocked on the door, ready to do whatever it might take to capture the necessary reference photos. Without a detailed series of images, I

The Story of Three Paintings

knew I'd never be able to produce a credible portrait, either of Rocky or any other animal you might choose to send my way.

Linda opened the door, and before we had a chance to get out of the way, Rocky—a massive boxer with sixty pounds of pure muscle and a tail like a pirate's whip—came bounding out from behind her, barking and lurching against us with all the force of a four-legged medicine ball.

"Oh, he's *harmless!*" laughed Linda. "Just a big, silly baby! Don't worry—he wouldn't hurt a flea. He just wants a little lovin' and hopes you're glad to see him!"

He was clearly an affectionate beast, but it's not easy petting the head of furry freight train of a dog, with teeth like a Tyrannosaurus rex. While Linda called off her sixty-pound puppy, I retreated to the living room and began setting up my camera and tripod.

"It'll be a serious challenge, drawing him," I laughed. "That's one monstrous canine!"

"Not monstrous at all!" she assured me. "And Ellie Mae's just as gentle. I've no doubt you'll love her, too!"

"Ellie Mae?" I said. "Who's Ellie Mae?"

"Oh, didn't I tell you?" she said. "We have two dogs, one big and one little. They're together constantly, and they'll make a great double portrait!"

Linda walked down the hallway and opened another door, and out rolled a tiny cannonball of a dog—a pug with short white hair, a tail like a pulsating croissant, and eyes both puppy-dog eager and hopelessly plaintive. It careened across the floor, bounced off the back of an easy chair, then leapt into Lisa's arms and began licking her furiously on the face.

"Say Hello to Ellie Mae!" Linda said, proudly but sheepishly. "I didn't realize you thought you were going to draw just one dog."

Apparently, I'd agreed to draw *both* dogs—a two-for-one, bargain basement sale—and for a paltry fifty dollars each. I wasn't upset about the money, only in shock about the formidable technical challenge I had ahead of me. One dog was enough for me, a relative newcomer to the art of portraiture. But *two*? I didn't know where to begin, even just to get the photos I'd need to pull this caper off.

No worry about Lisa, though: she jumped head-first into her assignment, chucking both dogs under their chins and making those quasi-musical, baby-talk sounds that have the power to transform a frenzied beast into something approaching a happy lapdog. Then, with Linda's help, she began coaching them to look toward the camera and smile their most captivating smiles.

Getting them to sit side by side, though, was another story. After several valiant attempts at canine camaraderie, the three of us abandoned the cause and focused instead on capturing photos of each dog alone in a wide array of positions. Once I'd gotten the images I needed, I packed up my camera and equipment, thanked Linda for her help with the sitting, and headed home to Berwick. Lisa, who by now had taken a severe but good-natured licking from both Rocky and Ellie Mae, bid them a good day and left for her home in South Berwick.

The next morning I crawled out of bed, poured myself a wake-up tea, and marched upstairs to my studio. I'd put a fresh canvas on my easel the night before and positioned my paints and brushes on a nearby table. Linda didn't know it, but I'd already decided to *paint* the portrait rather than settle for a drawing, convinced that with paints I'd be able to achieve a far more emotional, more authoritative portrait of her dogs than I'd be able to accomplish with pencils. It would be my surprise gift to her for trusting me with a project that meant so much to her.

First, though, I needed a plan. Should I paint each dog on its own canvas, or paint them side by side on one canvas? And if I were to paint the two dogs side by side, just the size they were in real life, I might be accused of causing Rocky to upstage his more diminutive friend.

I decided to work from close-up, star-quality photographs of each dog, them give them equal billing in the portrait, together on one canvas. Rocky would be rendered as the enormous, muscular animal he was in real life, while the tiny Ellie Mae would be right beside him in the painting and nearly as large as he was. The viewer, I decided, would understand intuitively that, in real life, Ellie Mae—who was after all a breed of dog that would never grow to be as big as Rocky—couldn't possibly be as massive as her boxer friend. Logic would prevail, and for both the dogs and their proud owners, all would be well.

I finally chose two strong images from the more than forty reference photos I'd taken, then had them printed at Photosmith Imaging in Dover, New Hampshire. It was time now for me to confront all of the problems a neophyte portrait artist could be expected to have.

To begin with, what would an ideal background color be? I tried a creamy white, but it seemed harsh and unemotional—lacking in the animal-to-human warmth that comes from loving and caring for a treasured pet. I decided on a subdued gray-green with a touch of aqua, and it worked like a charm, creating a European Old Masters effect that fit the dignity of my subjects as I envisioned them. The background, now free of even the

The Story of Three Paintings

suggestion of a romanticized landscape, horizon line, or other potential clutter, helped focus the visual energy where it really belonged—on Rocky and Ellie Mae. Now they were cast as the co-stars of their very own canine sitcom, and I began to think that, together, we had a better than slim chance to produce a hit.

The next step was to get the contours of the dogs onto my canvas. I cut each image out of its photograph with scissors, then adhered the cutouts to a sheet of card stock, positioning them precisely where I wanted them to be in the painting. Next, I drew a grid onto the surface of the card stock, repeated the process on my canvas, then transferred the image from card stock to canvas, block by block.

Once I'd laid in the underpainting of the two dogs, I began to tackle the details, beginning with the eyes. They were as difficult to render as I'd expected them to be, but the snouts and jowls were an even more formidable challenge. The deeper I got into the detailing, the more essential I realized it would be for me to get every single marking down pat. I knew there wasn't a dog owner in the world who didn't know the markings on his own dog's body as intimately as he knew the physical characteristics of both his children and himself. And the more distinct were the markings, the more daunting it was to get them to the point where there'd be no doubt whose dogs they belonged to.

The color of their fur, the configuration of their tails and ears, the exact proportioning of their paws, the precise arrangement of their whiskers—all had to be letter perfect. Add to these their collars and ID tags, objects with which dog owners are also intimately familiar, and you have the makings of a tension-filled, do-or-die commission.

Perhaps the most difficult challenge of all when painting an animal portrait is to capture the creature's unique temperament. All dogs have their very own unmistakable persona. They regularly exhibit behaviors unique to them and yet instantly familiar to their owners. And any dog owner will tell you that his or her pet has a distinctive aura—a full-blown personality, replete with charming quirks and annoying habits, no less identifiable than those of his human counterparts.

Alone in my studio, I worked hard to capture those essences, none of which I could have gleaned without having spent the time I did taking reference photos. So important was my on-site observation of them that I went back to the Skvirskys' home a second time, more to study the dogs' distinctive behaviors than to capture additional likenesses.

As the time for delivery of the painting drew nearer, I began to bear down obsessively on the last-minute details of the painting. Did I really get those marks on Rocky's chin right? Is Ellie Mae's snout really as pinched and abbreviated as I'd represented it in my painting? The more I scrutinized my work, the more flaws, both in detail and proportioning, I seemed to discover. December 24 was only five days away, and that's when Linda needed to have the portrait stored away in her closet, wrapped, beribboned, and ready to present to her husband on Christmas day.

On the evening of the twenty-first, shortly after supper, I began what I was certain would be my very last session with *Rocky and Ellie Mae*. I'd finally found the courage to declare my painting done, and yet, like nearly every artist I know, I couldn't resist the temptation to go over it one more time, checking the proportions, tweaking the colors, and praying I'd not find an error so egregious that it couldn't be repaired in the little time I had left to me. I was Woody Allen paranoid by now, exhausted from the long hours of labor and yearning to get the painting out of my house and into the hands of its soon-to-be owner.

I discovered at least three tiny mistakes that needed attention, and immediately set about the task of repairing them. Then, only twenty minutes into the session, the power went out—not only in my home but throughout our neighborhood and beyond.

Something had to be done. I tried lighting a candle and leaving it on a table near my easel, but it didn't come close to illuminating the trouble spots in my painting. Next, I lit the old kerosene lantern hanging from the rafters in our basement—the one we typically fired up during major winter storms—but it emitted more smoke than light.

After at least thirty minutes of cave-dwelling darkness, I realized my desperate wish for the return of light was not about to be granted. We were in it for the long haul, and it become more and more likely that I'd fail to get my painting to Linda by Christmas day.

And then I remembered Papa Gino's. The wintertime power outages for which the region is so infamous hardly ever extend to the far side of Dover. That meant that Papa's—for several years one of my favorite haunts because of the good food and friendly service—was likely still open. Better yet, it was only ten miles from my studio.

I checked my Timex Indiglo and discovered it was 6:30 p.m. Since Papa Gino's would close at 10:00 p.m., I knew I'd have just enough time to drive to Papa's, find an empty booth, and make the necessary repairs on my portrait.

In spite of the storm, I got there in record time, stomped the snow off my feet, and lurched through the door, balancing *Rocky and Ellie Mae* in one hand and my supply box in the other. Would they think I was just another maniacal drifter—the Vincent van Gogh of the Berwicks, homeless, deranged, and badly in need of shelter? At this point, their opinion didn't matter. I was badly in need of light, and Papa's had a more than sufficient supply of the stuff.

I set up shop in the corner booth near the jukebox—a pleasant place to be when visiting Papa's on a normal evening, but the very gates of heaven on this, my night of desperate need.

I ought not to have worried that the place would be crowded, or that anyone might disapprove of my decision to turn a pizza house into an art studio. There were very few people in the restaurant, and the employees knew me well enough by then to expect the unexpected whenever I walked into their establishment.

First, I'd work on Ellie Mae's snout. Her nostrils were slightly out of alignment and out of proportion with the rest of her face. I dipped my brush into the bottle of spring water I'd brought with me, then made the necessary adjustments, first with ebony black and then with a touch of pearl white to represent the flash of light playing off her nostrils in my reference photo.

Then it was time to repair Rocky's chin. Though I'd labored mightily to capture its distinctive marks, they still weren't convincing, so I painted over the entire chin with fast-drying titanium white—acrylic is perfectly suited for an artist in a hurry—then started over from scratch. If I'd left it the way it was before that night, Rocky would not have been Rocky, and for a portrait artist, that would have been an unpardonable sin.

Finally, I realized that neither of the dogs' paws were as accurately rendered as they needed to be. I pulled a 2H pencil from my supply box, sketched in the necessary adjustments to all four feet, then meticulously repainted them, paying much closer attention to both the color of the fur and the exact position of the claws.

Once I'd finished making corrections, I opened my precious jar of background paint—the warm, gray-green with a touch of aqua that I'd had the good sense to bring with me to the restaurant—and touched up the area around all four paws, using one of my prized Da Vinci Maestro detail brushes. Made in Germany and unusually expensive, they were worth every penny because of their durability and superior performance.

Once I'd finished the paws, everything clicked into place. I knew I'd finally achieved the level of precision that would allow my portrait of Rocky and Ellie Mae to sing like an opera star on Christmas morning.

Fig. 71. *Rocky and Ellie Mae* by Ross Bachelder.

I presented the portrait to Linda on the morning of December 24, while she was busy serving tables at Backstreet Kitchen. It was perhaps a little ironic that *Rocky and Ellie Mae* was conceived, completed, and presented in an eating establishment, true to my longtime practice of doing my most impassioned creative work in places that for centuries have fed both the bellies and the souls of their visitors.

When I pulled the shroud (actually a black plastic trash bag) off the portrait, Linda stared intently at it, smiled broadly, then registered her approval by marching it around the restaurant, showing it off to anyone—close friends and complete strangers—who might appreciate a portrait of the two dogs she loved as much as if they were her own children.

When Linda realized that I'd created a full-blown acrylic portrait of her pets instead of the pencil drawing she'd requested, she paid me five hundred dollars for my labors—an unprecedented amount for me and an enormous boost to my confidence as a fledgling artist.

The gallery world today is by and large openly hostile to the idea of animal portraits, considered by the movers and shakers within the fashion-conscious world of the arts to be anything but fashionable.

But the argument doesn't hold up under scrutiny. One has only to look back in the history of art to confirm that many world-renowned artists—including Albrecht Dürer (*Young Hare*), Franz Marc (*The Little Yellow Horses*), Rosa Bonheur (*Plowing in the Nivernais*), and Pablo Picasso (*Cat Eating a Bird*)—were more than happy to have chosen animals as the subject of many of their paintings.

Rocky and Ellie Mae will never be labeled a masterpiece, except perhaps in the late-night reveries of those two proud dogs. And yet, in spite of what anyone else might think, it had enormous significance for me. Technically, it far exceeded any portrait I'd painted up to that point—evidence of my undeniable growth as an artist. In the end, the only really important measure of an artist's worth is the measure against himself—the extent to which he or she has grown, through hard work and perseverance, in both artistic sensitivity and technical mastery.

I don't know if I'll ever take on another animal portrait commission, but if I do, I hope it will teach me as much about painting—and about the power and dignity of the bond between animals and humans—as *Rocky and Ellie Mae* taught me, one tentative brushstroke, canine yelp, and painterly lesson at a time.

Vito Ciccotelli, Age Ninety-Four: Portrait of a Diminutive Giant

Vito Ciccotelli may have been small in stature, but in all of the quiet, unspoken ways that contribute most importantly to a person's character, he was larger than life.

He was born in 1918 in Caramanico, Italy—now known as Caramanico Terme because of its proximity to a spa—then emigrated to the United States in 1931. After living many years with his wife and four sons in Ossipee, New Hampshire, and working at Portsmouth Naval Shipyard, he died in October of 2012, in nearby Wolfeboro, at the age of ninety-four.

From 1941 to 1946, Vito served with distinction in the U.S. Army, first as a member of the Antiaircraft Artillery Gun Battalion at Governor's Island in Upper Manhattan, in defense of New York City. Then, beginning in 1944, he took part in fierce battles and memorable campaigns in Normandy, northern France, the Rhineland, and the Ardennes. In 1945, near the end of his enlistment, he was promoted to the rank of captain.

I knew little about his wartime assignments except that he was immeasurably proud to have served in the army on behalf of his adopted country.

Vito was the father of my onetime employer, Dwight Ciccotelli. I first met Vito in 1997 when he stopped by one day at the frame shop and gallery I was managing at Ben Franklin Crafts. (I managed the shop first in Somersworth, New Hampshire, then in nearby Rochester, where it moved a few years later.) I've always had a keen interest in the parents of my adult friends, so when I heard Vito was in the store to visit his son, I asked Dwight to send him back to the shop to introduce himself to me. "All right," he said, "but it may take a while. He's pretty slow these days!"

Fig. 72. Captain Vito Ciccotelli, U. S. Army, December 1945.

I thought he was kidding, but soon learned otherwise. When I peeked out the door of the frame shop, I saw a man who had to have been Dwight's father coming toward me from halfway down the store, moving with all the speed of a snail trapped in a pool of molasses.

When he finally made it to the archway leading into the shop, he stepped toward me, greeted me with a warm smile, then extended his hand and said, "God bless you!" with a voice softer than velvet and sweeter than the chocolates he more than likely passed out to the children while on duty overseas.

In less than an hour, we established a kinship that was to last for all of the remaining years of his life. I asked a co-worker to take a photograph of the two of us, then shook Vito's hand and urged him to come back and visit me whenever he came down from Ossipee to visit the store and see his son.

He never failed to make the long, slow trek to the back of the store each time he was in town, and on every single occasion he'd step up to me, hold my hand between his two hands—the hands of a man in the ninth decade of his life and rich with experience—and say, "God bless you!"

One night, not long after meeting Vito, I was at home in my studio going over my list of completed paintings when I realized I had no acceptable portraits of humans to show prospective clients.

Something had to be done. For the next several weeks I kicked around the names of several friends who might be willing to sit for me, but came up empty.

I also began to worry that choosing a longtime friend as the subject of a sample painting wasn't a good idea. *Which of them would I really want to paint?* I thought to myself. *And would those I chose not to paint be offended?* I wasn't eager to mix business with friendship, so I eliminated my closest friends from the list, then continued without success to look for other, more appropriate candidates.

Then, one day in July, as I was working on a project in the frame shop, the bell at the service counter rang ever so slightly. "Probably a kid," I grumbled. "I wish they wouldn't do that!"

I left the project on the worktable and headed out the door, determined to catch the offender and tell him to cut it out, but there was no child in sight—only Vito, standing shyly at the service counter with his hand extended toward me in greeting. "God bless you!" he whispered, and I knew right away that Vito Ciccotelli would be the subject of my next portrait.

I immediately told him of my intentions and scheduled a photo session at his home in Ossipee. A week later I drove the thirty miles north for the appointment, and after iced tea and polite conversation with Vito and his wife, Arlene, I mounted my camera on a tripod and got down to the business of recording reference photos for the project.

Fig. 73. Vito Ciccotelli (candid photo by the author).

Less than a week later, I'd sketched the outline of Vito's face onto a blank canvas, arranged my colors on the palette—a panel of cardboard, cut from a grocery box—and begun to apply the flesh tones. By painting two or three hours each day after work, I made slow but steady progress, interrupted on occasion by foolish errors in both proportioning and color mixing.

I had no interest in idealizing Vito's face in my portrait. The deeply creased skin, the leopard-like assemblage of age spots, the deep bags beneath eyes that had seen fierce battle in World War II—all needed to be recorded in my portrait with uncompromising truth and meticulous attention to detail. Vito was Vito, and it was that inimitable countenance, deeply etched with feelings and memories gathered from more than eight decades of living, that I wanted badly to capture on canvas.

When I was reasonably certain I'd finished the first stage of my painting with credible success, I called my wife, Marilyn, into the studio to ask what she thought of my work.

"That left eye ..." she said with her usual soft-spoken bluntness. "That left eye is nearly an eighth of an inch too low, isn't it?"

"Damn!" I snarled. "I thought I'd really nailed down the proportions!"

"Well, almost—but not quite," she said, employing her exacting, woodworker eyes. "Better get back in there and make some repairs."

An hour or so later, after working through a shamefully protracted, self-pitying pout, I pulled myself together, went back to the studio, and performed major surgery on the offending eye. Then, since I was in such close proximity to the other eye, I made a few adjustments to that one as well.

Back to the studio came Marilyn, armed with her famously all-seeing eye and ready again to pass judgment on my work.

"Nice work on that eye!" she said. "Looks good!"

I quietly rejoiced. It was never easy to get less-than-perfect work past her, but this time I'd gone through the gauntlet and come out unscathed.

"It really does look good," she said. "But what happened with the *right* eye? It's bigger than the left one now, isn't it?"

I banged my head on the top of my easel, threw my brush across the room, and retired to my Morris chair to lick my wounds and summon the courage to return to combat with my faltering wannabe masterpiece.

Happily, the third inspection—painfully long and microscopically intense—yielded better results. The eyes were once again anatomically correct, and I was free to proceed with work on the skin, the eyebrows, and the ever-so-tricky curvature of the mouth. Vito's expression in the reference photo was caught somewhere between sunny smile and lingering sadness. It needed to be finely calibrated in order to be true to the mood I was determined to capture.

While my portrait of Vito wasn't a commission—I'd taken on the project voluntarily in order to add to my samples of portraiture—I dug deeply into the perfectionist component of my psyche and painted with laser-beam attention to detail. Every age spot had to be just the right shape and color, and in precisely the position it was in my reference photo. The eyebrows had to have just the right configuration in order to capture what I imagined to be Vito's emotions at the very moment I'd snapped the strongest photograph at his home in Ossipee. And every portrait artist knows just how daunting is the task of accurately rendering the corners of a mouth. I altered them over and over again, moving them up, and then down, to the left and then right, and back where they'd been in the first place. *Thank God for acrylic paint and hair dryers!* I thought to myself.

Finally, after intense concentration and thorough reviewing, I managed to pin down exactly what I'd seen that day in his poignant, emotionally complex, ninety-three-year-old expression.

By now Vito's physical condition had begun to deteriorate, so I worked feverishly to finish the portrait, then show it to him while he was still in a position to appreciate my work.

When the painting was finally done, I scheduled a meeting with Vito and his wife for the following Monday at 2:00 p.m.

This time, Arlene made sandwiches and tea, then brought out a stack of photo albums chronicling her husband's many colorful World War II adventures. As I studied photo after photo, with Arlene as my guide and interpreter, Vito was quieter than usual. Then, after we'd turned the last page of the last album, he repeated a ritual he'd begun to perform every time he saw me. Reaching ever so slowly into his pants pocket, he pulled out a key chain medallion with a faded sticker adhered to it. For some reason, he'd written my name—Ross—on the sticker. "See?" he, murmured, "This is the sticker you gave me!"

I immediately recognized it, but was surprised, then moved to think that he'd cared enough to save it. He put the medallion slowly back in his pocket, then settled into his favorite chair in the living room off the kitchen. It was time to show Vito the portrait.

I brought it in from the car, propped it up on a chair, and removed the plastic bag I'd transported it in. He said very little as he looked at the painting, but the smile on his face—broad as the side of a New England barn—told me all I needed to know about his feelings.

Once he'd seen the portrait, the mood in the Ciccotelli household became half celebratory and half reflective. To liven things up, I'd brought my flute and camera with me just for the occasion. I knew Vito loved "Edelweiss," a song written especially for Rodgers and Hammerstein's 1959 musical, *The Sound of Music*. He'd first heard the song many years ago while visiting Switzerland. It was inevitably linked in his mind to his favorite flower, and on countless occasions, no matter what the circumstances, he'd sing it to anyone who cared to listen. I'd decided in advance to record the two of us with my movie camera, playing and singing "Edelweiss" together.

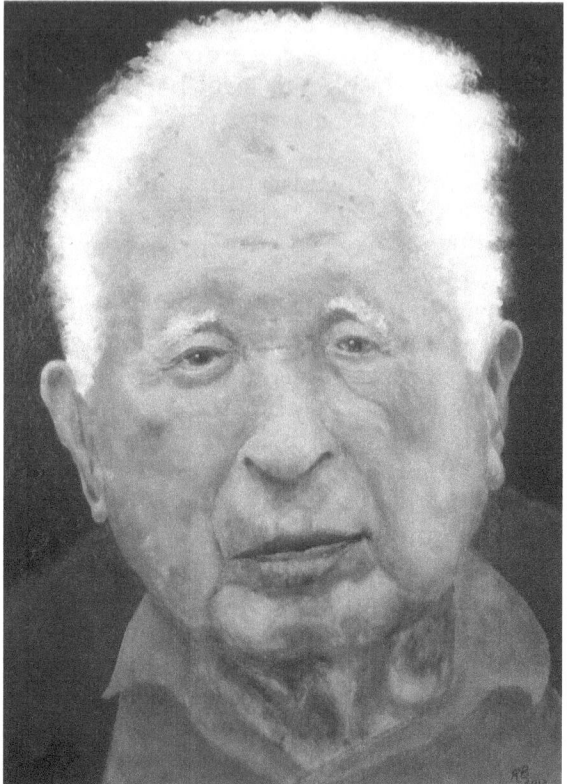

Fig. 74. *Vito Ciccotelli, Age Ninety-Four* by Ross Bachelder.

The moment Arlene activated the camera, he broke out in song. I grabbed my flute off the coffee table and jumped in with him, two measures late. It really didn't matter to me that we weren't in sync as musicians; the important thing was Vito, and he sang "Edelweiss" with consummate tenderness. As he finished the song, singing "Bless my homeland forever," his voice cracked and then trailed off. I knew I'd treasure that musical moment as much as I'd already begun to treasure the opportunity to paint him in the first place. I was a lucky man; it was my distinct honor and good fortune to have known Vito Ciccotelli.

In October of 2012, Vito finally passed away. On the day before his funeral in Rochester, his son Dwight got in touch with me and asked me if I might be willing to lend the painting to the family. He wanted it to be on exhibit, along with a large accumulation of mementos and photographs, in the lobby of the church in the moments leading up to the actual service.

I was exceedingly happy knowing the portrait I'd created to pay homage to Vito would actually be there with him at the church, helping the family reflect on his life and accomplishments and begin to work through the difficult grieving process.

The next morning I loaded the portrait into my Subaru and headed into Rochester to leave it with the family. As I approached the outskirts of the city, a call came in on my cell phone. It was Dwight.

"I know I asked you yesterday to lend us your portrait of my father," he said, "but there's been a change of plans. No need to bring it over. We'll be fine with what the family pulled together for the service."

I suppose I ought to have been angry, or at least indignant, but the only emotion I felt then was sadness. The next evening after work I attended Vito's wake and paid tribute to him by looking at the dozens of family photographs mounted on a display panel in the foyer of the funeral home. He'd clearly been playful and exuberant as a young man, and later, in his World War II uniform, he was strikingly handsome, with a quiet dignity that most men don't possess until much later in their lives.

What memorabilia the family chose to display at Vito's service was their business, not mine. I'll never know why they chose not to include my portrait in the service, but I did know with certainty that I'd painted it with love and Vito had seen it—and that was all that really mattered to me. In painting as well as in life, the trip is always more important than the destination. And in the few short years I knew Vito, I'd taken the trip of a lifetime, learning invaluable lessons about caring and decency along the way.

Chapter 16

The Flute Guy and the Juggler
Saying No to the One and Yes to the Many

I've been a flute player since the seventh grade—a very long time ago from the perspective of a seventy-year-old—but somewhere in the second year of my studies in the Department of Music at Eastern Michigan University, I began to realize that teaching and playing the flute for a living weren't going to be enough to satisfy my increasingly multi-layered appetite for creative work. I'd begun to discover other academic disciplines—especially writing—that had as much power as music to ignite my passion for learning. Eventually, it became clear to me that I was no longer just the Flute Guy. I'd become the Juggler, and playing the flute became only one of several endeavors in my life as a creative.

This is the story of my gradual transformation from specialist to generalist—from being the Flute Guy to being a confirmed and infinitely more fulfilled arts multiple.

When I entered seventh grade at Northwest High School in rural Jackson, Michigan, my hometown, I learned that I was eligible for the band program. I wanted to join, but hadn't a clue about choosing an instrument. Since my brother was already playing trombone in the band, I turned to him one day and said, "What instrument do you think I should play?"

He looked at me in his analytical, matter-of-fact way and replied, "Take the flute. The bus drivers don't like dealing with the big instruments. If you take the flute, you won't get any crap from anyone about how it won't fit on the bus."

I remember well the day my father, a factory supervisor with little real interest in music, came home with a flute—my very first musical instrument. It was an Armstrong—an affordable, widely popular student model—and came in a small, scuffed and tattered black case. Clearly it had been through more than one battle in the war against musical incompetence. And the fact that it was really small—roughly three-fourths the size of those trendy baguettes appearing so frequently in French art films—

The Flute Guy and the Juggler

meant that it was unlikely that Mrs. Cadwallader, our morning-route bus driver, would give me any of that crap my brother had warned me about.

Dad handed the flute to me with no fanfare—only a gruff "Here's your flute!" followed by an ominous "Better take good care of it." No romance, just the familiar bone-chilling, nuts-and-bolts imperative. It was okay, though. I'd just gotten the instrument I wanted most in the world, and I didn't really care how it was presented to me or what condition it was in.

Once the flute was out of its case, the evidence of its years of service was instantly on display. It was tarnished the color of root beer and covered from head joint to tail joint with unsightly blemishes and pockmarks. It had seldom been cleaned, so the natural oils from its player's fingers had eaten into the surface of its silver-nickel alloy and irreparably scarred its once-pristine surface. A few months after it came into my life, I began to wonder who'd taken such poor care of it and yet managed, somehow, to make tolerable music with it. Or perhaps the previous owner hadn't made tolerable music with it, which was why the instrument now belonged to me, and its original owner was now an accountant.

But that day, I shrugged off the deplorable condition of my new/old flute, concentrating instead on the magic I was certain was trapped in it, waiting to be brought out into the sunlight beginning first thing Monday morning. I was so new to the world of music and so excited about having become an actual musician that they could have told me my flute once belonged to Frederick the Great—an accomplished flute player when he wasn't being a king—and I'd have bought it hook, line, and sinker. I entered my school's instrumental music program right away, and my family supplemented the program with what became six consecutive years of private instruction—a gift from my parents that, in spite of our years of familial ups and downs, has never stopped giving.

I ought to have known that learning to play a musical instrument in a tiny, sports-obsessed Michigan farm town was going to be anything but a slam dunk. It was the mid-'50s, and rigid, puritanical ideas about the roles of both men and women were cemented irretrievably into the minds of most country folk. And where I grew up, near the sleepy, structurally decaying village of Rives Junction—a hotbed of evangelical conservatism—attitudes were even more regressive than usual.

The children of the congregants at Rives Baptist Church weren't allowed to participate in school dances. Even hayrides, which along with ice skating were among the most popular of leisure-time activities, were strictly off limits for them because—in the minds of the intimacy-phobic church elders and their flock—something bad might happen beneath the stacks of hay piled high and deep on the wagons. (As it turned out, I knew from both observation and experience on the hayride circuit that their hunch was more often than not right on the mark. If you knew what you were doing and didn't tell your parents, hayrides were the hottest thing in town.)

I had no idea, of course, that, in keeping with the area's oppressively stereotypical thinking, I was about to be subjected to a steady drumbeat of teasing and ridicule, all because a flute—not a snare drum or saxophone or trumpet, instruments thought to be the exclusive province of males—had become my instrument of choice.

Among the many insults I endured while hurrying down the hall to my daily band rehearsal was "Where'd ya get that thing—from a Cracker Jack box?" Another favorite was "Forget your dress today?" Such disparaging remarks would have crushed the spirit of a less intrepid boy than me, but somewhere along the line I'd managed to acquire ideals and ambitions too deeply entrenched to be tampered with. I dismissed the insults as plain jealousy—senseless malarkey from envious have-nots—and pushed ahead with my plan to be not just another small-town musician, but a damn good musician.

As it turned out, I had an answer for those pint-size purveyors of poison—youngsters conceived in the fetid petri dish of a Bible Belt community more worried about original sin than pride in accomplishment. I finished my six years of private instruction, left the band without ever having relinquished first chair, won a scholarship to attend a two-week summer session at Interlochen National Music Camp (now Interlochen Center for the Arts), then entered Eastern Michigan University as a full-time music student. I'd triumphed over the ridicule and proven the superiority of wholesome intellectual ambition over smug, sanctimonious, right-wing rectitude.

I proved to be a dedicated, highly driven student of music, spending several hours a day, seven days week in the practice room. It was my good fortune by then to have access to a much better, university-owned instrument—a Wm. S. Haynes open-tone-hole model that allowed me to produce a more robust tone than I'd ever been able to make with the Armstrong. Within the self-righteous hierarchy of the *flautist* community, if you were fortunate enough to have either a Haynes or a Powell, you were instantly taken seriously, and life was good. Anyone stuck with a lesser instrument—especially one without either open tone holes or a low B key—was seen as lacking ambition and doomed to labor without reward in the lowest echelons of the music industry.

As I got deeper and deeper into the music world and discovered just how much it was saturated with posturing and pretentiousness, I began to rebel against the longtime, well-meaning tendency of people, both within and outside the music world, to call flute players *flutists*—or worse, *flautists*. To my way of thinking, I was simply a man who happened to play the flute—a *flute player*—so the distinction in nomenclature became more and more important to me.

For the first time ever, I had to fight to hold first chair as a flute player, and I didn't always win. Dorothy Youells, my closest competitor, was a deadly serious musician—a very good player who was more married to her flute than a nun to the Lord Jesus. So completely was she immersed in the business of mastery that when I asked her one late-November day what she thought of the assassination of President Kennedy, she was at first puzzled, then genuinely surprised. "*Really!* I hadn't heard!" she said, assuring me that she'd been in the practice room for the entire weekend and hadn't heard any news at all. Dorothy, the imperturbable workhorse of the Department of Music, got all of the accolades because of her spectacular work ethic. No matter how hard I worked, I found myself scrambling to play catch-up.

It wasn't until I played flute under the baton of José Serebrier that I began to feel as if I was being taken seriously again as a flute player. Serebrier, an internationally respected, globe-hopping orchestral conductor, had eagerly accepted the positions of principle conductor and composer in residence of the university's orchestra—positions that would allow him the time and tranquility he needed to finish a new symphony he was composing.

It must have seemed to him like a can't-say-no, made-in-heaven opportunity. There, within the hallowed halls of a small but ambitious Midwestern university, he would finally be able to make beautiful music in a quiet setting, then have it tested in public performance, utilizing an orchestra of young, idealistic musicians so elated to be working under a renowned conductor that they'd pull out all the stops in order to please him. And they'd be simultaneously feathering their nests as aspiring orchestral professionals, so everyone would win.

It didn't quite work out the way he'd intended. At the time of Serebrier's residency, Eastern was by and large a working-class university—what was derisively called a commuter college—living under the ominous, often debilitating shadow of the world-renowned University of Michigan. It meant that an unpleasantly high portion of EMU's students didn't really share Dorothy Youells's relentless, red-hot drive to excel.

As one might expect, they didn't always arrive at rehearsals having thoroughly practiced the toughest passages of a given composition. This reality shocked and disillusioned Serebrier, and the disillusionment soon evolved into visible anger. He began to spend more time lecturing his musicians about the need for adequate preparation than he did about the way a given passage ought to be performed.

Because he was a native of South America, Serebrier had what some people raised in the ultraconservative, culturally homogeneous communities of rural southern Michigan considered a thick, often incomprehensible accent. The less knowledgeable musicians had difficulty understanding what he was asking them to do in rehearsals, so they stopped listening. Worse, he became the unspoken butt of ridicule for the peculiar way in which he conducted nearly every piece of music. Round and round he went with his baton, carving tight, concentric circles into the air, making his downbeat as elusive on some nights as the whereabouts of the kiwi in the wilds of New Zealand.

In spite of the temperamental stalemate between the conductor and his brood, the good news was that Serebrier liked me, and I liked him. He could sense that I was serious about the work of bettering myself as a musician, and I could see that he was a frustrated onetime musical prodigy, now well into adulthood and camping out in alien territory—a truly driven creative in the land of mediocrity. I liked to think he could feel my heartfelt empathy radiating from music stand to podium at each and every rehearsal.

Even better, he liked both my tone and the emotional intensity with which I delivered it. So, for an all-too-brief interlude, I was granted the title of principle flutist in the orchestra. I also had the good fortune to be employed in the university's work-study program as Serebrier's orchestra librarian—a fact that helped strengthen the bond between us.

I wanted badly for everything to work out for José Serebrier. Not only did I admire him for his impressive achievements as composer and conductor, I'd begun to see the celebrated but much maligned maestro as the one essential key to my eventual success as an aspiring ensemble musician. I was convinced, perhaps naively, that if I continued to impress him, he'd one day open unprecedented doors for me as a flute player.

But it clearly was not meant to be. Much to my chagrin, Serebrier—increasingly unhappy and unfulfilled as conductor and composer in residence—finally escaped from his year-long incarceration in what must have become for him more a prison for the underperforming than an institution for higher learning. He'd forsaken the life of an academic and moved up to far more friendly skies, flying from country to country to nurture his growing international prominence as conductor and composer.

I'd lost my champion, and Dorothy Youells—the student so completely devoted to her music that she hadn't noticed the assassination of a president—once again ascended to the throne of perceived superiority as the most ambitious, most respected musician in the department. Through no fault of either Youells or Serebrier, I'd in effect been demoted, both within the Department of Music and within my increasingly disenchanted self. I realized I'd soon need to find another way to shore up my sagging sense of self-worth as a young man in search of his identity.

I continued the demanding work of improving my proficiency as a flute player, but my long-held conviction that I was destined to become a music educator had begun to wane. Somewhere in my sophomore year, I began to nurture my growing passion for literature—a passion whose seeds had been planted first in high school under my English teacher, Barbara Locke, and then in college under my freshman composition instructor, Franklin Case.

I was having serious difficulty with the study of harmony under Dorothy James, who herself had studied with internationally renowned composer Howard Hanson. Soon afterward I ran headlong into the astronomically high expectations of my music history professor, Erich Goldschmidt, the university's gifted resident organist and an ardent worshipper of everything J. S. Bach. I emerged from those classroom experiences with less than impressive grades and a growing sense that I might be far more suited to live performance than esoteric scholarship and music theory.

I'd also begun to read novels, short stories, and poetry when not in the practice room, refining my technique as a flute player. At the same time I discovered *Cellar Roots*, the campus literary magazine overseen by Franklin Case, then submitted and saw published an embarrassingly pedantic essay about what I saw as the war in academia over the issue of whether language is inherently flexible or bound by certain inviolable rules. "Language is malleable and kinetic, not rigid and immoveable," I declared, then went on to make a string of long-forgotten assertions that, while sophomoric to some, had genuine meaning for me as a writer in development, struggling to find my voice.

It wasn't long before I decided to declare an English literature minor. I told no one at the time—not my parents, not my dorm mates, and not my professors in the Department of Music. It was an intensely personal decision for me, and for reasons I didn't fully understand, I was determined to keep it that way.

I quickly fell head-over-heels in love with all the lions of American literature—Stephen Crane, Sherwood Anderson, and John Updike among them. I read over coffee in local restaurants in the morning, over fries and burgers at lunch, and while waiting at Pease Auditorium for concerts to begin. Late at night, I lay awake wondering how on earth I was going to find the time away from my musical studies to meet the expectations of the English department faculty. The more deeply I immersed myself in literature, the less time and energy I had left over, either for music-related classwork or my critically important rehearsing as a flute player.

I decided something had to give. I made an appointment with the chairman of the music department, Dr. Howard Rarig—a patrician statue of a man with a booming voice and a flattop like a helicopter landing pad—and pleaded with him to be excused from required participation in the university's marching band. Without that responsibility on my academic schedule, I said, I'd be able to reclaim at least a dozen hours a week for required reading and the writing of essays so relevant and essential to the study of literature.

I could tell from the way he squirmed in his chair that he wasn't altogether impressed with my argument.

Time to pull out all the stops, I thought, then forged recklessly ahead, emptying the troubled contents of my aching heart onto his meticulously organized desk.

"To me," I said, "the marching band tradition in America is little more than a tiresome relic from this country's ultra-romanticized military history. It's a grueling, time-consuming activity, better suited to the goals of a physical education department than to the needs and aspirations of a performance major."

The growing smile on his face gave me hope that I was making progress, so I doubled my resolve and finished with a flourish worthy of crackerjack drummers at the Rose Bowl parade. "As I see it," I said, "stomping in lock-step down a football field and back again every Saturday afternoon does nothing for me as a student of music! I need the time for more relevant, more important work."

Rarig listened patiently to me, then politely but mercilessly dissected my argument while gazing down at me through stylish

The Flute Guy and the Juggler

half-moon glasses perched artfully on the tip of his sizable nose. When he'd finished his rebuttal, he cleared his throat, then stood up, straightened his lavender Italian silk necktie, and headed for the door.

"I hear your point of view," he bellowed, "but on reflection I think you'll understand that the decision is not really mine to make. I'm afraid you'll need to talk with Dr. Tyra, the head of our marching band program. I've no doubt he'll give you a fair hearing." I'd been vanquished in our little war of wills, then dismissed like a junior high miscreant.

The next morning I caught up with Dr. Thomas Tyra—known proudly throughout the Department of Music as "The Chief." He was a beefy, NFL tackle of a man, with a military buzz cut and the on-again, off-again smile of a Cheshire cat. He appeared always to be on the way to something important as he leaned precariously ahead of his feet, charging full-tilt down the halls of the Department of Music like a wayward beast from the running of the bulls.

"May I have a word with you, Dr. Tyra?" I peeped.

He stopped in his tracks, spun around, and looked straight down at me. "Yes, but I'm in a hurry. I have a marching band drill in ten minutes—and so do you!"

I steeled myself for my court appearance, then made my case to the magistrate. "I've declared a minor in English literature," I stammered, "and I'm having trouble keeping up with my work in both literature and music. I was hoping you'd understand if I dropped out of marching band. I need more time to study my subjects in both departments."

"Drop out of *marching band*? A *music major*?" By now his face had turned strawberry red, and he was glaring menacingly at me from beneath the visor of his EMU marching band cap. He'd dropped the kindly professor persona and become an angry drill sergeant.

"Not on your life!" he growled. "You're a *music* student, not a literature student. You've made a contract to be in marching band. It comes with the territory!"

"But I've been loyal to this department!" I snapped. "I work hard in every subject, and I really care about my studies. It's just that ..."

"Look!" he thundered. "You go right ahead and quit marching band if that's what you wish. But I'm telling you right now, you'll lose both of your music scholarships if you leave." He looked impatiently down at his wristwatch, then angrily back at me. "Gotta go," he said, and shot down the hall in his usual cannonball fashion, flanked by two of his loyal assistants, leaving me standing alone in the hallway, full of shame and foreboding. *What's to become of me?* I thought. I'd chosen honesty, and in return I'd taken a serious hit to both my pocketbook and my dignity.

I didn't need much time to make up my mind. The next morning I turned in my marching band uniform, and a week later I found a letter in my mailbox announcing that my scholarships would not be renewed for the next academic year.

"Thank you for your interest in the Department of Music programs," it said in the last paragraph. "And we want to wish you another successful year as an Eastern Michigan University student!"

The message to me was heartbreakingly clear: I wasn't wanted in the Department of Music if I wasn't entirely the intellectual property of the faculty, with a disturbingly parochial, utterly inflexible vision of what a good music student should be. Reading anything but books about sackbuts, ophicleides, and the origins of Medieval plainchant was off-limits and a waste of time. Independent thinking was not healthy for music students and other living things, and being literate was tantamount to being disloyal. As long as I knew how to march in a straight line, it didn't matter one whit if I couldn't tell the difference between a haiku and a heckelphone.

With the exception of conductor Bill Fitch, piano instructor Hershal Pyle, composer Anthony Iannaccone, and a handful of equally open-minded music educators, the Department of Music at EMU in the early '60s was top-heavy with professors hopelessly entrenched in their ways—career academics with an absurdly myopic vision, whose tastes in music were rigidly conventional and pathetically intolerant. To a few of them, classical music was the only really good music, and if a student—including me—was caught playing jazz alone in a practice room, it wasn't altogether uncommon for him to be reprimanded for wasting his time, then ordered to cease and desist.

Given the blinkered mindset of those times, I ought not to have been surprised at having been stripped of my scholarships for daring to aspire to a more well-rounded vision of the world than that of all too many of my instructors. I'd finally begun to realize that proficiency on one musical instrument, coupled with a broad but superficial knowledge of only one academic discipline, was simply not going to be enough for me.

I dropped out of school a short time after this incident because of personal struggles with my family and myself. And yet somehow, in spite of what was for me the department's unforgivable retribution, and in spite of a one-semester

The Flute Guy and the Juggler

Fig. 75. The author performing at Falmouth by the Sea Assisted Living, West Falmouth, Maine (photo by Anne Strout).

absence from school, I returned to EMU and carried on with my joyful immersion in music. By 1969 I'd earned a bachelor of science with a performance emphasis; then I took a teaching fellowship in EMU's Department of English, where I earned a master of arts in English and American literature while continuing formal, post-graduate study of the flute. That I was never going to be a specialist in any endeavor was becoming more and more clear to me.

It was no use denying I'd fallen in love with literature, so much so that I decided to become a university-level writing instructor. I got down to business, applied for doctoral programs in English literature, and was accepted for post-graduate studies at three area colleges—Wayne State University, the University of Toledo, and the University of Michigan. I'd found a new passion and was about to embark on what I imagined to be a sure-fire journey to occupational fulfillment.

But something about my plan was making me uneasy. I couldn't forget how disenchanted I'd become with the pomposity and intellectual narcissism of so many members of the English department faculty while earning my master's degree as a teaching fellow. It was essentially an unwelcome re-staging of the very same academic melodrama I'd lived through in the Department of Music only two years before.

Late at night, safely away from my more romantic illusions about "essential reading" and "a life of the mind," I began to wonder whether I'd ever be comfortable with so many scholarly peacocks preening and parading everywhere around me.

I was still very much a musician, though, and continued to harbor an equally powerful yearning to be a concertizing flute player. I'd heeded the siren call of both music and literature; my challenge now would be to find a way to achieve a reasonable balance between the two competing passions.

And that wasn't all. The struggle for balance was further complicated by the increasingly loud roarings of my very own entrepreneurial lion, lurking just under the surface of my young and ambitious self. More and more, I was drawn to the art of conceiving, organizing, and implementing creative projects, and that part of me refused to be silenced. How was I ever going to maintain the quality of my creative work—my writing, my music, my inner entrepreneur—while juggling so many creative endeavors? I began to look for a circumstance in which my multiple passions could be pursued with a reasonable chance of success, out from under the burdensome yoke of academia.

It wasn't long before the scenario I'd been yearning for began to take shape. My wife and I were both exhausted from several demanding years of university study. We were also haunted by the growing conviction that, by living in the Ypsilanti/Ann Arbor area—a densely populated, highly competitive academic jungle on the perimeter of metropolitan Detroit—we'd become infinitely more consumer than creator. We decided it was time to shake things up.

First, I rejected a tantalizing offer to pursue an all-expenses-paid doctorate in English literature at Shaw College in Detroit. It wasn't an easy decision; I'd have been put immediately on a tenure track as an instructor in English literature and composition, with all of the highly prized perks that come with the assignment. Then, in 1974, with our five-year-old daughter and our most ardent hopes and dreams in tow, we moved to a place light years away from the dense thicket of colleges and universities in southern Michigan—the tiny, blue-collar village of Berwick in the southern tip of Maine. My wife had just accepted an appointment as a music educator in the Berwick schools, and her hiring became the indispensable catalyst for our New England adventure.

Only a year or so after relocating to Maine, I landed a freelance assignment as weekly columnist and book reviewer for the long-established *Somersworth/Berwick Free Press* under its revered editor, Leola Pepler. I called my column Equal Time, and in it I'd review a book each week having something to do, however tangentially, with the changing roles of men and women. The Feminist revolution, with Gloria Steinem, Germaine Greer, and Bella Abzug at the helm, was well underway, and my own ideals as husband and father were being rapidly reconfigured by the country's debate over the rights of women and the part men would play in their liberation. It was a golden opportunity for me to explore male feminist issues that were remarkably well received, given that I'd landed in a politically conservative community.

I began to pick up speaking engagements at Unitarian churches, women's clubs, and other organizations, espousing what I called "active fatherhood" and the equal distribution of labor within marriage. On occasion I'd also agree to play the flute as a part of the same event—a development that eventually led me to work as a pit orchestra musician in area theaters.

Building on the success of both my writing and my public speaking, I decided to expand my efforts beyond the southern Maine / Seacoast New Hampshire region. Soon, by writing persuasive letters to various media outlets, I landed opportunities to discuss active fatherhood and male feminist issues on television programs in Boston, Bangor, and Buffalo.

When all of that work—the writing, the public speaking, the performing—failed to calm my restless spirit, I conceived and then founded the perfect business for the entrepreneurial part of me: Artful Endeavors. After years of giving away to people in the fine and performing arts my hard-won expertise in how to develop, market, and publicize creative skills, I decided to establish a freelance consulting service as a way to make additional money. As the director of Artful Endeavors—I was really a one-man band—I wrote business proposals, conducted workshops, and worked one-on-one with people from every walk of life who needed to jump-start their passion for whatever endeavor they were pursuing.

As I began to interact more and more with creative people from the Seacoast region, I hatched even more entrepreneurial schemes, including, for three hard-working years, a classical music booking agency. In that capacity, I wrote to the well-known South American conductor Antonia Brico—then the principal conductor of the Denver Symphony Orchestra—and offered to help her find engagements with orchestras in both North and South America. To my everlasting pleasure, she sent me a hundred dollars to cover my initial expenses, with the promise of more to come.

Unfortunately, Brico was in a hurry to advance her career, and when I failed to come up quickly enough with the opportunities she so badly wanted, the money stopped coming and she put an end to our relationship. Losing the Brico connection may have been a blow to my ego, but it was also an invaluable learning experience. It toughened me up, taught me a thing or two about the importance of dogged determination, and whetted my appetite for even more entrepreneurial ventures.

Just as I'd hoped when I chose to abandon the academic world and move from the Midwest to New England, I found myself gleefully immersed in a remarkably wide variety of creative endeavors, trying them on either simultaneously or one at a time, waiting for occupational lightning to strike. That it never really did—at least not in one well-defined, easy-to-manage package—was the story of my gradual but inevitable conversion from Flute Guy to arts multiple.

I'd taken various conventional assignments in order to help pay the bills—work as an art store manager-in-training, as a book store clerk, and, for seven years, as a teacher of public school music, teaching music privately on the side. But none of these endeavors could compete with the feeling I got when immersed in less conventional, more entrepreneurial schemes.

Founding and running my own summer theater for teens was among the most rewarding projects I'd ever taken on, but the best assignment I would ever have within the conventional work world came to me in 1995 after an exhilarating but punishing summer at Hackmatack Playhouse in Berwick. I found work as a picture framer, added an art gallery to the workplace, and for nearly nineteen years did freelance work in satellite mode, with the freelance work built around my frame shop and gallery employment.

My work as framer and gallery manager put me in constant proximity to artists, and from those interactions sprung yet another career within my arts-multiple lifestyle—work as a frequently exhibiting, multimedia visual artist. I was still the Flute Guy when the circumstances suited me, playing at art openings, performing in pit orchestras, and staging solo recitals. I was still a writer, taking assignments in a wide array of circumstances, including work as a newspaper columnist and an arts critic and as a part-time creative writing instructor at various colleges. But writing was only one piece of an increasingly complicated puzzle. I'd finally become the juggler I'd always wanted to be, and I couldn't have been happier about the serendipitous twists and turns that had begun unmistakably to define me as a true arts multiple.

One day at work, Tom Glover—a superb visual artist who, like me, supported his career as an artist with work as a framer—stopped what he was doing, and with a look of genuine perplexity, said, "Ya know, I can't quite figure out just what it is you're trying to *do*! I mean, the music, the writing, the art, the theater: Where's it all *leading* to?"

It was a defining moment in my life. Glover—a gifted artist whose energies were by choice and inclination devoted to just one highly specialized discipline—couldn't begin to see that there really was a pattern and a purpose in all of what I was doing in my multi-disciplinary life. I was never going to be the specialist he so naturally and inevitably had become; I was born to be a juggler—an arts multiple, through and through.

I knew with certainty that what I was doing—leaping from one endeavor to another and back again without apology, finding meaningful, richly rewarding connections between all of them—would never lead to the kind of notoriety that can come to an accomplished specialist in a specialization-crazed society. I've always played more than one genre of music in public performance; I've always worked in not one but several media as a visual artist; and for as long as I can remember I've been a writer for hire, willing to take on assignments in everything from poetry and cover art in literary journals to business proposals, theater company newsletters, press releases, and publicity posters.

There will always be those within and beyond the realm of the fine and performing arts who privately accuse people like me of being that odious creature no one wants to be—jack of all trades, master of none—but I've learned not to listen to their less-than-flattering characterizations of me.

As a visual artist, I'm always pleased and then proud when someone sees one of my multimedia solo exhibits and says in all earnestness, "Who are these artists? They're really interesting!" To be praised on occasion for doing so many things and doing them reasonably well is always music to my ears. It means that, in the minds of those whose opinions count, I'm as legitimate as the specialists. And when they discover that in addition to my work as an artist I'm also active as a writer and musician, I just might be even a little more interesting to them.

Long after I'd settled in New England and worked in several capacities as a creative, I stopped at Bull Moose in nearby Portsmouth, New Hampshire, one day and purchased an LP of orchestral works by Charles Ives, one of my all-time favorite American composers. To my delight, there on the record jacket, complete with bushy topknot and whimsical smile, was none other than José Serebrier, principal conductor of the prestigious American Symphony and champion of what was then called New American Music.

Seeing Mr. Serebrier on the jacket of that LP brought back a flood of Department of Music memories both delightful and disquieting. Along with these memories came a brief tidal wave of regrets about my years of study in Michigan—of imagining life as a tenured professor of English literature and concertizing flute player, then wondering just what I'd missed when Serebrier escaped his ivory tower, catapulted himself back onto the world stage as conductor and composer, then left me far behind him in the dust.

But that was then, and this is now. I'd never again be under the spell of Serebrier's quirky but inspired baton. I'd never again be in a position to incur the wrath of the esteemed Dr. Thomas Tyra, or suffer the indignity of being reprimanded for playing jazz riffs in what I'd erroneously presumed to be the unquestioned privacy of my rehearsal room. And yet all of it had finally begun not to matter. I had a brand-new life ahead of me in northern New England, and the seeds of creativity were about to flower in colors and configurations I could never have imagined in the years before my transformation.

It was a beautiful afternoon in early autumn, and as I crossed the street with the ghosts of Ives and Serebrier under my arm, got into my car, and headed home to Berwick, the regrets soon melted into insignificance, replaced by a late-in-life conviction that I really had done the right thing long ago by saying no to the one and yes to the many. Doing all of what I do still fits me like a well-made glove, and when on certain days I find myself absurdly over-booked and excessively stimulated, I couldn't be happier about my dilemma.

The Flute Guy and the Juggler

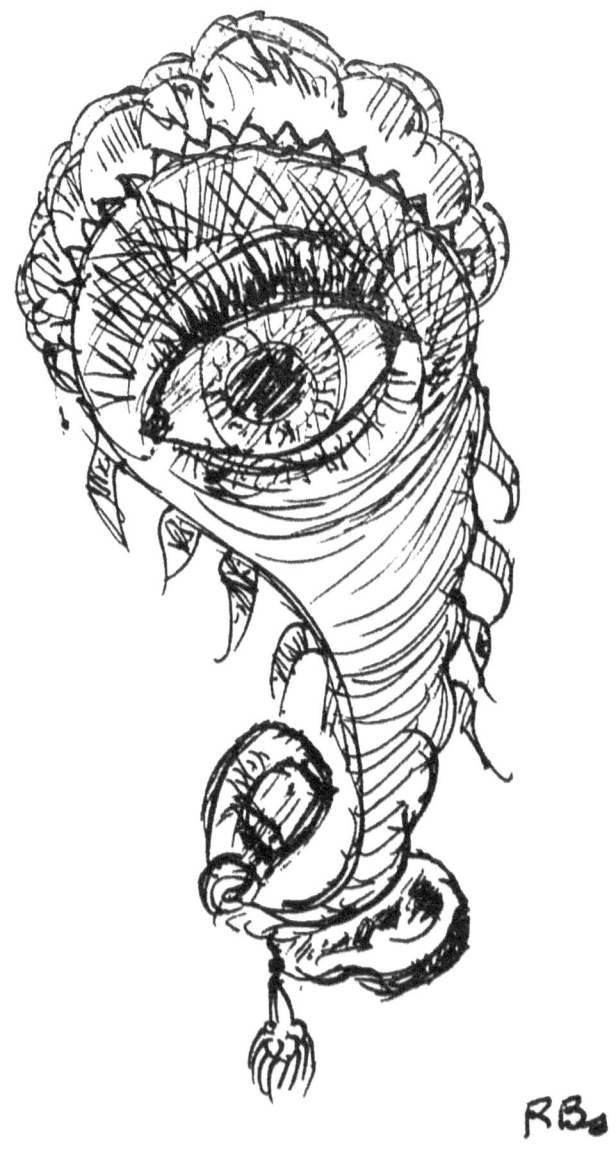

Fig. 76. *Little Miss One-Eye Finds a Lover* by Ross Bachelder.

✤ Tiny Novelette 8 ✤

Little Miss One-Eye Finds a Lover

Lilymae Scarfletter grew up during the Great Depression and spent nearly all of her life in Booger Hole, West Virginia, in a ramshackle two-room apartment above the offices of the town's most prominent physician, Dr. J. Rutherford Lewes.

It was Doc Lewes who brought her into the world, and he soon discovered that she had no feet, no arms, and no discernible mouth—only one great, luminous, all-seeing eye; one proud and magnificent toe; one exquisitely crafted ear; and one tiny, spider-like appendage, which he called a *grip-n-eater*, that would eventually double as both her mouth and her only means of locomotion.

But none of Lilymae's shortcomings mattered to Lewes. The moment he saw her he was enraptured, and he knew he'd one day be taking her under his wing. And sure enough, when Lilymae's mother was killed in a car crash one night while on the way to a bluegrass festival in Ivydale, Doc Lewes declared himself Lilymae's legal guardian—she was only two years old at the time—moved her into the upstairs apartment, and arranged to have his cousin Daisy Foglesong take care of her while he was downstairs examining his patients.

When Lilymae turned six, Lewes enrolled her in the one-room school down in Rush Fork Valley. Unfortunately, on the very first day of school, her classmates ganged up on her, dubbed her "Little Miss One-Eye," and refused to sit near her at lunchtime. To make matters worse, her teacher, Miss Petula Nightswang—a lumpy, disagreeable woman with hairy forearms and a chin like a turnip—showed her no affection at all. Worse, she kept her in from recess whenever she felt like it, and for no good reason. When Doc Lewes learned what was happening, he pulled Lilymae out of school and brought her home for good.

Lewes may have been a big-hearted fellow, but he was also notoriously tight with the dollar. While his own state-of-the-art flush toilet was the envy of the townspeople, Lily's place had no facilities at all. It meant that each morning, when nature called, she'd have to wobble down the stairs at the rear of the apartment and join Gertie Twombling and Leona Perks—always at precisely 7:45—in the town's only reputable three-holer, tucked behind Bobby Skanks's filling station. Depending on how you look at it, regularity can be either a blessing or a curse.

Because it was so hard for Lilymae to get around, by the age of twenty she'd become more than ever a recluse. Every evening she'd stretch out on the horsehair couch in her apartment, munch on elephant ears and funnel cakes from the local bakery, and play haunting melodies on the theremin Doc Lewes had picked up for her from Jigglin' Jimmy's, an odds-and-ends shop next to the cemetery. Her soulful music perfectly complemented the town of Booger Hole, which for as long as anyone could remember was rife with tales of unsolved murders and ghostly visitations. People all over town left their windows open late at night so they could hear her play, and the wolves added their melancholy descant to the mix.

Lonely and disillusioned with her life in Booger Hole, Lilymae yearned for romance and wrote passionate letters each night to the men in the Lonely Hearts column of *True Confessions*, hoping to find a lover. When after months of waiting by the mailbox she failed to get even one response to her enquiries, she tossed her stack of *True Confessions* into the trash, lay down on the couch with her face to the wall, and cried her heart out.

When she woke up the next morning, her nightgown was soaked with tears and her once-proud toe throbbed with foreboding. All seemed hopeless until she pulled the curtain back on the window above the couch, gazed across the rolling hills beyond Main Street, and, with the help of her astonishing visual acuity, saw a solitary figure wobbling precariously along the far ridge of Murder Mountain. He had one exquisitely crafted ear, one proud and magnificent toe, a powerful grip-n-eater, and one great, luminous, all-seeing eye.

"Just like me," she shouted to no one in particular. "So I'm not the only one after all!"

She couldn't help noticing that, unlike her, he had a dense, black beard and two short but serviceable arms. *The better to hold me with*, she thought to herself, giggling. *And with that beard, he looks like an ancient Scottish warrior. I'll call him Ian McWhiskers!*

She wriggled down off the couch, went to her theremin, and played a melody so hauntingly beautiful that McWhiskers—who could see and hear with the same astonishing acuity as Lilymae and just happened to have his bagpipe with him—whirled around, worked his way down Murder Mountain, and headed straight to Doc Lewes's place, playing "The Sweet, Sweet Pipes of Scotland" on his bagpipe as he went.

When he finally arrived, he teetered up the stairs with the help of his grip-in-eater, went straight to Lilymae, and wrapped his arms around the long, lithe figure of a woman more beautiful than he could ever have imagined. She didn't really mind that his beard tickled her to distraction; it was his warm, caring arms that meant the most to her.

The very next weekend, Ian and Lilymae were wed in Bobby Skanks's filling station, surrounded by a dense forest of grease guns, hub caps, and fan belts, all cleaned up for the occasion. Skanks, who worked as justice of the peace in his off hours, did the officiating. And Doc Lewes, who was best man in the ceremony, finally abandoned his parsimonious ways and had a deluxe, flushable two-holer installed in the upstairs apartment, complete with a hand-carved seat made of rare, splinter-proof bubinga wood imported from Bangui, Central Africa. They'd never again need to wobble down the staircase to use Skanks's three-holer: they'd do their business at precisely 7:45 every morning—in the privacy of their very own apartment—and Gertie Twombling and Leona Perks would just have to go it alone behind the filling station.

Little Miss One-Eye had finally found a lover, and from the moment they were married, Lilymae Scarfletter and Ian McWhiskers could be heard playing bagpipe and theremin duets each moonlit evening, always to the howling of the wolves and the beating of their own immensely grateful hearts.

Chapter 17

The Instructor and the Mailman
My Precipitous Fall into Academia's Underbelly, and How David Stupple Helped Me Get Out

In 1969, after completing a bachelor of science degree in music, I was awarded a graduate fellowship and became a teaching assistant in the Department of English at Eastern Michigan University, leading to a master of arts in English. It was an exciting time for me: I'd fallen in love with English and American literature while an undergraduate, and decided that for many reasons I was much more suited for teaching writing at the college level than teaching music in the public schools.

My time as a teaching assistant was three parts exhilarating and one part exasperating. On the one hand, I had the supreme pleasure of imparting my passion for literature to row upon row of freshman composition students, while simultaneously helping them gain basic competence as nonfiction writers. On the other hand, I was forced by circumstances to deal on occasion with students who were anything but eager to learn, tenured faculty who had little respect for teaching assistants, and administrators often too busy with their own higher-academic escapades to come to the aid of a fledgeling teaching assistant in need.

In spite of the setbacks and disappointments that inevitably came with the assignment, I persevered, savored my many victories in the classroom, and, in June of 1971, earned a master of arts in English literature.

Then, that summer, the exhilaration I felt at having succeeded as a college-level writing instructor quickly turned into occupational uncertainty, late-night worrying, and outright panic. I'd been so deeply immersed in my graduate studies, my teaching, and my all-important role as a father—and so certain that I'd easily find a full-time teaching position in a community college—that I'd done little if anything to actively prepare for life after my master's degree.

I'd suddenly become unemployed, and after a frantic, month-long search for meaningful employment, I took a job as a university postal worker—sorting and delivering mail at the same school where I'd just finished earning my graduate degree. Right away, I realized I would be delivering mail to the very same people who, only a few weeks before, I considered to be my colleagues. For me it was a dramatic drop in status within the university's hierarchy, and learning how to cope with the loss of prestige proved to be one of the more daunting challenges of my young life.

Determined to turn what had become a difficult emotional situation into a personal triumph, I dug in to my new assignment with great energy and idealism—but the feeling that I'd failed miserably as a budding academic would not go away.

Then, while delivering mail to the Department of Sociology one morning, I met faculty member Dr. David Stupple. Compared to the academics I dealt with every day while working as a teaching assistant, he was exceptionally warm and unpretentious whenever we crossed paths. That he was busy conducting research while I was driving a mail truck made the idea of a friendship seem highly unlikely, but things are not always as they seem. Everyone knows that friendships often blossom from within the daily rough-and-tumble of the workplace, but the majority of them are destined to be short-lived. And yet there are rare moments when a superficial, on-the-run encounter becomes a long-lasting, transformative relationship. Such was the case with David Stupple and me, and it could not have occurred at a more critical moment in my life.

It was in 1969—the year Kurt Vonnegut published *Slaughterhouse Five* and Neil Armstrong walked on the moon—that I finished my undergraduate degree in music with a performance emphasis, along with a minor in English literature. My gradual shift toward the study of literature was in some ways the inevitable result of my disaffection with the Department of Music, coupled with my growing love affair with books and the prospect of living the writing life.

For now, though, my fondest dreams would have to be put on hold. As a married man and the proud father of a very young daughter, I needed to find employment, and fast. I knew it wouldn't be in music education, because I'd abandoned my earlier plan to seek certification as an instrumental music teacher. I was now faced with a serious occupational dilemma: what truly worthwhile position could I hope to find, with so little time to find it? A look at our meager savings account reminded me that time was of the essence. I couldn't afford to be picky.

My first instinct was to go to the university's placement center and talk with the eternally optimistic director, Theophilus Hamilton. Theo was clearly in love with his work. Finding employment for EMU students was nothing less than a sacred mission for him. Because of his unceasing commitment to helping students find meaningful employment, he was beloved across every sector of the campus community. He was making a difference in people's lives, and my life was next in line for his heartfelt ministrations.

"Why don't you go down the hall and have a look at the job board?" he said, flashing his characteristic light-up-the-room, let's-get-it-done smile. "I'm certain you'll find lots of job opportunities there—something to tide you over until you land a full-time position!"

Each available job was typed the old-fashioned way onto its own white 3 x 5 card—likely the work of an employee in the work-study program—then added to the neatly arranged rows of cards. The less than exciting jobs—lawn care worker and pizza delivery man—held no interest for me. *Why would I want to fall so low*, I thought, *after having attained my coveted status as an academic-in-training?*

Then, as I was on the verge of kissing the job board goodbye and stomping indignantly out of the placement center, one bright yellow card near the bottom caught my interest: "Graduate teaching fellowship in freshman composition. Starts in September 1969. Contact the chairman of the Department of English for application procedure."

I went from deeply depressed to over-the-top ecstatic in less than one quick twitch of a mad cat's tail. I chanted *This is crazy!* to myself while driving home, determined to convince my wife that two impoverished grad students and a hungry toddler really could get by on $2,700 a year for two years while I earned a notoriously unemployable master of arts in English. Two dark, tension-filled days later, the crazy had won out over the practical, and I submitted my application for the fellowship.

In less than a month I'd landed the position, and late in August I reported to work as a wet-behind-the-ears, wildly optimistic teacher of Freshman Comp 101.

It didn't take long for that optimism to erode. I needed only a few visits to the faculty lounge to learn that, to the tenured faculty, the teaching assistants were merely briefcase-toting pretenders—men and women barely older than their students, lacking a terminal degree and therefore unworthy of acknowledgement as bona fide members of the department.

One morning, feeling more upbeat than usual about my prospects, I approached a dapper looking, middle-aged professor, waited until he was done stirring his cup of morning coffee, and asked him how I might best prepare to be a full-blown college professor. "Oh, I wouldn't worry about that," he smirked. "You'll never be a college professor anyway." Stung by the man's high-minded impertinence, I licked my wounds and headed down to my office.

Clearly, the status of teaching assistants within the departmental hierarchy was abysmally low. To cope with our less than rewarding place in the pecking order, we immersed themselves deeply in our lesson plans, showed up on time and thoroughly prepared for every class, and took care to dress in ways that might help us be taken more seriously as instructors. Along the way, we suffered all manner of indignities at the hands of our students, our fellow TAs, and even our administrators—injustices that came to be seen as an inevitable part of being a teaching assistant.

Mind over Footwear

During the time I taught freshman composition at EMU, the Department of English made very little effort to monitor the appearance, textbooks, or classroom techniques of the teaching assistants under their jurisdiction. Not only was their easygoing, hands-off policy a sign of the decade we were living through, with a growing distaste for bureaucratic restrictions of any kind, it was also the result of what I came to see as departmental indifference to anything the teaching assistants did as long as it didn't interfere with the daily affairs of the department or besmirch the reputation of the intensely status-conscious professors.

It took the department chairman many weeks, for instance, to learn that one of the more free-spirited teaching assistants—a brash young Kansan we'll call Jeffrey—was teaching freshman comp without benefit of shoes and socks.

That Jeffrey preferred to teach while barefoot didn't bother me in the least. I was charmed by his intellectual integrity, his romantic ideas about the world—he was fond of calling the vast, windblown wheat fields of his childhood "the oceans of the Midwest"—and even his brazen indifference to the rules that govern common-sense hygiene in a civilized society. It was the contents of his head, not the appearance of his feet, that mattered most to Jeffrey, and that was enough to cause me to trust him unconditionally as a colleague.

When Jeffrey approached me one morning and asked to borrow one of my dozens of 45rpm rock singles for use in a classroom project, I didn't hesitate to comply with his request.

"Sure!" I said. "Tell you what: I'll lend you one of my favorites—Elvis Presley's 'Hound Dog.' It has 'Don't Be Cruel' on the flip side. It's the first record I ever bought. That should generate plenty of discussion!"

"Perfect!" he said. Then he tucked the record into his briefcase, shuffled down the hall sans shoes, and waved goodbye to me as he stepped onto the elevator. "I'll have it back to you a week from today," he said. "Promise!"

Just as I expected, he showed up promptly at 5:00 p.m. the following Friday and handed me the record neatly wrapped in the Arts and Leisure section of the *Detroit News*. "Thanks!" he said. "Gotta run!"

Back in my office, thankful to have my record back again and proud of my trusting ways and unfailing generosity, I pulled off the tape and carefully unfolded the newspaper. Out fell the record—or more accurately, one jagged portion of the record—onto my lap. The rest of what was left of it crashed down onto the floor, then wobbled into the gap between my desk and a file cabinet full of theme papers. So much for trusting a transplanted Kansan without shoes, common sense, or respect for other people's property.

The Teacher-Student Conference: Shining Moment for the Caring Academic

Like any normal teaching assistant, I was often hungry for assurances from both students and administrators that I was performing at an acceptable level in the classroom, but praise was seldom available when I needed it most. When I felt especially under-appreciated, I could always go out of my way to help struggling students with their deficiencies as writers, then bask in the sunshine of their deep appreciation for the extra help.

The majority of my encounters were polite and perfunctory—brief sessions in which the student needed an assignment clarified or a grammatical error explained. There were moments, though, when I needed to call a struggling student up to my desk and arrange for some badly needed one-on-one tutoring.

Ernestine was among the neediest. Her essays—appallingly incoherent and nearly entirely lacking in complete sentences—were riddled with enough grammatical, punctuational, and syntactical errors to stretch my supply of red pencils to the limit.

I arranged immediately to have Ernestine meet me in my office—really just one of several desks for teaching assistants, strung along a forgotten corridor of the Pray-Harrold building and far removed from the offices of the "real" instructors.

Our first meeting went well enough. Ernestine was a fragile, self-effacing young woman—like so many students at Eastern, a blue collar fish out of water and painfully uncertain of herself.

I took her through every sentence and paragraph of her essay and showed her how she might have constructed each more carefully and convincingly. She accepted my recommendations without argument, then thanked me profusely for taking the time to help her with her writing. "I'd like to come again," she said. "You were so helpful!"

I couldn't say no—it would have been an unforgivable lapse in academic integrity—so I smiled, thanked her for meeting with me, and scheduled another meeting for the middle of the next week.

It was even more successful than the first one. "I'm really impressed with your progress, Ernestine!" I said. "You've clearly earned a higher grade for this assignment. But if you run into trouble again, don't hesitate to make an appointment with me. And don't worry, we'll get you through this course and on to other, more exciting challenges."

Another week went by, and sure enough, Ernestine was having trouble with the assignment to write a persuasive essay and needed to see me again. "I've a faculty meeting tomorrow," I said, "so I can't see you then. Would Wednesday morning at 8:00 be all right?"

Her elation was palpable. "Oh, yes!" she chirped. "I don't know what I'd have done without your help! You've been *sooo* good to me!"

Oddly, when I stepped into my office on Wednesday morning, Ernestine was nowhere in sight. "Probably got stuck in traffic," I figured. "I'll just correct some papers until she arrives."

As I popped open my briefcase, I noticed a single sheet of notebook paper, neatly folded and sticking out from under the pencil holder. I settled into my chair and opened the letter.

October 17, 1969

Dear Mr. Bachelder,

If you don't stop meeting with my girlfriend, I'm going to come down to your office and beat the crap out of you! Understand?

Sincerely,

Alvin McKindling

PS: Have a nice day!

Ernestine continued faithfully to attend my lectures. She sat quietly in the back of the room for the rest of the semester, fooling nervously with her textbooks and working overtime to avoid eye contact with me. She always managed to turn in her assignments—slightly more well written than in the past but still badly in need of repair—but never asked to meet with me again.

I figured I was a writing instructor, not a Miss Lonelyhearts, so I gave her a D- for the course. Someone would have to deal with Alvin McKindling again—and soon—but it wasn't going to be me.

It's All in the Words

I didn't really expect teaching writing to freshmen would be easy, and soon my worst fears and insecurities were borne out. In one harrowing first-semester session, I dug myself deep into the academic Slough of Despond by mispronouncing one of those million-dollar words that every university writing instructor worth his or her salt is expected to know and understand.

"One can choose a wide array of strategies for breathing life into one's writing," I intoned to the rows of faces looking straight through me with glazed-over eyes. "Take, for instance, the literary device known as hyperbole." I pronounced it HI-per-bowl instead of hi-PER-bo-lee.

Next came an eerie silence punctured by a cacophony of knee-slapping *haw-haws*. I felt suddenly like some malodorous evolutionary misfit and wanted desperately to crawl out of the classroom and back to the swamp I came from.

Had it not been for the intercession of one lone sympathizer—John Mifsud, recently arrived on campus from the island of Malta—I might very well have bolted from the room, run crazily across campus to the dean of liberal arts, and submitted my resignation on the spot.

But this was the real world, and I had a class to teach. Once the laughter had begun to subside, Mifsud—a strapping young man with a warm smile and a prominent, Jay Leno jaw—stood up and began to speak, firmly and earnestly, to everyone in the room.

"You're not being fair!" he said, flashing an indignant glare from student to student. "Mr. Bachelder may have mispronounced a word—we all do that on occasion—but he's our instructor, and mispronunciations or not, the man really knows what he's doing. So we need to respect him!"

So eloquent was Mifsud's plea that the entire roomful of students sat up straight in their chairs, wiped the sneers off their faces, and became eager learners once again. A miracle had been performed, and a caring young man from a faraway land was the unlikely agent of my salvation as a budding academic.

Administrative Support: Safe Haven or Endangered Species?

I seldom had problems with discipline while working as a teaching assistant—after all, this was college, not junior high school—but a series of incidents occurred in one of my classes that caused me to wonder if I might be in imminent danger of losing control as a disciplinarian.

At the time, the Vietnam war was raging, the Black Power movement was in full swing, and youthful rebellion was widespread on the nation's college campuses. Two of my students—one black, one white—began carrying on a love affair while class was in session, holding hands, passing notes, and gazing starry-eyed at each other across the aisle, utterly indifferent to anyone else in the classroom, including me.

When I asked them one day to put an end to their displays of affection during class time, they refused outright, then began embedding childish diatribes into their required essays, accusing me of being incompetent and racist.

When I confronted them with the absurdity and impropriety of their behavior, they refused to stop, so I went straight to the chairman of the Department of English, told him I was going to remove them from my class, and asked for his support.

He refused, saying the offending students had a right to be in my class and express themselves as they saw fit—even in their essays—and that it was my responsibility to deal with the issue.

His refusal to step in and actively support me as a member in good standing, however fleetingly, of the Department of English was just one more piece of evidence that, in this department, teaching assistants were not really important, and therefore not worthy of support in issues of critical importance to the preservation of academic integrity. Like many college administrators during a time of political unrest, the chairman was running scared, and I was left to clean up the mess caused by his indifference to my dilemma.

Somehow, in spite of this and other inevitable setbacks, I managed to gain the trust of nearly all of my students, impress my academic advisors with the quality of my writing, and complete my master of arts degree in June of 1971.

All very nice, but now I had no place to teach, no extra money in the bank, a daughter to raise, and little hope of finding relevant employment by the fall. There was no choice in the matter: I'd have to go back to that job board and find tolerable work to tide us over and keep the familial ship afloat.

I called Theo, and a week later I'd landed a job in the mailroom at the same university where I'd just finished my graduate work. For me—an ambitious young professional with soaring dreams of academic tenure—it was a precipitous fall from grace. I'd gone from college writing instructor to campus mailman in less time than it took to put a stamp on an envelope and push it through the slot.

In the beginning, I was in anguish. How could this have happened to me, a dashing young post-graduate with briefcase, sport coat, stylish tie, and a fierce determination to be the best damn writing instructor a student could ever hope to have? The proud collegiate attire was quickly consigned to my closet, replaced by the required uniform for non-academic laborers, army green pants and matching shirt with EMU mailroom logo. To me, it was more like a clown costume than a uniform. To make things worse, our delivery van was identical in color. When we climbed into it, we were awash in an olive green sea and stripped of any appearance of individuality.

To counter the regimentation, I decided to grow a beard. I figured it would be a real dinger, too—long, red, and bushy enough to spill down onto my shirt and neatly camouflage the logo I so detested.

I was also certain that having a bearded mailman on campus would be a nice touch. After all, universities have always championed diversity, and individuality was a cherished ideal. My conviction was reinforced when my immediate supervisor, Malone Hall—a likable but diffident fellow, up only recently

The Instructor and the Mailman

from the hills of Kentucky—confessed that he liked my new foliage. "Y'all look like one o' them college perfessah types, now," he said, laughing. "You'll be a big man on campus!"

Things were going smoothly in the mailroom until Ed, the only African American on the mailroom staff, showed up one day wearing a shiny red-and-turquoise pendant on a gold chain. He looked smashing with that pendant displayed conspicuously beneath his chin, and when he donned his lemon-yellow sunglasses, he was strictly lady-killer material.

The pendant lasted less than a week. When an administrator with campus-wide jurisdiction over non-academic affairs stopped by the mailroom one morning and saw Ed's unorthodox neckwear, he flew into a rage. "That pendant you're wearing is inappropriate for any on-the-job university employee," he bellowed. "No jewelry allowed. Either *it* goes or *you* go!"

Ed needed his job as badly as I needed mine, so he didn't fight back. I tried on the spot to defend his right to wear the pendant—after all, the women on the mailroom staff were allowed to wear necklaces and earrings—but my argument fell on deaf ears. As for Malone, he really didn't care about the pendant. Nevertheless, in keeping with his easygoing, unassertive temperament, he chose to remain silent rather than rock the boat.

On the day Ed's pendant met its demise, the administrator was too frothed up to notice the beginnings of my beard. It was only a matter of time, though.

Sure enough, a few weeks later—after my beard had assumed Bunyanesque proportions—I encountered him in a corridor of the science building while delivering a case of test tubes to the chemistry department.

"Step over here, Mr. Bachelder!" he said, with beet-red face and ominous brow. He was at least six foot two and built like an NFL fullback. Without warning, he walked me to the nearest wall, pressed his chest against mine, and lowered the boom on me. "I want that beard off your face immediately! Go home right now and shave it off, then come back to work. I'll be checking on you to see to it that you've shaved. And incidentally, tuck your shirt in! We can't have sloppy-looking employees at our school."

I made a feeble attempt to defend my right to have a beard and wear my shirttail untucked—I genuinely thought it looked better outside my pants—but he'd have none of it. Then, suddenly, he decided to take a more convivial tack.

"Look, I've got a tip for you—a technique you can use to keep your shirttail tucked in at all times. I learned it in the Army, and it works like a charm!" By now he was acting more chummy than the head counselor in a church camp, and feeling mighty good about himself.

"What you *do*," he whispered conspiratorially, "is get yourself a large safety pin, then pin the shirttail between your legs before you put your pants on. You'll never again have to worry about looking sloppy at work!"

I did go home as ordered that afternoon and shave off my beard to keep my job. I also vowed to remember to tuck my shirt in each morning before reporting to work. But I nixed the safety-pin strategy. The fellow who ordered me to remove my whiskers might be a jerk, I reasoned, but he wasn't about to check to see if I'd done his bidding south of the equator. There had to be laws against that sort of thing, even when you're the proud possessor of administrative clout.

Dr. Stupple to the Rescue

Over the next few months, I went about my affairs with a grim determination to be the best damn university mailman in the business, hoping my daughter would someday be proud of me for my stoicism and the dignity with which I approached my labors. I sorted mail with astronomical speed and astounding precision. Twice a day, I lugged boxes full of textbooks and canvas bags full of letters up dozens of flights of stairs, never failing to be prompt, courteous, and accommodating. I'd become an olive-green, non-academic Santa, bearing gifts for the learned to every academic department on campus. And as an unexpected bonus, I lost thirty pounds in the process.

While barreling around campus in my mailroom van, I vacillated wildly between feelings of pride in a job well done and acute embarrassment at the downward turn my life had taken. One day I'd remember Emerson's admonition to know a man not by what he does but by who he is, then rejoice in my ability to see the dignity in all labor. The next day I'd come home at night with my tail between my legs—not my shirttail, I assure you—angry at the world for having orchestrated my tumble from the halls of academe to the bowels of servitude. I knew I'd taken the mailroom job to be a responsible husband and father, but no matter how idealistic were my motives, the bad taste in my mouth wouldn't go away.

Then, while delivering mail to the sociology department one morning, a ray of sunshine finally broke through my foul-weather, self-pitying mood.

The Instructor and the Mailman

The sociology department was seven stories up in the Pray-Harrold building. I had to wheel box after box of obscenely heavy textbooks ahead of me onto a crowded elevator, where I would then burrow my way into a tweed-and-polyester labyrinth of legs belonging to nattily dressed academics on the way to their lectures. My olive green uniform, along with the dolly I was pushing ahead of me, stacked with boxes of textbooks, branded me as one of the Untouchables. While I was reasonably sure I was there, I was for all intents and purposes the Invisible Man.

Once I'd wormed my way off the elevator, I headed toward the department to announce my arrival and ask where to leave the boxes. The secretary was nowhere to be seen, so I flagged down the only other person in the reception room—a sandy-haired, professorial looking man, probably in his late thirties, leaning against a chair and perusing page one of the *New York Times*.

"May I help you?" he said warmly. A professor of anything, willing to help a common laborer? It hadn't been my usual experience since becoming mailman to the stars.

"Yes! I was wondering where I should leave these textbooks. Can't just drop 'em off anywhere."

He tossed the newspaper down on a nearby couch and grabbed a box off the top of the dolly. "Come with me!" he said. "I can keep them in my office until the secretary comes back. I'll give her the bill of lading then."

I thanked him profusely for helping me with the boxes. "No big deal," he said. "Glad to help! Besides, I can use the exercise. By the way, I'm David Stupple, one of the teachers here." He smiled while giving me an industrial-strength handshake. "And you?"

I mumbled my name to him while shrinking down to nothingness inside my uniform. The gulf between his circumstances and mine was immense, and, today at least, I didn't know if I even wanted to try to cross it.

"I've been delivering mail to make ends meet after finishing my M.A.," I said. "I was a teaching assistant in the English department. I had to find employment right away—I've a two-year-old daughter to support."

"Aha! *That's* where I've seen you!" he said. "I have friends on the sixth floor, and when I went down to visit with them, I'd see you on occasion, heading down the hall with your briefcase. Thought you were a prof!"

By now my discomfort had morphed into outright distress. "Big drop in status," I said quietly, feeling more conspicuous than that odious insect in Kafka's *Metamorphosis*.

Fig. 77. My friend Dr. David Stupple, Eastern Michigan University sociologist.

"Not necessarily!" he said, smiling. "Not necessarily."

He went back to his newspaper, and when I was finished stacking the boxes I went on my way. I hadn't consciously intended to ask for the man's pity, and yet something inside me had undoubtedly been craving any evidence, however small, of understanding. I was at a low point in my self-esteem, hungering for any word or gesture that might offer reassurances that I hadn't failed after completing my fellowship. I didn't want to believe that this job and this uniform actually had the power to define me.

Over the next few weeks, while delivering mail to the sociology department, I'd see David on occasion, talking with colleagues or sitting quietly in the lounge. He never failed to acknowledge me, always saying, "Hello, Ross! How are things with you?"

I began to look forward to his stop on my route. Here, at least, was someone who genuinely respected me—who wasn't judging me on the basis of either my uniform or my occupation. Whenever he happened to see me, he'd invariably take a moment to engage me in conversation, asking me what I was reading and how my family was doing. He'd even talk at length about his work as teacher and researcher, making me feel almost like an equal.

Then, one day, he asked me if I'd like to come over to his house. I was thrilled, and I instantly accepted his invitation. "Next Thursday?" he said. "Bring your wife and daughter, and we'll have a meal together." I went to my next delivery humming to myself and savoring the cloudless blue sky and blazing sunlight. I'd not felt so good in weeks.

Our first visit to the Stupples' home was a revelation. To my great delight, I learned that as a sociologist he was interested in two very different subjects—the inner workings of flying saucer cults and the writings of advice columnist Ann Landers. Clearly, his quirky research interests fit like a glove with his own mild eccentricities.

To do his flying saucer research, he'd infiltrate various cults in the Upper Peninsula of Michigan, hundreds of miles north of Ypsilanti, pretend with remarkable success to be a believer, then leave the group and publish his analyses, which were written from a sociological perspective. His articles appeared in a small, influential magazine called *FATE* and in other topically relevant magazines.

I never learned why David was drawn to Ann Landers, a wildly popular advice columnist for nearly sixty years, as the subject of serious sociological research. I suspect it was not just Landers herself, but the people who depended so obsequiously on her advice that drove him to study the Ann Landers phenomenon.

One night, after we shared a meal with David and his family at their home, he asked me if I'd like to come down and see his basement.

David was what medical professionals at the time called physically exceptional, so I couldn't help wondering how easy it was going to be for him to make the descent with what were obviously severely impaired legs.

I learned later that while a teenager he'd suffered a debilitating, inexplicable illness. His parents, who were Christian Scientists, initially refused medical help because of their religion's belief that only prayer has the power to heal the sick. He eventually got the medical attention he needed, but not soon enough to help him.

Doctors were convinced that he'd contracted paralytic poliomyelitis, or polio—a mysterious disease that erupted in the early '50s, killed more than three thousand children in 1952 alone, and terrified the nation—so they put him in an iron lung for a year. He then developed what would prove to be a permanent walking disability, and while his illness was never diagnosed with certainty, doctors eventually decided that he may very well have been the victim of viral encephalitis.

Watching him walk around his home that day, I couldn't help feeling bad for him, but when he scrambled down the stairs to the basement with such remarkable speed and agility, I had to wonder just how much or how little he even thought about his disability. I eventually learned that he thought a great deal about it, but never in a self-pitying way. He was passionate about the idea that the public needed to be better educated about *exceptionality*—a word that meant a lot to him because it was, he thought, a badly needed antidote to the popular perception that people like him were cripples, unable to function successfully in normal society.

Differently abled was another frequently used term in the '70s, but I don't remember ever having heard David use that term in conversation. One thing is certain, though: he thoroughly disapproved of the term *disability*. I learned quickly never to use it while in his company.

Once down the stairs, he flipped on the basement light switch, and there in the center of the room, lit by a suspended pool table lamp, was a well-worn Ping-Pong table with paddles on either end, at the ready.

I scratched my head at the sight of that table. Given what seemed to me the obvious limitations in David's mobility, I wondered how could he could hope to play a credible game of Ping-Pong. I figured the table must be there for his children—something they could do with friends on occasion to burn off their youthful energy.

"Wanna play a game?" he said, employing his usual gentle, sandpapery voice. Because of his posture, his back was noticeably lower to the ground than mine as he scrambled around the far end of the table and picked up a paddle.

Why not? I figured. *It'll be good fun, and I'm pretty good at Ping-Pong.* I picked up my paddle and got into position, and before I even had time to think, the ball came crashing over the net, hot as a blowtorch and straight as a laser beam. It caught the far right corner of the table, near my right leg—a perfectly aimed volley.

"Well, that was a damn good shot!" I said, hoping it was a fluke and would be followed by something more normal—something I could actually handle.

It was no fluke. From that point on, every one of David's deliveries was like a bolt of lightning from an angry Zeus. I quickly realized I'd be helpless to compete in any meaningful way with his killer serve and upper-body adroitness. He beat me soundly, 21-3, in that very first contest.

The truth was that I was more exhausted than embarrassed. "Where's that bathroom, again?" I panted. "I need to take a break!" (Anything to get me away from the scene of the slaughter.) "Upstairs and to the left," he said, chuckling both to himself and to the victim of his full frontal assault. "I'll give you a couple of minutes to rest before the next set."

By now I figured that Dr. David Stupple, professor of sociology, flying saucer researcher, and Olympic-caliber paddle wizard, was quietly gloating down there in the basement. He had good reason, too. He'd just shown me by example what someone with alleged disabilities can actually accomplish. The man was a natural-born teacher, and I had a feeling I was going to learn a lot from him—and not just how to win at Ping-Pong.

While upstairs and heading down the hall to the bathroom, I noted that the Stupple household was not at all pretentious. In fact, it was rather average—a little frayed at the edges, with predictable '60s-era swivel chairs around the dining room table, Danish modern end tables, and off-white shag carpeting. *He keeps the wild side to himself,* I thought as I reached inside the bathroom door and flipped the light switch.

When the lights came on, I felt like I'd just been blinded by the passing of a meteor sent by otherworldly beings from one of Stupple's flying saucer cults. The entire bathroom was black-lit, pulsing with psychedelic posters, glow-in-the-dark accessories, and the eerie glow of a lava lamp. David Stupple: so full of surprises—so utterly unacademic!

Fig. 78. The Stupples—David, June, Kyle, and Kelly—Ypsilanti, Michigan (1975).

Over the next few months, David and I and our families became the best of friends. We nearly always got together at their home rather than ours, simply because it was more spacious and they were the ones with the Ping-Pong table. Kelly and Kyle, David's children, got along well with our daughter Amy, and they soon became inseparable playmates.

David's wife, June, and my wife, Marilyn, were the quieter members of the foursome, but no less assertive and opinionated than the two of us in matters political and intellectual. Because our views on a wide range of social issues were remarkably compatible, we had many lively after-dinner discussions. The Vietnam war was coming to a close, Detroit was still trying to recover from the devastating effects of the 1967 12th Street riot and a host of related social and economic ills, and the rights of blacks, women, and physically exceptional people were being hotly debated in intellectual circles, analyzed by behavioral scientists, and confronted aggressively on the streets in the form of sometimes violent demonstrations.

David proved to be an exceptionally empathetic listener. When we were alone, I began to talk with him in considerable detail about my often troubled childhood: about the tensions within the walls of our tiny, claustrophobic, post–World War II home; about my struggle to be taken seriously as a unique human being with a right to my own opinions; and about my inability to penetrate the layers of emotional armor around my symbiotically connected parents. Together they were a fierce, impenetrable fortress, and as children my brother and I were seldom if ever allowed to scale its walls and learn what was inside that the two of us might actually share with them on an equal basis.

In the course of our frequent one-on-one conversations, David taught me many things that helped me feel better about myself. Emotionally, I was still very much a work in progress, and in his wise, unpretentious way he went quietly about repairing the damage to my self-esteem, lesson by lesson.

The first lesson—never to work from false assumptions—came over the flat, green expanse of David's Ping-Pong table. In the beginning, I'd arrogantly presumed that, given the condition of his legs, David would never be able to play Ping-Pong with any authority. But after many months of being soundly and repeatedly whipped by the master, I finally came to understand that for David, the possibilities of living were limitless.

The second lesson—more nuanced and harder to learn—manifested itself in his uncanny ability to listen, fully and compassionately, to what I was telling him about myself. David had come into my life at an especially vulnerable time for me, and he quickly revealed himself as the skilled, caring listener I so badly needed. His unbridled empathy—an open-door policy he maintained for friends and students alike—was one of his greatest gifts to me and, I'm certain, countless others in his life.

The third lesson—just as powerful and life-changing as the others—had to do with his rare ability as an academic to live and work outside the suffocating walls of ivory tower superiority that imprison so many socially ambitious college instructors. Stupple was not a social climber; Vance Packard, author of the groundbreaking 1959 book on social stratification, *The Status Seekers*, would have been proud of him. The academic hierarchy might have been an unavoidable reality for him as a professor, but he never allowed it to restrict him—not in his intellectual endeavors, not in his personal relationships, and not in his inimitable ways of looking at the world.

This meant that David was that rarest of breeds on campus—a man as open as a flower to the personal qualities and intellectual gifts of everyone around him, regardless of each person's place in the human pecking order. The characteristic humility with which he dispensed his wisdom—accompanied by his twinkling eyes and an asymmetrical smile—made him seem almost Buddha-like on occasion.

The astonishing thing about David was that, unlike the pompous administrator who had a violent aversion to pendants and whiskers, and unlike the peacock professor who so arrogantly pronounced me unfit to be a true academic, David saw straight through my mailroom shirt and deep into the heart of me. To him I was an intellectual equal, and I couldn't recall having gotten a greater gift than that from anyone I'd known.

Examples of his egalitarian way of thinking would show up in surprising ways. When he discovered one day that I was a prolific and competent writer—I'd shown him many of my writing samples—he didn't hesitate to make me an offer: "I've a proposal," he said. "Would you be interested in helping me edit my research articles before I submit them for publication?"

The thought that Dr. David Stupple, a well-published, highly respected academic, would ask me to help him prepare his work for submission to publishing houses astounded and then thrilled me. To him I wasn't just a lugger of boxes and sorter of mail. In spite of having lost my status as a member of the academic community, I was no less a thinker and an idealist than he was. Like Emerson and his fellow New England Transcendentalists, David saw no reason why working with one's hands should be incompatible with a life of the mind. As much as Emerson—and perhaps even more—David Stupple was my kind of man.

Our friendship had shored up the greater portion of my sagging self-esteem, and because of it I felt deeply indebted to him. But I was still a young man, just out of grad school and in search of occupational fulfillment. No matter how much I tried to idealize my work as mailroom clerk, I knew it was only temporary. It wasn't where I belonged.

Something would have to change. At home, my wife and I put our heads together and made a pact: whichever one of us found a professional position with a livable wage first, the other would follow unconditionally, without complaint. There was no time to waste, and we got to work right away.

I labored mightily to find employment as a community college writing instructor, sending out hundreds of letters of inquiry that landed me interviews at a half dozen colleges in the Southeast. At the same time, Marilyn, who had just finished a master of arts in music theory and literature, began looking aggressively for work as an instrumental music teacher. To help her with her search, I composed, typed, and sent out hundreds of her letters of inquiry in addition to my own.

She got there first. After driving alone for two weeks across the eastern U.S. to interview with the superintendents of eight school systems from New York State to northern New England, she finally landed a position in the tiny, southern Maine town of Berwick. Our dream of a new and exciting adventure had become a reality, and within the month we began planning and packing for the journey.

Not surprisingly, the prospect of leaving the Midwest wasn't all sunshine and roses. It would soon be time to break the news to David and June that we'd found a chance for another, more productive life in northern New England.

It happened on our very next get-together. "I've something difficult to tell you," I said after yet another epic, gladiatorial contest of Ping-Pong—a game in which David soundly trashed me for what seemed like the three-hundredth time.

"All right," he said. "But it can't be as bad as what I heard at the faculty meeting last night. Seems like we've got budget problems. They're talking staff reductions again."

"Maybe worse!" I said. "Marilyn has finally found a job. We're moving to Maine in just a few weeks."

David paused, his back toward me as he hung the paddles up on the pegboard near the table, ready for his next inevitable conquest.

"Ah, yes!" He said quietly. "The land of the cultural overlay!"

I didn't fully understand—something about the migration of modern-day Midwesterners to old New England, he said, followed by their slow but inevitable assimilation into the centuries-old local culture. The scholarly David was always just beneath the surface of his more playful self, waiting to be engaged.

"This wasn't an easy decision!" I told him almost pleadingly. "I couldn't go on being a postal worker, and Marilyn needed to find her footing as an educator."

"I understand!" he said gently. "We had to make the same sort of decision when we moved from Missouri to Michigan. But sometimes the hardest decisions prove to be the wisest. I'm sure you'll do fine up in Maine."

We spent the better part of a month packing our belongings, then arranged for one last get-together with the Stupples. This time, instead of having dinner in their home, we picnicked on the living room floor of our empty apartment. It was a sad, emotionally awkward afternoon. The children played with each oth-

The Instructor and the Mailman

er in a distant corner of the apartment while we made small talk together, pretending we weren't about to say goodbye to what had become an enormously rewarding friendship.

A week later we were in New England, cheering wildly as we drove over the Piscataqua River bridge between Portsmouth, New Hampshire, and Kittery, Maine. With our rented U-Haul crammed to the ceiling with everything from bedsprings to bicycles, we worked our way twenty additional miles to the village of Berwick.

Two weeks after our arrival, Marilyn began the first of what would prove to be thirty-eight years as a gifted, highly motivated, and universally loved music educator. I stayed home with Amy, got her enrolled in kindergarten in the same school system, then began seeking freelance assignments as a writer and musician.

In the excitement that inevitably comes with moving to a new and unfamiliar place, my memories of David had begun to recede. Then, sometime in October, when the leaves had just begun to reveal their spectacular fall colors, the reality of what I'd left behind—a fine young friendship with an extraordinary man—finally set in.

Awake at night in our sparsely appointed apartment, blanketed against the invigorating chill of a New England autumn, I realized I missed the Stupples—and especially David—more than I ever could have imagined. In the name of financial stability and self-renewal, I'd forfeited our hard-won camaraderie, and now, far away from him in New England, I felt as if I'd committed an inexcusable act of betrayal.

By midwinter, feeling increasingly guilty for having left David behind, I sat down and wrote my first letter to him, lamenting that I'd not seen him for many months. Then, with what I hoped were carefully chosen words, I gently chastised him for expressing little interest in coming to Maine. He wrote back soon afterward, reminding me of what I ought to have known unequivocally—he had professional obligations as a university professor, and because of his limited mobility, travel wasn't always easy for him.

It was a foolish accusation, born of what were then my own persistent insecurities, and I was immediately ashamed for having made it. Not surprisingly, our correspondence came to an abrupt halt, and I had only myself to blame for it.

Many months later, a letter arrived in our mailbox, not from David but from his wife, June. *How good of her to write to us!* I thought. *David must be too busy at school to stop and write.*

I eagerly tore open the letter, and in the very first sentence learned what no friend wants to hear: David had been hospitalized for surgery to remove a tumor on his back, but had contracted pneumonia and died unexpectedly in the hospital on the very weekend of his admittance.

In the letter, June was very matter-of-fact about the situation. "Would you like to claim his research papers," she wrote, "then compile and edit them for possible publication? I think he would have liked that."

If I'd been less preoccupied with my own affairs—more mature, more compassionate, and more certain of my abilities—I would undoubtedly have jumped at the chance to edit those papers. But I didn't, and now, nearly four decades after his passing, I continue to harbor equal amounts of guilt and regret for having failed to take on the project. I'd let David down yet again, and I doubt I'll ever completely forgive myself for my behavior.

Many years later, while visiting relatives in Michigan, I looked up June's new street address in Ypsilanti, then knocked on her door, hoping to stand before her and apologize for my transgressions. Unfortunately, she wasn't home. Once back in Maine, I wrote a note explaining that I'd tried to visit her, but I never heard from her again.

What was it about David Stupple that influenced me in such a lasting way? It was not one thing, but many. The best things in life are never simple either in their appearance or in the depth and breadth of their influence. His gentle demeanor; the deceptively casual way in which he interacted with others, taking a genuine interest in their lives; his complete lack of interest in social status and material things; and the wise, unpretentious way he shared his observations of the world—all were woven unselfconsciously into the fabric of the man, and a beautiful fabric it was.

More than once, when he heard me saying things about myself that laid bare the insecurities that plagued me, David would smile in his distinctive way, then offer up some sage advice from his treasure chest of Truths Only David Knows. It was pretty much the same familiar litany each time, delivered with a certain musical lilt that reached inevitably into the heart of me, and I never really tired of hearing it.

"Ross!" he'd say to me right after whipping me at yet another hour-long Ping-Pong extravaganza, "There's no need for you to be so hard on yourself! I want you to get up every morning, stand in front of your mirror, and say to yourself, 'I am beautiful! I am somebody! And I'm making a lasting difference in the world!'"

I could have said it over and over to him, too, but David didn't really need his own advice. He was already somebody, he was already a beautiful human being, and he'd already made a lasting difference in the lives of countless people, including me, just by being David.

I've come to believe that the best teachers, whether in or out of the classroom, never really stop teaching. They just teach by example, and their own hard-earned lessons, in partnership with their fundamental decency, are tailor-made to last a lifetime. David Stupple was a teacher's teacher, and even after all these years, his influence has continued to make all the difference in my life.

Chapter 18

Other People's Art
My Years as a Picture Framer

From September of 1995 until December of 2013, I made the greater portion of my living as a picture framer at Ben Franklin Crafts, first in Somersworth, New Hampshire, then in nearby Rochester, the city the store moved to in August 2007. A dozen of those years were spent as manager of the frame shop and Franklin Gallery. Framing was for me a challenging and rewarding occupation, a superb complement to my freelance work in the fine and performing arts.

Years ago, when I'd only just begun to taste the fruits of the framer's life, a friend and fellow framer from another shop said, "Once you become a framer, it'll get into your blood. You'll keep your job for life!" As it turned out, my friend was right about the blood, but wrong about the longevity. Though I loved nearly everything about my work as a framer, I never really planned to keep the job for life. Nevertheless, I consider myself remarkably fortunate to have found such relevant employment at a critical time in my creative life—work that was for every one of those more than eighteen years woven inextricably into my life as an arts multiple.

It was the summer of 1995. I'd just finished three months as actor, publicist, and set-builder at Hackmatack Playhouse in Berwick, Maine. While the work was immensely rewarding—surely one of the finest multidisciplinary assignments I'd ever had—I knew that since Hackmatack is strictly a summer theater, I'd be out of a job the moment the curtain went down on the final show of the season. To compound my troubles, my mother had finally lost her eight-year battle with cancer. I flew home twice that summer to deal with the crisis, then came back to Berwick in time to finish my work at the theater—including a cameo role as Mr. Beckman in the musical *Gypsy*—while simultaneously looking for a job to replace my work at Hackmatack. The inquiries I'd made early in 1995 had yielded only a handful of responses, so occupationally, things were not encouraging.

Then, only a day or two after I'd walked off the set of *Gypsy* and turned in my costume, I got a call from Dwight Ciccotelli, the owner of Ben Franklin Crafts in nearby Somersworth, New Hampshire. Apparently, he'd finally had a look at the résumé I'd sent him more than six months before in response to a help-wanted advertisement in the local newspaper.

"I've got your résumé here on my desk," he said with his distinctive *basso profundo*, jackhammer voice. "We need to hire a framer. Come on down and we'll talk about the work."

The interview lasted twenty minutes. "Sounds like you could be good with color and design and stuff," he said, "and with people, too. But there are a lot of other things to learn in the shop besides sales and design. You'll need training." He paused, then made an offer. "I can start you off at minimum wage—$5.50 an hour—and if you do okay, you'll get a raise."

Minimum wage? For a man of fifty-two, who'd taught public school music and college writing, it felt a little like a lethal dose of humiliation—but not for long.

I quickly shrugged off the idea that I was somehow being wronged. Who was I to think I could take a job doing something I'd never done before, then expect to be high on the pay scale at the outset, just because I was older? Besides, I reasoned, I'd just been offered a rare opportunity to train in a line of work not all that far removed from my work a few years before as set designer with my own theater company. And it would get me a step closer to the visual arts, to which I'd had a decades-long, armchair attraction. I'd wanted for years to do more than just read about art and artists, and here was my chance to test the waters.

I took the job, and on my very first day, the frame shop manager—a cranky, dyspeptic young man—greeted me not with a smile, and not with a warm ritual welcome, but with a peevish, openly hostile observation. "My God," he said, "you're old enough to be my *father!*"

I needed only a handful of days to discover that I was clearly going to be the odd man out in the deeply entrenched, male-bonding chemistry of the frame shop. It wasn't just the disparity in our ages that contributed to the subtle but ever-present gulf in our relationship. I was repeatedly accused, either by supercilious intimidation or verbal swipes, of talking too much, wasting time, and having too much fun with my customers. I began to sense that both the store's owner and my grudging colleagues in the frame shop saw me as little more than an avuncular, smiley-faced oldster, on the verge of retirement and in need of something to do to while frittering away what little time he had left to him on the planet.

For the first few months I struggled mightily with the fundamental tasks of a framer busy framing. For me, a man accustomed to a very different kind of thinking—spontaneous, playful, imaginative, empirical—the sudden, everyday need to measure precisely, understand spatial relationships, and master the settings for mat cutters and underpinners proved to be a formidable challenge.

I've no doubt that my obvious discomfort with those tasks, in combination with my propensity to actually enjoy my time with my customers, made me seem like a questionable hire for a team of framers for whom technical proficiency was vastly more important than the one concern of greatest importance to me—warm, friendly, caring service.

I finally got enough control over the technical demands of framing to relax, settle into the everyday requirements of my job, and contribute with qualified success to the constant flow of projects. Still, the chilly atmosphere within the shop often made me want to walk out the door and never come back again.

I actually left the place twice and worked briefly at two other frame shops, but neither place could offer me the job security I needed. And so, even though working at Ben Franklin Crafts had begun to feel remarkably like a fraternity hazing, I swallowed my pride and returned to the frame shop both times. Dwight, aware that I'd begun to build a formidable stable of satisfied clients at his store, was glad to have me back. It also helped that I'd fallen in love with both the designing of projects and the satisfaction that comes with giving customers considerably more than what was merely required of me as an employee.

I soon adopted that above-and-beyond philosophy in my relationship with every employee and every department of the store, working from an assumption that, no matter what our occupational specialties, we were after all a family and needed to support and encourage each other in the workplace.

There was, however, still one area in which I had a lot of growing to do. I'd yet to be sufficiently baptized in the art of defusing a customer's anger. When things got difficult with customers—and it happened with alarming regularity in the early years—I would occasionally lose my temper. Dwight and his wife, Jean, assured me that I wasn't alone in my disenchantment with rude and bellicose customers.

One morning, Jean took me aside after I'd suffered a particularly nasty encounter—a moment in which a notoriously difficult customer had just admonished me in front of a half dozen other customers to "shut up and get me what I want!" To her everlasting credit, Jean extended her sympathies, then imparted to me one precious nugget of the wisdom she'd acquired from years of battle in the world of retail.

"People like that make it their profession to go from store to store, being obnoxious and unreasonable," she said. "Don't you worry! Whenever there's a conflict, we'll back you 100 percent." I realized then that Jean and her husband trusted me to make the right calls, and I calmed down and learned to control my temper when provoked into anger. I'd finally learned how to handle a difficult customer well enough to become known not as Mr. Explosion but as that nice older man in the frame shop who seems to know what he's doing.

But it wasn't enough. The more I observed about the areas of dysfunction within the shop, the more I began to form a vision of the many ways the shop could be made to work more successfully. In general, it was wildly disorganized and poorly maintained. Worse, the atmosphere, both within the shop and at the service counter, was anything but warm and welcoming.

I finally had to admit to myself that my own growing disenchantment was contributing to the chilly atmosphere of the shop. The downturn in my mood had begun to seep into the workplace and affect the mood of my fellow employees, and to me—a man long committed to the ideal of being a force for good in the workplace—such a state of affairs was unacceptable. I knew I had to do something about it, and fast.

The answer to my disenchantment, both with the tone of the shop and myself, came to me one day just three years after I'd begun framing. I looked at an unsightly, underutilized short wall to the left of the service counter and thought, *I could create a gallery there!*

I went straight to Dwight that afternoon and pitched my idea, and he was receptive. Five minutes later, I left his office with a mutually agreed-upon plan: we'd ask for a 20 percent commission from the sale of artworks, with half going to me as the gallery manager and half going to him for offering me the rent-free space in which to establish a gallery. I was certain the project would boost my morale. I also knew it would be good for area artists, good for the store (which, like any enterprise, welcomed favorable, cost-free publicity), and good for the city of Somersworth.

Humble as it was, the Franklin Gallery was an immediate hit, and my feelings about working at Ben Franklin Crafts improved dramatically. But the reality that I now had a pet project to nurture still wasn't enough for me. To grow as a framer and make a really meaningful contribution to the enterprise, I needed not only to learn how to put up with the

Fig. 79. The frame shop and Franklin Gallery at Ben Franklin Crafts, featuring works by artist Judith Heller Cassell of Rochester, New Hampshire (October, 2011).

workplace negatives, but to identify my own negative behaviors and work to eliminate them.

To that end, I plunged headlong into both the development of the gallery and the rehabilitation of my less than appealing disposition as an employee. I finally became more agreeable with everyone around me, including my customers, and over time, the financial and marketing value of my hyper-attentive, chatterbox relationship with them began to prove itself to the owners, if not always to my fellow framers.

Whenever my customers came by, I'd make it a point to ask them how they were doing, then talk with them about their interests and aspirations. If they happened to have lost a favorite relative or pet and were there to frame a cherished photograph or memento, I'd always express my sympathies, then give them a substantial discount on the cost of the project. It was the best possible kind of goodwill advertising, and because of it they returned again and again to the frame shop.

Because I worked so hard to take care of my customers—an entirely unscripted approach that came naturally to me—a growing number of them began to call and ask when I was scheduled to work. As a result, an undercurrent of resentment began to seep quietly into the frame shop.

In the beginning, I found myself apologizing in subtle ways for my popularity. Then one day I decided that, rather than feel guilty about my success with customers, I ought not only to take pride in it, but to see it as an opportunity to demonstrate to others—by example—what works and doesn't work when serving the public. One ought never feel embarrassed about being genuinely good at something. Competence in any endeavor doesn't come easily—it's earned, and it deserves to be admired and emulated.

It didn't take long for me to learn that, when people are shopping for goods or services of any kind, they're really shopping for much, much more than that. No matter what our age or circumstances, we never really grow out of our childhood yearning for praise and approbation. When all is said and done, shoppers are really just people of every imaginable background and circumstance who happen to be shopping and need competent, caring assistance. Their hunger for warm human interaction and the approval of strangers doesn't evaporate the moment they enter a store.

As things began to come together for me in every phase of my work, I came to realize that, in spite of the inevitable frictions that play themselves out in the workplace, the work of a framer was a finer occupational fit for me than many things I'd done before—better in some respects than teaching writing in three colleges; better than my many years of undependable work in professional theater as actor, musician, director, playwright, and publicist; and better for me than pretty much anything you could have suggested to a man in need of reliable employment and yearning for fulfillment.

When the current manager decided one day that he'd had enough of managing and wanted to focus entirely on design and production, I was chosen to replace him as manager. It was an enormous boost to my self-esteem in the workplace, and the fact that I was happy again at work—that I was clearly having a good time with my customers—was written all over my face. If money were my greatest concern when finding employment, framing would have been near the bottom of the list of potential occupations. But satisfaction—not money or status—has always been my most important requirement when looking for meaningful work.

Ironically, what I consider to have been my greatest accomplishment as a BFC employee really had nothing to do with the world of framing.

Only a few weeks into my tenure at the frame shop, I discovered that Dwight and Jean, the people who wrote my check each week, lived on an entirely different ideological planet. They and a handful of other BFC employees began to reveal themselves as ardent and unabashed disciples of Rush Limbaugh. Even the rabid, high-decibel fulminations of Michael Savage—the Prince of Darkness of conservative talk radio—didn't seem too diabolical to fit within their brash, take-no-prisoners approach to politics.

I'd joined the frame shop as a dyed-in-the-wool political progressive—a true child of the '60s who'd voted for George McGovern and supported Jesse Jackson in his failed bid for the presidency. I thought Bill Clinton was the best thing to happen to America since Elvis and ice cream. And then, when Barack Obama was elected President, I was beside myself with glee because of pretty much everything he stood for. Finally, this country had shown the world that it could actually learn to be color blind in its quest for a more than capable, genuinely inspiring leader and problem-solver.

No matter what Dwight and Jean and their like-minded colleagues had to say about Obama and his fellow political progressives—and some of it would never have made it past the censors, even at Fox News—I didn't allow their opinions to interfere with what I considered the most important characteristics of a successful workplace: civility, cooperation, and mutual respect.

It was Thomas Jefferson who in the embryonic years of our Democracy said, "I never considered a difference of opinion in politics, in religion, [or] in philosophy, as cause for withdrawing from a friend." I've always been determined to live that belief to the fullest, and at Ben Franklin Crafts the veracity of my political convictions was tested as never before. In spite of our profound political differences, I worked hard to build a bridge of tolerance over the vast philosophical gulf between us—a way of thinking and behaving that, instead of exploiting our differences for personal gain and self-aggrandizement, capitalized on our shared values for the good of all. As I saw it, by concentrating on the things that really mattered in the workplace, we were far more likely to succeed as a business endeavor without squandering the always precious opportunity to build lasting friendships.

There were many reasons why picture framing became such an ideal late-in-life, arts-oriented occupation for me, but some deserve special attention.

To begin with, my time at the service counter was always a chance for me to connect with, listen to, and learn from nearly every person I met. It was also a remarkably effective place for networking in the arts. My antennae were always up for opportunities either to collaborate or to initiate projects of my own. I learned through constant vigilance to take advantage of the steady flow of those opportunities—everything from solo exhibits and group shows to freelance graphic design work and gigs as musician and public speaker. Altogether, these extra-curricular endeavors significantly increased my monthly income.

The service counter also proved over time to be a powerful secular humanist pulpit for me—an evangelical forum from which I could dispense advice, offer encouragement, experience the joy of shared passions, and express my sympathy for people who for various reasons were down on their luck and wanted to talk about it with someone. It wasn't about wanting to change people; it was rather about being as aware as possible of the needs, interests, and passions of anyone who crossed my path in the workplace.

One of the less obvious benefits of being a picture framer was the chance to watch an astonishingly wide variety of artworks come across the service counter each day—works ranging from the highly sophisticated to the truly incompetent. Artists who've received formal training or who work in a college setting tend to see only a steady stream of technically proficient, academically informed works, but as a framer I got a wildly fluctuating dose of the full painterly monty each and every day at work, and I'm happy to confess that I reveled in it.

What was I as a framer to think of the artworks I saw in the course of a typical day's labor, some exhilarating and sublime, others bordering on visual atrocity? I realized early on that I had a choice as a public servant: I could either puff up my chest and pray for the souls of anyone less trained and less informed than me, or choose instead to celebrate the indisputable fact that these men and women were using whatever spare time they could find in their overworked lives to express their very own idea of beauty, no matter how much that idea conflicted with mine.

There will always be artists who are certain their works are superior to the works of others. I cannot in good conscience exempt myself from membership in that group. Our human tendency to rank ourselves in relation to others is inescapable. The important thing is to remember just how subjective the idea of excellence in the fine and performing arts really is, then proceed with caution when making any claims of the superiority of your work. With close observation, a firm commitment to objectivity, and a healthy dose of humility,

I always managed to find something beautiful in everything that came across my counter, no matter how naive or ill-conceived it might be.

To my delight, I discovered right away that there was also a built-in educational component in my work as framer. A long-established truism holds that, once you've been a teacher, you'll always be a teacher. Having taught both music and writing in a wide variety of situations for many years, it was inevitable that I'd find pleasure in sharing my creative strategies and insights with frame shop customers and, along the way, empowering them to make informed judgments, no matter where they chose to do business.

People who came to ask for help with the framing of their artworks didn't want passivity or indifference. They wanted informed, enthusiastic opinions—multiple approaches that would finally help them decide just what they wanted their artwork to look like once it was out of the shop and into their home. The interactive approach to designing fostered a sense of ownership in my customers, increasing the likelihood that they'd go away feeling proud of their contribution to the design. And once they learned that I was there not to convert them to my way of thinking but to advise them, they were far more likely to return as customers.

Once I became manager, it became clear to me that my responsibility was no longer merely about technical competence and customer satisfaction. It was also about profit and how to increase it without compromising either my personal integrity or the reputation of the frame shop. I'd always worked hard to draw in more customers—for me it was a matter of pride in workmanship, managerial success, and job security for everyone in the shop—but I also knew it wasn't enough just to make each customer happy, one by one. I needed to study the numbers carefully each week, then find ways, often in the midst of a severe economic downturn, to increase profits. It is one of a manager's most important hats, and I had to learn to wear mine with pride and as much competence as I could muster.

Every few months, some well-meaning customer would look me in the eye and say, "You seem like a pretty smart guy. Why on earth are you working in retail?" My response to those well-intended critiques soon became a mantra: "You know, I've done a great many things in my life to make money, including teaching writing in three colleges, managing two professional theaters, and founding one of my own, but the truth is that my work as a framer is the best damn job I've ever had!"

And then, if the moment was right, I'd deliver a homily of sorts, having to do with the public's ignorance of—and the arts community's occasional contempt for—the world of retail.

"Creativity is not the exclusive province of the artist, writer, or musician," I'd say to anyone who'd listen. "It can happen anywhere—in science, medicine, academia, city planning, infrastructure design and maintenance, and yes, even in the world of business. And within any human endeavor, sound management is also a form of creativity—no less impressive, when done exceptionally well, than anything one can find in an art gallery, concert hall, or theater."

Then I'd zero in on the importance of managerial competence within the retail establishment: "A genuinely creative manager—one who solves problems, increases profits, and treats his employees at every turn with dignity, respect, and a sense of fair play—is at the heart of any successful business enterprise," I'd say. "Conversely, business failure is the inevitable result of managerial incompetence, and it can nearly always be traced to a lack of creativity."

My hope was that, after hearing my well-intended sermonette, my customers would begin not only to have more respect for the business world, but to appreciate how remarkably varied are the modes of creativity everywhere in civilized society. People in retail—the men and women who sell you essential goods and services every day—are often highly skilled in their particular disciplines and take great pride in their expertise. They're not the one-dimensional, underachieving, insignificant clerks and functionaries that the economists and the popular media have painted them to be.

After serving visual artists and lovers of art as a framer for nearly nineteen years—and after mounting nearly two hundred exhibits as manager of the Franklin Gallery I'd founded and nurtured—I yearned to spend the rest of my life concentrating more intensely on my own creative work. The time to move on had come.

It wasn't altogether easy to say goodbye. One by one, I announced my intentions to the longtime frame shop customers who'd come to mean so much to me. I knew I'd miss the vast majority of the people whose artworks I helped frame, whether they were regulars or one-timers. Many of them had become valued friends and collaborators, so my work as a framer has continued to spread its concentric circles of pleasure into other areas of my creative life.

Just six months after I left my job as frame shop and gallery manager—and after a severe nationwide downturn in the economy—Ben Franklin Crafts threw in the towel, liquidated its assets, and after twenty-seven years of service closed its doors forever. The energy and idealism I'd brought to my job as framer was now diverted to my work as writer, visual artist, public speaker, musician, and fine and performing arts advocate.

People don't expect retail employees to care deeply about their work—to have within themselves the same supreme idealism that motivates doctors and educators, scientists and clerics—but a great many retail employees do care. I never really thought of myself as a retail employee while working as a framer. I was a craftsman, passionate about my work and driven to excel. And like every other man or woman who's created beautiful things for a living, I asked only for basic respect and some quiet evidence of appreciation for the quality of my work and the idealism that I brought to it day after day.

When we care enough to invest emotionally in the people we serve in any occupation, a connection is achieved and a bond is formed. Once I'd finished my work as a framer, I took a deep breath and looked back on the depth of my caring for so many frame shop customers from every walk of life and realized they'd collectively made an enormous contribution to the quality of my life.

For me, at least, they were family. Their loyalty to me, along with their obvious trust in my design abilities, helped reinforce my sense of worth as a creative. Just as importantly, they'd contributed significantly to my vision as an artist simply by sharing themselves with me so generously in the course of our design sessions. They also increased my fundamental respect for all well-intentioned attempts at creativity, no matter how humble the results.

Other than being with treated with dignity, then paid what one is actually worth—circumstances in the world of retail more rare than a one-legged dog or a straight-talking politician—what more can any employee ask for beyond professional fulfillment and pride in a job well done?

I found creative fulfillment as a framer—the perfect complement to my work as writer, artist, and musician—and along the way, my work with my customers and with artworks of every imaginable kind and quality enriched my life immeasurably.

Other People's Art

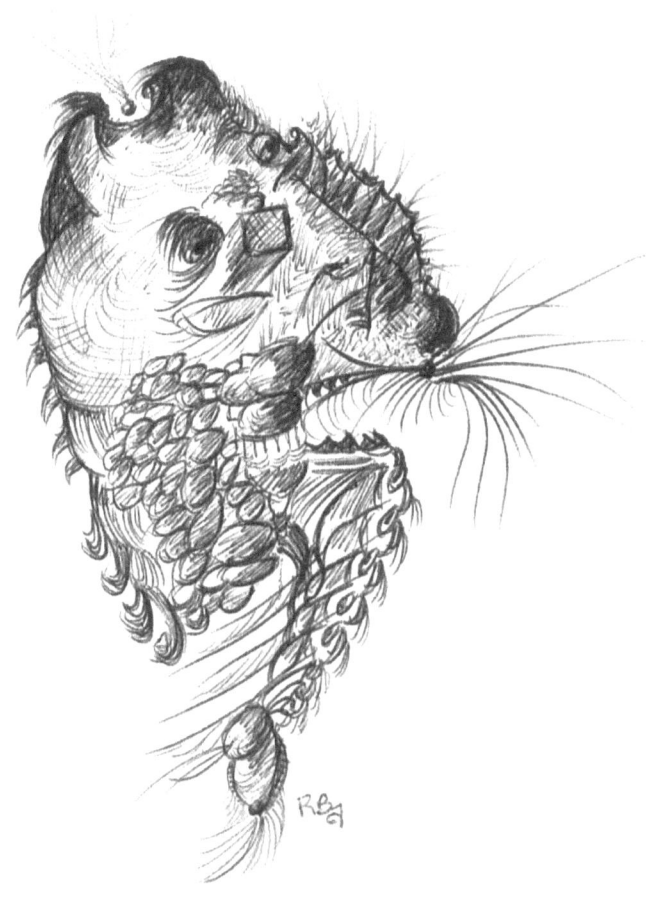

Fig. 80. *Reginald Ruffington's New Look* by Ross Bachelder.

❄ Tiny Novelette 9 ❄

Reginald Ruffington's New Look

The teachers at Smugbridge Arms Preparatory School, nestled in the rolling, patchwork hills of Chesterfield-on-Thames, England, noticed very early on that Reginald Ruffington III wasn't quite like the other boys in his class.

While his classmates were outside on recess, either smashing heads in rugby matches or making fun of anyone who appeared to be less athletic than they were, Master Ruffington—a remarkably erudite twelve-year-old—preferred to stay inside and read books like Milton's *Paradise Lost*, Boccaccio's *The Decameron*, and Dostoevsky's *Crime and Punishment*, then dangle the participles and mangle the modifiers, just for sport.

While Ruffington was proud of his intellectual abilities, he was also painfully aware of his delicate features, wan complexion, and wispy physique. And because he'd been roughed up repeatedly by the worst of his classmates, he seldom if ever ventured onto the playground.

One boy in particular—Wadleigh Peebles, the spoiled son of Scottish millionaire industrialist Gofton Marcellus Peebles—was the very prototype of the schoolyard bully. And at five feet eleven inches and more than two hundred pounds, he never needed to worry about coming out on the short end of a playground scuffle.

Clearly, Peebles and his classmates had pegged Ruffington as a sissy—too timid to come outside and face his tormenters like a man—but Ruffington figured the advent of puberty would soon take care of that problem. Any day now, he expected to wake up not as some pint-size British dandy, but as a full-blown, strapping adolescent with massive, rippling biceps and a chest like a beer barrel. Then, on the very next recess, he'd sneak up on Wadleigh Peebles, spin him around, pin him to the stone wall encircling the commons, and soundly thump him as fair retribution for years of shameless bullying.

And yet, for some inexplicable reason, the outward signs of puberty never arrived. While the other boys grew overnight into young men of beefy, Adonisian splendor, Ruffington continued to be more fragile than the flower girl in a wedding. He reached the age of twenty, then twenty-five, and then thirty—and yet, when he looked anxiously into his mirror each morning, he saw only the same sallow cheeks, pencil-thin arms, and pasty complexion that had defined him as long as he could remember.

Enough is enough, he thought to himself while leaning over the sink one morning, brushing his teeth. Sick, depressed, and desperate for a change in his appearance, he decided to consult a shaman and move things along more expeditiously.

That night he traveled to the village of Lustleigh, Devon; found a candlelit corner table at Lustleigh's favorite public house, the Cleave; and met with Madame Solipsis, the wise and ancient shaman known throughout the British Isles for her uncanny ability to solve the most inscrutable mysteries of existence.

"What precisely is your need, my son?" asked the magnificently attired Madame Solipsis while cupping Reginald's velvet-smooth face in her bony, bird-like hands. Her beloved shaman's drum, scuffed and discolored from untold years of use, lay in wait on the chair next to her.

A small ocean of tears welled up suddenly in Ruffington's pale green eyes. "For the first time in my life," he said, "I want to look into my mirror and see a *man*! I want everyone I encounter—especially Wadleigh Peebles, if I should ever see him again—to know that I'm not some pusillanimous pushover, but a force to be reckoned with!"

Without saying a word, Madame Solipsis picked up her drum and began tapping a hypnotic, steadily accelerating rhythm. When the tapping reached seven beats per second—a rate only the most gifted shamans are capable of achieving—Ruffington thrashed about in ecstasy, then fell headlong into a deep and cleansing trance. Such euphoria! It was by far the most delicious, otherworldly state of mind he'd ever experienced.

As the tapping slowed steadily down, an unmistakable aura of serenity enveloped the room. Then, as soon as Ruffington emerged from his trance, Madame Solipsis pulled a priceless, pearl-inlaid mirror from her handbag and held it up in front of his face.

"Look deep within," she whispered, "and tell me what you see!"

Ruffington saw immediately that his delicate features and wan complexion had vanished. In their place was a face more wolflike than human. His eyes had shed their pale hues and turned dark and penetrating; his skin, once soft as a marshmallow, was now more coarse than a sheet of sandpaper; his chin and jowls were carpeted with thick, interlocking scales; and his facial hair, for years more soft than the fur on a newborn kitten, had become more bristly than the spines on a cactus.

"And those are not the only changes you'll see," said Madame Solipsis, smiling proudly as she put away her drum. "You'll soon be witness to another, and in the very near future!"

Ruffington had no idea what she was talking about, but it didn't really matter; he couldn't have been happier about the changes Madame Solipsis had wrought in his appearance. He thanked her profusely, paid her handsomely for her services, then raced home and leafed frantically through the latest issue of the *Smugbridge Arms Alumni Newsletter*, hoping to learn the whereabouts of Wadleigh Peebles. In the "Smugbridge Notables" section, he learned that, in spite of being expelled from Smugbridge Arms years ago for conduct unbecoming a student, Peebles had managed somehow to climb to the top of the corporate ladder and become CEO of RugbyQuipment International, the world-renowned, London-based manufacturer of rugby boots, mouth guards, and custom-embroidered hoodies—essential equipment for stylish rugby players everywhere, including even the most reprehensible bullies.

Right away, Ruffington vowed to track Peebles down and exact revenge on him for the awful way he'd treated his classmates. The very next evening he arrived at RugbyQuipment headquarters just before closing, strode angrily into the plush-carpeted lobby, and demanded to see Peebles. The secretary, too stunned and terrified by Ruffington's wolflike appearance to say no, ushered him immediately into the executive suite, where Ruffington found Peebles standing at a grand Palladian window in the half-darkness, staring twenty stories down toward the traffic-choked avenues and twinkling lights of central London. *I might be wrong,* thought Ruffington, *but the man doesn't seem to be quite as tall and muscular as I remember him.*

"Who *is* it?" said Peebles without turning around.

Ruffington slipped quietly up behind him, tapped him on the shoulder, clenched his fist, and prepared to deliver the most powerful blow he could muster straight to the chin of the bully he so detested for his years of inexcusable behavior.

But when Peebles whirled around, annoyed at having an intruder, Ruffington was astonished to see that his onetime tormentor had been transformed into little more than a wafer-thin, prepubescent weakling with the same delicate features, wan complexion, and wispy physique that Ruffington himself had wanted so desperately to be rid of for so many years.

Madame Solipsis, he marveled. It just *had* to be her doing!

Some might be tempted to think Peebles's obvious misfortune was cause for celebration, but happily, there are moments in life when the worst of human propensities are thwarted and decency wins the day. Ruffington saw only sadness and insecurity in Peebles's eyes, remembered how painful it was to be bullied, and felt not vengeful pleasure but genuine pity for the man's predicament.

Wadleigh Peebles was rich and successful now, to be sure—but all the wealth and notoriety in the world cannot guarantee happiness. Suddenly, the animosity Ruffington had harbored for his classmate for so many years began to evaporate like an early morning mist over the Thames. He dropped his clenched fist to his side, extended a more peaceable hand in friendship, and together they left RugbyQuipment International, stepped across the street to a pub, ordered two foaming tankards of ale and a bucket of onion rings, and prepared to build a bridge of understanding between two longtime enemies who had suddenly and inexplicably become friends.

Chapter 19

Happy Dawg and the Sad Man
Art, Inhumanity, and the Quest for Happiness

Happiness: it's both endlessly tantalizing and maddeningly elusive. We all want it, but few of us ever learn how to sustain it for very long when it makes an appearance in our otherwise prosaic lives. So preoccupied are we with the idea of happiness in our culture that, at least within the closely aligned, mutually beneficial worlds of marketing and advertising, the search for it has become both a cliché and a commodity—as if happiness can somehow be purchased.

This state of affairs ought not to come as a surprise. As a species, we aspire to more than mere survival, and humankind's never-ending search for happiness is one precious way for us to give voice to our deepest longings while simultaneously erecting a wall against the violence, cruelty, and inhumanity we see around us every day. When we do manage, whether collectively or individually, to find moments of happiness, we hold on to them for dear life, knowing that without them, our lives would be stripped of any real meaning.

Artists in particular have believed for centuries that the simple act of creating beautiful things is one sure way to take a courageous stand against violence and cruelty, alleviate sadness, and contribute meaningfully to human happiness.

But some of the most important and most persistent questions within the worldwide community of artists may never be answered. What is beauty? Can it ever really be defined? Can an artist whose works never confront the uglier realities of human existence really be called a genuine artist? And must artists feel obligated in any way to confront those realities in their work? Since these and other closely related questions have profound implications for us as a society, they deserve to be discussed. And if that discussion can contribute in any lasting way to human happiness, then the effort will have proven to be more than worthwhile.

The idea of happiness and how to achieve it has been explored throughout recorded history in myriad ways: in literature and the behavioral sciences, in religion and philosophy, in music and the visual arts.

The most universally recognizable symbol of happiness—one with which every man, woman, and child is intimately familiar—can be found at the tail end of a well-adjusted dog. When he's happy, his tail wags so furiously that one is tempted to think he's about to lift off the ground like a helicopter and rise up triumphantly into the clouds. It's that supreme moment of exhilaration that we all wish we could capture and then hold on to for ourselves—not just for a short time, but forever.

Some of us do manage to wag with remarkable frequency, but to wag perpetually is the stuff of unattainable dreams. To pretend that the world we live in is or ever will be entirely free of sadness—such as the monumental indignities reported without cease on the nightly news—will get us nowhere.

The depth and breadth of that sadness, at any given moment, everywhere on earth, is really quite staggering. Has there ever been a time in history when vast segments of our planet weren't either up in flames, riddled with bullets, or writhing in agony from some intractable conflict between warring factions? To a creature from another galaxy, we must at times appear to be little more than a seething ball of violent, self-loathing dystopians, here on earth only to build and then destroy in one vicious, never-ending cycle.

Lift your telescope, my friends, then point it toward any country in the world, including your own. You'll find sadness that's either intensely individual or alarmingly widespread.

Stoning, mass rape, genital mutilation; sexual slavery, torture, genocide. In cultures both "backward" and "advanced," we're forced every day to bear witness, in both print and electronic media, to a truly demonic smorgasbord of child abuse, elder abuse, domestic abuse, or human trafficking. The menu is chock full of entrées for the evil epicurean with time on his hands and an insatiable appetite for inflicting pain and spreading misery.

To establish a safe emotional distance from the steady bombardment of violent incidents—and the sadness we inevitably feel when they occur—we've no choice, as caring, sentient beings, but to turn away, numb our feelings, and get on with our lives.

Or must we? Can it ever be truly constructive to turn away from intractable social problems begging to be solved?

A great many courageous, caring people from every walk of life—doctors and scientists, teachers and inventors—expend enormous energy every day on such problems, always hoping their important work will help solve the most daunting of them, alleviate the sadness we feel, and bring greater happiness to the world.

And artists in particular—painters and playwrights, dancers and photographers, sculptors and musicians—have for centuries believed that the simple act of creating beautiful things has enormous power as an agent of happiness—a powerful antidote to the violence we experience and the sadness it engenders.

It's tempting, of course, for those artists to play it safe and produce only the sunniest, most uplifting works. After all, such works have proven to be immensely popular, and the more conservative galleries know they sell.

Fig. 81. *Happy Dawg Walks the Sad Man* by Ross Bachelder.

Artists, writers, and other creatives always have a difficult choice when they get up in the morning: they can either keep their distance from the ugliest of life's realities by creating only the prettiest, most demonstrably salable things, or confront those realities aggressively through their art. The latter approach clearly appears to be the most courageous one.

But this brings up an enormously important question: Must artists feel obligated in any way to acknowledge, through their art, the existence of the worst that humankind can inflict on itself?

Given my longtime existentialist leanings, it would be next to impossible for me to argue that such a thing *should* or *must* be done—unless, of course, I as an individual, entirely on my own initiative, based on my own personal convictions, and without the interference of a church or other hierarchical institution, decide that I simply want to do it.

Søren Aabye Kierkegaard, generally considered to have been the first existentialist philosopher, was convinced that each one of us—not society or religion—is solely responsible for giving meaning to life, then living it passionately and sincerely. As I see it, Kierkegaard and I are speaking the same life-affirming, secular humanist language.

Whatever our personal philosophies or creative inclinations, the questions persist: Can an artist create a body of works entirely without evidence of a social conscience, then legitimately call himself or herself an artist? Can showering the world with never-ending sweetness ever be fully sufficient as an artist's contribution to the welfare of humankind? These questions are tough to ask and even tougher to answer.

Like the vast majority of artists, I have moments when I enjoy creating landscapes, still lifes, and other noncontroversial subject matter—"safe" images intended to celebrate the beauty of nature in all of its myriad forms. But there is another part of me that can't help but see arresting beauty in things that people in the conventional art world consider disturbing, violent, or just plain ugly. It is here where the role of artist as provocateur comes in, and it need not be incompatible with either our love of beautiful things or the never-ending quest for human happiness.

Can depictions of violence be beautiful? History tells us they most emphatically can. Over the centuries, innumerable artists have captured violent subjects on canvas, often to address important political and moral issues of the time. They and other, like-minded artists have had little trouble seeing the beauty of a well-painted subject, no matter how repugnant that subject might be. But many people—including a surprising number of practicing artists—find it impossible to reconcile the violence of a given subject with the beauty with which it has been rendered.

Michelangelo Caravaggio's *Salome with the Head of John the Baptist*—an artwork inspired by the biblical parable and painted between 1607 and 1610—will inevitably shock and disgust some viewers because of its violence, but it will exhilarate others because of both its undeniable poignancy as a morality tale and its exquisite beauty as a painting.

Théodore Géricault's painting *Anatomical Pieces*, one of his most violent works, was completed in 1819 and features a ghoulish mound of severed limbs. To achieve such realism, Géricault painted from actual body parts lent to him by a Paris morgue for the purpose of anatomical study—a common practice of the time. *Anatomical Pieces* was one of several artworks in a series Géricault embarked on to help prepare him for the painting of his acclaimed masterpiece, *The Raft of the Medusa*.

The story behind *The Raft of the Medusa* is itself a powerful testament to tragedy. When the *Medusa*, a French naval vessel, ran aground on a sand bar near Mauritania in July 1816, the crew and passengers—altogether four hundred people—needed to abandon ship. The six available lifeboats had a capacity of only 250, so 146 men and one woman had no choice but to scramble onto a poorly constructed raft. After thirteen hellish days at sea, with very few provisions and much infighting that resulted in passengers being thrown overboard, passengers jumping overboard, and cannibalism, only fifteen of the people on the raft survived the ordeal. The incident created a storm of protest against a government accused of being too slow to respond to the crisis. And yet, in spite of the heartrending violence depicted in Géricault's painting, it is celebrated today as one of the great narrative masterpieces of nineteenth-century art.

Pablo Picasso's *Guernica*, a monumental painting he completed in 1937, was the artist's passionate response to the Nazi bombing of the town of Guernica during the Spanish Civil War. In it he dramatized the tragedy of military conflict throughout history, with special attention to the slaughter of innocent civilians. Ironically, though *Guernica* is obviously full of violence, it has become the most famous anti-war symbol in the world, and it is considered a masterpiece.

That some can see the beauty in a violent painting while others can see only the horror should be a reminder to all of us that the idea of beauty has always been and will always be profoundly subjective.

Whether a given work of art has aesthetic merit really has little if anything to do with the nature of its subject matter. The more artworks we're exposed to, the greater is the likelihood that we'll begin to see beauty where we once saw only ugliness, even in the most horrifically violent subjects. And out of beauty, whatever form it takes, comes happiness.

Examples of things considered either beautiful or ugly are everywhere around us, and yet the line between beautiful and ugly can be difficult, if not impossible, to define.

This really shouldn't surprise anyone. Unlike other creatures in the animal kingdom, we have the gift of metaphor in our blood, and because of it, wherever we turn, we see objects—animal, vegetable, and mineral—that can be perceived in more than one way. A lawn-obsessed homeowner sees only ugliness in a weed—the wicked stepsister to a flower—but to the botanist, and to the artist as well, that same weed can be no less beautiful than the award-winning chrysanthemum in an ornamental garden. A duck-billed platypus may seem a genetic abomination to some, but to a zoologist—and indeed to a platypus in mating season—it's a creature of stunning beauty and endless fascination.

In his painting entitled *That Which I Should Have Done I Did Not Do (The Door)*, the American surrealist artist Ivan Albright (1897–1983) used an arrangement of desiccated flowers on a funeral wreath as a metaphor for decay and death. Some would think this a truly morbid painting, but who is to say with any authority that the flowers of French pastel artist Odilon Redon are beautiful, while the flowers of Ivan Albright are ugly? Once again, it's entirely a matter of opinion.

The legendary photographer Diane Arbus was unusually fascinated with the grotesque—things thought to be so ugly or distorted that they're repulsive. At one point in her career, she was a regular at Hubert's Museum, a freak show and flea circus in Times Square, New York City. For Arbus, the grotesque was not really grotesque at all. It was quietly, stunningly beautiful—magnificent according to its very own, disarmingly unconventional rules. Arbus understood the subjectivity of beauty better than nearly everyone around her. Her poignant photographs of people with unusual physical characteristics offered incontrovertible evidence of both her bottomless capacity for beauty and her enduring compassion for all of God's children.

Some subjects can be especially hard, at least on first viewing, for anyone to categorize as beautiful. In the Art of the Americas wing of the Museum of Fine Arts in Boston is a painting by Hyman Bloom entitled *Female Corpse, Back View*—one of three portraits of decaying corpses Bloom painted after going in 1943 with fellow artist David Aronson to the onetime Boston Psychopathic Hospital in Kendall Square to sketch cadavers. The painting must have been deeply offensive to the vast majority of viewers when it was first exhibited—and no less disturbing for many of those who see it today—and yet to Mr. Bloom, a painter of exquisite sensibilities and technical virtuosity, the subject was no less a thing of beauty than Wordsworth's cottage in England's Lake District or Picasso's beloved Montmartre in the Right Bank of Paris.

"On the one hand, [seeing the corpse] was harrowing," he said. "On the other it was beautiful—iridescent and pearly. It opened up avenues for feelings not yet gelled.... I felt something inside that I could express through color. As a subject it would synthesize things for me. The paradox of the harrowing and the beautiful could be brought into unity."

Anyone can recognize the exterior touchstones of the female anatomy in that painting—a view of the back of a corpse being dissected—and be horrified. But to an anatomist, and to artists like Aronson or Bloom, who are open to experience and wired for all things beautiful, it can be a visual feast of form, texture, and raging, multitudinous color. Disturbing? Without question. Ugly? It depends entirely on who's doing the looking.

Just ask the moralists—those pit-bull social engineers whose most urgent mission is to force their own righteous ideas of beauty and propriety onto the rest of society. Remember Andres Serrano's *Piss Christ* and the whole distasteful flap over Robert Mapplethorpe's beautifully rendered homoerotic male nudes? Serrano and Mapplethorpe proudly took up the cause of creative freedom—the right to live by one's very own hard-won definition of beauty—in the Reagan era of growing intolerance of anything that might deviate from socially acceptable norms.

Because the idea of beauty is so overwhelmingly subjective, the champions of artistic freedom must always remain vigilant in the face of attacks from any individual or group—preachers or politicians, scholars or scoundrels—who seek to silence the tongues and banish the artworks of creative people everywhere. "I know what good art is," they say with maddening but indefensible certainty.

Unlike the avowed moralists from any walk of life, artists—perhaps especially within the realm of aesthetics—tend to have fewer hidebound opinions and less judgmental ways of seeing and interpreting the world. Of course, there are a great many artists who are far too certain of what is and isn't beautiful; just being an artist does not somehow make a person magically immune to pigheadedness.

But as I see it, a genuine artist cannot help but see beauty wherever he or she turns, regardless of where and why it occurs and what form it might take. And if an artwork does depict violence, like Picasso's *Guernica*—or something merely repugnant, like Bloom's *Female Corpse* or Albright's haunting portrait of the door with the funeral wreath on it—one can nearly always trust that those images were conceived and brought to life on canvas not to celebrate violence but to encourage loving ways and peaceful coexistence.

If we as artists accept the argument that, like doctors, scientists, and teachers, we're here on earth to serve others—not just ourselves—then, within commonsense limits, we need to stop worrying about the propriety of our subject matter and get down to the work of doing what artists do: making beautiful things. It's our job to choose subjects we ourselves think beautiful, record them lovingly, in the medium of our choice, no matter how repugnant or controversial they might seem to others, then release them without apology into the aesthetic marketplace.

The good news is that, if we've brought all of our available expertise, empathy, and imaginative powers to the creation of a given work, then the result will nearly always find an audience. It is then that we'll know the Happy Dawg is walking the Sad Man, and not the other way around.

Chapter 20

Our Incomparable Jennie
Fragments of a Life

One must never doubt the ability of people well into their nineties—and more—to have a lasting influence on the people and events around them. Some nonagenarians are more physically active and intellectually engaged than people half their age. Consider these three late-in-life high achievers: Nola Ochs, born in Jetmore, Kansas, in 1911, set a world record for being the world's oldest college graduate at the age of ninety-five. Celebrated American composer Eliot Carter published more than forty works between the ages of ninety and one hundred, and another twenty after he turned one hundred in 2008. German-born American photographer Ruth Bernhard, hailed by Ansel Adams as "the greatest photographer of the nude," was still photographing when she died in 2006 at the age of a hundred and one.

They're no longer an isolated phenomenon. Thanks to advances in preventive medicine and nearly every area of healthcare, the number of productive, deeply engaged people from all walks of life will continue to grow dramatically around the world. We must learn to adjust to that reality.

Of course, there are legions of people well into their nineties and beyond, who, while leading less than glamorous lives, have made invaluable contributions to their families, their communities, and their professions simply by being productive citizens and caring neighbors. Jennie Gay of Berwick, Maine, was one of them. And the power of her influence on us—three recent transplants from the Midwest to northern New England, suddenly in need of a warm home and a friendly face—cannot be overestimated.

I knew Jennie Gay for just four short years—some of the best years of the four decades in which I've called New England home. As I look back on those years, I'm glad I and my family decided long ago to leave the Midwest and settle in Maine. If we'd not moved here, we'd not have had the pleasure of knowing

Jennie, and without her in our lives, even for just four years, we'd have become very different people.

My wife, Marilyn, and my daughter, Amy, and I moved to the village of Berwick from the densely populated college town of Ypsilanti, Michigan, in 1974. Marilyn, only twenty-eight years old at the time, had just taken the job of music teacher in the Berwick schools after completing a master's degree in music theory and literature at Eastern Michigan University. I'd just turned thirty and had only recently completed a graduate teaching fellowship in English literature at the same school. We were more than ready for an occupational adventure in a brand new place.

Within just two weeks of our arrival in Berwick, Marilyn reported to two schools—the Estabrook School and Noble Junior High (now known as Noble Middle School)—where she would be responsible for twenty sessions per week of K-8 classroom music, small-group instrumental and choral rehearsals, and full band/chorus rehearsals. It was an exceedingly demanding assignment, but she was more than thoroughly prepared to handle the work, and she plunged eagerly into her new life as public school music educator.

Amy would enter the Estabrook School as a kindergartner, and, simply by circumstance, her mother would be her music teacher. I was responsible for getting Amy off to school each morning and welcoming her home in the afternoon. I'd become what people in the '60s and early '70s called a house husband, and I approached my assignment with a keen sense of adventure and a profound awareness of the importance of my role in the scheme of things. When not performing my duties as father and contributor to household maintenance, I began finding opportunities to write, speak publicly about male feminism and active fatherhood, and perform as a freelance musician.

Our first home in Berwick was actually a small apartment on Maple Drive—one of four connected units across the street from one of the town's two cemeteries. The landlord fit the classic stereotype of the small-town New Englander: aloof, laconic, and even a little grumpy at times. We didn't know quite what to make of him, and he knew even less what to make of us. Not only was I from away, I had long red hair, a bushy beard, and a bumper sticker on my car that said "War Is Not Healthy for Children and Other Living Things." (It spoke volumes about where I'd just come from and what I stood for.) Nevertheless, we got along well enough and went about our respective lives without incident.

Over the next three years, Marilyn settled into the rough-and-tumble of her work as music teacher. I began to write for the local Somersworth/Berwick Free Press and pick up assignments as a pit orchestra musician. Amy was doing well in school, wowing her teachers with her writing and speaking abilities and her highly inquisitive mind. She became a proud second-grader whose teacher at the Estabrook School, Margaret M. Linton, loved her obvious excitement about learning and took exceptionally good care of her as she adjusted to living far away from her original home in Michigan. Margaret soon become our friend, and from then on we—and Amy, too—knew her as Peggy. We looked to her for solutions to our everyday problems—everything from where to find a reliable plumber to how to renew a driver's license.

Each day after school, our daughter would dash home with me and reunite with Olga, the plump orange tabby we took into our home after Toty, Amy's pet mouse, died. (We tucked Amy's mouse-mate into a discarded Timex watch box, then laid him to rest in a tearful ceremony in our backyard. His resting place was topped off with a grave marker Amy had made expressly for the occasion out of two popsicle sticks.)

Everything was going well for us on Maple Drive until one morning when the landlord was collecting the trash and discovered Olga purring nonchalantly on a windowsill at the rear of our apartment, dreaming of sparrows, chipmunks, and other creatures any self-respecting cat would want for supper.

Less than a minute later, he was pounding furiously on our front door. When we answered, he exploded in anger—not at all the quiet, withdrawn man we'd grown accustomed to as his tenants.

"You have a *cat* in your apartment!" he bellowed. "The lease on your apartment says no animals allowed. I want you out of here by the end of the month!"

Amy cowered in a corner of the living room, her hands cupped tightly over her ears, saying nothing. Olga had long ago scampered off the windowsill, dashed into the nearest bedroom, and worked her way under the bed to wait out the tempest.

Once the landlord had caught his breath and reined in his rant, I tried to explain to him what seemed so obvious to the three of us—that a seven-year-old loves animals, and, like any other human being, yearns for companionship.

"It's natural for a child to have a pet!" I shouted, fighting back. "The cat isn't making messes anywhere in our apartment. We take good care of her. She's harmless! I'm sure you'll understand that, under the circumstances, it would be best that she be allowed to stay!"

By now, the veins on his forehead had grown even more pronounced. "No animals allowed!" he roared. "Be out by the end of the month. And by the way, your last month's rent is due this coming Thursday!"

He slammed the door, stomped away, and returned to his daily trash round. Olga came out from under the bed and reestablished her territory, curling up next to Amy on the threadbare couch we'd brought with us from our apartment in Ypsilanti. The three of us then sat together in our living room and talked about what we should do next.

Right away, Amy had an idea. "We should call Mrs. Linton! She's lived here for a long time and knows everybody. Maybe *she'll* be able to help us find a place." It was a fine idea, and we praised her for her quick thinking.

Then an indignant frown formed itself on her usually cherubic face. "But I don't like that landlord. He's a *mean man!*" Then she reached down, swept Olga up onto her lap, and hugged her as if she'd just returned home after a year on the run.

I called Peggy the next morning, and sure enough, she had what she thought would be the perfect solution. "Jennie Gay," she said. "She lives just across town in a nice white Victorian on River Street. There's a tiny, two-story apartment attached to the rear of her home, and it's for rent. If I were you, I'd get over there right away and talk to her. And tell her I sent you!"

We had less than a week to find a place. If we came up empty, we'd almost immediately become homeless, and that would create a host of additional problems for the three of us. It was a dire situation, but I'd devised a plan overnight and was reasonably certain I could pull it off. I might be all books and music, but I was no dummy.

The next day, right after school, I headed over to River Street with my checkbook in one hand and my daughter's hand in the other, full of an unsettling mixture of hope and trepidation. I figured the sight of us together would melt the heart of an ice maiden, so I didn't see why it wouldn't work on Miss Jennie Gay, too.

I turned to Amy, offered her a smile of reassurance, then marched up the steps to Jennie's place with her hand in mine. Amy rang the doorbell, and a moment later a stern-faced, immaculately groomed woman, dressed in a blue and white flower-print dress and wearing an apron, opened the door and stood ramrod straight before us. She looked as if she might be fast approaching ninety. She also struck me right away as having no appetite for nonsense of any kind.

"Ayup!" she said, with a Down East accent thick enough to cut into bricks and use for a sidewalk.

"Hello!" I chirped, a trifle intimidated by her quasi-military demeanor—General Patton in a flower-print dress. "I'm Ross, and this is my daughter, Amy."

I watched as the two of them, one just seven years old, the other well into the last proud lap of her life journey, smiled ever so slightly at each other, testing the waters.

"Peggy Linton said you might have an apartment for rent, and we're badly in need of a place to live."

"Ayup," she said again. "I know Peggy. Good woman!" (Not a waster of words, this Jennie, but she sure had that Down East accent down pat.)

She paused, then stared down at us from the top step of her porch. She would need to assess us.

"You married?" she asked. (The interrogation was now underway.)

"Yup," I said. "Nine years now."

"Got more kids?"

"Nope. Just the three of us. I'm a writer and musician. My wife Marilyn teaches music here in town. And Amy's in second grade now, same school!"

"Uh-*huh*! And where've you been livin'?"

"Maple Drive—top of the hill on 236, across from the cemetery," I said. "Our landlord threw us out yesterday when he discovered we have a cat."

A surge of genuine warmth—the first indication of a more sensitive side—crept into her chiseled, Mt. Rushmore demeanor.

"A cat!" she said. "Don't see why that ought to have bothered him. Myself, I *love* cats!"

"We couldn't do without a cat in the family!" I said. I was feeling better already. *She's an animal lover! And she just might be an ideal replacement for the two grannies we left back in Michigan.*

"Well," she said, "rent's $150 a month, plus an extra month up front as a deposit to cover any damage to the apartment." She finished her assessment, then got down to business. "If Peggy sent you, I guess I can trust you to be good about paying on time. The apartment's yours if you want it, but I'll need a few days to get it ready for you."

My guess is that she'd seen her long-ago self in Amy that day: a fragile young girl with auburn hair, an irresistible smile, and her entire future ahead of her. It was true, then—my greatest weapon really was Amy, and she'd won the war for us just by being next to me at the base of Jennie's stairs, pouring on the charm.

Fig. 82. Our home on River Street in Berwick, 1978 to 1982.

Three days later, we loaded all our possessions into a U-Haul, left our Maple Street apartment for good, and set up house at the corner of Bridge and River.

In spite of its tumbledown condition, we immediately fell in love with the place. It was sparkling clean the day we moved in— Jennie had clearly made sure of that—but the decades of exposure to New England winters had taken their toll on its structural integrity. It sagged here and there, the clapboards were badly in need of paint, the home was drafty from top to bottom, and the chimney leaned a little too eastward for its own good. Nevertheless, it had a homey feeling that our old place could never have matched.

Inside, the living room featured 1920s wallpaper with a miniature rose pattern interrupted here and there with water stains and a half-dozen minor separations along the seams. At the very center of the floor was a cast iron furnace grate beneath which we could easily see—and regularly hear—a tangle of heating ducts that groaned like an injured mastodon on the colder mornings when we fired up the furnace. One late-summer morning, while preparing to replace the grate after a good cleaning, I backed into the gaping hole in the floor and nearly broke my wrists in an attempt to halt my fall. It was a slapstick Descent into the Maelström, and Laurel and Hardy couldn't have done it better.

On the right side of the first floor, not far from the shower that inevitably snorted and snarled when we turned on the spigot, was a spacious, wraparound screen porch with battleship gray floorboards, forest green trim, and a couple of creaky, banged-up folding chairs for our moments of leisure. In the evenings we'd run a power cord out one window, drag a floor lamp out onto the porch, and read to the tune of neighborhood children at play amidst the magical twinkling of fireflies.

Not long after we'd settled into our River Street home, we began to discover in Jennie a long list of endearing quirks and anomalies.

The first had to do with the peculiar manner in which she handled phone calls, combined with the special nature of her generosity. One afternoon the telephone rang while I was upstairs, tidying up the bedrooms. *Probably another parent calling*, I mused. Calls were coming in like flack in a ground war in recent weeks, all having to do with questions about band or chorus or the date of the next Band Parents meeting.

I got down the stairs as fast as I could, picked up the receiver, and waited for the familiar hello that's built into the typical phone call, but it never arrived. Instead, an ear-splitting declaration stabbed through the silence and penetrated my ear: "Your suppah's ready!" she bellowed. "It's on the PO-ach!"

Suppah? Po-ach? I hadn't the foggiest idea either who was calling or what she'd just said. "Enough calls already!" I grumbled.

I forgot about the call and settled into my favorite chair for a moment of reading. While reaching for a magazine, I glanced absentmindedly out the window overlooking the screen porch and saw three plates of piping hot food—chicken, biscuits with gravy, and garden-fresh peas—all steaming away on the railing nearest our front lawn.

It was Jennie. Suddenly, the fact that she'd not bothered to say hello didn't matter anymore. With just one kind gesture, she'd won us over for all eternity. I rescued the three plates of food from the screen porch, marched them into the kitchen, and set the table for what turned out to be a delicious, utterly unexpected after-school meal. And it would be only the first in a long list of homespun banquets delivered from the kitchen of Jennie to the humble apartment behind her home.

But few things in this world come without a price. In return for her generosity, certain expectations began to manifest themselves—hard-and-fast presumptions that as her tenants we were expected be available, on call and without warning, to help her with the more difficult chores.

She'd pick up the phone on a hot summer day and shout, "Company's comin' up from Cambridge! Lawn across the street needs mowin'!'" then hang up without saying goodbye. Her nephew, Hollis Gerrish, president of the Cambridge-based Squirrel Brand company—famous throughout New England for the quality of its peanuts and confections—would be up in a day or two from Massachusetts to pay her a visit, and everything had to be just right for the occasion.

I walked our lawnmower across the street, and half an hour later I'd trimmed the lawn to perfection. And when the first River Street winter set in, I needed no prompting to step around the corner and shovel snow off her porch and sidewalk after every storm.

We may have been inconvenienced on occasion by her ad hoc, four-season imperatives, but her heartfelt appreciation for our assistance—and the inevitable bags of Squirrel Brand peanuts left on our screen porch whenever Hollis Gerrish came up from Cambridge—made the moments of servitude more than worth the aggravation. It was our very own version of the Yankee swap—peanuts in return for yard maintenance—and we loved being a part of it.

Jennie loved not just manicured lawns and colorful flowers, but nature in all its glorious plant and animal forms. She was an indefatigable gardener, and on many a morning in the spring, we'd wake to the sound of her fast at work in the garden she'd planted just beyond our kitchen window, wearing either a flower-print dress or little more than a slip and a sunbonnet. One morning in early autumn, we stepped outside our front door, wondering who or what was making the persistent scraping sound on the roof of our apartment. Sure enough, it was Jennie, then more than ninety years old, all decked out in bedroom slippers and a tattered nightgown, perched nonchalantly on the edge of the sloping roof and raking down the fallen leaves.

As for the animals, Jennie was a longtime member of the SPCA and a fierce defender of anything with four legs or a pair of wings. On more than one occasion, we saw her outside in the dead of winter, sweeping a shivering cat up into her arms and delivering it to the door of a neighbor, along with a stern, inviolable message: "Either take your cat in right now," she'd say, "or I'll be delivering it to the shelter down in Kennebunk—and you'll be gettin' a bill in the mail!"

Her gifts to us were legendary for their eccentricity. In spite of her unfailing generosity with the intangibles—the little things that matter the most—she was notoriously tight with her finances. If she was moved on occasion to give us something, it never came with holiday-themed wrapping paper, topped off with a ribbon.

On special occasions, we'd often get a greeting card from Jennie, not delivered by the post office—a service that would have forced her to invest in a postage stamp—but left quietly on our screen porch for us to discover. She was unfailingly parsimonious: instead of squandering her well-deserved retirement income on costly Hallmark cards, she'd simply remove the back of a pre-owned card with a pair of scissors, then sign the surviving front panel on the back and deliver it to us as a single-sheet token of her unswerving devotion.

One morning she called and delivered a message to us in her usual perfunctory manner. "I've got somethin' for you," she shouted. "Come round my front door and pick it up. Got some fresh-made cookies, too!" The cookies—classic sugar cookies with a raisin at the center—were fresh out of the oven and delicious. The other gift turned out to be a white ceramic cat wrapped in a tabletop ironing board cover. It was just what we'd have asked Santa for, if only we'd had the good sense to think of it.

Another colorful example of her chronic penny-pinching, related to us by a neighbor across the street from our River Street home, occurred one day while she was dining with a group of women friends at Suzelle Restaurant, at the time a well-known family-style restaurant in nearby Somersworth, New Hampshire. They'd just enjoyed a meal of chicken wings, macaroni salad, and apple pie, and it was time for everyone to gather up their belongings, pay the waitress, and move along home. One by one, they stood up and slipped into their winter coats, laughing and chitchatting as they prepared to leave. When Jennie stood up, a chorus of gasps rang out around the table as a mound of stockpiled chicken wings tumbled onto the floor from the napkin across her lap.

While frugality was always high on the list of Jennie's priorities, she was interested in much, much more than guarding her nest egg. Not only was she a skillful artist, with examples of her precisely rendered works displayed prominently in various rooms of her home, she was also an avid reader. Over the years, she'd collected many valuable, historically significant books penned by local and regional writers. It was when she discovered that our daughter, Amy, was also an avid reader that the books began to make their journey from her home to ours. We still have a few of the finest she either lent to us or gave us outright in her more generous moments, but one in particular stood out as the pick of the literary litter.

She'd called us one evening, in her usual out-of-the-blue manner, with what sounded like an important announcement. "I know you love books," she shouted. "I've one he-ah that I want all of you, and especially Amy, to see. For now I'm going to lend it to you, but someday I might even let you keep it for good." She paused for a moment, then delivered the kind of chilling proviso only a nonagenarian, utterly certain of her priorities, can make without apology: "You'll just have to promise me you'll take *good care* of that book!"

What she had for us was an enormous leather-bound journal written by a soldier from nearby York, Maine, while he was serving on the front lines in Virginia during the Revolutionary War. It was undoubtedly a precious document, worth hundreds of dollars or more, and we were first stunned and then deeply moved to realize that she thought enough of us to trust us with it.

From that moment on, we couldn't get enough of that journal. On quiet evenings we'd leaf through it and read to each other from its poignant, action-packed narrative. It was a rare opportunity to experience living history from the pages of a one-of-a-kind journal, written by a local resident and chronicling the uniquely American experience for which New Englanders have so much respect and affection. With the aid of breathtakingly beautiful penmanship, the soldier recorded story after story of moments in the heat of battle, along with reassurances that he was safe and well-fed, missed his family, and wanted desperately to be home again in the village of York.

One evening, not long after the Memorial Day parade, Jennie called us and declared her intention to sell the journal to a rare-book collector up from Boston. We had one last emotional encounter with it, returned it to her the next morning, and never saw it again.

As much as we loved having Jennie Gay as our landlady, the return of the journal would prove to be one of our last meaningful interactions with her as her tenants. We'd always wanted our own home, so in the summer of 1982 we qualified for a Maine State Housing Authority loan, and by Labor Day we'd signed the contract and begun construction on a one-acre plot six miles out into the countryside around Berwick.

Our Incomparable Jennie

I dreaded the day when I'd need to tell her of our decision to leave River Street. We knew we'd also be leaving behind a woman who'd unhesitatingly taken us in just four years earlier at a time when we'd just been evicted and were desperately in need of a home. Overnight, she'd become our loving, caring rent-a-granny, just when the three of us, building a new life more than nine hundred miles from our Michigan home, needed her the most.

When I approached her to deliver the news of our departure, she was standing on the front steps of her home—the same steps she was standing on the day I first met her—talking with yet another collector up from Boston to appraise her valuable furniture, antiques, and paintings. I apologized for interrupting the conversation, then meekly informed her of our intentions. I oughtn't to have worried about her reaction; she took the news with quiet dignity, then wished us well in our new home.

I stood at the base of the stairs, feeling enormously guilty for what had begun to feel like an out-and-out abandonment—the squandering of what had been a beautiful, mutually rewarding friendship. Jennie, always on the high side of human decency, showed her understanding with a comforting wave of her hand.

"It's been good having you he-ah," she said with equal helpings of nobility and wistfulness in her smile. "And someday you'll know just how much the three of you meant to me!"

I thanked her for her kind words, then walked across the lawn, slipped around the corner onto River Street, and stepped into the living room of our apartment. All around me were the memorable attributes of the sagging, paint-starved home that had given us such pleasure over the past four years. The furnace grate I'd fallen into in a moment of recklessness; the rose-flowered, water-stained wallpaper, coming apart at the seams; the always noisy shower; and the wraparound screen porch with its battleship gray floorboards, forest green trim, and flickering constellations of fireflies: all had become indelibly, irresistibly New England to me. I knew with terrible finality that our next home, more austerely modern than Jennie's apartment, would never have in it the quaint eccentricities and incomparable warmth-of-Jennie that made 2 River Street such a magical place in which to raise our daughter.

A few months after we'd settled into our new place in the country, we learned that Jennie had finally gone to live in a nursing home in Rochester. We visited her several times over the next year, and each time she'd come down to the common area and sit near us on the couch—a warm, indulgent hostess, dressed in another of her elegant flower-print dresses and adorned with an unpretentious string of pearls. Seeing her sitting there, so beautiful and strong in the ninth decade of her life, we wanted to believe she'd soon be heading over to the Suzelle to have yet another round of chicken wings and late-in-life merriment with her friends.

On each visit, she'd remind us how much she missed her home. "I loved that home," she said, in a voice still strong but tinged with regret. "I knew I could no longer keep the place up. I had to let it go, but I still find myself wishing I could be back there again someday."

In the spring of 1987, we learned that Jennie Gay had finally passed away at the age of ninety-six, strong, courageous, and fully engaged to the very end. The handsome, meticulously maintained Victorian on Bridge Street in Berwick would never again have the pleasure of her stewardship, and everyone in the neighborhood, including the stray cats and dogs she cared so much about, would need to accept the fact that Jennie would never again be their neighbor.

While we greatly missed Jennie—her absence had created an enormous void in our lives—we needed for everyone's sake to tend to our own affairs. Our new home, unfinished when we first moved into it, needed constant attention to make it fully livable. Marilyn was more immersed than ever in her teaching, and me in my freelance work as writer and musician. Amy was now in junior high school, serious about her classwork and well on her way to what would eventually be a successful career as a writer and editor in faraway Cincinnati, Ohio.

Many years ago, when Amy was still with us in Maine and preparing to enter junior high school, she interviewed Jennie, then wrote a paean to her, entitled "My Favorite Person, and Why," for an assignment in Mrs. Crandall's sixth-grade class. Not long ago, while visiting Amy in Cincinnati, I asked her what she remembered best about that interview and her other encounters with Jennie.

"More than anything else," she said, "I remember the grandfather clock that was always ticking in the background when I came by to see her. And on the day I interviewed her, I learned many fascinating things about her long-ago life in Berwick. As a youngster she was able to take the train from downtown Berwick all the way to Boston and back again. Her husband, Vernon, was a prominent chiropractor, well-regarded throughout the southern Maine / Seacoast New Hampshire region. Her longtime handyman was known to have installed the very first flush toilet across the border in Somersworth. And she had a really impressive collection of memorabilia tucked here and there around the house, including a souvenir photograph of President Abraham Lincoln!"

A few months after we'd finally settled into our new home, we found an official-looking envelope in our mailbox, addressed to Ross, Marilyn, and Amy Bachelder. It was from the Coolidge Law Firm in Somersworth, New Hampshire.

Why would we ever need to hear from a bunch of attorneys, of all people! I wondered. I tore the envelope apart and unfolded the letter. It read as follows:

> The Coolidge Law Firm
> 98 High Street
> Somersworth, New Hampshire
>
> RE: Estate of Jennie G. Gay
>
> July 6, 1987
>
> Dear Mr. Bachelder:
>
> This office represents Hollis and Catherine Gerrish, Personal Representatives named in the will of Jennie G. Gay.
>
> Mr. and Mrs. Gerrish have asked us to advise you of the portion of the will of the late Jennie Gay that pertains to you, which is as follows:
>
> "To my friend, Ross Bachelder of Berwick, Maine, the sum of One Thousand Dollars ($1,000.00) if he survives me, but if he does not survive me, then to his wife, Marilyn Bachelder, but if she does not survive me, then to their daughter, Amy Bachelder."
>
> You will be therefore notified in due course regarding the payment of the above request.
>
> Very truly yours,
>
> Clyde R. Coolidge

Shortly afterward I received a second letter from Mr. Coolidge, instructing me to drive to York County Courthouse in Alfred, Maine, and sign the necessary papers. A few days later I met with the courthouse clerk in Alfred, signed the papers, and picked up the check from Jennie's estate.

Fig. 83. Jennie Gay in 1987, the year of her death.
(Photo by Amy Bachelder Jeynes).

It took only a moment for us to decide as a family how the money would be dispersed. Marilyn and I knew Jennie cared as much for our daughter as she did for the two of us—and perhaps even more—so we divided the bequeathal evenly amongst the three of us.

I doubt that any of us could tell you with any certainly what we did with the money, though I'm sure it was something both responsible and meaningful. The only thing that really mattered to us was the knowledge that Jennie Gay, our penny-pinching landlady and loving rent-a-granny—the woman who'd come so valiantly to our rescue in a time of need—had cared enough for us to include us in her will. True to her unimpeachable character, she'd found yet another way to show her appreciation for our friendship—this time from beyond the grave. Her kindness gave us one more reason to be deeply thankful for our life in New England.

Early in 2015, long after Jennie's passing, I drove past our old apartment on River Street to see how it was faring at the hands of its new and very different owners.

The neighborhood appeared to have undergone a minor renaissance, with fresh coats of paint on several homes, and lawns more manicured than I remembered them. Both Jennie's place and the attached apartment we'd called home had new, weather-resistant siding, and the house proper was buzzing with activity.

And yet, in spite of the cosmetic improvements here and there, the apartment had managed somehow to lose nearly all of its turn-of-the-century charm. The garden Jennie had so lovingly planted and maintained was nowhere to be seen, and the wraparound porch where we'd spent so many pleasurable mid-summer evenings was now little more than a dumping ground for broken toys, failed appliances, and unwanted furniture. Remembering the Jennie we knew and loved, I've no doubt she would have been heartbroken to witness the downward arc of her once-proud River Street home.

Time, neglect, and deterioration can rob us of many of our most cherished memories—a beautiful home gone sour, a way of life under siege—but nothing can take from us the enduring power of a finely crafted, lovingly maintained friendship.

Our lives were immeasurably enriched by our association with Jennie Gay. We were three young, wide-eyed immigrants from the Midwest, freshly evicted for the sin of harboring a cat, and badly in need of a home. She was a woman of enormous dignity and high moral character, in the ninth decade of her life, and badly in need of a tenant. Without really needing to try, we quickly became a family, finding ways to support and encourage each other, turning our inevitable setbacks into moments of triumph—all on an unpretentious street in a quiet New England village.

One could argue that we owed our good fortune not just to Jennie Gay, but to our dear friend Peggy, who knew a happy alliance when she saw it and sent us to Jennie; to Olga the cat, a shrewd, all-knowing feline who must have known ahead of time just how to get us out of a less than ideal situation; and to a grumpy, rules-obsessed landlord who would never know what an enormous favor he did for us when he tossed us out of his apartment.

We continue to lead a rewarding life together in our home in the Berwick countryside. Jennie may have been known for her tightness, but we quickly learned that there was another, remarkably generous side to her, and we were often the beneficiaries. After her passing, we had several generous gifts to remember her by, including the porcelain cat, a stereopticon and the dozens of cards that went with it, and a priceless collection of keys of every size and shape, mounted on sheets of cardboard and hanging now in our home.

Our daughter, Amy, now married and raising a family in Cincinnati, has found her happiness there. But in the hearts of all three of us, that sagging, paint-starved apartment on River Street—the one with the wraparound porch and the fireflies—will always be our home.

Afterword

Happy Dawg Walks the Sad Man was conceived in 2010 as I lay trembling with cold one winter night in Maine, trying without success to fall asleep. The problem wasn't just the cold. My lofty goals and nagging insecurities were in full nocturnal combat, and once again I had to seriously wonder if I would ever get down to business and write the book I'd wanted for so long to write.

I tossed and turned for what seemed like hours, and then, all alone in my bedroom, I finally came to my senses. *No more excuses!* I thought to myself while staring into the darkness. *Your very own, unique ways of thinking—your fondest dreams, your most incisive ideas, your most passionate convictions—are no less worthy of landing between the covers of a book than anyone else's!* Then, with socks worthy of an Iditarod musher on my feet and my favorite patchwork quilt tucked under my chin, I hunkered down for the night, more content in spite of the cold than I'd been in a very long time.

The next morning I drove straight to my favorite restaurant, ordered my ritual toast and tea, tore a sheet of lined notebook paper from my tablet, and sketched out a tentative list of chapters. Four years of intense labor, twenty heartfelt essays, and nine tiny novelettes later, I had my book.

But why, and how? Just what was it that drove me, finally, to pour the contents of my heart and soul onto those blank, thirsty pages?

One simple answer can be found in my age. As I approached my seventh decade of living, I finally figured out that it probably

Fig. 84. Caricature of the author by artist Tom Glover.

wasn't going to be easy to write my book from within the dismal confines of an urn with my name engraved on it. A heightened sense of urgency—of time being wasted and dreams gone fallow—turned me overnight into a round-the-clock writing machine. I was fiercely determined to have a book under my belt while I was still around to appreciate it, and nothing was going to stop me from writing.

But the truth is that it wasn't just my age that made me do it. It was also a series of passionately held convictions, stashed away for far too many years in a mind remarkably like an overstuffed attic, crammed to the rafters with memorable experiences in the fine and performing arts. Suddenly, my convictions were demanding to be brought down the stairs and out into the warm glow of sunlight, to be shared with anyone, from anywhere and from any walk of life, who might be inclined to hear them.

A few of those convictions—the ephemerality of fame, the scourge of the nay-sayers, and the problem of specialization (and its attendant curse, credentials)—proved to be especially relevant as I began writing *Happy Dawg Walks the Sad Man*.

As I see it, fame has always been and will always be little more than a hollow, short-lived, maddeningly elusive goal. After all, competence and hard work aren't the only qualities we need if we're to achieve fame; to become truly famous also requires a generous helping of plain, old-fashioned dumb luck—and only a handful of us can count on ever having enough of it to make a lasting difference.

But all is not lost. The more intimate, close-to-home kind of fame—the respect of our peers and the admiration of friends and neighbors—is the only goal with any real staying power, truly worth achieving. And while it's nice to be known well beyond our respective neighborhoods as people of high achievement, the only really worthwhile measure of success is the measure against ourselves.

To that end, it's always a good idea to sit down on occasion and sketch your very own, up-to-date plan for self-improvement. Not to do so is to trap yourself in a never-ending, guilt-inducing cycle of *didn't do*. Better to get up each morning knowing you are better at something today than you were yesterday. It's undoubtedly the most satisfying accomplishment of all.

Side by side with my inherent distrust of fame is an equally powerful conviction that listening to the shrill chorus of the nay-sayers around you—the boss you've always hated, that pompous, know-it-all uncle of yours down in Albuquerque, or even, God forbid, a short-sighted, insensitive teacher—is an enormous waste of human potential. People like that are fond of telling you, either subtly or overtly, that you've nothing really important to contribute to the world. So do yourself a favor and stop listening.

And worst of all, I think, is for you to have allowed anyone, including yourself, to convince you that, at your age (whatever that is), it's too late for you to make a lasting contribution. Every human mind, no matter what body it inhabits, is a marvelously sophisticated, endlessly curious vessel, waiting eagerly to be filled. And as far as I know, other than in the minds of fools, nowhere is it written that only the young have within themselves ideas, impressions, and experiences worth sharing. It stands to reason, then, that age ought never to be an excuse for shutting down the intellect and waiting, patiently and resignedly, for the arrival of the undertaker.

Finally, one of my most cherished convictions is that specialization—and its close and problematic cousin, the professional credential—are together doing more to stifle individual expression and undermine creativity than any other force in the world of employment.

In reality, credentials—the inevitable outgrowth of a specialization-crazed economy—are neither a reliable measure of competence nor a guarantee of employability. And the pressure to specialize is not rampant merely in the corporate world, or in academia and medicine; it has also wormed its way, deeply and perversely, into the fine and performing arts. It means, for instance, that, in the minds of many employers, job applicants with the "proper" credentials, from the "right" schools, are likely to be considered perfectly suited for a position in arts management or administration, while applicants without those credentials—but bursting with fresh ideas, healthy ambition, and a spectacular work ethic—often can't get their foot in the door to plead their case. Does someone really need an MFA in writing to be a good writer, or a PhD in education to be a good teacher? These are laudable credentials to have, I suppose, but they ought never to be the only available way a job applicant can and should be evaluated.

These three long-held convictions of mine—that the idea of fame is not worth the paper it's printed on; that people must learn to ignore the nay-sayers and believe, fully and passionately, in their own unique creative abilities; and that credentials, hand-in-hand with the pressure to specialize, are not always healthy for artists and other living things—are the very heart of *Happy Dawg Walks the Sad Man*.

I'd like to close now by saying that, if this book has managed somehow to cause you to have a more favorable view of your creative potential, I'll feel good about having written it. If it has inspired you to immerse yourself in areas of the fine and performing arts that you always thought were entirely beyond your reach, then I'll feel even better. And finally, if it has helped to rid even one or two of you of the erroneous idea that certain of your attributes—your age, your sexual orientation, your racial or ethnic identity, your social status, or your lack of the right credentials—should disqualify you from being actively creative, I'll feel like a million dollars and probably even more. And just think! Thanks to you, I'll be more fired up than ever to write my next book and release it joyfully into the marketplace of ideas. Won't you join me there?

Ross Alan Bachelder

About the Author

Photo by Michael Penney

Ross Alan Bachelder grew up in Jackson, Michigan, earned degrees in music and English literature from Eastern Michigan University in Ypsilanti, then moved with his wife and daughter to the southern Maine village of Berwick in 1974.

Since moving to New England, he's been deeply immersed in the fine and performing arts as writer, musician, theater professional, visual artist, and arts advocate. He has published essays, poetry, magazine profiles, and fine and performing arts reviews; performed widely as a pit orchestra musician, at special events, and as a solo recitalist; worked as either manager or publicist for several theater companies, including his own; founded and coordinated a group for abstract and experimental artists; run a consulting service for creatives of every kind; traveled widely in the service of the arts; and exhibited his multimedia artworks in Maine, New Hampshire, and Massachusetts.

Happy Dawg Walks the Sad Man is his first book. His next project will be a collection of short stories at least as quirky and mysterious as the tiny novelettes in *Happy Dawg Walks the Sad Man*, and—if he has anything to say about it—more so.

library page • musical instrument repairman • mental hospital orderly • children's summer camp counselor • tester of sonubuoy underwater submarine detectors • Air Force cargo net weaver • university orchestra librarian • FM radio classical music programmer • injection-molded plastic stereo case maker • clothing salesman • babysitter • lawn maintenance worker • construction site accountant • restaurant dish washer • soap sample delivery boy • bookstore sales clerk • male feminist writer/lecturer and women's rights advocate • department store bicycle assembler • theater company general manager • technical theater laborer • editor, theater company newsletter • art, music, and theater critic • songwriter • playwright • music educator • private flute teacher • teen theater founder/director • writer/producer of musical comedies • college writing instructor • freelance magazine writer • picture framer • gallery manager • abstract artist association founder/coordinator • poet • elementary reading tutor • substitute teacher • Ogunquit Playhouse publicity director • actor • Edwin Booth Theatre general manager and publicist • solo and ensemble flute recitalist • theatrical set designer • traveling musical instrument demonstrator • civic band musician • abstractor of criminology research articles • founder/director of Artful Endeavors

www.ingramcontent.com/pod-product-compliance
Lightning Source LLC
Chambersburg PA
CBHW020603300426
44113CB00007B/490